Dietrich W. R. Paulus
Joachim Hornegger

W0077391

Pattern Recognition of Images and Speech in C++

vieweg

All rights reserved
© Springer Fachmedien Wiesbaden, 1997
Ursprünglich Erschienen bei **Friedr. Vieweg & Sohn Verlagsgesellschaft mbH,
Braunschweig/Wiesbaden, 1997**

Vieweg is a subsidiary company of the Bertelsmann Professional
Information.

No part of the publication may be reproduced, stored in
a retrieval system or transmitted, mechanical, photo-
copying or otherwise, without prior permission of the
copyright holder.

http://www.vieweg.de

Ursprünglich Erschienen bei

ISBN 978-3-528-05558-5   ISBN 978-3-663-13991-1 (eBook)
DOI 10.1007/978-3-663-13991-1

To Dorothea, Belinda, and Dominik

In the text we use the following names which are protected, trademarks owned by a company or should be emphasized otherwise: GNU, HP, AT&T, Unix, PostScript LaTeX, HTK, Entropic, Corel Draw.

Part I Introductions   3

Part III Object–Oriented Image Processing   195

Part IV Speech and Pattern Analysis   291

Part V Appendix   363

Preface

This book emphasizes practical experiences with image and speech processing. It offers a comprehensive study of

- image processing and image analysis,
- basics of speech processing,
- object–oriented software design and programming,
- and programming in C++.

The theoretical background is introduced in an order respecting the requirements of programmers, which have to deal with pattern recognition problems. The mathematical exposition is self–contained and the prerequisites are some basic analysis and probability theory.

The book is divided into five parts.

In the first part we introduce speech and image processing, programming tools, elementary statistics, and the basics of C++.

In the second part we describe object–oriented programming in general and possible applications of object–oriented concepts to image and speech processing. The new features of C++ are introduced entirely by the use of examples. Some details are only mentioned in the exercises. Therefore, the book is not a manual of C++, but a guide to its use for pattern analysis.

The third part describes a complete system for image segmentation. Some of the material covered refers to the exercises found in the first and second parts: this verifies our belief that an image segmentation system can be developed while simultaneously acquainting others with C++. We combine the data representation described in the second part with the algorithms that use and manipulate them here in the third part.

In the fourth part we apply the object–oriented ideas to speech processing and pattern recognition. We implement statistical models in C++ and show the applications to feature extraction and classification.

In part five — the appendix — we give additional technical informations.

The introduction of the C++ programming language is done in an informal way. We do not specify all the language details.[1] However, everything the reader needs is described in sufficient detail to cover most applications of image and speech analysis programs.

---

[1] Footnotes provide references for those who want to know the details.

A basic knowledge of the C programming language is required. We assume that the readers of our book are interested in both pattern recognition and programming in C++.

C++ is, by itself, *not* an object–oriented programming language. It needs further tools such as class libraries. We use the NIHCL class library that is found in the public domain. A brief introduction is given in chapter 15.

The input of images or signals and the output to screen or sound devices are not treated here. These strictly hardware–dependent issues have to be solved differently on every computer. Some locations of sources for image display programs using the windowed environment X11 are also listed in the appendix.

Parts of this text were used for several years by students in a two–term undergraduate course in computer science. The book was also used in several lectures on the graduate level, for compact courses in applied programming, and for lectures on applied pattern recognition. The students had to prepare projects in small groups (2–4 students).[2] This book teaches not only C++ but *real object–oriented* programming and algorithms for image and speech processing.

The authors wish to express their special thanks to all those who helped to make this book. First of all, Prof. Dr. H. Niemann, the head of our department, for his constant advice and support. Furthermore, U. Ahlrichs, R. Beß, Dr. J. Denzler, and B. Heigl helped to keep PUMA (the common system, Sect. 3.9) running. Dr. E. Nöth and S. Harbeck helped with the speech processing sections; J. Haas and V. Warnke computed the spectrograms and supported us when we wrote the chapters on spectral features and classification. The chapters on edge detection and contour tracking (21 and 21) use figures and text which were taken partially from [Brü90] — with permission of the author.

Our special thanks goes to Carey Butler who carefully revised the text of the first version and did his best to improve our English and style. After a complete revision of the text and of the structure, Dr. Michael G. Brown again read the whole book; he corrected many errors and gave us most valuable hint to improve style and contents. All remaining errors are our fault and we apologize for them. Last not least we thank our students for their comments and their suggestions for improvement.

Erlangen, Germany   D. Paulus and J. Hornegger
June 1997

The pictures were drawn with xfig (by Brian V. Smith), occasionally using clip arts from Corel Draw. Pstricks (by Timothy Van Zandt) greatly simplified layout and formatting of the text.

---

[2]Some projects are included here as exercises. Further course materials (slides in Postscript or TEX as well as all programming examples) are available upon request (see page 370 for details).

Part I

"We must begin inquiring whether the distinction between what can and what cannot be seen in the pictures by 'merely looking at them' is entirely clear. (...) Does merely looking, then, mean looking without the use of any instrument? This seems a little unfair to the man who needs glasses to tell a painting from a hippopotamus."
Nelson Goodman, [Goo69]

The goal of this part of the book is to provide the basic background knowledge required for the more sophisticated applications in those that follow. Details are left to footnotes and to the references. Only those subjects relevant for part II, III and IV are introduced.

In this part of the book we will cover three different topics:

- Principles of pattern recognition and their applications to image and speech processing,
- Mathematical techniques for image and speech processing,
- The conventional part of the C++ programming language with simple applications to image and speech processing,
- Software engineering principles and tools in Unix and PC operating systems, C++, and pattern recognition applications.

1 Pattern Recognition

In this chapter we will briefly introduce the basic ideas and the models used in pattern recognition. We exclude biological aspects and treat only the mathematical and technical aspects of perception. This is done in a very informal way, since it is not within the scope of this book to present a rigorous discussion of pattern recognition theory. We put our main emphasis on explaining image and speech processing concepts. The research problems treated are motivated by practical examples. After a brief introduction to the applications of pattern recognition, a sketched mathematical description of patterns, problem domain, and environment is given. Due to the fact that modern computer systems need digital data, we will also discuss the central problem on how continuous, observable signals can be transformed into digital signals. A more technical description can be found in the literature (e.g., in [Pra91]).

1.1 Images and Sound

The basic input data to any pattern recognition system are recorded in the form of digitized signals. These digitized signals are then processed by the system. Images as well as speech are typical examples of input data and represent the most important areas in the research and application of pattern recognition.

Digital images and speech signals are very common in today's computer and audio–visual equipment. Digital high–definition video is becoming a huge market. Almost all personal computers have video and audio capabilities and publishing programs now enable the mixing of digital images with text, thereby creating new so called *hypertext* documents. PC users are familiar with the JPEG and MPEG standards[1] which are often used for image transmission. Image data formats (like TIFF e.g., [Poy92]) are compatible across hardware borders. Special hardware for video conferences using personal computers and standard computer communication networks also now is being sold. Several types of media are commonly used in conjunction with each other: text, speech, pictures, movies, etc. The combination of these many media sources and uses is called *multimedia*.

---

[1]see the reference website for MPEG http://www.bok.net/~tristan/MPEG/ for further information

Digital signals can be *synthesized* by a computer based upon a description given to it; sound can be generated by a synthesizer or a voice generator and images can be created by *computer graphics*. Natural signals are *recorded* by special devices; sound, for instance, is recorded by microphones and images are captured by cameras. The quality of sensor data is dependent on the used sensor.

The treatment of sensor data is called *signal processing*. If a computer tries to "understand" what a natural signal "means", then we call this process pattern recognition and analysis. The terms "image processing" and "speech processing" are used as general terms for signal processing as well as the analysis of images and speech. The relation between graphics and image analysis is shown in Figure 1.1. In this book, we cover image and speech processing and the recognition of visual and audio signals: this is different from algorithms that treat visualization or sound generation.

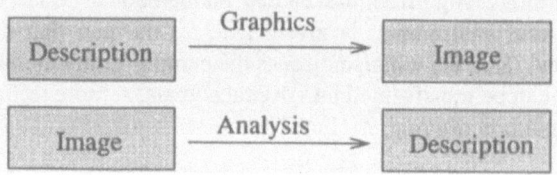

Figure 1.1 Graphics and image analysis

1.2 Applications of Pattern Recognition

Applications of pattern recognition can be found in several areas. For instance, industry, medicine, and military make extensive use of pattern recognition techniques. Image processing of satellite images [Jäh93], automatic and computer–aided medical diagnosis based on X–ray or MR–images [Udu91, Wel95], robot control using visual information [Rim91], and autonomous vehicles [Mey91, Tal93] serve as common examples. Other applications are automatic postal address reading systems [Sch78] or the development of an electronic appointment diary [Bub96], where the interface is a system for handwritten character recognition. Bar code readers are commonly used in banks and shopping centers.

Acoustic communication with computers, dialogue systems, and speaker recognition are potential applications of speech processing. You can already buy car telephones with which you can dial using just your voice.

Other applications may be found, for example, in seismic processing where the input signal comes from a seismic sensor. Other signals are processed in medicine like sounds of the heart or signals from the brain (which have more similarity to speech processing than to images).

1.3 Environment, Problem Domain, and Patterns

Human beings use their eyes, ears, skin, nose, and taste buds as sensors to perceive their environment. These sensors provide our brains with the stimulation necessary for perception. Technically speaking, we model the environment as a large number of variables, or dimensions, whose values cover a specific range that can be recorded by sensors like CCD cameras or microphones. Dimensions will not be considered, if they are not measurable by sensors.

Algorithmic approaches to pattern recognition problems require the presentation of a mathematical framework and a formalization of each problem domain being examined. We now briefly provide a general mathematical approach to pattern recognition [Nie90a].

We describe the environment U by the following set

$$U = \{b_r(x)|r = 1, 2, \ldots\} \quad , \tag{1.1}$$

using vector functions $b_r(x)$. The dimension D_r of $b_r(x) \in \mathbf{R}^{D_r}$ may be different for every r. The components are by definition real numbers. To give some examples:

- $b_1(x, y)$: sea–level (x = geogr. degrees longitude, y = geogr. degrees latitude)
- $b_2(x, y, z)$: temperature, (x, y, z) position in 3–D space
- $b_3(x, y, z, t)$: wind–force / wind–direction (vector!) of the 3–D position (x, y, z) at a certain time t

The aim of pattern recognition is not the description of the *complete* environment. Instead, we limit ourselves to special application domains or parts of the environment, i.e., the so called *problem domain* Ω:

$$U \supset \Omega = \{f_r(x)|r = 1, 2, \ldots\} \tag{1.2}$$

The dimensions of $f_r(x)$ and x are now fixed and adjusted for each application. Examples are color still images, movies (image sequence), and speech:

- color image (three color channels R(ed) = 1, G(reen) = 2, B(lue) = 3):
  $f_r(x, y), f_g(x, y), f_b(x, y)$.
- TV image sequence (time dependent): $f_r(x, y, t), f_g(x, y, t), f_b(x, y, t)$.
- speech signal: $f(t)$.

Elements of the task domain Ω are called *patterns* $\boldsymbol{f}_r(\boldsymbol{x})$ and they are represented as multivariate vector–functions.

$$\boldsymbol{f}_r(\boldsymbol{x}) = \begin{pmatrix} f_{r_1}(x_1, x_2, \ldots, x_n) \\ f_{r_2}(x_1, x_2, \ldots, x_n) \\ \vdots \\ f_{r_m}(x_1, x_2, \ldots, x_n) \end{pmatrix} \tag{1.3}$$

1.4   Characterization of Pattern Recognition

H. Niemann characterizes the field of pattern recognition in [Nie90a; p.4] as follows:

> "Pattern recognition deals with the mathematical and technical aspects of automatic derivation of logical pictures of facts. At the present state of the art this comprises classification of simple patterns as well as analysis and understanding of complex patterns."

In general, the patterns we are working with can be divided up into different categories. On the left of Figure 1.2 an example for a simple pattern is presented. In contrast, the other two images show more complex patterns; these patterns have more detail and require a distinction of background and foreground.

Figure 1.2   Simple pattern (left), complex patterns (middle, right)

During the *analysis* process, an *individual* symbolic description is computed for each pattern. This description may be different for any two patterns. In pattern classification, a fixed label (namely the class index) is assigned to every pattern. Formal details are provided in chapter 6.

If simple patterns are given, our primary interest is in classifying the complete image into one class. A typical example is the recognition of written characters. The decomposition of images and a symbolic description of the observed scene appear during the analysis of a complex scene. A simple classification of a complex pattern is usually not useful since this will not be sufficient for a complete description of the scene. For instance, satellite images can be decomposed into regions — like "forest", "street", "water", and "town" — before a subsequent processing step begins. In some applications a general classification can still be the ultimate goal, for example, for the classification of complicated medical image into "critical" or "healthy".

1.5 Speech Recording

Before we describe how digital signals are computed from continuous ones, we will briefly introduce some basics of the recording of speech signals and images. Speech signals are usually recorded using microphones. The quality of a recording device can be measured partially by the signal to noise ratio (c.f. Sect. 8.9). Microphones try to copy the mechanism of the human ear (see Figure 1.3), where a membrane (approximately 0.1 mm thick) is used to transform the sound. The human ear consists of three main parts:

- the outer,
- the middle,
- and the inner ears.

The outer ear consists of the ear lobe and the meatus. The ear lobe channels sounds into the ear and supports the localization of sound sources. The meatus transmits the received sound signal to the middle ear drum, and its length is approximately 2.7 cm. This transmission channel can be considered as an acoustic tube with a resonance frequency of about 3000 Hz. As the tympanic membrane moves, so does the three bone structure, the bone chain, which results in a movement of the stapes of the middle ear and transmits the signal to the inner ear. Inside the Cochlea, the main part of the inner ear, there is the so–called Basilar membrane. This membrane converts the mechanical signal into the corresponding neural signal. A very interesting and important feature is the fact that different frequencies excite different parts of the Basilar membrane. This allows the analysis of frequencies. For that reason, the ear is considered to work like a spectrum analyzer, and the use of spectral features for speech recognition purposes seems advantageous. However, the conversion of mechanical signals into neural signals works in a way that is not yet completely understood. Indeed, little is known about how the brain decodes the acoustic information it receives.

In the case of microphones, a diaphragm is made to be stimulated by impulses in the frequency range from 10–25000 Hz. The diaphragm's physical movement is then converted to an electrical signal. Unfortunately, due to the mechanical parts in the transmission, the device does not respond to all frequencies equally. Digital filters can be used to compensate this effect. A typical speech signal recorded with a microphone is shown in Figure 1.4.

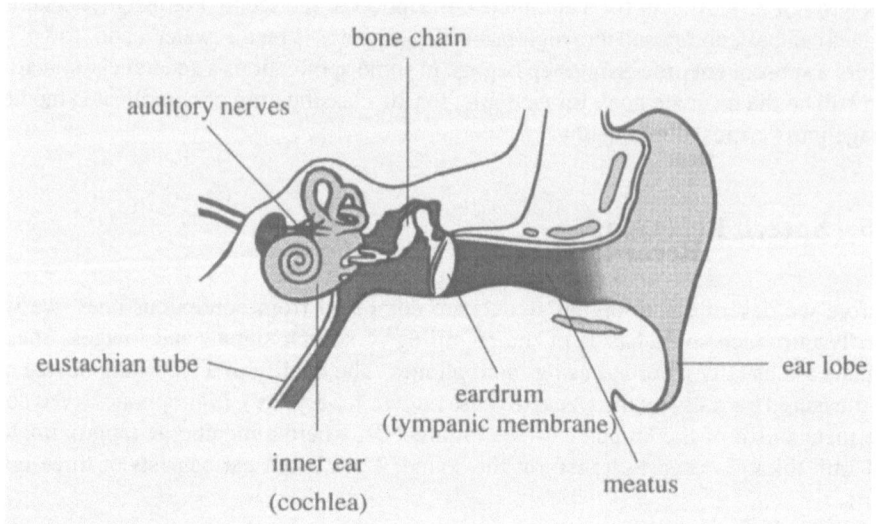

Figure 1.3 Human ear

1.6 Video Cameras and Projections

Many image processing systems use gray–level images as input data for their recognition and analysis algorithms. These images can be recorded by a video camera or similar sensors which project a three-dimensional scene onto a two-dimensional plane. We will consider two different kinds of projections here which are commonly used for modeling the real projection onto a CCD–chip. The most realistic way cameras capture images is using perspective projection. This kind of projection is also the way that images are projected onto the human eye. The simplest model of a camera with perspective projection is the so called *pinhole camera* (Figure 1.5).

In the pinhole camera model, we have a focal point lying behind an image plane. Three-dimensional points are projected onto points in an image plane in such a way that the lines starting from the focal point to the 3–D scene points intersect the image plane; this indicates the locations of the projected points. The resulting image coordinates (x_p, y_p) can be written in terms of the camera focal length f and the three-dimensional object coordinates (x_c, y_c, z_c) in the following manner:

$$x_p = \frac{f\,x_c}{z_c} \qquad\qquad y_p = \frac{f\,y_c}{z_c}, \tag{1.4}$$

where z_c represents the *depth* of the observed 3–D point.

The so called *scaled orthographic projection* (or *weak perspective projection*) provides an approximation to perspective projection. Scene points are simply projected orthog-

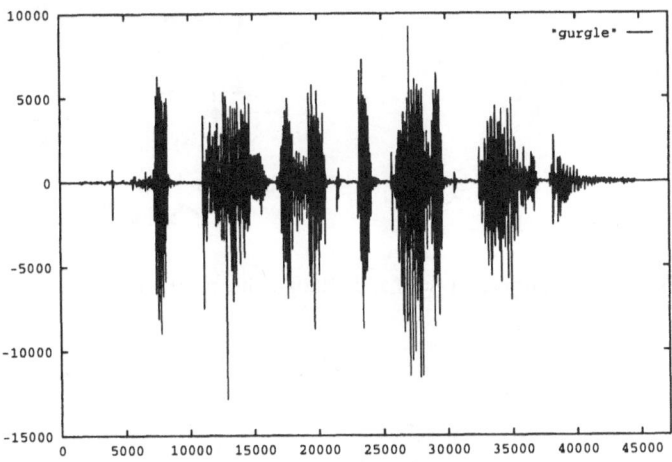

Figure 1.4 Part of the utterance "The pan galactic gurgle blaster".

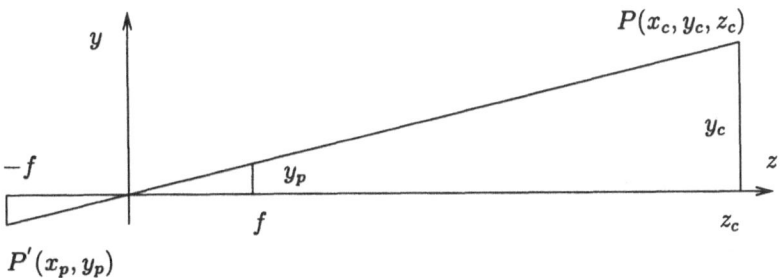

Figure 1.5 The pinhole camera model

onally from the observed three-dimensional scene onto the image plane. The projected point of the 3–D point (x_c, y_c, z_c) is therefore (x_c, y_c). In perspective projection, the size of the object in the image plane varies for different distances, so the resulting orthographic projection image has to be scaled by a factor, to simulate the changes in perceived size. Nevertheless, weak perspective projection does not capture perspective distortion. Figure 1.6 shows the principles of perspective and orthogonal[2] projection in two dimensions.

---

[2] Also called *orthographic projection*

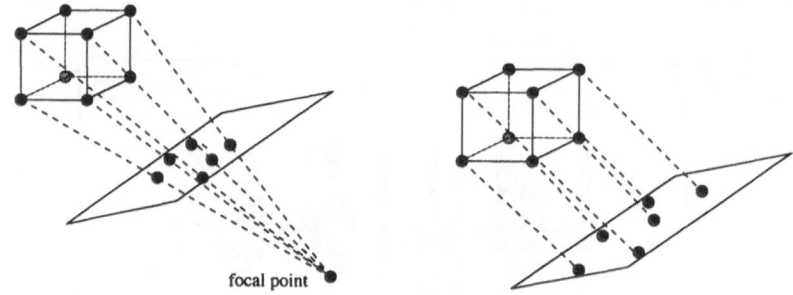

focal point

Figure 1.6 Perspective projection (left) and orthographic projection (right)

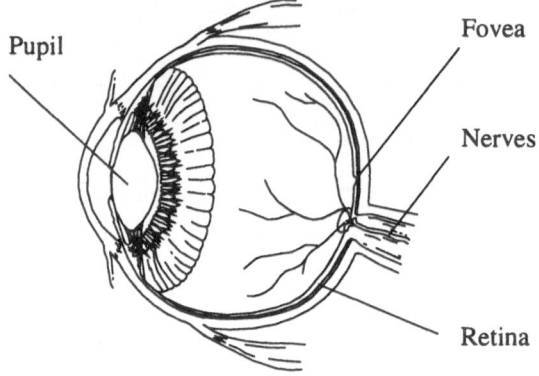

Pupil

Fovea

Nerves

Retina

Figure 1.7 Human eye

Human beings use their eyes for the perception of visual data which is shown in Figure 1.7. Indeed the projection model of eyes can by approximated by perspective projection. The image of the scene is projected through the pupil to the retina, which of course is not plane; the resolution on the retina is also not constant, it is much higher in the area of the fovea.

1.7   From Continuous to Digital Signals

The vectors (1.1) and (1.3) represent continuous signals. However, today's computer systems usually process digital data with finite precision. Therefore, we have to convert analog to digital signals by so–called A/D converters. Figure 1.8 shows an example of a color image converted to three discrete matrices and a transition of an analog speech signal to its digital version.

In everyday life, we watch movies at the cinema which are composed of sequences of discrete images (25 images per second). Our brain does not recognize the discrete structure; we observe continuous sequences. This illustrates the aim of the so called *sampling theorem*. It seems to be sufficient to take a certain number of discrete states for the reconstruction, i,e., interpolation, of a continuous signal.

For an obvious distinction between analog and digital signals it is necessary to introduce the following notation. For continuous signals we use $f(x, y)$ for two-dimensional and $f(t)$ for one-dimensional signals. For the discrete signals we make use of indices, i.e., f_{ij} resp. f_t for representing matrix and vector elements.

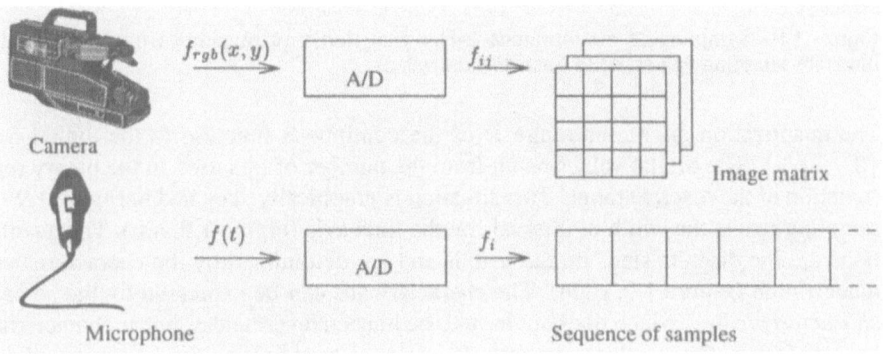

Figure 1.8 A/D-conversion for pattern recognition. The continuous signals $f(x, y)$ resp. $f(t)$ are converted to the discrete values f_{ij} resp. f_t.

The conversion of continuous to digital signals is characterized by two parameters:

1. The *sampling rate*, which follows immediately from the sampling theorem.
2. The *quantization* of the signal value, which is responsible for the quality of the sampled signal.

The quality of signals is measured by the *signal–to–noise–ratio* measured in decibels (dB). The sampling theorem states that after the transition of an analog signal to a digital version of a band limited signal with the frequency bound ω_G, the original signal can be exactly interpolated by a discrete sum, if the sampling period was lower than $1/(2\omega_G)$. The error of this quantization has to be zero. We will see more about this topic in Sect. 12.

Of course for real signals, like natural speech, the band limitation is not generally satisfied. But band limitation can be forced artificially using band pass filters. If the sampling rate is too low, *aliasing* occurs.

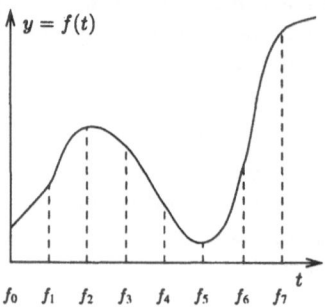 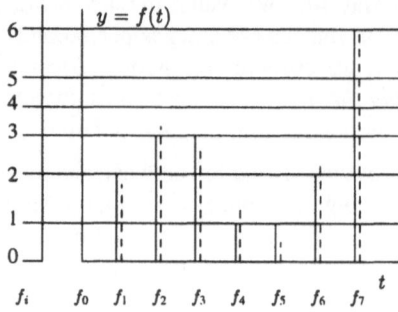

Figure 1.9 Sampling of a continuous 1–D signal (left); quantization (right): dashed lines illustrate sampling values, solid lines discrete values.

The quantization aligns the range R of the continuous function to the digital range $\{0, \ldots, N\}$. The digital values result from the number of bits used in the binary representation of the discrete range. This situation is graphically sketched in Figure 1.9. The sampling rate is the width of intervals on the time axis (Figure 1.9, left). The quantizations are the discrete steps on the y–axis and are determined by the characteristics of quantization (Figure 1.9, right). The characteristics can be expressed by the so called *characteristic line*, which does not have to be linear. Nevertheless, linear characteristics are satisfactory for practical purposes. The error of quantization can be computed using the distance between the continuous and discrete function values, e.g., the euclidian distance. A more comprehensive mathematical discussion of the sampling theorem can be found e.g., in [Nie90a, Nie83].

1.8 Sampling Theorem in Practice

For practical applications in image processing, quantization and sampling rate are usually non–parametric; the technical equipment, like CCD–chips or the resolution of a monitor, has fixed values for these parameters which cannot be modified by users. For images, the sample rate is determined by the distance of the CCD elements on the chip. One additional difficulty is the fact that these pixels usually are not of quadratic shape (c.f. Exercise 1.g).

In the field of speech recognition nonlinear quantization has noticeably improved the recognition quality; in many cases, logarithmic quantization is done as well [Rab93, ST95].

For simplicity, we assume only linear quantization characteristics in the following chapters. The processed images will be gray–level images, i.e., they have just one channel.

The movie example introduced above is also suitable for showing the necessity of the sampling theorem and the connection between the sampling period and the limited frequency. Assume in a movie, which shows 25 discrete images a second, you observe a wheel rotating with the frequency f. Everyone of us has observed the phenomenon: Depending on the speed of a car, the wheels rotate forward or backward. The explanation is simple using the sampling theorem. Only when the frequency f of the wheel is smaller than or equal to $25/2$, then it is possible to reproduce the continuous rotation of the wheel; if the frequency f is greater than the sampling rate of $25/2$, the continuous signals cannot be reconstructed. In these cases it is possible that the wheels seem to rotate backwards.

1.9   Visualization and Sound Generation

For visualization and acoustic control, e.g., in a multimedia application, we also need a conversion from digital to analog signals. This D/A–conversion is shown in Figure 1.10. Theoretically, the sampling theorem guarantees a faultless reconstruction of the continuous signal.

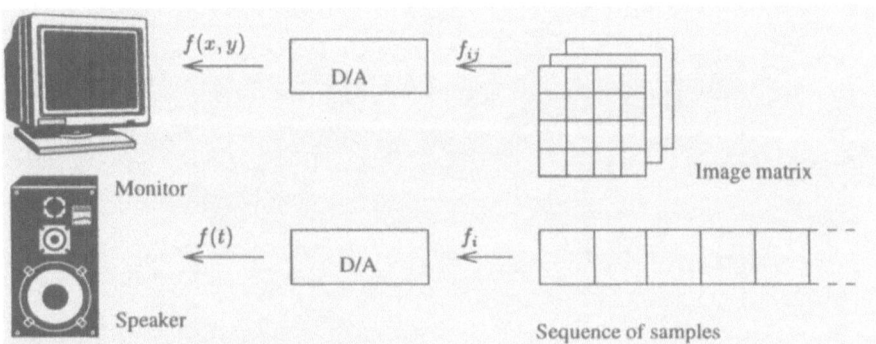

Figure 1.10 D/A–Conversion for visualization and acoustic control. The discrete values f_{ij} resp. f_t. are converted to analog signals $f(x, y)$ resp. $f(t)$.

Typical problems occur, if the signal is visualized with another size than the original recording. In this case, care has to be taken that the sampling theorem is not violated.

Exercises

1.a   Verbally describe the pictures in Figure 1.2. What would be an appropriate symbolic description?

1.b   Which problems will arise with respect to the sampling theorem if a digital image has to be resized (shrunken or expanded)?

1.c   Let Ω be a discrete task domain of size n. How many different ways exist to define a k class partition on this set?

1.d   Which sampling rate is needed for a signal with a limited frequency of 10 kHz?

1.e   What happens if, in perspective projection, the focal length is very large? What do we get in the limit?

1.f   Describe the effects of the sampling theorem on your audio, TV, and video equipment. Does the CD player obey the rules of the sampling theorem?

1.g   Look up the horizontal and vertical size of your TV screen and your PC monitor in the technical documentation. Also check the number of pixels on these devices. Can these pixels have a quadratic shape? What is the ratio width to height?

2   From C to C++

In this chapter we do a quick transition from C to C++, treating C++ as an extension of ANSI–C [Joh93]. It will enable readers to write very simple C++ programs.[1] As stated in the introduction, the description of the language does not cover all the details: the syntax definitions are incomplete with respect to the language definition; they are complete, however, in the sense that they contain all the applications which can be found in this book. In Sect. 2.1 we introduce some notation to be used throughout this volume. In Sect. 2.2 we explain the basic principles for compilation and in Sect. 2.3 we show simple function calls. Some C++ extensions to C declaration syntax are listed in Sect. 2.4. In the remaining sections of this chapter we describe basic features of C and set them in a new context for C++. Sect. 2.5 describes standard formatted input and output which is part of the C programming language and available in C++ as well. Basic data types, the main program, function definition, and scope are described in the final sections.

2.1   Syntax Notation

The C programming language [Ker78] has become very popular and is used in many pattern processing systems. More recently, attention has shifted towards object–oriented programming. C++ is the natural choice for those who want to do object–oriented programming and have a C background or want to reuse their existing C program sources. Most ANSI–C programs will compile with the C++ compiler, i.e. they *are* themselves C++ programs. C programs of course, do not contain all the new object–oriented features which enrich the C++ language.

Some kind of notation has to be used when a new syntax for a programming language is to be introduced. We use the following simple syntactical conventions:

- syntactic structures in square brackets are optional,
- alternatives are separated by a bar "|",
- an * indicates arbitrary repetition (including omission),
- if necessary, { } pairs are used to indicate what is to be repeated, or where the alternatives refer to

---

[1] ... as long as they don't ask too much about what's going on ...

- a $^+$ indicates at least one repetition,
- terminal strings (i.e. those strings which will literally appear in the source code) are typed in teletype and are underlined.

An example including several of these features is shown in the syntax of floating point numbers. Verbally, it reads as "an integer number is a sequence of at least one digit, a real number can either have a sequence of digits before an optional dot followed by the fraction which may be omitted, or the integral part may be omitted, in which case the fraction has to be present".

Syntax:

digit := 0 | 1 | 2 | 3 | 4 | 5 | 6 | 7 | 8 | 9

int_number := *digit*$^+$

real_number := {*int_number*$^+$. *int_number**} | {*int_number** [.] *int_number*$^+$}

signed_real_number := [{+ | -}] *real_number*

When an intuitive description is simpler than a formal definition, we either mix the style or use a verbal description only. The following is an example of a syntax definition for comments in C++.

Syntax: *comment* := // *any text until end of line*

The syntax description do often not cover all variants but serve as a guideline for the most common cases. A complete formal definition of the C++ language can be found in the appendix of [Str91].

2.2   Principle of C++ Compilation

The source code of C++ programs and, similarly, of C programs is translated by a compiler.[2] By convention, C source files have the extension .c and the C++ files end in .C. Initially, sources are preprocessed by a program called cpp.[3] In this step all lines beginning with the symbol # are evaluated. Except for comments, no information other than preprocessor directives may be present on these lines.[4]

First, we consider the lines starting with #include followed by a filename in angle brackets as <system-file> or in quotes as in "personal-file". In both cases,

---

[2]In contrast to interpreted languages.

[3]Some non–Unix systems may call it differently or work without it. The principle of compilation is, however, the same. Usually, C code is preprocessed by a program called cpp; C++ compilers use the same preprocessor.

[4]Some systems also allow compiler directives such as hints for optimization or parallel implementation here.

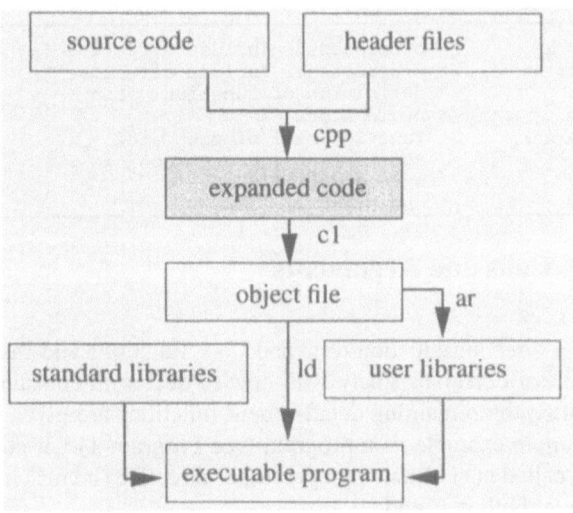

Figure 2.1 From source code to executable programs

a temporary file is generated by the compiler, where the corresponding system and personal files are explicitly inserted (gray box in Figure 2.1). By convention, included files usually have the extension ".h"; they are called *header–files*. The path entries of the compiler are searched for the files included by #include <file>. When #include "file" is used, the compiler searches for the file in the current directory first before looking at the default compiler path.

Most of the files searched for by <file.h> are part of the environment for the compiler or operating system. They may be found at a common place for all users of the system. Private files "file.h" will often be used by only one user.

The temporary file produced is then compiled successively by one or more programs contained in the compiler. Usually, two compiler passes produce an object module, which has the extension .o. Executables are then created by a linker which resolves external symbols from the system libraries and adds the interface to the operating system. Alternatively, the object module may be added to create or modify a library (usually with extension .a). Figure 2.1 shows the data flow of the compile process annotated by the required programs.[5]

---

[5]If dynamic linkage is used (so called "shared libraries"), the resolution of external symbols from the libraries happens at program runtime.

```
#include <stdio.h>        /* preprocessor include directive */
#include <stdlib.h>       /* preprocessor include directive */
main()                    /* definition of function: main */
{                         /* begin block */
    puts("hello\n");      /* function call of puts with
                             constant string argument */
    exit(0);              /* exit gracefully */
}                         /* end block */
```

2.3   Function Calls and Arguments

We now present a brief introduction to C and C++ functions and their arguments. In doing so, we concern ourselves solely with how to deal with constant arguments and function call syntax; the remaining details about functions are given later (Sect. 2.8). Here is a very simple example of a program (see Program 1).[6] It consists of a main function (always called main) and a preprocessor directive (#include). The code is syntactically correct both in C and C++.

The file stdio.h allows the inclusion of common input and output functions (I/O) by inserting their declarations into the source code.[7] The imported file is placed within the compiler environment and is inserted in the program by the preprocessor.

Input and output functions are not part of the language definition of C++. They are made available from standard libraries via function calls. The function call puts stands for *put string* and prints its sole argument on the screen; the program, when executed, will produce the output "hello" followed by a new line. The compiler "knows" about this function because it is declared in the file stdio.h. A call to the function exit with argument 0 ends the execution and flushes all open files. By convention, the argument 0 indicates proper program termination, whereas any other value would indicate some sort of error condition. The compiler knows about this function from the declaration found in stdlib.h.

Note that a function can be called by just giving its name.[8] The arguments that are passed to the function must be enclosed in parentheses. In Figure 1 we see a function with only one argument: later, we will use functions with several arguments separated by commas and sometimes even functions with a variable number of arguments.

Actually, main is also a function. The program above *defines* the function main; the other functions referred to are only called and are defined somewhere else. Their definitions are attached to the executable by linking it with the system libraries (see Figure 2.2).

---

[6]The examples for programs are numbered consecutively. An index can be found on 397.

[7]Of course, streams in C++ are safer and nicer (Sect. 15.4). But for teaching purposes we explain standard function calls rather than introducing things like cout << without proper preparation.

[8]As in Pascal and other languages based on the ideas of Algol 60.

```
int i;              // definition of i uninitialized!!
long l = 3, 12 = -4L;  // definition and initialization
char * str0 = "abc";   // string variables are char *
char * str1 = "cde",   // a string
     * str2 = "ax",    // another string
       c   = 'a';      // this is not a string!
const int ci = 3;      // regular integer
```

②

2.4 Declaration and Definition of Variables

Each identifier has to be declared before it can be used. The *declaration* merely introduces the name and its associated attributes to the compiler. The *definition* of a variable,
however, requests a storage location for the value as well; the definition also serves as
a declaration.

- In C, variables have to be declared and defined at the beginning of a block. C++
  allows this nearly everywhere,[9] since declarations are now syntactically treated as
  statements. The declaration is valid only inside the current block.

- If identifiers are declared outside of functions, they are *global* and are valid in every
  function following the declaration. Global variables should be used very carefully.

Simple variables can be defined and initialized at the same time. The initialization's
validity will not be checked by all compilers (i.e., uninitialized variables will not always
produce a compiler warning). Some compilers initialize variables with default values,
others do not. These compiler dependencies should be avoided since they do not ensure
portability of the software and show bad programming style.

The basic syntax of the variable definition is as follows:

Syntax: ▌ [const] *type* [*ptr*] *var1* [≡ *val*] [, [*ptr*] *var2* [≡ *val*]]* ;

This means that we first specify the type of an identifier, and optionally, *something*
which will be introduced later (called ptr here) followed by the identifier's name.
Optionally, we may then list any additional identifiers. Any of the variables in the list
may be initialized to the value given after the "=" sign. It is recommended that all
variables are initialized immediately along with the definition. The relaxed placement
rules for declarations (with respect to C) simplify this task, since some computation can
be programmed in between two subsequent declarations and definitions.

Fundamental data types in C and C++ are char, short, int, long, float, and
double with their unsigned variants for the integer types.

Program 2 shows some definitions and declarations. Strings are denoted by char *
and can be assigned a constant value; the * is repeated for the subsequent definitions;

---

[9]In the following chapters we will note occasional exceptions, where declarations are not allowed.

the * corresponds to the `ptr` in the above program fragment. Strings are explained in detail in Sect. 5.6. In the last line, `str1` and `str2` are strings, whereas `c` is a single character. Constant values — such as the variable `ci` in the example — can be declared as such with the keyword const and have to be initialized immediately. Long integer constants are given as a sequence of digits followed optionally by an `L`.

2.5   Unix–File Access via Standard Functions

Most (useful) programs need some sort of input and output. The C–language was developed together with the Unix operating system. Input and output were originally separated from the language definition. However, most programmers use the standard interface provided in the `stdio.h` header file.

The Unix naming conventions and the basic philosophy for file and terminal I/O were used when C was ported to other operating systems (even to MS-DOS). We may thus talk about files as if we all were using Unix.

Unix offers — as one of its remarkable features — a uniform file concept which includes directories and devices in a homogeneous way. Access of files in C is done by function calls. C++ encapsulates the I/O operations by streams.[10] The `stdio`–interface is, however, still available in C++ allowing existing C routines to be reused. Three channels in Unix exist, which are always ready for input and output; they are referred to as a `FILE*`:[11]

- `stdout`: this is the destination for regular output, (output may be delayed due to buffering)

- `stdin`: this is the primary source for input (e.g. from the keyboard),

- `stderr`: errors should be printed here; they will be printed instantly, i.e. no buffering.

New output and input channels are opened by a function call to `fopen` with two string arguments: the first is the file name and the second is the access mode (`"w"` for write and `"r"` for read).[12] Existing files will be destroyed by the use of `"w"`! The function `fclose` closes a channel which was opened by `fopen`; the argument is the `FILE*` (see Program 3).

---

[10]This will be treated in Sect. 15.4.

[11]What type is a `FILE`? What does the * mean? As we told you, don't worry (footnote 1 on p. 17)!

[12]Depending on the operating system, there may be more choices or the distinction for binary and text mode.

```
const char * terminal = "/dev/tty";    // constant string
FILE * tty = fopen(terminal,"w");      // open console output
fclose(tty);                           // close the stream
```

```
int i = 30;  float f = 1.3;
printf("%d students were marked %f\n", i, f);
printf("%s%c %f %%\n", "that i", 's', 33.0);
```

The function printf prints to the current standard output device (stdout). It provides a general facility for the conversion of data to text. The declaration of this function is included in the file stdio.h. The number of arguments to this function is dependent on the first argument, which is used to format the text. In this string, there may be several substrings beginning with a percent sign (%) which are treated specially.

The characters immediately following the percent sign determine the format of the text and the type of the required arguments (Table 2.1). The actual arguments corresponding to those specified in that string are listed next. For every percent sign, except for %% which prints a percent sign (Program 4), there is one argument.[13] Further options exist for the format string which are less commonly used.

%x	output of integral value hexadecimal
%d	output of integral value decimal
%ld	output of long–value decimal
%c	output of character
%s	output of string
%%	output of %
%f	output of double or float value as integer plus fraction
%e	output of double or float value scientific notation

Table 2.1 Format control strings

The percent sign can be followed by a numerical value specifying the length of the output text. This value precedes the character of the specified type. The output length of integers and strings can be given as integer values. Negative values for width means left adjustment. Floats and doubles are formatted using float values: the number before the decimal point specifies the overall width and the value after the decimal point stands for the number of decimal places (Program 5).

The additional first argument of the function fprintf specifies the output file. A function call to fprintf(stdout,...) and printf(...) is equivalent (Program 4 and Program 6).

---

[13]Another exception is %* not mentioned in the table (c.f., for example, [Str91; p. 357]).

```
printf("%5d students were marked %3.1f\n", i, f);
printf("%-20s %7.2f %%\n", "that is ", 33.0);
```
⑤

```
fprintf(stdout,"%5d students were marked %3.1f \n", i, f);
fprintf(stderr,"Fatal Error %d\n", errno);
```
⑥

One basic property of this input/output concept is that data transform to files is buffered, i.e. not every read or write function call will immediately result in disk access. As a consequence, an output to stdout will not directly show up on the screen. The error channel (stderr), however, is unbuffered.[14] Alternatively, the function call fflush(stdout) can be used to print all information currently accumulated in the buffer.

2.6   Numeric Expressions

For short int, float long, and double the binary operators +, -, *, / have their usual intuitive semantics. The operator precedence is identical to the operator rules of mathematics, i.e. * and / bind tighter than + and -; parentheses are used for grouping as well. Exponentiation does not exist as an operator. Mathematical operations are also admissible for variables of type char. Characters are converted to integers in C and treated as tiny integers in C++. Range checking and the overflow of integers are not detected by the system at runtime so if data–types are mixed in an expression, an automatic adjustment of types is performed.[15] This process is known as *implicit conversion*. Automatic type conversion is a complicated topic. We recommend, therefore, to use explicit conversion whenever in doubt.

The C++ syntax for type conversion is simple and looks like a function call:

Syntax: *type (expression)*

Alternatively, the C–syntax can still be used (and in some cases must be used):[16]

Syntax: *(type) expression*

Conversion from float or double to integer types truncates to the appropriate range. When rounding is required, add 0.5 to the float value. Conversion and casts are shown in Program 7.

---

[14]This is important and useful when you trace a program with control output!

[15]There exist different rules for the conversion in C and C++, due to the fact that in C, for example, there is no char–valued expression.

[16]The C–version of the cast must be used when the type cast to is not a simple type name, e.g. in (byte **) ptr.

```
int i = 3 * 5;                    /* value: 15  */
float f = 0.7 + 3;                /* value: 3.7 */
int j = int(f) * ( i + 2 );       /* value: 51  */
```
⑦

```
#include <stdio.h> /* will not C++ compile without it! */
main(int argc, char ** argv)
{
        int i = argc;
        char * progname = argv[0];
        FILE * out = fopen("/dev/tty", "w");
        fprintf(out,"Program name \"%s\" %d args\n",
                   progname, i - 1);
        exit(0);
}
```
⑧

Instructions are terminated with semicolons. The assignment operator is "=". Integer division is performed with "/" when the operands are integers; the modulus operation is "%".

2.7   Main Program

The function main has to be defined once in each complete C++ program. The function represents the main part of the program (see also Program 1). Usually, it is defined with two arguments called argc and argv. Theses variables contain the arguments given by the operating system interface (e.g. the command line processor). The variable argc contains the number of arguments; argv provides the locations of the argument strings (c.f. Sect. 5.9 for more details). The first value is the name of the program (as it is known to the operating system); it is referred to as argv[0].

In Program 8, the variable i is defined and initialized to the number of arguments. A string variable progname will be assigned the name of the program. An output file is opened with a fixed name (a device in Unix). The program name and the number of arguments are printed to this file which is then closed automatically before the end of execution of the program by the call to the exit routine. It is, however, good practice to close all open files explicitly. Also, note that \ " in the format string of the fprintf function call prints ".

2.8   Function Definition

Modular programs split the code into functions and procedures which group a series of statements or expressions together. Functions are used in expressions and may return a

```
void printij(int i,int j)              // definition
{                                      // function body
   if (i < 0) return;                  // conditional return
   printf("I is %d, J is %d\n", i, j); // print something
}                                      // return

main()                                 // main function
{                                      // body
   printij(1,2);                       // call other function
}                                      // return
```
⑨

value; procedure calls are considered statements in their own right. Their actions can be controlled by *parameters* called *arguments* for functions.

The void type is a key word and prefixes a procedure[17] declaration in C++. A procedure definition in C++ looks like the following:

| Syntax: | void *identifier* ([*type argument*] [*, type argument*]*) *block* |

The block in the procedure definition is called the *body* of the function. A function may be called using its name followed by a possibly empty list of arguments included in parentheses. The arguments have to correspond in number and type to the list given in the declaration. These arguments are passed to the function and their values are substituted for the variables in the function body.[18] The control returns to the location following the call after termination of the function. This happens when the last statement of the function body is executed or upon encountering a return statement, as shown in Program 9. It is admissible for functions to call themselves, i.e., recursion is possible.

Functions may have a return value. This already happened in Program 8 where the variable out was initialized with the return value from the call to fopen. The syntax for functions is as follows:

| Syntax: |

returntype identifier ([*type argument*] [*, type argument*]*) *block*

The execution of the function can be terminated at any point inside the function body with a return statement which now has to specify a value to be passed back:

| Syntax: | return *expression* |

The expression has to be of the type given by the *return type* in the function declaration. The use of functions is exemplified in Program 10; this also shows how access is made to command line arguments. The (external) function atoi has one string argument taken from the command line. It *returns* an integer value — namely the conversion of its string argument to a number.

---

[17]The term *procedure* is used here as in Pascal. Procedures are functions which do not return a value.

[18]At this point we consider only passing arguments by value. Later we will see other possible mechanisms (Sect. 7.3).

```
int sign(int i)                  // sign function definition
{
     if (i < 0) return -1;       // case 1
     if (i == 0) return 0;       // case 2
     return 1;                   // otherwise
}
main(int argc, char ** argv)     // main function
{
     int j=argc+sign(atoi(argv[1])); // function calls
}
```
10

```
void a(int);                            // declaration
void b(int,int);                        // declaration
void a(int i)        { /* ... */ b(i,1); }   // definition
void b(int i,int j) { /* ... */  a(i); }     // definition
```
11

If the return type is omitted from a function definition (as in the previous examples with the functions `main`), it is assumed for historical reasons to be of type `int`. If the use of a function is intended where no return value is needed, then the function should be declared as `void`; this will disallow its use in expressions.

Since procedures are just special cases of functions — returning the type `void` — in the following we talk about functions and arguments only and omit the terms *procedure* and *parameters*.

2.9   Scope and Lifetime

As already noted, identifiers have to be declared prior to their use. Functions, for example, may be declared first and then defined later. In this way it becomes possible for two or more functions to call each other mutually (Program 11).

The name of a variable becomes known to the compiler as soon as it compiles the declaration statement. Variables declared inside a block are invisible from the outside. The value and the storage location of these variables is lost when the block is left. It will be reallocated upon reentering the block where the declaration occurs.[19]

Declarations outside of any function are called *global*. These names are visible in any function following the declaration. It is considered bad programming style to use many global variables across different files.

As in many other programming languages, the name of a variable that has already been declared outside of a given block may be reused within this block for a completely different purpose. The closest declaration (with respect to scope) will be the one referenced

---

[19]Depending on compiler implementations.

to within the block. In Figure 2.2, we depict functions by two nested blocks; the first introduces the names of the arguments, the second corresponds to the function body. Inside a function, the argument names can overwrite global name bindings. Inside the function body, new declarations may then introduce new names. Declaration 1 will be known in Functions 1 and 2. Declaration 2 will be known only in Function 2. Local variable 1 will be visible only in Function 1. Local variable 2 will be visible only in Function 2. Program 12 shows how variable names can be overwritten in nested blocks and by function definitions. Such style — of course — does not improve readability of your code!

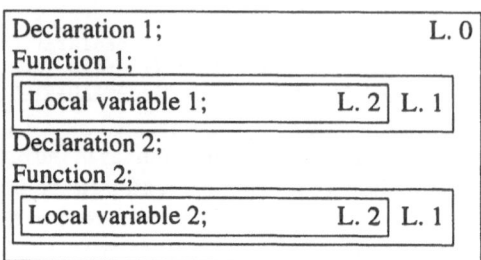

Figure 2.2   Declaration inside blocks

If a local variable is tagged `static`, it will keep its value even if the program control passes out of the block (Program 13). When the block is entered again, the variable will be accessible with its old value. The name, however, is nevertheless invisible from the outside.

```
int i, l;                          // global variables (bad style!)
void fct(int i, int j, int k)      // global i will be invisible
{
  int l;                           // will overwrite global l
  { int j; }                       // will overwrite argument j
}
```
12

```
void fct()
{  static int counter = 0;                  // keep the value
   printf("fct called for the %d-th time\n", ++counter);
}
```
13

```
char*s="char*s=%c%s%c;main(){printf(s,34,s,34);}";
main(){printf(s,34,s,34);}
```
14

Exercises

2.a   Write a program that prints your address including the date and place of your birth and your profession into a file named "my_address". Try different ways of formatting the output!

2.b   Arguments can be passed from the command line to a program as program execution begins. The variable `argv` contains all parameters given on the command line when the program was called. The ith argument can be retrieved by `argv[i]`. Standard functions are provided for converting strings to integers or floats such as `atoi` and `atof` respectively.

The following line assigns the converted first argument string to the variable `i`:

```
int i= atoi(argv[1]);   // assign return value of call
```

Write a program that prints its number of arguments and interprets the first argument as an integer `i`. Also print the ith argument.

2.c   What happens if you provide an illegal value of `i` at runtime, (e.g. you provide the argument line "4 a b")?[20] Will the system warn you?

2.d   What is the shortest complete C++ program?

2.e   Try to understand the following C–program listed in Program 14.
Run the program and send the output to a file! Can you invent something similar? Why is it a C program and not a C++ program?

2.f   *Syntactic Macros*
It is tempting for a Pascal programmer to write a program as in Program 15. This is, however, bad programming style for C++ and C. In particular, some tools like the "C–beautifier" `cb` will not work with this code.
Rewrite this program to standard C++. Pascal programers also note the if—else syntax; there is no `then`!

---

[20]Be sure to remove the file `core` if you create one!

```
#define BEGIN {
#define END }
#define IF if(
#define THEN )
#define ELSE  else
main ()
BEGIN
     int i = 1;
     IF i < 0
     THEN BEGIN i = 0; END
     ELSE i = 1;
END
```

15

3 Software Development

In this chapter we introduce the basic principles of software development with a special emphasis on pattern recognition programs and object–oriented programming. Basic concepts of documentation and program design are also explained.

3.1 Software for Pattern Recognition

Digital images, represented as matrices of fixed size, are the basic data for computer vision. Usually, gray–level images have 256^2 or 512^2 pixels with 256 different gray–levels, i.e. each image contains, 64 KBytes resp. 256 KBytes of data. For color images, such as RGB–images with three color channels, three–dimensional arrays are required for representing an image. The number of two–dimensional arrays needed for color images depends on the number of color channels. For motion analysis, an image sequence of 25 images per second has to be processed. If we use 512^2 color images, one second of the image stream would need 18.75 MBytes.

Speech recognition algorithms are based on a *sequence* of sample values. When considered as a certain interval of time, these sequences can be interpreted as vectors. Very often, the sample frequency of speech signals is 16 kHz with a quantization of 12 or 16 Bits. Consequently, the amount of information per second is 23.4 to 31.25 KBytes.

These examples show the large amount of data pattern recognition algorithms have to process. Implementations of pattern recognition systems are often huge programs with many lines of source code. Even if the systems described in this book seem to be small, they will rapidly grow in size if they are applied to real world problems. Therefore, it is essential that the rules of good software production are strictly obeyed.

Large systems must have a sufficient amount of documentation concerning their behavior in order to be useful for other users. To facilitate further improvements, the code should have been extensively commented by its implementors. The structure of such systems must be modular and this modularity should be based upon recent developments in the field of software–engineering. Each programmer contributes a small part of the complete system, using all implemented modules. It is crucial to guarantee compatibility between program code, documentation, and comments as well.

3.2 Software Development and Testing

Figure 3.1 shows the classical cycle of software development. Recent research in the field of software-engineering such as CASE (*C*omputer *A*ided *S*oftware *E*ngineering, [Fis88]) differs from this established approach. CASE–tools make it possible to generate code automatically during the planning and design phases. Additionally, automatic code generation influences its own documentation.

With the analysis of the problem, we also start with the documentation of the software (box 0). The documentation is finished within the final version of the code (box 10).

Syntactical errors in the source code are taken into consideration in box 7–9. In box 9, the syntax check of the source code is done, for instance, by the compiler. If errors are found, we will proceed with box 8. More serious problems, e.g. logical mistakes, make a complete revision necessary, symbolized in box 5.

In the first phase of a project a computer is not needed. In the planning phase (box 4–6), the computer can be used for supporting the work because there are software tools available to generate structograms or flow diagrams. The test phase of the program is generally done in a development environment using *debugging* tools.

The common principle of *stepwise refinement* for software development can be seen in box 4 and box 6. Here we start with an abstract top–level description of the problem, e.g., a function interface with a dummy implementation, and then iteratively refine the implementation, adding new functions and supplying the code for the dummy functions.

Object–oriented programming is associated with the keywords "class", "object", and "inheritance" and will be discussed in more detail in Chapter 9. Several changes in the classical development cycle and the terminology were introduced in the course of object–oriented programming and are talked about in Chapter 9 as well. In order to judge the improvement gained by object–oriented software, it is useful to know about the classical ideas and principles for software development.

The test phase is a very crucial part of software design and programming. It should not be ignored, neglected, or underestimated. Systematically organized tests will increase the reliability of software for real–world applications. Problems not considered during the analysis might be detected during tests. A general problem is the following fact:

> Tests can reveal the existence of bugs, but generally cannot be used to prove that there are no errors in a program.

The more you test, however, the lower will be the chance that there is a hidden bug in your code. Some general guidelines will help you testing your software:[1]

---

[1]Collected from the world wide web, from lecture notes, and from personal experience.

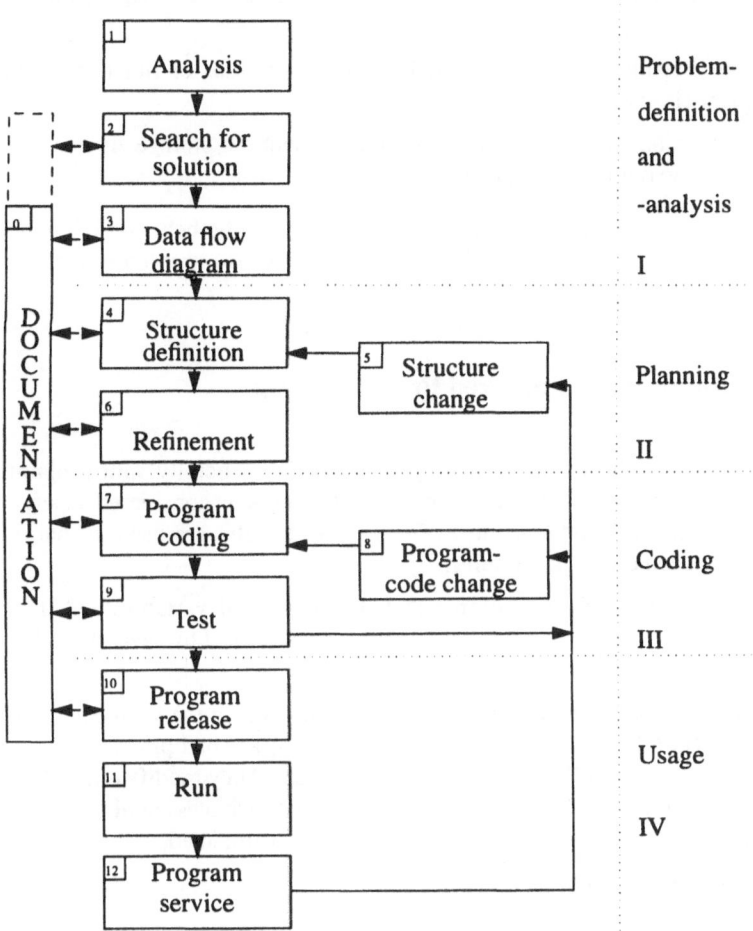

Figure 3.1 Classical cycle of software development

1. Each branch in the program should be activated at least once during the test. This comprises the parts for rare error conditions as well!

2. Every loop should be used at least twice.

3. Try to imagine irregular, unexpected, wrong, inconsistent input and test your routines with such data, for example, images of size 1×10000 or even of size 0×0.

4. Use more than one data set for testing.

5. Use at least one data set as input for which you know the expected output of the program.

6. Test predictable special cases, such as discontinuities of functions, division by numbers close to zero, etc.

7. Keep in mind the limitations of resources, such as storage or execution time. Estimate the required resources.

There are some cases in which one can formally prove the behavior of functions and routines; this is called program verification. In real world problems, such proofs are usually not possible.

3.3   Modular and Structured Programming

Obeying the principles of modular programming, we generally split program source code into several parts. Most often, implementation code is considered separately from the interfaces that will influence it. In C/C++, header files are used to share common interfaces between different modules.

Unfortunately, C++ does not enforce that the sharing of variables and data is controlled by a clean interface definition. Global variables used by several modules create dependencies which are often hard to understand.

The flow of information naturally follows the statements in the source code. Unconditional jumps (in C/C++ this means the use of goto) are bad practice. Function calls return to the statement following the calling statement. They modify only what is specified in the function definition. Modifications of global variables should be the exception (due to potential "side effects") and should be well documented.

We state the following default rules:

- no goto's,
- no side effects of function calls, and
- no global variables.

The aim of modularizing programs is guided by well defined interfaces (in C/C++: the use of header files). The principle of local changes states that as long as the interfaces are not involved in those changes, the changes have no (undesirable) influence on other modules. Well defined dependencies for source code fragments and interchangeability of modules are primary goals of modularization.

3.4   Comments and Program Layout

Comments in source code are neglected by many programers. Nevertheless, good and sufficient comments aid in the reuse and maintenance of software. Programs should at least contain text covering the following:[2]

- description of the module (description of the file, revision number, state of the project, name of the author, etc.)
- description of the functions, their arguments, and their semantics,
- description of the main part of the program including the command line options.

Mnemonic identifiers for variables and files as well as comprehensible comments should be used; this supports and facilitates documentation and the chance of producing reusable software.[3]

Proper indentation of code lines makes the code a lot more readable. Usually, statements in the same block of code are lined up vertically. New blocks are indented by one tabulator position.[4]

C++ assists commenting with its a syntax; comments can be added to the end of each line (see page 18). It is highly recommended to add terse and descriptive notes to each code line, or at least to each group of closely related lines (e.g. one comment for a small loop is usually ideal).

3.5   Documentation

The components of useful documentation are textual descriptions of the program semantics as well as the abstract structure of the modules and interfaces.

The flow of control can be visualized by structograms as introduced in [Jen85]. Be careful to avoid the use of C syntax within graphical visualizations of algorithms; this description should be an *alternative* to reading program code. The basic components of structograms are blocks which can be nested or stacked on each other. A sequence of statements is called a *block* and can be depicted as in Figure 3.2.

---

[2]Some of this information can be added automatically, e.g. by rcs (A.4, Sect. 3.8, Exercise 3.d).

[3]We once got a program, properly commented and documented, doing its job perfectly — but the variable names were all in a foreign language...

[4]For C and C++ two styles for indentation are common. Most Unix systems provide the program cb which is a C–beautifier. Therefore it makes little sense to invent your own style! See the manual of this program for the description of the styles.

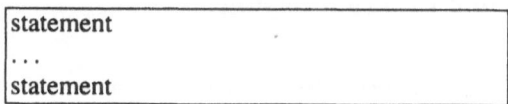

statement
. . .
statement

Figure 3.2 Structogram element for sequential execution

Three types of loops are shown in Figure 3.3. The FOR loop is used for iteration, the WHILE loop checks the condition before the loop is entered, and the UNTIL loop checks it at the end, i.e. the loop is executed at least once in an UNTIL loop.

FOR rejecting loop
block

WHILE condition
block

block
UNTIL condition

Figure 3.3 Three types of loops

The graphical presentation of a branching in the flow of control shown in Figure 3.4 is not the standard form, but available in the `strukto–`TEX`–style.`[5] For more than two branches (i.e., for a `switch`), another component is available which is not shown here.

IF	condition
THEN	block
ELSE	block

Figure 3.4 Conditional execution

Algorithms designed using structograms will almost automatically result in well structured code. There is no way to express a `goto` in a structogram!

Data flow can be documented with data flow diagrams. Especially in object–oriented systems, special care has to be taken on the documentation of data structures. Entity–Relation Diagrams (ER) which are common in data base design can be used. Modern object–oriented software development provides extensions of these ideas (Sect. 9.1).

3.6   Teamwork

The design and implementation of large or huge software systems, such as for image analysis or speech processing, cannot be finished by a single person. Such work will only succeed if the project is properly coordinated and planned.

---

[5]Available from most TEX–archives.

We have to partition the complete problem into independent parts, and define the interfaces of each partition. For implementation purposes, modules and classes are suitable concepts for information hiding. If more than one person modifies the files, we need to implement version and access control. This guarantees that no conflicts will occur – for example, when two partners edit the same file at the same time. Furthermore, all changes and their authors should be taken down.

3.7 Efficiency

Efficient programming is often neglected by computer programmers. It is, however, very important for image and speech processing. Especially for real–time processing of images and speech, the huge data rates require efficient code. Efficiency has to be a major *design goal* for image and speech analysis programs and should almost never interfere with structured and clean programming. Any "dirty tricks" have to be well commented and should have only local influence on the program. [Sch90] gives some examples of efficiency considerations for segmented programs.

The test phase of a program (box 9 in Figure 3.1) reveals inefficient parts of a program which have to be changed. High modularity helps to keep the required updates local. On modern computer processors, the costs of calling a function and passing arguments to it are small and performed in few processor cycles. When the function called computes more than just a trivial expression, the relative computation time of the function body is high compared to the time needed for calling and returning. Thus, no reduction of the efficiency is to be expected if programs split the code in many small functions, which are in turn easier to be optimized.

C++ additionally provides functional syntax and semantics even for trivial computations, which can be executed *without* loss of efficiency (Sect. 7.7).[6] Efficiency is one reason for C to be used in so many image and speech processing systems. C++ seems to be the right extension as it keeps the speed and adds a lot to structuring and modularization.

3.8 Tools for Software Development

Unixis more than just an operating system kernel that provides an interface between the user and the hardware. Unix also includes several tools for program development which are not directly related to the hardware. For example, the operating system itself provides access facilities for teamwork. Unix groups can be built who share rights on individual files or directories. Locking mechanisms are present in newer versions of

---

[6]In Unix there are tools which can be used to find the part of the program where most of the computation time is spent.

Unix to avoid conflicts. Such mechanisms are also available for other recent operating systems.

For software development, the following features and commands are useful for software production, especially in a team with shared resources:

- `groups` (ask your system administrator)
- `newgrp` (change your current group in system V based Unix)
- `umask` (can be set to grant access to a group by default)

The following tools are useful for every programmer. They should be used in any project, no matter whether in a team or working alone.

- `make` is a program maintenance tool. `make` will do all the required actions such as compiling or linking after a change in the program source code.
- `rcs` is the abbreviation for "revision control system". `rcs` will record your changes and in addition grant or deny access to source files shared by several users. Various related tools exist.

In appendix A we briefly describe these common Unix tools which are also available on almost any other computer operating system.

3.9   PUMA

Program development and experiments in the field of pattern recognition are costly and time consuming. For simplifying this process, the programming environment PUMA[7] was designed and developed [Pau92b]. PUMA is machine independent; consequently, experiments and programs can be implemented without considering special hardware constraints. Special mechanisms — like the automatic generation of documentation — support the implementation of the software engineering principles discussed above. The system is used as a pool for common functions, classes, and programs for image and speech analysis.

PUMA includes (**AN IM**age **A**na**L**ysis System) ANIMALS (see Chapter 17). The implemented classes are named „hippos" (**HI**erarchy of **P**icture **P**rocessing **O**bject**S**), from now on written with Greek letters ἵππος (pronounce as: „hippos") [Pau92b]. In ANIMALS we define common command line interfaces. Different programs doing similar things look similar to the user.

---

[7]Programmier-Umgebung für die Muster–Analyse — in English: a programming environment for pattern analysis

```
> co -l test.C,v
> co -l test.C
> ci Makefile
> chmod ugo-rwx *
> chmod +w test.C,v
> make love
> got a light?
```
16

In Part II and in Part III of this book we present a subset of the ἵππος–interface which is tailored to simple applications, but fully compatible with the larger ἵππος system. The algorithms in Part III are implemented in ANIMALS. The functions and classes can serve as an example for modularity.

Implementation as well as data storage of a program should be machine–independent. For the system described in this book, we show how this can be implemented.

We experienced that program documentation which is kept in separate files from the source code almost never reflects the actual status of the project. Therefore we put all the documentation into the source and header files, as close as possible to the implementation. Consistency of documentation with the actual programs was enhanced considerably. An implementation of this idea is left as Exercise 3.e.

Exercises

3.a   Write a Makefile which compiles the C++ program my_program.C, adds the object file to the library, and generates an executable program test using the library.

3.b   Decide and discuss which commands are useful or nonsense in Program 16. Try them on your machine!

3.c   Huge programs are divided up in modules and the C++ source code can be found in different directories.
       Assume we have the following directories:
       filters, segmentation, models, classification.
       Each subdirectory contains C++ code and a Makefile for compilation, building libraries and executable programs. Write a Makefile in the actual directory which automatically updates the complete program system by calling make world.

3.d   Check the rcs manual and find out which of the information in the module header of a program (Sect. 3.4) can be added automatically.

3.e   Write an awk script which extracts the module head from program and header files and creates a readable layout from this information. Include general information about the program, its usage, and its purpose.

If necessary, mark this information appropriately, e.g. by DOC_BEG text DOC_END, to help extraction with awk.

Add this command script to the makefile and program in Exercise 3.a.

4 Control and Data Structures

In this chapter we briefly describe the data structure definitions which are already available in conventional C. We explain how these data structures and control statements can be used in C++.

4.1 Structures

Like most modern programming languages, C++ has a mechanism for gluing already known data types together into a new data type. In C++ this is called a `struct` and usually has a type name.[1] The syntax is basically as follows:

Syntax:	`struct` [*sname*] `{` *declaration** `}` [*vdef*] `;`

This introduces a new type name (*sname*). The semicolon at the end is very important and is a common source of errors, when it is forgotten. Declarations of variables inside the braces declare storage locations which are the *members* of the data structure; the names are called *structure tags*. Variables may be immediately defined with a type declaration (*vdef*); more commonly, they are defined separately using the structure name (*sname*). Program 17 shows the new data type `PointXY` for point coordinates. The variable p0 is defined using this new data type. Access to the members of a structure is possible via a variable followed by a dot and the member tag.

Static or global data can be initialized by values listed in curly brackets, as shown in Program 17 for the variable p.

In contrast to C, the structure name can be used as a type without a `typedef` (c.f. Sect. 7.1).

---

[1]Occasionally the name is left out; c.f. Program 136 for an example.

```
struct PointXY {        // declare new data type
   int x,y;             // members are x and y
};                      // do not forget the ;

PointXY p0;             // define a variable
p0.x = 1;               // access member x
p0.y = 1;               // access member y
PointXY p = { 1, 2 };   // initialize a variable
```
17

```
enum A {
        voiced = 1,
        fricative = 2,
        voiced_fricative = 3,
        stop = 0
     } ;
A a = voiced;
enum ZoomSetting {wide = 0, portrait = 1, tele = 2};
ZoomSetting z = wide;
```
18

4.2 Enumerations

Enumeration data types allow constant integer data with a very small range to be explicitly named. They are a handy feature to use to associate several constant values with their own name. The syntax is as follows:

Syntax: enum [*typename*] { {*name* [$\equiv$ *int_value,*] }* } [*vdef*] ;

Variables can be defined using the *typename*. If no initialization is specified with the *int_value*, the next free integer value is chosen by the compiler.[2] An example for labeling phonemes and lens positions is shown in Program 18.

Enumeration data can be used in many cases where formerly defines were used in traditional C.

4.3 Scope Resolution

In Sect. 2.9 we saw how global names can be avoided when the declarations are inside a block or local to a file.

Enumerations, as in Program 18, introduce many global names. This is generally bad software practice and may cause problems when linking different modules together. A solution is to declare enumerations within a structure scope (Program 19). The names are now visible only inside the structure. They can still be used from the outside by the *scope resolution operator* ": :".[3] An artificial example is shown in Program 19; we will see more practical examples later. Of course, enum definitions do not require any storage during run time of a program.

The scope resolution operator — like all other two character operators — may not be separated by a blank character.

---

[2]It is even possible to assign the same value twice to different names with explicit initialization.

[3]Another application of this operator is to access a name which was overwritten by the same name in a closer block, as later in Program 121. Various other sophisticated applications of this operator are possible but not treated in this book.

```
struct X {                      // artificial example
    enum A { i = 1, j = 2, k, 1};  // enum within structure
    A a0;                       // variable of this type
} x;                            // structure variable
X::A a1;          // use type defined in structure scope
int i = X::i;     // use value defined in structure scope
```
⟨19⟩

```
union numbers { long a; double b; char c; };
numbers n;
```
⟨20⟩

4.4 Unions

Another language feature in C/C++ is called a union Inside a union, several fields can be specified. The syntax looks exactly like the syntax for structures. Fields declared inside the union are accessed just like the fields inside a structure. Similarly, methods can be declared inside unions as with structures and classes of C++.

Syntax: union [*sname*] { *declaration** } [*vdef*] ;

In contrast to structures, all the fields in a union share the *same* location in memory and can only be used alternatively.[4] The overall memory requirement is calculated from the longest entry. In Program 20 the size will be based on the length of the double field. There is no compiler generated run time information about which field is used and how many bits are valid.[5] If such information is required, it has to be coded explicitly.

Unions are in some sense a low–level language feature and should be used with care![6]

4.5 Bit– and Shift–Operations

Often operations are defined on integer values so that they can be used to inspect data bit by bit. They are used this way mainly in operating system or hardware interfaces or in highly efficient parts of a program.

Bit– and shift–operations for C and C++ are listed in Table 4.1. A zero value is inserted on left shift operations (LSH). A right shift (RSH) of an unsigned value will insert a zero in the highest bit. A right shift of a signed integer will do an arithmetic shift corresponding to a division by two; i.e., the highest bit is left unchanged and the second

---

[4]The fields in structures can be used simultaneously!

[5]In Program 20 one can create illegal bit patterns for the double field when the union is written with the long field and then read using the double field.

[6]Inheritance in C++ (Chapter 13) can in many cases substitute unions in C.

```
int b = -2;           // not spectacular
int a = b | 0x33;     // bitwise OR connection
int c = a << 4;       // see the operator precedence
b ^= (a & 0xffff);    // parentheses look better
b = a || c;           // logical connection
```

21

highest is filled with the value of the highest bit.[7] The operators & and | combine their operands bitwise. In contrast, the boolean operators && and || combine the values of their operands logically.

Syntax		Example
&=	AND	a &= 0xff
|=	OR	a |= 0x13ff
^=	XOR	a ^= b
<<=	LSH	a <<= 3
>>=	RSH	a >>= 2

Syntax		Example
&	AND	a & 0xff
|	OR	a | 0x13ff
^	XOR	a ^ b
<<	LSH	a << 3
>>	RSH	a >> 2
~	NOT	~0

Table 4.1 Bit operations on integer values

Binary bit and shift operations can be combined with an assignment as shown in Program 21.

4.6 Bit Fields

When dealing with hardware — e.g. the interface to a frame grabber — it is often required to request exactly a certain number of *bits* — for example, 8 or 16. One implementation could use a structure containing a byte and a short. Since the size of a short may vary between machine architectures, it is better to request 16 bits. The language construct in C++ and C is a so called *bit field*. An example is shown in Program 22. Inside a structure the number of bits for a field may be specified. There is no difference to this structure members in access in comparison to regular members as in Sect. 4.1. Their type is always unsigned int.

Depending on compiler or hardware restrictions, there may be limitations on the number of bits which can be requested in bit fields.

Bit fields are, of course, also a low–level feature of a this programming language. If they are used properly, they may be very useful for efficient programming — as is required for pattern recognition purposes. In combination with unions (Sect. 4.4) the use of bit

---

[7]This behavior is machine dependent; you should not rely on it.

```
struct SubPixCoord {        // subpixel coordinates for images with
    unsigned int x: 12;      // size MxN
    unsigned int y: 12;      // M,N in [1..4096]
    unsigned int xfract: 4;  // subpixel accuracy 1/8 pixel
    unsigned int yfract: 4;
};
SubPixelCoord p;             // a variable
unsigned int x0 = p.x;       // access bit field as unsigned integer
```
(22)

fields can be even trickier; only if such tricks are properly encapsulated, they can add efficiency to a program while still maintain its clarity.

4.7 Logical Values and Conditionals

Neither C nor C++ supply the data–type boolean: instead, integer values can be used as truth values. The value 0 stands for FALSE, everything else is interpreted as TRUE. Operators for comparison are:

| Syntax: | $expr1 > | >= | < | <= | != | == expr2$

The operator == checks whether two values are equal. A common mistake is to confuse the assignment operator = and the equality operator ==. Inequality can be tested using !=. The operator < (> >= <=) checks whether the expression on the left is smaller (greater, greater or equal, smaller or equal) than the expression on the right side.

Logical values — i.e., integer expressions — can be combined by operations as listed in Table 4.2. The precedence of operators is complicated and a common source for errors. We suggest the use of parentheses to make the wanted precedence obvious.

Operator	Explanation	Example
&&	AND	`((i>1) && (i<2)) ...`
||	OR	`((i>1) || (i<-2)) ...`
!	NOT	`((i>1) && (!(i<2))) ...`

Table 4.2 Logical operators

Often it is necessary to control a program through the use of validity tests with boolean expressions. Normally, statements are executed in the sequence given in the program. Expressions are evaluated from left to right. Conditional execution as well as loops and function calls can alter this sequence. Unconditional jumps (goto) are almost never needed and considered bad programming style. Jumps are often accepted in C to deal with exceptional cases (c.f. the function longjmp in most C libraries). C++ provides

```
if (i > 2)                      // if #1
    if ((i == 5) || (j < 3))    // if #2
        j = 4;
    else                        // belongs to if #2
        j = 8;
```
(23)

```
if (i > 2)
    j = 3;
else if ((i == 5) || (j < 3))   // if cascade
    j = 4;
else {                          // here we use a block
        j = 8;
        i = 2;
                                // we end the cascade
}
```
(24)

alternatives by exception handling as a more structured way of handling errors. We leave this feature to the references [Str91].

Conditional execution can be done using the if statement:

Syntax: if (*expression*) *statement1* [else *statement2*]

Statement1 is executed if the expression evaluates to an integer value other than 0. Otherwise if the else clause is present, *statement2* is executed. Nesting of conditional statements is possible. As in Pascal, the "else" is assumed to belong to the next possible "if". Program 23 shows this situation.

Of course, the statements in the conditional branches can be blocks (c.f. Program 24). Also note the typical indentation style for if and else cascades in the following example (see also Sect. 3.4) which puts the last else under the previous else. Cascades of if–else–if–else etc. thereby can be aligned.

4.8   Loops

Three types of loops exist in C++ corresponding to the structograms in Sect. 3.5. The syntax of the while and the do loops are as follows:

Syntax:

         1) while *(expression)* *statement*
         2) do *statement* while *(expression)* ;

We call the *statement* in the loop the *loop body*; it may of course be a block containing several statements. In the while–loop the statement is executed as long as the expression evaluates to something other than 0. The do–loop terminates when the expression

```
while ( i > 2) {
      printf("%d ", --i);
}
// next loop
do {
      printf("%d ", --i);
} while (i > 0);
```
⟨25⟩

```
for (int k = 0; k < 10; ++k) {   // declare loop variable
      int j = fct();             // get some value
      if (j == -1) break;        // exit the hard way
      if (j == 0) continue;      // skip the following
      printf("%d %d", i, j);     // otherwise: print
}
```
⟨26⟩

evaluates to 0; the do–loop body is executed at least once. Since both loops use the keyword `while`, it is crucial to use proper indentation (Program 25, see also Sect. 3.4)

The third loop syntax is the `for`–loop, which is a special type of the `while`–loop:

Syntax: `for` (*statement1* ; *expression* ; *statement2*) *statement3*

This is equivalent to a while loop

`statement1; while(expression){statement3; statement2;}`.

The `for`–loop contains two assignments and one boolean expression. The first assignment initializes the loop variable, the second assignment can be used to change the loop variable, and if the boolean expression becomes false (i.e., zero), the loop terminates. Any of the statements may be empty.

Since declarations are statements in C++, they can be used in the loop to introduce a new variable. This style of writing is very common in C++; it is exemplified in Program 26.

Any loop can be terminated by a `break` statement. The `continue` statement skips the rest of the loop body and continues with the next iteration. These constructs help to avoid goto's. They are commonly used but in principle unstructured (no symbol exists in standard structograms, Sect. 3.5). Program 26 shows these constructs.

4.9   Switches

Instead of cascading numerous levels of `if else if else ...`, a switch can be used when all the conditionals depend on the same integer variable. The value of this variable can be used to dispatch to several *constant* integer values. These values are used as case labels. The execution of such a branch can be terminated with a `break` statement. If the break is missing, the control continues with the next statement. When

```
void fct2(int c)        // function will modify global i and j
{   extern int i,j;     // GLOBAL VARIABLES
    switch(c) {
        case 1:  ++i;   // fall into next case
        case 0:  ++j;
             break;
        case 3:  --j;   // fall into next case
        case 2:  ++i;
             break;
        case 5:  --i;   // fall into next case
        case 4:  --j;
             break;
        case 7:  ++j;   // fall into next case
        case 6:  --i;
             break;
        default: fprintf(stderr,"Illegal direction (%d)\n",c);
    }
}
```
                                                                            27

this is desired it should always be commented. Otherwise, it might look like one of many common programming errors in C. A default case can be specified which is applied if none of the switch values are matched (assuming switches contain a break). The most common form of the syntax is:

Syntax:

switch *(expression)* { *case_stms** [default:] *statement** }

case_stms: {case *const-expr:*}* *statement** [break;]

After the opening curly bracket of a switch, a declaration is possible. These variables may not be initialized. Inside the switch, declarations are not allowed, except when they are inside a new block.

A function including a large switch is shown in Program 27. Note, that some of the statements "fall into the next case", which is commented, as required. We will use this example later on (Sect. 16.4, page 200); then we will be able to understand the meaning of the error message in the default case of the switch.

Exercises

4.a   Graphically show the dependencies of the files in Program 29–32.

4.b   Write and test a makefile for the shown examples. Include the dependencies for version control with rcs (Appendix A.4).

4.c   How can the break and continue statements be avoided? Transform the code in Program 26 into an equivalent program without break and continue and draw the structogram.

```
* M1.h */
extern void fct();
```
28

```
/* M2.h */
extern int verbose;
```
29

```
/* M1.C */
#include "M1.h"
#include "M2.h"
void fct()
{
  if (verbose) printf("fct() called\n");
}
```
30

```
/* M2.C */
#include "M2.h"
int verbose = 0;
```
31

```
/* M0.C */
#include "M1.h"
#include "M2.h"
main(int argc, char ** argv)     // nonsense example
{
    int verbose = (argc > 1);    // verbose used as boolean
    if (verbose) fct();          // conditional call
}
```
32

5 Arrays and Pointers

In the first chapter we explained that discrete speech signals can be represented by vectors. Images are usually stored as matrices or as higher dimensional arrays. Therefore vectors and matrices are very important data–structures in the field of pattern recognition and should be discussed in detail.

5.1 Vectors and Matrices

In general, C++–arrays are indexed by unsigned integers beginning with 0. A one–dimensional array f of size n therefore has the elements $f_0, f_1, \ldots, f_{n-1}$. Neither the compiler nor the runtime system check the range of the subscripts; nasty errors may occur with the use of improper values (see also Exercise 2.b on page 29).[1]

A variable is declared as an array by placing the constant number of elements within square brackets following the variable name. With multidimensional arrays the size specification is repeated.

Syntax:	*type ID* [*size*]*;

Examples of the declaration of arrays are given in Program 33. For two–dimensional arrays, the first size specifies the number of rows, the second specifies the number of columns. Access to single elements is done by supplying an index of range $0, 1, \ldots, n-1$ for each dimension,[2] as shown in Program 33, which also shows how eight bit gray level images are represented in C and C++, i.e., pixels are unsigned char represented as

---

[1] In Sect.10.8 we will learn how to avoid this "feature" in C++.

[2] The expression image[2,4] is also syntactically correct, but is equal to image[4]! (Cmp. 7.9)

```
int    a[10];          // integer array size 10
char   c[20];          // character array size 20
float  f[20][10];      // float matrix size 20 * 10
int i = 9;             // integer variable

unsigned char image[256][256]; // a typical image
a[4] = 3;       c[9] = 'c';       f[4][2]     = 4.33;
a[0] = a[4];    a[0] += 4;        image[1][i] = 0;

a[++i] = 10; // syntactically correct, but wrong index! (i>9)
```

33

```
#define COLUMNS 256
#define ROWS    256
static unsigned char image[ROWS][COLUMNS];  // global image
main(int argc, char ** argv)                // main program
{
    int s = atoi(argv[1]);                  // should check argc!
    for (int i = 0; i < ROWS; ++i )         // loop over lines
      for (int j = 0; j < COLUMNS; ++j )    // loop over columns
        image[i][j] = (i * s) ^ j;          // ^ introduced later
    fwrite(image[0],COLUMNS,ROWS,stdout);   // ugly - raw write
    exit(0);                                // good exit code
}
```
(34)

byte. The size of the image is fixed to 256^2 elements. A change of image size would most likely cause many changes in the source code. It is a little better to use macros (Program 34). C++ also introduces constants which can be used as array sizes; we will learn about this feature later in Sect. 7.3.

The program in Program 34 creates a fancy synthetic image and writes it — the hard way — to stdout.[3] It combines the indices i and j with the xor–operator ^ introduced in Sect. 4.5. The result for two different values of s is shown in Figure 5.1.

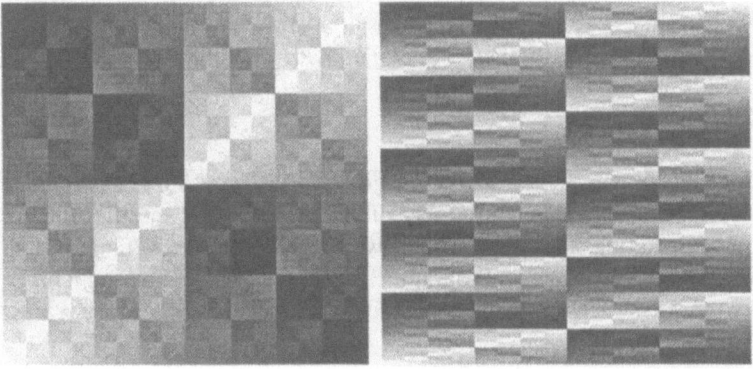

Figure 5.1 Result of Program 34 with argument 1 and 5

5.2 Pointers

People often are very suspicious of using pointers. Especially those whose "native language" is Pascal. Nevertheless, the essence of C and C++ is in the usage of pointers.

---

[3]We will see better ways of storing images in Chapter 11.

```
int * a, b, *c;    // Pointers to int a and c, normal int b
```
35

```
int b = 3;    char a = 'a';   // memory filled with values
int *bp;      char * ap;      // pointers (not initialized)
int *cp;                      // i.e., undefined value
bp = &b;                      // *bp == b
cp = bp;                      // *bp == *cp
ap = &a;                      // *ap == a
*ap = 'x';                    // a == 'x'
ap = NULL;                    // NULL-pointer
```
36

"First of all, don't panic".

Pointers in C and C++ are declared as variables pointing to data of a known type, i.e. there are no pointers *per se*, but pointers to integers, pointers to floating point numbers, pointers to characters, etc.. The syntax was already introduced in Sect. 2.4.[4] The * declares the variable immediately following as a pointer to the type.

Syntax: *type* [*] *var1* [≡ *expr*] [, [*] *var2* [≡ *expr*]]* ;

Program 35 shows the definition of two pointer variables to integers (a and c); the variable b is a normal integer variable.

After the definition of a pointer variable, the value of the variable is undefined (as it is the case with normal values), i.e. the address in the value cell is arbitrary and — in general — not valid. Pointer values can be set by assigning one pointer to another of the same type. Pointers can be set to any location in memory where data of the expected type is present. In contrast to Pascal, for example, this location can be assigned by the address operator & on a normal variable and does not have to be allocated dynamically. The access of the data pointed to by the pointer is done using a *. Program 36 illustrates the various uses of pointers.

If a pointer is not initialized, it points *somewhere* — which is usually an illegal location. It is often required to have a pointer point *nowhere*; in Pascal this is done with the *nil*–pointer value. In C/C++ there is a macro in the file `stdio.h` or `stdlib.h` named `NULL`; we then call the pointer a "NULL–pointer".

5.3   Vectors vs. Pointers

Vectors and Pointers are very similar in C/C++ and their syntax is the same in many cases. A vector can be seen as a constant pointer to the first element of an array. Applications can be seen in Program 37.

---

[4]There we did not specify, what `ptr` was.

```
char carray[64];
char * cptr, *cptr1;
cptr = carray;
cptr = &(carray[3]);
carray = cptr ;            // ILLEGAL
carray[3] = *cptr;
cptr[3] = 'a';             // [ offset ] is legal for pointers
```
37

```
int iarray0[10] = {1,2,3,4,0,1,2,3,4,5}; // all values specified
int iarray2[10] = {1,2,3,4,5};            // remaining values 0
int iarray1[]   = {1,2,3,4,5};            // int iarray1[5]
```
38

```
unsigned char image[4][3] =     // image variable
    { {  1,  0 ,   1},          // row 0
      { -1,  0 ,  -1},          // row 1
      { -1,  0 ,  -1},          // row 2
      {  1,  0 ,   1} };        // row 3
```
39

Assignment to the whole vector with one operator is not possible (see the illegal line in the example), since an array is a *constant* pointer. However, a pointer can be set to an array. Assignment to single elements is obviously possible as well. Data pointed to by a pointer can be accessed using [index] as in an array.

Global or static arrays of simple types can be initialized during the variable's definition. The values assigned are listed in curly brackets separated by commas. The size of the array can be implicitly determined by the number of initial values. If a size is specified, it may not be smaller than the size indicated by the number of elements in the initialization (Program 38).

Static multidimensional arrays are initialized by nested lists of values as shown in Program 39. For two–dimensional arrays, the inner lists initialize the rows, one after another.

5.4   Pointer Operations and Allocation

Pointers can be manipulated by various operators; for example, they can be compared using the relational operators (> >= == != < <=, cmp. Sect. 4.7). If an integer is added to a pointer, the address is incremented by the given number of elements; i.e. if 4 is added to a pointer pointing to an integer (int *), the result of the addition points to the fourth integer following the actual position of the pointer. The same holds for subtraction. This can be understood best if we look at the index operator [index

```
cptr = &(carray[0]);
*cptr = 'a';
cptr++;
*cptr = 'b';
*++cptr = 'c';
cptr = new char[10];       // allocate 10 characters
cptr1 = cptr + 3;          // third element of array
int d = cptr1 - cptr;      // number of elements between pointers
delete [] cptr;            // discard allocation
cptr = new char;           // allocate 1 characters
delete cptr;               // discard allocation
```
40

```
void strcpy(char * to, char * from)
{
    while((*(to++) = *(from++)) != '\0')   // zero character terminates string
        /* empty body */ ;
}
```
41

]; the expression `carray[3]` is identical to `*(carray+3)`.[5] Subtraction of two pointers (of the same type) yields the number of elements between the two positions.

Like in addition and subtraction of numbers, pointers can also be incremented and decremented. These operations are often combined with * to access the element pointed to as can be seen in Program 40. A pointer can be set to a legal address by assigning the address of a variable using the address operator. Alternatively, the pointer may be set to unnamed memory requested by new; the memory will be sufficiently large and aligned for the requested data type. The allocation can be discarded by the operator delete. When the type given to the operator is a structure, sufficient storage is requested.

Syntax:

> *ptr* = new *type* [[*nelem*]]
> delete [[]] *ptr*

A summary of the operations on pointers is given in Table 5.1. When arrays are created with new type[size] the corresponding delete operation has to use the syntax delete [].

The function in Program 41 is a very common application for strings. It also shows the combination of assignment and relational comparison. The first string had better be long enough! When a loop's body is empty (as in Program 41), this should be marked and commented clearly, so other readers will not suspect an error there.

---

[5]Together with the commutativity of addition, this implies a[i] == i[a]. This is not a joke!

operator	operand 1	operator	operand 2	Explanation
*	ptr			Dereference
&	var			Address of
++	ptr			Increment
--	ptr			Decrement
	ptr	=	ptr	Assignment
	ptr	=	& var	Assignment
	ptr	=	new type [number]	Array allocation
	ptr	=	new type	Allocation
delete	ptr			Disposal
delete[]	ptr			Array disposal
	ptr	[number]		Array access
	ptr	+	int	Addition
	ptr	–	int	Subtraction
	ptr	–	ptr	Distance
	ptr	rel–op	ptr	Compare addr.

Table 5.1 Operations on pointers; rel–op stands for any relational operator (Sect. 4.7).

5.5 Pointer to Structures

As with standard data types, pointers may be set to user defined data types. Structure members can be accessed by the use of pointers to structures. The combination of pointer access and member ((*ptr).member) can be abbreviated by a new operator -> (Program 42). Like arrays, the structures can be initialized by lists in curly brackets.

Incrementing a pointer to a structure naturally advances the pointer by the number of bytes occupied by the structure. This value can be found by the sizeof operator, which returns the size (measured in byte) of its argument at *compile–time*. The argument can be a variable, an expression, or a type name. This operator again shows the difference between vectors and pointers. Applied to a pointer, the operator will give the number of bytes required for storing an address; applied to an array, it will give the size of the array. Program 43 shows how to enquire the number of elements in an array at compile time. The result of the sizeof operator cannot be used in preprocessor directives, since it is evaluated by the compiler, not by the preprocessor (c.f. Figure 2.1).

As can be seen in Program 43, the sizeof operator may be used to write machine–independent programs which adjust their behavior according to the size of the same data type found on a different machine architecture.

```
PointXY p = { 1, 2 };        // initialize a variable
PointXY *pp = &p;            // define a pointer variable
p.x = 1;                     // access via variable
(*pp).y = 1;                 // access via pointer
pp->x = 2;                   // short hand for (*pp).x = 2;
```
42

```
static char string[] = "abc";        // initialize static array
static char * cptr   = string;       // pointer
static int  arrayp[] = {1,2,3,4};     // initialize static array
int asize = sizeof(arrayp)/sizeof(int); // number of elements
int slen  = sizeof string;            // no () required
int plen  = sizeof cptr;              // plen != slen
```
43

```
char string0[10];                     // constant length 10
char string1[] = { 'a', 'b', 'c', '\0'}; // length 4
char string2[] = "abc";               // also length 4
```
44

5.6 Strings

In Program 33, the array c represents a string, i.e. strings are vectors (one–dimensional arrays) of characters. They are always delimited by the trailing ' \ 0 ' character. Initialization of a string (i.e. an array of characters) can be done using the lists described in Sect. 5.3; it also can be simplified by supplying a string in double quotes (Program 44). In the first case, the ' \ 0 ' has to be added explicitly; in the later case, the ' \ 0 ' is added automatically, the array will thus be one element longer than the number of characters provided in the initialization.

Useful functions on strings can be found in the standard libraries. Comparison and manipulation of strings is facilitated by the following routines: strcmp compares two strings, strlen returns the length of the string, and strcpy copies one string to another (Program 41). These functions are declared in string.h and can be inserted into the program with #include <string.h>. Refer to the compiler or operating system manual for further information on these functions.

5.7 Pointer and Array Arguments

The C programming language passes *all* function arguments by value. Changes to the arguments in the function body are therefore local and have no global effect.

Functions can change global data using pointer arguments. In Program 41 the pointers to and from are incremented; this does not, however, change the value of the pointers

```
void swapint(int * a, int *b) // swap the value of two integers
{
    int tmp = *a; *a = *b; *b = tmp;
}

void fct()
{   int i = 3, j = 4;
    swapint (&i,&j);              // now i == 4, j == 3
}
```
45

```
void fct(unsigned char m[][3], unsigned char f[][256])
{
    f[3][4] *= m[1][1];
}
```
46

```
int i, * ip, ** ipp;
i = 3; ip = &i; ipp = &ip;
*ip = 4; ** ipp = 5;              /* i == *ip == **ipp == 5 */
```
47

provided in the call which are passed to the function by value! The changes occur in the data pointed to by the arguments! This is shown in Program 45.

Of course, global variables may be accessed inside a block or function. This is generally not the best software practice, however. The return value of a function can be used in the calling sequence to promote the changes of a function. Later we will see other argument parsing facilities for C++ (Sect. 7.3).

When a multi–dimensional array is to be passed to a function, the size of the argument has to be provided to the compiler; only the first size of the argument may be left unspecified. An example is given in Program 46. For image processing, this is of course completely unsatisfactory. Several text books treat images as one–dimensional arrays and do pointer arithmetic for the interpretation of lines and columns. There is, however, a nice *trick* for circumventing the problems with multidimensional arrays (see e.g., [Pre92]) which we will exploit in Sect. 10.8.

5.8   Pointer to Pointer

Pointers are tied to a given type. Naturally, the data the pointer points to can again be a pointer. The declaration and application of a pointer to a pointer to an integer is shown in Program 47.

Because of the dual nature of pointers and vectors, a twofold pointer can be seen as a two–dimensional array, i.e. it can be accessed using two indices. Although this looks

```
#include <stdlib.h>
main(int argc, char ** argv)
{
    while ( argc-- > 0 )
      printf("%s\n", *(argv++));
    exit(0);
}
```
48

```
#include "image.h"          /* defines for XS and YS */
unsigned char image[YS][XS];  // global definition of an image
main(int argc, char ** argv)
{
    char * in, * out;
    // get args
    readimage(in,image);
    // etc.
}
```
49

similar as an array access (Program 33), it has a different meaning to the compiler. For static arrays, indices are evaluated using the type sizes contained in the array declaration; after an arithmetic expression, this will result in the address of the array element. Generally, addition and multiplication is required here. We will use this feature later in Sect. 11.1 to access matrix elements efficiently.

For pointers to pointers, the indices are offsets to the pointer. The first index will be an offset to the pointer. This will yield an address to which the second offset is applied. No arithmetic other than addition is required here.

5.9   Command Line Arguments

In Sect. 2.7 we used the main function with two arguments argc and argv; argc is already known as the number of arguments on the command line; we can now explain argv.

The argument argv is an array of strings, i.e. a pointer to a pointer to a character. It is passed to main as a pointer to the first string which contains the name of the program. The length of each string is known by the trailing '\0' in the string. Program 48 shows a program that prints its own arguments. When argv is declared as char **, it is common to scan all arguments by *++argv as shown in Program 48.

There exist several handy functions for parsing the arguments of a program. In the following chapters we will use extensions of the functions defined in the following exercises.

```
#include "image.h"              /* defines for XS and YS */
void readimage(char*filename,unsigned char image[YS][XS])
{
   FILE * file = fopen(filename,"r");
   if (file == NULL) {
     fprintf(stderr,"Could not open file %s\n",filename);
     exit(1);
   }
   fread(image[0],YS,XS,file); // ugly - raw binary read
   fclose(file);
}
```
50

Exercises

5.a   Declare, define, and initialize a static array of strings with its size determined
       by the number of initialization strings. Write a NULL string as the last string.

5.b   Write a routine cmp_arg with one string as an argument called opt. Compare
       opt to all the strings of Exercise 5.a. If the string is a unique prefix of a string in
       the list, return its index in the array. If it is a prefix, but not a unique one, return
       -1; If it is not found in the list, return -2.
       Hint: use the function strncmp.

5.c   Write a routine printargs which prints all the strings of the list in Exercise 5.a.

5.d   Write a routine check_args(argc,argv) which is called from main.
       Every command line argument starting with a '-' should be checked by the
       routine of Exercise 5.b. Skip the '-' for that purpose. Use a switch on the return
       value of cmp_arg. In case of failure, use printargs and print an appropriate
       error message.

5.e   Write a simple function which generates a synthetic image containing a filled
       circle. Your main program could look as in Program 49. Use a fixed size for the
       image. Provide filename, center, and radius from the command line. Write the
       image to a file using the raw write function in Program 34 — but hide the call in
       a separate function write_image and put the defines for the image sizes in a
       separate header file as shown in Program 50.
       Make sure that your program works with arbitrary image sizes. Write a makefile
       and use rcs (c.f. Appendix A).

5.f   Write a program that applies a simple *filter* (c.f. Chapter 19) to an image: replace
       every pixel by the mean of its left and right neighbor. For argument handling,
       input and output, proceed as in the previous exercise.

6   Classification and Pattern Analysis

Depending on the input data and the problem to be solved, there exist three major areas in pattern recognition and pattern analysis:

1. classification of simple patterns,

2. classification of complex patterns, and

3. analysis of complex patterns.

In the subsequent parts of this book we will emphasize our discussion on the first and third point above, even though we will briefly introduce all of them. A comprehensive discussion is presented in e.g. [Nie83]. In this chapter we give an overview of the architecture of pattern recognition and analysis systems. We outline the relation of knowledge based pattern understanding systems to the general problems of artificial intelligence.

6.1   Classification

The goal of pattern classification is to associate a class with the given input pattern (Sect. 1.4). With respect to the classification process, the task domain (see Sect. 1.3) is partitioned into k disjunctive classes Ω_λ ($\lambda = 1, \ldots, k$), i.e. $\Omega_\mu \cap \Omega_\nu = \emptyset$ for $\nu \neq \mu$. The classification assigns each observed pattern exactly one class of this partition. Several applications suggest the insertion of a *reject class* Ω_0; for example, for those applications where rejection will bring about lower costs than misclassification.

Some examples can illustrate the goal of classification:

1. classes $A - Z$ and "unknown" for character recognition,

2. forest, street, field, water for the automatic generation of maps using satellite images,

3. the phoneme classification to the classes vowel, plosive, fricative, nasal, and silence for word recognition.

The classification algorithms can be divided into two classes: syntactical classifiers and numerical classifiers. If the features of the patterns are real numbers, vectors, sets or other structures on the field of reals, the resulting classification system will be a numerical one. Typically, statistical principles are used for the design of numerical classifiers to be used speech recognition [Hua90]. Based on the geometric nature of objects, numerical classifiers in the field of image processing are often based on some distance measures [Mar82]. Basic statistical methods for pattern classification will be introduced in Chapter 8. Spectral features for speech classification are presented in Chapter 25. Alternatively, artificial neural networks can be used for classification purposes. We briefly mention this subject in Sect. 26.7.

Syntactical classification uses the results of parsing a syntactic description of the pattern using a formal language. Examples for syntactical image classification can be found in [Bun92]; syntactic classifiers for speech recognition are used in [Nie83].

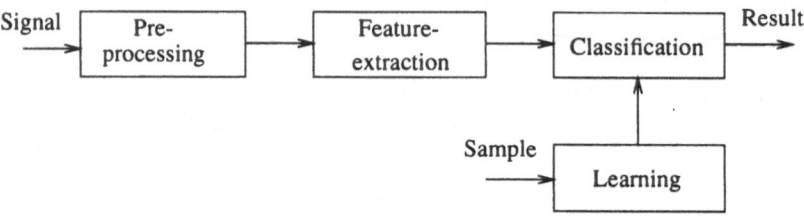

Figure 6.1 The architecture of a simple classification system [Nie83]

Figure 6.1 shows the modules of a classification system for simple patterns. The classification module decides which class fits best to the computed features. Usually, a training set (sample) is used so that the parameters of the classification process can be adapted by a learning module.

6.2 Preprocessing

Before features can be extracted, the signal is *preprocessed*. Usually preprocessing operations are problem–independent. Patterns are transformed into patterns, i.e. an image matrix into an image matrix or a speech signal into a speech signal. In other words, the type of representation does not change.

The goal of preprocessing is to simplify the computation which will have to be done in later stages of the analysis. The signal may be enhanced, normalized, filtered, etc. in order to reach this goal. For example, smoothing of patterns represents a typical operation in the preprocessing stage. Smoothing will eventually reduce unnecessary details or noise and may thus speed up succeeding processing. Other examples of preprocessing operations are things such as filters or changes of the size of images or the duration of speech signals.

Another common preprocessing technique is the normalization of the input signals. Energy normalization, for example, would adjust the loudness of speech signals or the darkness of an image. Size normalization of patterns or rotation of a given sub–pattern into a normal position is common, e.g. in character recognition.[1]

6.3   Feature Extraction

Numerical features can be vectors of real numbers or a set of vectors which characterize the class of a pattern. For speech signals one can use the zero–crossings or Fourier descriptors (Chapter 25). The average gray level of a region in an image can be significant in the classification of objects. Some simple statistical features are, for example, the average intensity in a local spatial neighborhood of a picture region or the variance in the temporal proximity of a speech sampling value. In some applications it is better to use symbolic features instead of numerical ones.

The process of feature extraction can be characterized as problem–independent. Patterns are transformed into features; numerical values are computed in statistical feature extraction; the mean of gray levels for example. A symbolic representation of a feature is, for instance, the attribute "convex" of a specific surface patch. The computed features are used decisively in the classification process. Symbolic features once extracted are fundamental for syntactical classifiers [Bun92].

6.4   Analysis

The analysis of complex pattern searches to obtain the individual description of an input pattern. In general, this requires a knowledge–based processing of the patterns, i.e. the system is based on knowledge about the range of the application. The first part of the analysis requires no application dependent knowledge. The general structure of the analysis is shown in Figure 6.2. Preprocessing can be done problem–independently. The parameter setting and selection of the appropriate preprocessing method may, however, be based on assumptions about the signal, i.e. on knowledge about the problem. The preprocessing operations correspond to those used for the classification of the simple patterns. The search for the characteristic and simple parts of patterns is called *segmentation*.

Like preprocessing, image segmentation algorithms mostly require no knowledge about the objects in the scene. Speech can be segmented solely based on the information in the signal. The choice of the best suited algorithm and its parameters can be guided by knowledge.

---

[1]This is not a trivial problem. Consider the sampling theorem!

Model driven analysis (the upper two blocks in Figure 6.2) can be understood as a search and optimization process during which optimal correspondences between the knowledge about the given scene — represented as models in the knowledge base — and a segmented image are found [Nie90a].

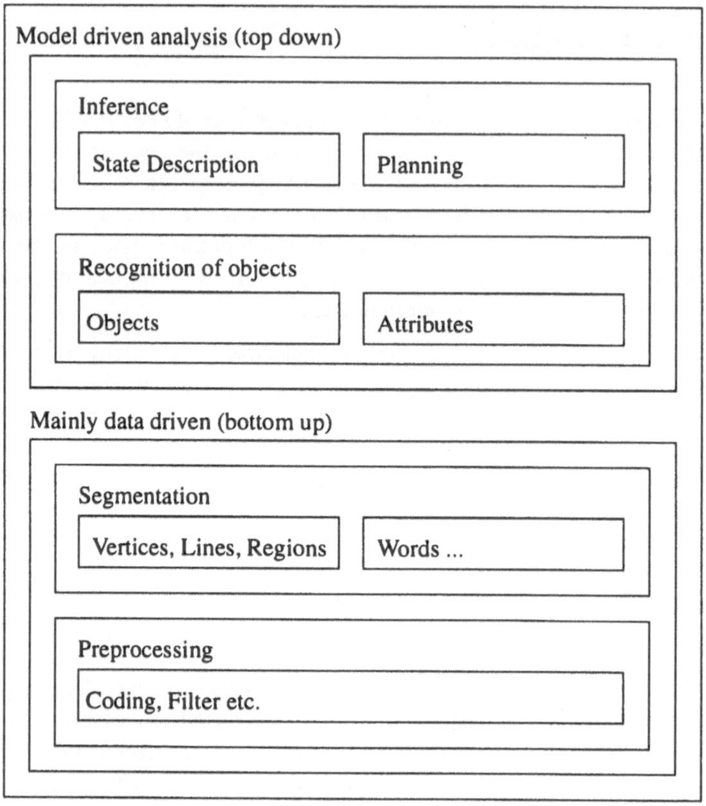

Figure 6.2 Structure of a knowledge based system for pattern analysis. The left part represents the image analysis process, the right one the speech analysis (from [Nie90a]).

6.5   Image Segmentation

Segmentation is frequently a data driven process where knowledge about the application domain is not required. In this book, we mainly cover these problem–independent segmentation techniques. In a model driven approach, problem dependent knowledge for segmentation can be used.

Image segmentation can be based on homogeneities; namely, homogeneous regions that are detected in the image. Alternatively, discontinuities can be used for the detection of primitives. It is assumed that these correspond to contours in the real objects. Line based segmentation is the result of this way of looking at images. We will cover techniques for line segmentation in chapters 14, 21, and 21.

The resulting primitives of the segmentation are dependent upon the methods used. Some examples are lines, regions, or vertices: the latter being a result of the intersection of two or more lines.

Figure 6.3   Image segmentation 1: input and edge candidates

Indications are that simple geometric objects are an important part of human visual perception as can be seen from Figure 6.3. Usually, the segmentation into lines process is carried out in a series of computational steps. First the edge candidates are extracted from the image (Figure 6.3). These candidates are then linked to lines. The corners and intersections (vertices) are located and the lines are approximated by circular arcs or straight lines (Figure 6.4). All of these objects are represented and stored in a common interface for image segmentation called a *segmentation object* (Sect. 16.8). We will cover the representation of such data in Part II; in Part III we describe algorithms for the computation of such data.

Alternatively, segmentation can be based on the detection of homogeneous regions. Contours of these regions are further inspected but the interface as a segmentation object remains the same.

Every segmented part has to be judged for its reliability; this measure will be used by the image analysis module (Sect. 6.7) in advanced recognition tasks.

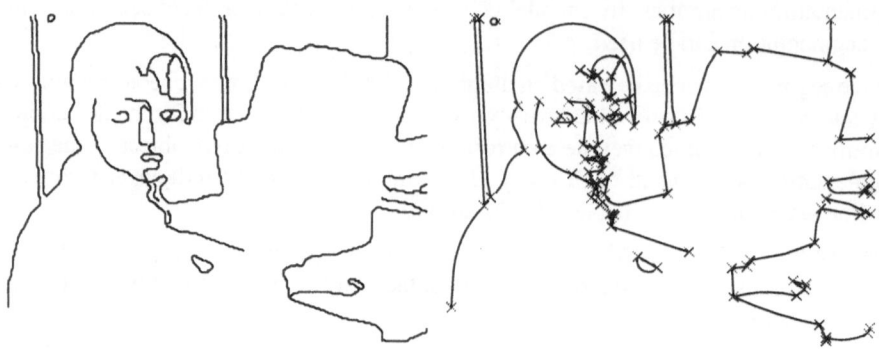

Figure 6.4 Image segmentation 2: lines and corners

Data abstraction of these objects yields a series of processing steps, which are shown in Figure 6.5. Proceeding from one level to the next means the introduction of a new class of data. This idea is further pursued in Part III.

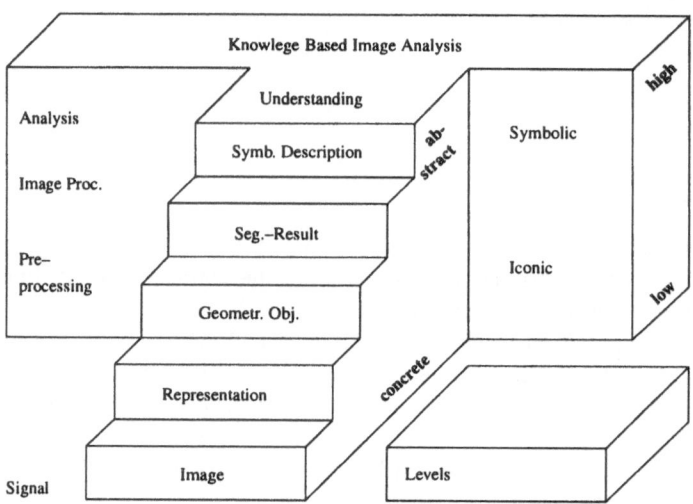

Figure 6.5 Levels of Abstraction with respect to data structures in image processing [Pau92b]

6.6   Speech Segmentation

The segmentation of speech signals is correlated to a decomposition of the time ordered signal into linguistic units. Each unit represents an interval of the signal and can
be, for instance, a single word or a syllable of a continuous spoken utterance. In general, those units computed by segmentation operators symbolize parts which are either
homogeneous in some sense when they are compared to their neighbors, or they are heterogeneous regarding some other criterion. Different approaches for the segmentation
of speech signals can be found in [Nie90a, Nöt90].

With the triumphal success of Hidden Markov Models (see Chapter 25) speech segmentation operations became of minor interest for speech recognition systems. It turned
out that statistical methods give better recognition results than structural analysis of the
speech signal. The speech signal is divided into frames of equal length for which features are computed; we introduce common methods for this computation in Chapter 25.
These features are input for a statistical analysis; we introduce basics of statistics for
this purpose in Chapter 8 and apply them to speech processing in Chapter 25.

6.7   Pattern Understanding

Understanding a pattern within the present context requires knowledge stored explicitly
in a knowledge base.

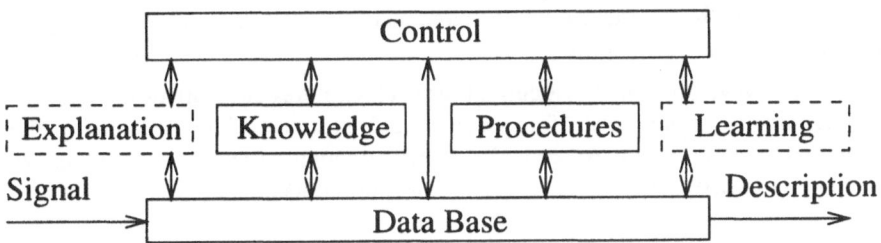

Figure 6.6   General structure of pattern analysis systems [Nie90a].

Image processing methods are applied to the data and are eventually transformed into a
description as shown in Figure 6.6. This process is *controlled* by a separate module. The
principle is generally observed through the *matching* of model data from the knowledge
base with the segmentation data.

It is essential for the control module that the results of the segmentation are judged
according to their quality and reliability. This problem dependent measure has to be

provided by the segmentation methods. The search problem mentioned in Sect. 6.4 can then be solved by general search strategies in the control module, like the A^*–graph search or dynamic programming (see e.g. [Nie90a]).

Knowledge based pattern analysis as well as pattern understanding is related to problems of artificial intelligence (AI). In fact, speech understanding and vision were one of the first major ideas for machine intelligence. One of the important journals for speech and image analysis is called "Pattern Analysis and Machine Intelligence".

The following problems are directly connected to AI and refer to its central ideas (knowledge representation, searching, matching):

- representation scheme for the knowledge base
- matching of patterns with models
- search for best matching object
- dealing with uncertainty and false assumptions
- planning

In image analysis, the recovery of three–dimensional information from the visual data can be assisted by spatial or geometric reasoning. Speech analysis will use linguistic knowledge and dialogue strategies.

Object–oriented programming can assist to keep track of software dependencies in a large knowledge based system. C++ provides the extreme computational efficiency which is also required for pattern understanding. Matching and optimization can be nicely implemented with object–oriented techniques; we will see an example in Sect. 25.2. Steps toward an object–oriented implementation of the knowledge base for image analysis are outlined in Chapter 26.

It should, however, be noted that current research explores alternatives to "traditional" AI. Instead of an explicit model for speech or objects, statistical information is gathered and used for understanding. AI methods are left to dialogue strategies or planning, which is required in active vision tasks; active vision is introduced next.

6.8   Active Vision and Real Time Processing

Instead of, or in addition to a symbolic description (which was the result of the system in Figure 6.5 and Figure 6.6), in active vision systems a series of commands for the active device is required. This will result in a top–down data flow all the way from control to low–level image processing (Figure 6.2).

Typical active methods change the focal length of a zoom lens; the aperture, or the focus (Sect. 1.6). Changes of the camera position are also possible if the lens is mounted on a robot. Examples can be found in [Den94]. One idea motivated by the human eye is to use a higher resolution in the area where interesting objects are expected (see the fovea in Figure 1.7). Technically, this can be achieved by two cameras with different focal length, or by changing the zoom setting of a single camera.

Active vision usually requires a response of the system within fractions of a second; otherwise a feedback of the information cannot be accomplished. It is crucial that the response delay is guaranteed not to exceed a maximum period. This is commonly called real–time processing if the time period is reasonably short. Of course, this again relates to efficiency (Sect. 3.7, 6.8). Typically, the images are captured at 25 frames per second (Sect. 1.7). A delay of less than 40 ms is therefore usually sufficient for real–time processing. Since common algorithms require more computing time, other control algorithms with a shorter delay period have to be found.

In real–time speech analysis, the maximum computation time is determined by a human's senses while communicating with a machine. This can be used as an upper limit for the analysis of a complete utterance.

6.9   Software Systems

Software engineering in the field of image processing has been a topic for several years. Data structures and more recently object–oriented programming have been proposed e.g. in [Car91, Cog87, Dob91, Pau92b, Pip88, Jak94]. A somewhat longer summary can be found in [Pau94]. Since this problem is currently discussed widely, the list of references above and systems below can of course not be complete.

Several commercial and free software systems are available for image processing; some of them we will now briefly introduce.

A very popular system is the Khoros system [Ras92] which has a large library of image processing functions and a nice graphical interface. It now also has a C++–interface.

The book [Zim96] comes with a CD ROM for image processing on a PC. The system described in [Koe96] is said to be available from a company. Both systems are written in C++ and encompass large hierarchies for image processing.

The so called "Image Understanding Environment" (IUE) has been discussed and planned for several years, e.g. in [Har92]. It is now available on the internet in the public domain (c.f., for example, various articles in the proceedings of the *Image Understanding Workshop*, e.g., [Mun92]). It provides a large C++ library and has a graphical user interface. Real time processing is explicitly excluded.

All those systems have nice user interfaces; none of them is dedicated to real–time applications or high efficiency (c.f. Sect. 3.7). In this sense, the very basic approach presented in this book differs from them.

In contrast to image processing there are not so many free software packages for speech processing. Most of the currently available systems were free several years ago and became commercial, as, for example, the Entropic's HTK toolkit[2] which provides utilities for building speech recognition systems using Hidden Markov Models. Another product offered by Entropics is the ESPS/Waves package with basic signal processing functions and visualization tools.

The ISADORA system (Integrated System for Automatic Decoding of Observation Sequences of Real-values Arrays) [ST95] is another toolset for working with one–dimensional signals, especially for the use with HMM based speech recognition. It integrates Markov modelling and hierarchical representation of phonetic, lexical and syntactic knowledge into one network.

The OGI Speech Tools are free software and provide a set of speech data manipulation tools developed at the Center for Spoken Language Understanding (CSLU). They can be used to compute and display signal representations and train neural networks.[3]

There are, of course, several systems for knowledge representation used in image and speech understanding. Most of them result from some AI project. Only one general system is known to the authors which is tailored for its application in pattern analysis: the system is called ERNEST [Nie90b] and some implementation details are discussed in Sect. 26.5.

Exercises

6.a   Explain differences and similarities of feature extraction and segmentation!

6.b   Think about formalisms for representing domain knowledge. Which techniques would you prefer?

6.c   Discuss the objectives of classification and analysis in detail!

6.d   **Top–Level Loop for Speech Analysis**
       Start writing a program using the control structures introduced in Program 51 that waits until a speech signal is recorded by a microphone and then tries to analyze the data until a spoken end command is heard. Assume that isolated words are spoken (in contrast to a continuously spoken language), and that each word is analyzed separately.
       Following the idea of stepwise refinement (Sect. 3.2), specify a top–level loop (see Program 51) and leave some details to be filled in later.
       Fill in variables needed for the speech signal. In the initialization, the actual settings of the device and the noise level in the background should be measured. Waiting for the word to start can be simply done by adding up the absolute values

---

[2] http://www.entropic.com
[3] URL: http://www.cse.ogi.edu/CSLU.

```
main(int argc, char **argv)
{
    int word;              // words may be identified by numbers
    init_micro();          // start up recording
    wait_for_speech();     // record speech frames until
                           // speech is observed
    do {
        get_frames();      // record until a pause is observed
        word = analyze();  // find word number from frames
        action(word);      // show some reaction on the input
    } while(wordNumber!=0); // 0 means "QUIT"
}
```
51

of all sampled values in the present frame. If the computed number is considerably higher than a comparable computation for a frame in the initialization, we assume that a word has been spoken.

Use separate files for the function dummies which are called from the main program. Make sure that a header file defines all the required interfaces. Use a Makefile to build the program.

7 C++ as a better C

In this chapter we conclude the description of the conventional programming part of C++. We include the new features of C++, which amend some of the defects of C. Most of the important features of C which are also valid for C++ will have been mentioned by the end of this chapter. The exercises in this chapter introduce some very useful tools.

7.1 Type Declaration

New types can be introduced using already known declarations with the keyword typedef.[1] Program 52 shows common types declarations of the new types byte, string, and GrayValue. For structures, a typedef — as in C — is no longer required in C++ (c.f. Sect. 4.1).

Type definitions may enhance the readability and portability of a program. Imagine, for example, a change of your image data format from eight to sixteen bits.

7.2 Type Conversion for Pointers

As was already explained in Sect. 2.6, types can be converted to others through the use of a type cast. Numerical values are then adjusted to the given type. A change of size and value is sometimes necessary (e.g. when converting from an unsigned character to a double value).

Pointers can also be converted using cast expressions. Normally, the size of the result is the same as before, i.e. a pointer requires the same number of bytes for storing the address no matter to which type it points. An example of type conversion for pointers is shown in Program 53. A special notation void * can be used for a generic pointer pointing to *any* type. Before the data pointed to can be accessed, however, the pointer

---

[1]Although it sounds like "type definition" it is really a *declaration*!

```
typedef unsigned char byte;   // byte now identical to uns. char
typedef byte GrayValue;       // gray value identical to byte
typedef char * CString;       // string type
```
52

```
char * cpt;              // some pointer definitions
int * iptr, i;           // not initialized
void * anyptr;           // can point anywhere
iptr = &i;               // pointer to an int
cpt = (char*) iptr;      // explicit conversion
anyptr = &i;             // now points to an int
* (int*) anyptr = 3;     // cast required
```
53

has to be cast to the appropriate type. The cast thus tells the compiler that the pointer is set to data of another type than the one deduced from the syntax. This is a potentially dangerous thing! The result of a pointer cast may in some cases give illegal values of the address or may even change the value of the pointer. For example, on most machines you should not try to cast a character pointer to an integer pointer, if the character pointer has an odd address.[2]

7.3   Type Specifiers and Variable Declaration

Variables can be *specified* with additional keywords in the declarations. C++ offers several choices: const declares the variable to have a constant value,[3] & makes it a reference, register is used for compiler optimization, extern, auto, and static control scope and lifetime. These modifications are valid for function arguments as well. When a variable is declared extern, the statement is a declaration and not a definition.

Reference arguments in function declarations provide a twofold benefit. First, changes to a non–local variable can be done through the use of reference arguments. This introduces arguments with the "call by reference" semantics as found, for example, in Pascal or Fortran. An example is shown in Program 54 (compare to Program 45).

Secondly, it is often advantageous not to pass large objects to a function. Arguments passed by value require a copy operation on the data. Argument references are not copied when they are passed as arguments; only a reference to the object is passed to the function. To make this intention explicit, a combination of reference and const should be used as shown in Program 55.

Reference variables provide alternative names for accessing data (Program 56). They have to be initialized upon definition. The keywords auto and static are used as in C.

---

[2]Try for example:
```
float f=1, * fp=&f; char * cp=1 + (char *) fp; fp=(float*) cp;
*fp=3;
```
Do not forget to remove the core file!

[3]Enumeration data types provide alternative ways for the definition of integer constants.

```
void swapint(int &a, int &b)
{                        // swap the value of two integers
    int tmp = a; a = b; b = tmp;
}

void fct()
{   int i = 3, j = 4;
    swapint (i,j);      // now i == 4, j == 3
}
```
54

```
static int globalint = 0;  // local in this module
static void fct(int a,     // pass by value
        int & b,           // pass by reference
        const int & c,     // pass by constant reference
        int * d,           // pass as a pointer
        const int * e)     // pass as pointer to constant
{
    auto     int i = 0;    // same as int i = 0;
    register int k = 10;   // hint to the compiler
    static   int j = 1;
    const    int l = 0;
    a  =  i;               // local effect
    b  =  i;               // will change the referenced arg
    c  =  i;               // error
    *d =  1;               // global effect
    e  =  d;               // ok, only data pointed to is const
    *e =  *d;              // error
}
```
55

```
PointXY p;
int & px = p.x;
px = 3;    // now: p.x == 3;
```
56

We can now specify a more complex (but still incomplete, see [Str91]) syntax for a variable declaration; for simplicity we leave out initialization and multiple variables in one declaration statement.[4]

```
c++decl> explain int * const f[10]
declare f as array 10 of const pointer to int
```
⟨57⟩

```
extern "C" int verbose;
extern "C" int fct(int);
main(int argc, char **argv)
{
  if (verbose) printf("%d\n", fct(argc)); // call C function
}
```
⟨58⟩

Syntax:

[__extern__ |__static__ |__register__ |__auto__] [__const__] *type* [__*__*|__&__] *var1* [[__size__]]*

Various combinations of * and [ ] can result in cryptic sequences of characters. Through the use of typedef's it is often possible to reduce the complexity of such expressions. A declaration and an explanation[5] is shown in Program 57.

7.4   Type–Safe Linkage

When using different modules, inevitably names for functions and variables have to be shared between different files. In C, only the name is exported to the linker. For example, if a function fct is defined in one module and used as an integer fct in another module, this will not result in a linkage error. The runtime system will, however, show the disastrous effects.

C++ introduces type-safe linkage and treats the integer fct different from the function fct(). The technique used generates function names that include an encoding the function's argument types into the external name (Sect. 7.3). It does this through the use of a unique naming scheme (called "name mangling"). Occasionally, the linker will report such unresolved symbols. A program called demangle can normally be used to decode these cryptic messages into more readable ones.

A special notation extern "C" can be used to circumvent the coding of arguments into the external name. This is useful when modules compiled in the C language have to be linked with C++–modules. Program 59 and Program 58 show a C and a C++ program which can be linked together into one program which will most likely *not* print what the programer expects. Since the C++ system has no information about the argument's type

---

[4]We still miss the possibility to express pointers to functions etc.

[5]The program c++decl is in the public domain (see Sect. B.1). It explains in clear English a given variable definition or declaration or cast expression for C or C++.

```
/* ANSI C Program */
int verbose;                            /* global variable */
int fct(float f) { return (int) f; }  /* converts its argument to int */
```
⟨59⟩

```
/* C++ subroutine */
extern "C" {
#include <stdio.h> /* should be C anyhow ... */
int c_function(int);
}
extern "C" int cplusfcn(int i) { return i*i; }
main(int ac, char **av)
{
    printf("%d\n",c_function(ac));
}
```
⟨60⟩

```
/* C Subroutine */
extern int cplusfcn(int);
int c_function(int i) { return cplusfcn(i); }
```
⟨61⟩

for the function fct, it will just put an integer number on the stack.[6] The C function will not "know" about the type of the data on the stack and will just handle it as if it were a floating point number. Name mangling ensures that such errors can be detected by the compiler and linker. However, differences in the return value between declaration and definition will still not be detected.

It is also possible to include complete files as C code into a C++ program such as the stdio.h file in Program 60.

If you want to provide a C++ function for a C subroutine, you will have to circumvent name mangling as well. Using the prefix extern "C" this is also possible. These techniques are shown in Program 60 and 61

7.5 Overloaded Function Names

Several different functions may share a common name as long as the function can be uniquely identified by its arguments. Of course, this only makes sense for groups of functions which essentially do the same thing, e.g. as those in Program 62. Name mangling ensures that such functions can be distinguished by the linker. A difference of two functions in the return type alone, i.e. with no difference in the argument lists,

---

[6]Most compilers pass arguments to a function via a stack pointer which is not directly accessible to the user.

```
double square(double a) { return a*a; }   // square for double and float
int    square(int a)    { return a*a; }   // for int
```

```
typedef unsigned char byte;
double square(unsigned char a) { return a*a; }
int    square(byte a)          { return a*a; } // error
```

```
void fct0(int i, int j = 3) {}                 // definition
void fct1(int i, char c = ' ', float f = 0.0); // declaration
int  fct2(int i ... );                         // declaration

void fct1(int i, char c, float f) {}           // definition

main()
{
    fct0 (1);           // call fct0(1,3)
    fct2 (1,2,3,4,5);   // fct2 will have to take care of the args
    fct0 (1,2);
}
```

is not allowed since this would cause no change in the mangled names. A distinction could be made neither by the compiler, nor the linker.

Functions which cannot be distinguished by the compiler are shown in Program 63.

7.6   Return Value and Arguments

A function can have a variable number of arguments in the call syntax, such as the function printf. The implementation of such functions in C is possible using macros from an include file varargs.h. This is, however, error prone, since the compiler cannot check whether a sufficient number of arguments is provided when the function is called. A safe and easy solution in C++ is to provide default values for the arguments in the *declaration* of the function. These values can then be left out when the function is called. Only the trailing arguments can have initial default values. Another possibility is the use of ". . ." which declares the function with an unspecified number and type of arguments.[7] This should be avoided in general; but it is necessary for both C and the Unix interface of the language. Program 64 shows these features.[8]

The specifiers described in Sect. 7.3 are valid when declaring the return value of a function as well. Returning a reference is rather interesting, because the return value of the function can be assigned a value as if it were a variable (Program 65); this

---

[7]The function then has to use varargs to recover the argument list.

[8]See varargs and [Str91] for details of a possible implementation for fct2.

```
#include <assert.h>              /* useful macros for debugging */
int & elem(unsigned int i)
{
    static int f[10];  // must be static
    assert(i < 10);    // check index
    return f[i];       // return reference to local data
}
void fct(int i)
{
    elem(i) = 3;       // see the function call on the left!
}
```
65

```
#define square(a) a*a          /* a dangerous macro */
main()
{
    int    i = 3;
    float g = 3.0;
    int    j = square(++i);     // surprise
    float f = square(g+2);      // surprise
    printf("%d %f\n", j, f);    // prints 20 11.0
}
```
66

example also shows the use of the macro `assert` which is very useful during program development. If the expression passed to the macro evaluates to `false`, the program stops at this point and gives a message that the assertion failed at this point in the source code.[9]

Above example also shows a new return type: a reference to an integer. It is an error to return a reference to a function's local variable, which is not static, upon its return, since the memory location is no longer valid after the return from the function that was called. This is a common mistake, but usually compilers print warnings, which give hints to programmers.

7.7 Macros and Inline Functions

Macros are often a source of nasty errors, especially if they have side effects as shown in Program 66.

Although it looks like a function call, `square` in Program 66 is just a textual substitution and has no function semantics. C++ introduces `inline` functions, which in many cases replace the use of macros with a safer tool.

---

[9]The macros can be defined to an empty statement when the program is compiled with -DNDEBUG; see your local compiler manual. Compare also Exercise 7.c.

```
#include<stdlib.h>
inline int    square(int a)    { return a*a; }   // square 1
inline double square(double a) { return a*a; }   // square 2
main(int argc, char ** argv)
{
    int   j = square(atoi(*++argv));        // call square 1
    float f = square(atof(*++argv)+2);      // call square 2
    printf("%d %f\n", j, f);                // works as expected
}
```
67

Inline functions provide the runtime efficiency of macros and the flexibility of functional semantics including local variables and scoping rules. Program 67 shows the new version of Program 66 which now works as expected. However, we need two function definitions in order to provide the square of integral numbers and of floating point numbers. Of course, inline functions can be overloaded just as regular functions.

The function `atof` in Program 67 works like `atoi` but returns a floating point value. Inline functions are "expanded" like macros but provide functional semantics. They should be used in C++ instead of macros wherever possible.

7.8   Function Pointers

In Chapter 5 we introduced pointers to data. Pointers may also set to functions. The syntax of the declaration is basically as follows:

| **Syntax:** | [extern | static] *return_type* (* *name*) (*arguments*)

This means that a function pointer variable is declared which can be set to a function of a given type; this declaration includes the return type and the argument declaration of the function. It is possible to circumvent this kind of type checking by a cast, but in general this can introduce problems during run time of a program.

Functions can be called *indirectly* via pointers as shown in Program 68. This technique is very powerful and used in large C programs. In C++, other mechanisms exist which are safer with respect to type checking and simpler in terms of programming. We will hear more about that in Part II.

Since C++ provides better features than function pointers, we will not go into details here. This language feature is, however, required if functions from the system libraries are to be used, for example, a quick–sort function as declared in Program 69 and used in Program 70.

A complicated cast of the function pointer `compare` is required to bypass C++ argument type checking. Such casts can occasionally be made more readable by a `typedef` for a function pointer.

```
static int fct1(int i) { return i; }
static int fct2(int i) { return i*i; }

static int (*fptr) (int)     // declare fptr as ptr to function
          = fct1;            // and initialize to fct1

main()
{
    printf("%d\n", fptr(2)); // indirect function call to fct1
    fptr = fct2;
    printf("%d\n", fptr(2)); // indirect function call to fct2
}
```

68

```
extern "C" void
qsrt(                        // extern C quick sort function
    void *base,              // pointer to start of data
    int nel,                 // number of elements
    int size,                // size of an element
    int (*compar)(const void *, const void *) // compare function
);
```

69

```
static int cmp(const int* i1,const int* i2) {return (*i1)-(*i2);}
main()
{
    int * ia = new int[20];
    // do something with ia
    qsrt(ia,20,sizeof(int), (int(*)(const void*,const void*))cmp);
}
```

70

7.9 Comma Operator and Conditional Expressions

Two minor features of C and C++ conclude this chapter. The *comma operator* is mostly used in tricky macros and should be avoided in general. Only the common use in a for—loop is recommended (in Program 71) the two expressions left and right of the comma are evaluated both). The result of the first expression is discarded.

The *conditional expression* is used more often. Depending on the result of the expression before the "?" the result is either the value of the next expression or of the one following the ":". It is clearly defined what happens if the comma operator and conditional expressions have side effects. Such things are very hard to read and understand; they should thus be avoided.

```
int i, j = (argc > 2) ? 2 : argc ;
for (i = 0, j = 0; i < 10; ++i, ++j) {}
```

71

```
int i; char c; float f;
char buffer[256];
fgets(buffer,sizeof(buffer),stdin);
sscanf(buffer,"I = %d, F = %7.2f, c = %c",&i,&f,&c);
```
(72)

Exercises

7.a   **The Functions** sscanf **and** fgets
      The function sscanf extracts values from a string and is part of most C libraries.
      This function can be used when atof and atoi is not sufficient.
      In combination with the function fgets which reads a string into a buffer,
      simple formatted input can be parsed. The formatting parameters are essentially
      the same as for printf (Table 2.1). However, the arguments have to be provided
      as pointers to be filled with values. An example is shown in Program 72.
      The functions fscanf and scanf read directly from a stream and are not as
      safe as sscanf and fgets. C++ provides other facilities for input from streams
      ([Str91; pp. 325], c.f. Sect. 15.4).
      Declare the functions fgets, fscanf, and sscanf with their argument lists.
      Check your result against the declarations in the file <stdio.h>.

7.b   *Repeat Macro*
      One syntactic macro — in contrast to Program 73 — will make code more
      readable,[10] since the multiple use of the keyword while is avoided:
      Write a macro repeat and until (expression) which will work as
      expected (refer to the Pascal manual). Use proper parentheses for the expression!

7.c   *Debug Macro*
      Even if your system has a nice debugger, messages for debugging a program
      are often very handy. On the other hand, it is a nuisance to remove them for the
      final run. Efficiency requires that such lines disappear completely from the code
      after debugging.
      Define a simple macro called DEBUGMSG.
      It should have one (!) argument which is used for the function printf. Since
      printf directs its output to stdout — which is a buffered file — messages
      are delayed until the buffer is full. Use the function fflush to avoid this
      behavior.
      Hints:

      • Create two files:

          – debugmsg.h containing the macros
          – debugmsg.C containing the functions

        Write a test program, use a makefile and rcs.

---

[10]This is at least the opinion of the authors of this book.

```
#include "debugmsg.h"
main (int argc, char** argv)
{
    DEBUGMSG(("starting main %s\n", *argv));
    // do something
    DEBUGMSG(("End of main\n"));
}
```
73

- The resulting lines in the program should look as in Program 73.

- Check the file <assert.h> for further ideas. Try man assert as well.

Then redefine the macro in a way that

- No output is printed

- Absolutely no code is generated for this line

8 Statistics for Pattern Recognition

Applications of image and speech processing have to deal with uncertainty and noise effects. These factors can be partially suppressed by suitable preprocessing operations. You can, for example, normalize the intensity of light, which is ordinarily different under varying illumination conditions, or the energy of speech signals. Probability theory and statistics provide a mathematical framework to handle these phenomena. As outlined in Sect. 1.4, pattern analysis deals with the *mathematical* part of perception. It is, therefore, natural to use all kinds of mathematical tools for solving pattern recognition problems. In addition to preprocessing, typical applications of probability theory in pattern recognition are statistical learning and pattern classification (Sect. 6.1). Lots of examples can be found in [Dud73, Nie83, Fuk90, Vap96].

The subsequent sections explain the basics of probability theory and statistics that are useful for the understanding of the algorithms and principles of Chapter 19, Chapter 25 and Part III. For more mathematical details, we refer to [Bre88, Fuk90, Pap91].

8.1 Axioms

Many concepts of probability theory are inspired by numerical phenomena. You can, for instance, *measure* the energy of a speech signal or the intensities for each pixel of a gray–level image. Such measurable quantities are called *random variables*.

The basic object in probability theory is the *probability space* $(S, \mathcal{F}, p)$, where S represents the set of all possible outcomes of an experiment, $\mathcal{F} \subseteq 2^S$ is the family of events, i.e. a set of subsets of S and p is a probability function assigning to each event $A \in \mathcal{F}$ its probability $p(A) \in [0, 1] \subset \mathbf{R}$.

The introduced probability space has to satisfy the axioms of probability theory summarized in Table 8.1.

Depending on the applications, the range of random variables can be discrete or continuous. Both cases are important for pattern recognition applications and discussed separately in the following two sections.

Axioms of Probability Theory:

1. $\mathcal{S} \in \mathcal{F}$

2. if $A \in \mathcal{F}$, then $\bar{A} \in \mathcal{F}$

3. if for all elements of the sequence $(A_n)_{n \geq 0}$ we have $A_n \in \mathcal{F}$, then $\bigcup_{n \geq 0} A_n \in \mathcal{F}$.

4. $p(\mathcal{S}) = 1$

5. for any sequence $(A_n)_{n \geq 0}$ of pairwise disjoint events the following additivity condition is valid

$$p \left(\bigcup_{n \geq 0} A_n \right) = \sum_{n \geq 0} p(A_n) \quad .$$

Table 8.1 Axioms of probability theory

8.2 Discrete Random Variables

The probability to observe a discrete random variable is written as $p(X)$; similarly, the probability that the value of X is in the interval $[A, B]$ is denoted by $p(A \leq X \leq B)$. Using above axioms of probability theory the following equation obviously holds:

$$p(X \leq A) = 1 - p(X > A) \quad . \tag{8.1}$$

In many practical situations it is necessary to *estimate* the probability $p(X)$ for each random variable X from the training samples. This is done using the relative frequency of the observed random variables. Let M be the set of observed random variables and $|M|$ the cardinality of the training set. For each random variable $X \in M$ we can compute

$$p(X) = \frac{|\{Y \in M \mid Y = X\}|}{|M|} \quad . \tag{8.2}$$

This quotient is called the *relative frequency* of X.

The *cumulative distribution function* $P(x)$ for the random variable X is defined by

$$P(x) \quad = \quad p(X \leq x) = \sum_{X \leq x} p(X) \quad . \tag{8.3}$$

A cumulative distribution function is monotonic and increasing; its maximum value equals 1.

One fundamental result of probability theory states that the estimated probability converges for $|M| \to \infty$ to the real probability. The difference between the real probability

$p(X)$ of observing X and the estimated relative frequency is lower or equal to an arbitrary small positive number and converges to zero for an infinite sample set (see e.g. [Bre88]).

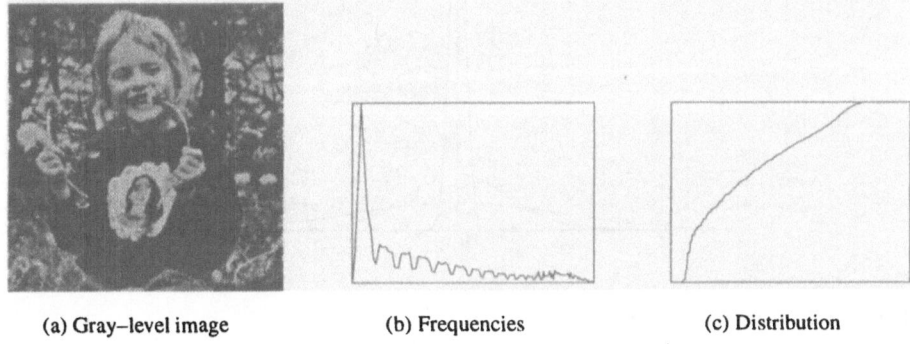

| (a) Gray–level image | (b) Frequencies | (c) Distribution |

Figure 8.1 Frequencies and the associated cumulative distribution function for a gray–level image

The following example will clarify some of the introduced concepts: In image processing applications random variables often are the gray–levels of image pixels. Figure 8.1 shows a gray–level image, its frequencies of gray–levels, and the associated distribution function. The relative frequency of each gray–level can be computed by dividing the value of the ordinate in the histogram by the number of image pixels. Each gray–level in the histogram is related with the number of pixels having this value. You can also see that the distribution has the value 1 for the gray–level 255, i.e. the probability to observe a gray–level lower or equal to 255 is 1 (as expected!).

8.3   Continuous Random Variables

Suppose now that we are working on analog image data. In this case the random variable *gray–level* will have a real value, i.e. we have a set of random variables of infinite cardinality. From the axioms of probability theory we conclude that the probability of observing a specific gray–level equals zero. Of course, for each point in the image plane, we can measure a gray–level; nevertheless the probability of observing exactly this gray–level is zero. The sum over the probabilities of all possible outcomes has to be equal to one. Due to the fact that the cardinality of the set of random variables is infinite, the summands cannot be nonzero.

In analogy to the discrete case, we define the cumulative distribution function

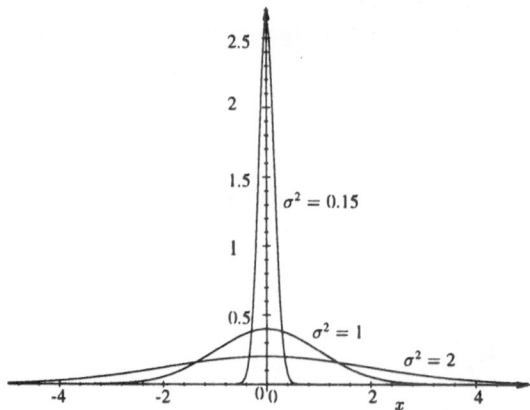

Figure 8.2 Gaussian densities with $\mu = 0$ and $\sigma^2 = 0.15, 1, 2$

$$F(x) \;=\; p(X \leq x). \tag{8.4}$$

If there exists a nonnegative function f such that,

$$F(x) \;=\; \int_{-\infty}^{x} f(z)\, dz, \tag{8.5}$$

then we call $f(x)$ the *density function* of the continuous random variable X.

One of the most famous probability densities is the *Gaussian density*

$$f(x|\mu, \sigma^2) \;=\; \frac{1}{\sigma\sqrt{2\pi}}\, \exp\left(-\frac{1}{2}\frac{(x-\mu)^2}{\sigma^2}\right)\quad . \tag{8.6}$$

This density function defines a parametric family of densities $\{f(x|\mu, \sigma^2)|\mu, \sigma^2 \in \mathbf{R}\}$. The parameters μ and σ^2 are called the *mean* and *variance* of the given distribution. A probabilistic interpretation of these two parameters will be given in the next section. Figure 8.2 shows some representative elements of this parametric family. It is fairly easy to see that the value of the density function $f(x)$ for $x = \mu$ can be greater than 1, if $\sigma < 1/\sqrt{2\pi}$. So $f(x)$ should not be confused with the probability function p of the probability space (Sect. 8.1).

The cumulative distribution of normal or Gaussian distributed random variable is

$$F(x) \;=\; \frac{1}{\sigma\sqrt{2\pi}} \int_{-\infty}^{x} \exp\left(-\frac{1}{2}\frac{(z-\mu)^2}{\sigma^2}\right)\, dz\quad . \tag{8.7}$$

For the integral in (8.7) there exists no closed form solution. That is the reason why numerical methods are used to evaluate this integral.

```
#include <math.h>            // import constants and functions
double gauss(double x, double sigma, double mu)
{
   return ( 1 / (sigma /
            sqrt(              // sqrt: square root function
              2 * M_PI         // M_PI: from math.h
            )) *
          exp ((               // exp(..) exponentiation function
            - 0.5 *
            sqr(x - mu)        // sqr: square function
          ) / sqr(sigma)));
}
```
74

In the field of pattern recognition, Gaussian densities are widely used [Dev96, Nie83, Dud73]. Normally distributed random variables are mathematically easy to handle, and most applications take advantage of the approximation of density functions by Gaussian densities or variations [Nie83]. Gaussian distributions are suitable to model noise effects (Chapter 18, [Bel89]). In speech recognition Gaussian distributions describe the statistical behavior of features [ST95]. The probabilistic modeling of point features for object recognition purposes is often based on normally distributed random vectors [Sar94]; this probabilistic model leads to reliable recognition results.

The support of mathematical functions and operations in the language definition of C++ is small compared to other languages, like e.g Fortran [Bra78]. For the computation of function values with e.g. the formula in (8.7) we need the constant π, exponentiation, etc. These values and functions can be found in a header file math.h and a mathematical library which has to be added by the linker (Sect. 7.4).[1] Program 74 shows an implementation of the Gaussian density function $f(x|\mu, \sigma^2)$ as defined in (8.6).

8.4 Mean and Variance

In general, the underlying statistics of gray–levels or other observable sensor data is not known. Nevertheless, the statistical quantities mean and variance can be estimated from k observed random samples. The *mean* of given samples can be computed by

$$\mu \;=\; \frac{1}{k}\sum_{i=1}^{k} f_i \;\;, \tag{8.8}$$

and the *variance* is estimated using

$$\sigma^2 \;=\; \frac{1}{k}\sum_{i=1}^{k} (f_i - \mu)^2 \;\;. \tag{8.9}$$

---

[1]Usually, a flag has to be passed to the linker like -1m to inform it that this library is needed.

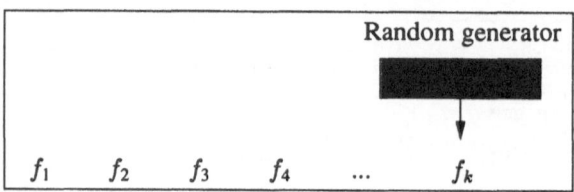

Figure 8.3 Random generator for normally distributed variables

Although, these formulas are often used for arbitrary distributions of random values, they are true only if they are normally distributed. Both values can be computed assuming that the gray–levels f_i, $1 \leq i \leq k$, are normally distributed or not. A proof of the estimation formulas (8.8) and (8.9) can be done by a so called *maximum likelihood estimation* of the parameters μ and σ^2 (c.f. [Fah94, Tan93]). If a random generator is given and if it is known that all generated observations are normally distributed (see the "black box" in Figure 8.3), the parameters μ and σ^2 can be estimated by maximizing the likelihood function

$$L(\{f_1, f_2, \ldots, f_k\}, \mu, \sigma^2) = \prod_{i=1}^{k} f(f_i | \mu, \sigma^2)$$

$$= \left(\frac{1}{\sigma\sqrt{2\pi}}\right)^k \exp\left(-\frac{1}{2\sigma^2}\sum_{i=1}^{k}(f_i - \mu)^2\right) \qquad (8.10)$$

for the observed set of gray–levels. Here, we assume that all observations are pairwise statistically independent (see Sect. 8.7). Thus, the density function for observing the training set $\{f_1, f_2, \ldots, f_k\}$ is the product over all single density values $f(f_i | \mu, \sigma^2)$.

A common way for the optimization of continuous functions, such as the likelihood function or its logarithm, with respect to some parameters is the computation of zero–crossings of the partial derivatives with respect to the unknown parameters μ and σ^2.

To give an example, the computation of mean and variance of the gray–levels of the video image shown in Figure 8.1 yields $\mu = 143.417$ and $\sigma^2 = 1959.78$. This is a kind of obvious, since the image has a balanced ratio of dark and light gray–levels.

8.5 Moments of a Distribution

The cumulative distribution or the density function characterize the distribution completely. The mean and variance introduced in the previous section can be computed using the above formulas. Even if the underlying distribution of the observed sample data is not Gaussian, we get a result for μ and σ. Therefore, we cannot conclude from these values the underlying distribution of the sample data. The mean and variance are coarse measures of the distribution. Therefore, we generalize these measures.

Let k be a natural number and $f(x)$ the density function of a distribution. If the function $g(z) = z^k f(z)$ is absolutely integrable, then we call

$$m_k(p) \quad = \quad \int z^k f(z)dz \qquad (8.11)$$

the k–th absolute moment of the distribution p. Analogously, we call

$$\widehat{m}_k(p) = \int (z - m_1(p))^k f(z)dz \qquad (8.12)$$

the k–th central moment of the distribution p, if $g(z) = (z - m_1(p))^k f(z)$ is absolutely integrable.

The first absolute moment is called *expectation* and we commonly write $E[X]$ for the expectation of the random variable X. Above definitions are valid for continuous random variables. In the discrete case, one has to substitute the integral sign with a discrete summation. The first absolute moment and the second central moment are the mean and variance in the discrete situation.

The definition of moments is not only restricted to univariate density functions. Moments can also be applied for higher dimensional, arbitrary functions. For instance, assume a discrete gray–level function $(f_{i,j})_{0 \leq i,j \leq 255}$, where $f_{i,j} \in \{0, 1, \ldots, 255\}$. The discrete sum

$$m_{r,s} \quad = \quad \sum_{i,j=0}^{255} i^r j^s f_{i,j} \qquad (8.13)$$

introduces the (r, s)–moment of the given gray–level image. The center of gravity (x_S, y_S) of $f_{i,j}$, for example, can be computed by first moments, i.e.

$$x_S \quad = \quad \frac{m_{1,0}}{m_{0,0}} \quad \text{and} \quad y_S \quad = \quad \frac{m_{0,1}}{m_{0,0}} \quad . \qquad (8.14)$$

The normalization of geometric patterns is usually done by pattern transforms based on moments (8.13) for various values of r and s [Nie83; p.64].

8.6 Random Vectors

The definition of random variables can be used for generalization purposes. We call a vector $\boldsymbol{X} = (X_1, X_2, \ldots, X_n)$ a *random vector* of dimension n, if the components $X_1, X_2, \ldots, X_n$ are real valued random variables. The multivariate cumulative distribution function of $\boldsymbol{X}$ is similar to the one–dimensional case. It is defined as

$$F_{\boldsymbol{X}}(x_1, x_2, \ldots, x_n) \quad = \quad P(X_1 \leq x_1, X_2 \leq x_2, \ldots, X_n \leq x_n). \qquad (8.15)$$

The nonnegative multivariate density function $f_{\boldsymbol{X}}(x_1, x_2, \ldots, x_n)$ can be computed from the following n–dimensional integral equation

$$F_X(x_1,\ldots,x_n) \;=\; \int_{-\infty}^{x_n}\cdots\int_{-\infty}^{x_1} f_X(y_1,\ldots,y_n)\,dy_1\ldots dy_n. \tag{8.16}$$

The formulas for discrete random vectors follow immediately, if the integral signs are substituted with sums over all possible values of the discrete random variables.

For example, a gray–level image of size $M \times N$ can be viewed as a discrete random vector of size $n = M*N$, where the gray–levels of the image represent the components of the vector.

Let $X = (X_1, X_2, \ldots, X_n)$ be an n–dimensional random vector. The *mean vector* is now defined by the vector of means of each component, i.e.

$$E[X] \;=\; \begin{pmatrix} E[X_1] \\ E[X_2] \\ \vdots \\ E[X_n] \end{pmatrix}. \tag{8.17}$$

The generalization of the variance is done by the *covariance* of two random variables X_i and X_j by

$$\sigma_{i,j} \;=\; E[(X_i - E[X_i])(X_j - E[X_j])]. \tag{8.18}$$

Obviously this results in the variance, if $i = j$. The *covariance matrix* is now given by

$$\Sigma \;=\; \begin{pmatrix} \sigma_{11} & \cdots & \sigma_{1n} \\ \vdots & & \vdots \\ \sigma_{n1} & \cdots & \sigma_{nn} \end{pmatrix}. \tag{8.19}$$

It is symmetric (see (8.18)) and positive definite.

To continue with the famous Gaussian density function, its generalization to n dimensions is

$$f_X(x) = \frac{1}{\sqrt{2^n\pi^n|\det\,\Sigma|}}\;\exp\left(-\frac{(x-\mu)^T\Sigma^{-1}(x-\mu)}{2}\right)\;, \tag{8.20}$$

where $x = (x_1, x_2, \ldots, x_n)^T$, μ is the n–dimensional mean vector, and $\Sigma \in \mathbf{R}^{n\times n}$ the covariance matrix. Figure 8.4 shows an example of a two–dimensional Gaussian density.

In general, arbitrary one–dimensional densities $f(x)$ $(x \in \mathbf{R})$ can be lifted to higher dimensional density functions $\tilde{f}_X(x)$ $(x \in \mathbf{R}^n)$. For that, we define a $(n\times n)$–dimensional matrix Σ and a n–dimensional mean vector μ, compute the quadratic form

$$x^T\Sigma x \;\in\; \mathbf{R}\;, \tag{8.21}$$

and get the n–dimensional density function

$$\tilde{f}_X(x) \;=\; \frac{\alpha}{\sqrt{|\det\,\Sigma|}} f((x-\mu)^T\Sigma^{-1}(x-\mu))\;, \tag{8.22}$$

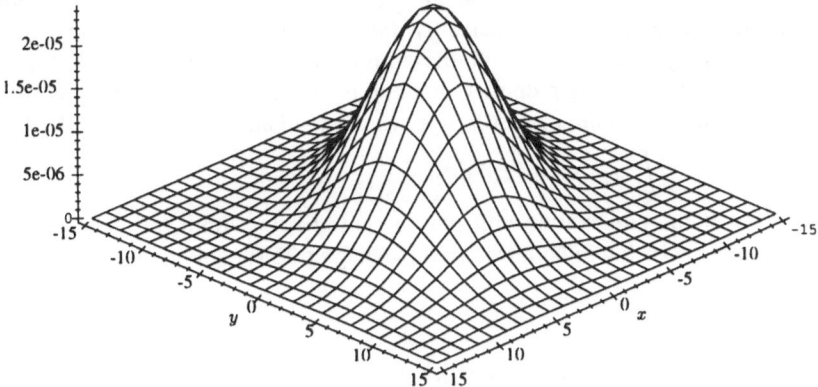

Figure 8.4 2–D Gaussian density

where the variable α has to be chosen such that

$$\int_{x} \tilde{f}_{X}(x)\, dx \;\; = \;\; 1 \quad . \tag{8.23}$$

For the n–dimensional Gaussian density, we have $\alpha = (2\pi)^{-\frac{n}{2}}$.

8.7   Independence and Marginal Densities

Axiom 5 (Table 8.1) shows that for pairwise disjoint events the additivity condition is valid. Real random variables $X_1, X_2, \ldots, X_n$, or the components of a random vector $X = (X_1, X_2, \ldots, X_n)^T$ are said to be statistically independent, if for all $x_1, x_2, \ldots, x_n \in \mathbf{R}$

$$f_X((x_1, x_2, \ldots, x_n)) \;\; = \;\; \prod_{i=1}^{n} f_{X_i}(x_i) \quad . \tag{8.24}$$

If random variables do not satisfy the independency condition, the probability function can be factorized using conditional probabilities:

$$
\begin{aligned}
f_X((x_1, x_2, \ldots, x_n)) \;\; = \;\; & f_{X_1}(x_1) f_{X_2|X_1}(x_2|x_1) \\
& f_{X_3|X_1,X_2}(x_3|x_1, x_2) \\
& \vdots \\
& f_{X_n|X_1,X_2,\ldots,X_{n-1}}(x_n|x_1, x_2, \ldots, x_{n-1}) \quad ,
\end{aligned}
\tag{8.25}
$$

where the conditional probabilities hold

$$f_{X_i|X_j}(x_i|x_j) \;\; = \;\; \frac{f_{X_i,X_j}(x_i, x_j)}{f_{X_j}(x_j)} \quad . \tag{8.26}$$

Assume that the bivariate density function $f_{X_1,X_2}(x_1, x_2)$ is given, and we are looking for $f_{X_1}(x_1)$. If X_1 and X_2 are statistically independent and if f_{X_2} is known, a simple division gives us $f_{X_1}(x_1)$. In general, these prerequisites are not satisfied. A common way to compute the unknown density function is *marginalization*. We integrate in the continuous domain and sum in the discrete case over all admissible values of x_2 and get

$$f_{X_1}(x_1) = \int_{x_2} f_{X_1,X_2}(x_1, x_2)\, dx_2 \quad . \tag{8.27}$$

The process of marginalization will play a central role within the theory of hidden Markov models, which will be introduced in Chapter 25 for solving single word recognition problems.

8.8   Statistical Features and Entropy

The defined statistical distribution characteristics constitute possible features of patterns. For example, a speech signal is divided into intervals of fixed size, usually at a sampling rate of 10 kHz or disjunctive windows of a duration of about 12.8 ms. In general, the interval size should be motivated by phonetics and has an averaged duration of 10–20 ms. For each signal frame, features like the mean number of zero–crossings can be used. Images can be decomposed into blocks of fixed size, for example, 16×16 pixels. Statistical measures like moments can be computed for subimage. These are suitable features for the given patterns and can be applied for pattern classification (Sect. 6.1).

When we observe a random measure x_i of the random variable X_i, the information derivable from the outcome will depend on its probability. If the probability of observing the random variable is small, a large degree of information can be concluded, since the occurrence of this random variable is very rare. In contrast to that, random variables with a large probability of being observed have a very small degree of information. In coding and information theory the amount of *information* is defined as

$$I(x_i) = -\log p(x_i) \quad . \tag{8.28}$$

The important property of a randomized information source is the *entropy* which is defined as the average amount of information, i.e.

$$H(S) = -\sum_{x_i \in S} p(x_i) \log p(x_i) \quad , \tag{8.29}$$

where S denotes the set of observations. The entropy is the measure of the amount of information required in specifying which random variable has occurred on average. The entropy $H(S)$ holds the inequality $H(S) \geq 0$, if and only if $p(x_i) = 1$ for some $x_i \in S$. A probability is called *degenerated*, if $p(x_i) = 1$ for some x_i and $p(x_j) = 0$ for all $x_j \in S$, where $i \neq j$. Thus, the entropy is minimal for degenerated probabilities. The maximum value of $H(S)$ depends on k, where k denotes the cardinality of S. Obviously, $H(S) = \log k$ if and only if $p(x_i) = p(x_j)$ for all $1 \leq i, j \leq k$.

8.9   Signal–to–Noise Ratio

For the representation of a real value f_i in the computer we have to use the discrete value f_i'. The error between the discrete and the real value is called *quantization noise* (c.f. Figure 1.9) and is given by

$$n_i \;\; = \;\; f_i - f_i'. \tag{8.30}$$

A measure for the accuracy of this quantization is the *signal–to–noise ratio* (SNR). For the quantization of continuous signals the SNR is defined by a quotient of means:

$$\text{SNR} \;\; = \;\; \frac{E[f_i^2]}{E[n_i^2]} \tag{8.31}$$

The assumptions that the quantization error is uniformly distributed, the quantizer is not saturated and the quantization is fine enough, leads to the following formula for the SNR:

$$\text{SNR} = 12 \cdot 2^{2B-6} \quad , \tag{8.32}$$

where B is the number of bits used for quantization, i.e. we have 2^B different values for the digital range [Nie83; p. 29]. B is typically greater than 6. Thus, an additional bit improves the quantization error by 6 dB. The signal–to–noise ratio is used as an objective measure for the "quality" of a signal. It may happen, however, that a signal with high SNR looks or sounds worse than one with a lower ratio.

Exercises

8.a   Compute the probability that in a gray–level image of size $n \times m$ all pixels have the same gray–level. Assume that the discrete gray–levels are uniformly distributed on the integers $[0, g]$.

8.b   Usually, mathematical function libraries provide a random function which generates uniformly distributed random numbers from a fixed interval [min, max].[2] Sketch an algorithm which permits the computation of uniformly distributed numbers out of a parameterized interval $[l, u]$ using the available random generator.

8.c   Write a program which plots the *Cauchy probability density*

$$f(x) \;\; = \;\; \frac{1}{\pi}\,\frac{1}{1 + x^2} \tag{8.33}$$

and compare the graph with the Gaussian density. Show that there exist no mean and variance for the Cauchy density! Do you think Gaussians should be approximated by Cauchy densities?

---

[2]Try rand() or random() on your machine.

8.d   Give a proof of (8.8) and (8.9) as suggested in the text!

8.e   Compute the SNR for music with CD quality (16 bit).

8.f   Define a vector for the speech signal locally in the main function. Pass the vector and its length as arguments to all the functions which need it.

       If your computer has an audio input device, put all the device dependent code into a separate module and run the program. Try to recognize three different, isolated spoken words:

       - "Start"

       - "Stop"

       - "Quit"

       Use simple features, like the duration of the speech signal, or the mean number of zero–crossings.

Part II
Object–Oriented Pattern Recognition

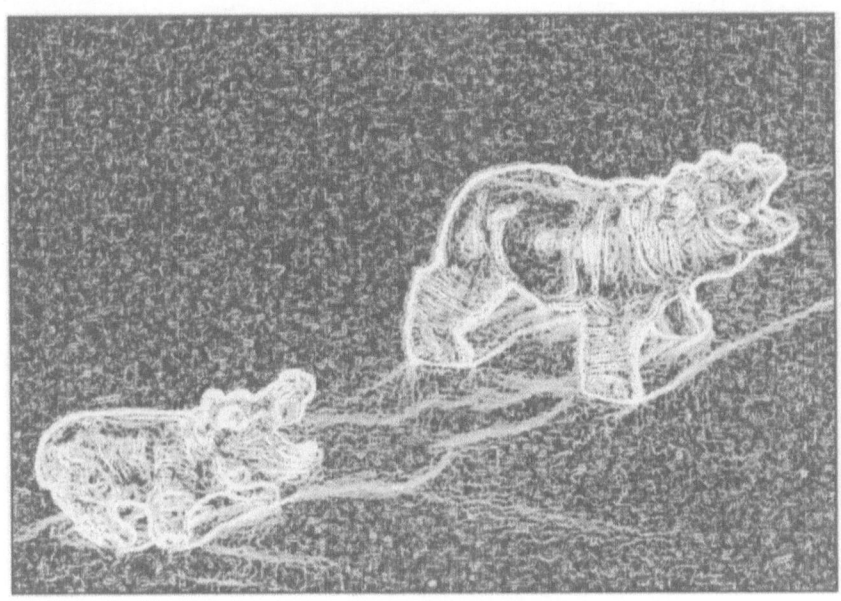

Edge strength computed on the image on page 3.

Part II of the book introduces C++ as an object–oriented language. We describe class hierarchies for general object–oriented programming (NIHCL) and for object–oriented image processing and analysis.

9   Object–Oriented Programming

In this chapter we introduce the object–oriented programming paradigm and other related subjects for object–oriented software construction. The term "object–oriented programming" has recently become very popular. Many applications of object–oriented programming and software design principles exist and there are many journals and scientific publications which are specialized in the philosophy and the possibilities of object–oriented systems. The following sections can only summarize the fundamental concepts of object–oriented programming languages. The interested reader may find more information in the references. A recommended summary can be found in [Bus92].

9.1   Object–Oriented Software Techniques

The object–oriented programming style involves the decomposition of a problem domain into a hierarchy of classes and a set of communicating objects, which are themselves instances of classes. The object–oriented programmer then specifies *what* is done with the objects. The procedural way of programming uses aspects of *how* something gets done. The advantage of object–oriented software design is that a one–to–one correspondence between objects of the real world and the objects in the program can be made. Even the analysis of the problem domain has to be involved in this mapping. Analysis and program design are no longer separated in the software development process (c.f. Chapter 3); object–oriented analysis and design share the same terminology and tools.

The first phase of object–oriented software development is to define the requirements (RD). In the object–oriented analysis (OOA) stage of a problem, concepts of the problem domain and their correspondences are identified and specified. Hierarchical relations between the concepts are used; information which can be shared by several special concepts will be included in a general concept and passed to the special cases through *inheritance*. In the object–oriented design (OOD) phase, the conceptual class hierarchy is overlayed with additional links which are meaningful for the implementation only. This provides a transition from the problem domain to the *solution* domain. After analysis and design, the object–oriented coding can take place (object–oriented programming, OOP). Conventional tools as well as the corresponding object–oriented terms are shown in Figure 9.1; structured design (SD, [DeM79, PJ80]) and structured programming (SP) are now integrated into the new object–oriented techniques. Whereas conventional software engineering is mostly sequential with some optional loops (Figure 3.1), object–oriented software development has a main stream from RD to OOP, with possibly feedback at every stage.

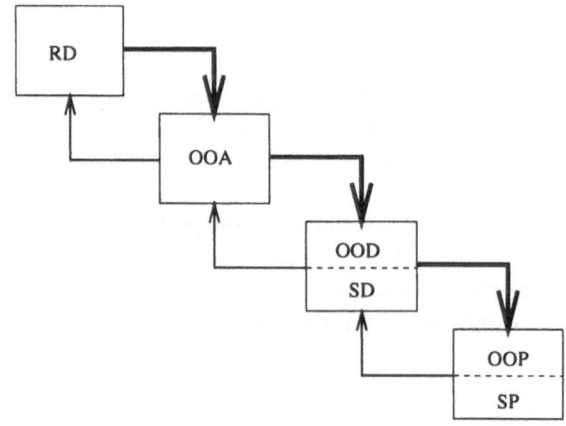

Figure 9.1   Object–oriented software engineering techniques (explained in the text)

Several graphical representations and mechanisms have been proposed for OOA and OOD. The books of Booch [Boo91], Coad & Yourdon [Coa90], Rumbaugh et al. [Rum91], and Shlaer & Mellor [Shl88] are commonly suggested in this stage of software development. Recently, the methods of Booch and Rumbaugh have been unified [Rum96].

9.2   Basic Concepts

According to [Weg87], the characteristical features of the object–oriented programming paradigm are:

- objects,
- classes,
- inheritance,

- data abstraction,
- polymorphism,
- message passing,

- methods,
- types, and
- durability.

Objects can be, for example, integers, reals, gray–level images, lines, addresses, or any other concept conceivable in the problem domain. Objects are *instances* of classes. Classes consist, in general, of data (member variables) and methods (functions) which can be used for manipulating the member variables. Classes describe the layout of objects.

For example, a class "gray–level image" has member variables like a matrix including intensity–values and the focal length of the camera used to capture the image (c.f. Chapter 11). Necessary methods are, for instance, selectors for reading a gray–value at a certain location and a method which returns the focal length of the camera. The matrix can also be an instance of a class. The image class for gray–level images is derived from a more general class, where the information common to all types of images is specified. The provided technique for the implementation of such dependencies is inheritance. Data and common methods shared by all variants of images — e.g. a recording time stamp — can be defined in the common base class.

Another basic feature of object–oriented paradigm is the concept of polymorphism. In combination with inheritance, objects may exhibit "polymorphic" behavior and react on messages differently depending on the class the object actually belongs to. For example, matrix elements of a general matrix class can be integers, reals, gray–levels, or of some other type. The addition of two matrices is defined by a component–wise addition; this is the case for all data types of the matrix entries. Thus, the code should be written independently of the types of the matrix entries. If a programming language supports parameterized member variables, a general matrix class can be implemented, where the type of the matrix entry is not specified. A set of operators for matrix elements is assumed. Each specialization of a matrix defines the type of the matrix elements and redefines this set of operators.

Operator overloading, where functions with the same function name are distinguished by their arguments, is also a common technique in object–oriented systems. For instance, addition and multiplication are denoted by + and * for arbitrary numbers like integers, reals or complex numbers. The used implementation depends on the arguments' type.

In the following sections we will elaborate on the above features a little further and relate them to C++.

9.3 Data Abstraction and Modules

One of the aims of object–oriented software design is to provide an abstract interface for programmers using the technique of *information hiding*. The user of a class only needs to know the methods of a class and their semantics. The internal data representation and the implementation details of several methods should not be in the scope of the user. The method of information hiding renders a high degree of modularity and supports the teamwork required in large programming projects.

Data abstraction facilitates modular programming. For example, you want to add two matrices in a part of a function. Since the matrix class provides a method for the addition of two matrices, you will not have to reimplement the addition using the components of the matrix. Furthermore, the code becomes more readable and thus reusable for other programmers (presupposing that the code is well documented). Changes in a special operation, e.g. addition of matrices, can be done locally in the method's definition. The code which uses this function has only to be recompiled or linked.

Computer scientists invented the concept of *Abstract Data Types* (ADT). In this concept, data and the operations which read or alter the data are strongly connected. The data representation is no longer relevant. All access to the information is done using the operations provided in the data type. This is what we mean by information hiding. The definition of ADT is a more theoretical concept that combines data representation with formal aspects of implementation and representation [Gut78]. Some programming languages have implemented this concept; a typical example is Modula 2 [Wir83]. Abstract data types are defined in some programming structures together along with the appropriate functions which define the interface for the given data type. Variables of this type can now be defined. The programmer can operate on these variables using only the methods which were associated with the ADT.

Using the graphical elements of [Coa90], an ADT can be depicted as in Figure 9.2. If one data type A uses or references another type B, this can be visualized by a line connecting the two corresponding boxes, marked with a triangle pointing to A. This link is often used for the "part–of" or "has–a" relationship. Type A has to apply the operations associated with B in order to access data of B.

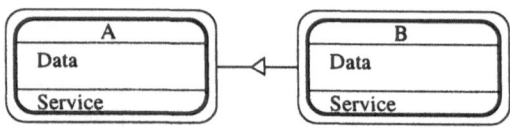

Figure 9.2 Two related abstract data types (ADT)

9.4   Inheritance

Classes, as well as ADTs, may be understood as descriptions of terms which describe the problem domain. Objects result from classes by aligning special values to their descriptions. Classes can arise by inheritance from one or more base classes. This process is generally called the derivation of a new class. In the terminology of object–oriented programming the base class is often called a *superclass* and a derived class a *subclass*. We call this inheritance graph a *hierarchy*, no matter whether it is actually a directed acyclic graph or really a tree.

The use of class hierarchies and inheritance forces programmers to think about an ordered structure of the underlying problem domain. The resulting source code is more structured and has a higher degree of reusability. Since the implementor of a class should provide a complete definition, i.e. not only those functions needed immediately but all reasonable functions for future uses of the class, the number of code lines may increase for object–oriented programming. This is compensated by the use of inheritance which reduces the number of lines needed for the implementation.

Inheritance can appear in two different ways: on the one hand we have *simple* inheritance. If a class is derived from one super–class, we call the inheritance simple. On the other hand, if a class has more than one base class, multiple inheritance is being used. Derived classes inherit both the methods and the members. Furthermore, inheritance grants more insight to a class than the usage relation in Figure 9.2. Many authors suggest the use of simple inheritance because there exist fewer conflicts, e.g. if a member of the same name is inherited from two classes.[1]

One class may contain members of another class. We call the classes of the member objects *clients*. Instead of inheriting classes we may also in some cases use a client and define all the methods of the client in the new class. These methods will just pass the arguments to the corresponding methods of the clients. This is called *delegation*. In many cases multiple inheritance can be avoided using delegation.

Often, a system contains several classes which are identical except for the type or class of some member variables. *Parametric types* allow to create classes from a description including parameters. A general scheme is expanded to the actual classes. In C++, this can be done with templates (Sect. 11.2). For instance, matrix classes can be defined using parametric components. The specialization of the used element type should be done within the definition of objects (c.f. Chapter 11).

Artificial intelligence tries to organize knowledge in some structured formalism. Most frameworks use special/general, concrete/abstract, and has–a/part–of relations. The semantic network system ERNEST [Nie90b] imposes restrictions on these links, e.g. that concepts related by a part–of relation must be on the same level of abstraction. For class design and inheritance planning, such thoughts are also very useful (c.f. also Sect. 6.7).

To summarize, a provisional and simplified characterization of object–oriented programming can be itemized as follows:

- classes (represent abstract units),
- inheritance of classes (abstract generic terms), and
- objects (concrete terms associated with values).

---

[1] We will not further elaborate this problem here.

Using the graphical elements of [Coa90], inheritance of two classes Integer and Real from Number can be depicted as in Figure 9.3. The line between the boxes now contains a semi–circle with the round edge towards the base class.

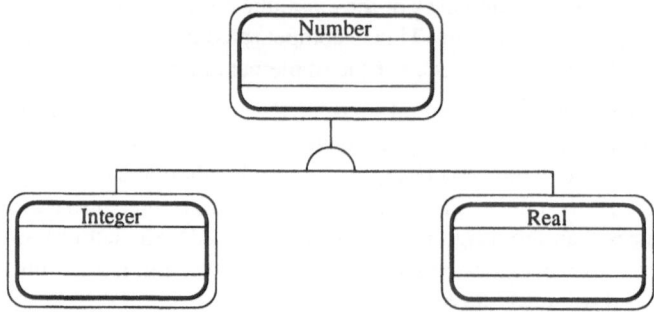

Figure 9.3 Inheritance for numbers

9.5   Abstract Classes

The examples explained so far were concrete classes including methods which are explicitly suitable for implementation purposes. Assume you have to implement a class for lines. Obviously there are different possibilities for representing lines. For instance, you can use polygons, arcs, or a set of affine functions. Furthermore, you have to distinguish between lines of different dimensions. Independent of the internal representation, a class for lines should include methods for the determination of its length or for traversing the points along the line. It cannot be the aim of an object–oriented programming system to implement all different classes for lines without the use of the more abstract concept of lines. Abstract classes provide the declaration of a class where no concrete members have to be specified and the methods can be declared in an abstract manner. In these abstract classes no implementation of the methods has to be made. The concrete definition of the methods then must be developed in derived classes, where the explicit line representation is known. The advantage of abstract classes is the development of modular and well structured software, where classes which depend on each other in an abstract way are reflected within the network of classes. Abstract classes may specify concrete members and methods which are shared by all derived classes — even without redeclaration.

The class Number in Figure 9.3 had better be an abstract class, since an object is not simply a "number" but either a real number or an integer or whatever class of concrete numbers are used in the program. Using the graphical elements of [Coa90], an abstract class looks as in Figure 9.4.

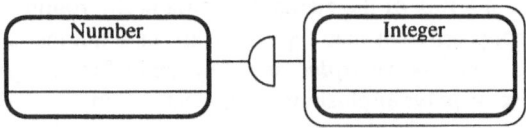

Figure 9.4 Abstract class and concrete derived classes

9.6   Object–Oriented Classification

The term "classification" was introduced in conjunction with pattern analysis in Sect. 6.1. This term is also used in the description of object–oriented systems. Object classes can be defined as representatives of a class of objects. The universe of objects is divided into classes by a partition. Objects of similar purpose are grouped into equivalence classes. Object–oriented classes in this sense correspond to the term "class" in set theory.

> A class is a set of objects that share a common structure and a common behavior.

This definition allows for the distinction of types and classes.[2] Classification is thus a fundamental problem of OOA. Objects have to be grouped according to their behavioral and structural similarity. However, it is context–dependent, which kind of behavior is regarded as similar. Class boundaries in the real world tend to be fuzzy rather than clear.

9.7   Polymorphism

Another basic concept of object–oriented programming languages is the use of poly-morphism.

> Polymorphism: A concept in type theory, according to which a name (such as a variable declaration) may denote objects of many different classes that are related by some common superclass; thus, any object denoted by this name is able to respond to some common set of operations in different ways, [Boo91; p. 517].

---

[2]Objects belonging to one class may still have separate types. However, this is relevant only in some object–oriented programming languages. In C++ we can handle classes as types.

Sometimes an algorithm can be formulated in an abstract manner independent of the data types it operates on. Mathematicians are well versed in those problems. For example, the determination of the maximum element of a set or a sort algorithm on a set of elements depends only on the ordering of the elements' domain. So, routines are needed which can be applied to many different data types, for instance numbers, letters, or vectors. These functions are called *polymorphic* and they serve for the sparing source code. Another consequence of polymorphism is a compact and more easily surveyed source code, which can easily be reused by others.

Polymorphism together with dynamic binding and inheritance is a key concept in object–oriented programming. Often operator overloading is called weak polymorphism. Examples for overloaded operators are addition and multiplication for integers, reals and complex numbers which share the same symbol.

9.8   C++ as an Object–Oriented Language

The ideas of Smalltalk [Gol83] should be familiar to everyone who wants to do object–oriented programming. Simula [Bir83] and Smalltalk can be seen as the 'parents' of object–oriented programming. Both language definitions describe the syntax and provide extensive class libraries for various applications. Most object–oriented concepts such as classes, objects, methods, inheritance, polymorphism, etc. were introduced in Smalltalk. The even older root of object–oriented programming can be found in Simula which introduced virtual functions and the class concept which are now similarly available in C++.

The ancestor of object–oriented languages Smalltalk did not allow multiple base classes. Several modern object–oriented programming languages do, however, implement this concept. It is by far more complex to maintain a class hierarchy with multiple inheritance, than with single inheritance.

Another major influence on the new standard C++ library originates from Ada which is said not to be an object–oriented language, since in its first revision it misses inheritance. The generic modules in Ada have a similarity to templates in C++. The new revision of the language standard supports single inheritance [Kem97].

C++, like Simula, is a compiled language and thus has to omit some features which can be realized only in interpreted languages like Smalltalk. C++, as defined in [Str91], provides no such environment as Smalltalk. C++ combines several features from various languages to a mixture of conventional and object–oriented ideas which can be used to write highly efficient yet modular programs and modules for pattern processing and analysis.

Already now, the first descendents of C++ exist. The programming language Java [Dec95] is mostly used in world–wide–web applications but its application for other purposes is increasing. This language has many similarities with C++ and avoids some of the weaknesses of C++, for example, it supports automatic garbage collection. Java is an interpreted object–oriented language and thus lacks the required runtime efficiency for pattern recognition purposes; compiled Java can be as efficient as C++.

9.9   Class Libraries

Object–oriented programming has been used to define various libraries. For example, object–oriented ideas are used in the implementation of the X11 graphics system or the XDR data representation scheme, even if no object–oriented language is used.[3]

The Smalltalk system is distributed with an extensive library for graphics and all common programming applications. It includes sets, collections, dictionaries, all sorts of mathematical applications etc. It also contains a windowing environment.

In contrast, C++ in its original form is a programming language without any advanced programming libraries. The only classes contained in the standard distribution are those for input and output with streams. This is a great disadvantage for those who want to start with object–oriented programming. Every little concept has to be individually programmed. There are, however, class libraries in the public domain which add some of the power of Smalltalk to C++. We will see more about this in Chapter 15. New versions of the language include a more elaborate standard library, e.g. the STL library (c.f. Chapter15).

System designers have to select from available libraries carefully. They are the major source of software reuse.

Exercises

9.a   Develop a class hierarchy for lines. Which methods should be declared in the abstract class? Is it useful to use multiple inheritance? Where can concepts like polymorphism and operator overloading be used in this example?

9.b   Check the advertisements in your favorite computer journal for occurrences of the term "object–oriented". Try to find out whether this term is correctly applied there.

9.c   Compare different graphical descriptions of object–oriented programming such as those mentioned in the text. Which one do you prefer? Why?

---

[3]XDR is available in C++ as RPC++.

10 Classes in C++

C++ is not an object–oriented language. It *allows* for object–oriented programming. The features of object–oriented programming introduced in chapter 9 can be mapped to features of the C++ language. In this chapter we introduce the design of classes in C++ and show the use of abstract data types for encapsulation.

10.1 Methods and ADT's

Program 17 (p. 41) showed the data structure PointXY consisting of two data entries. This basically looks like Pascal. No restrictions on the access, modification, and use of the structure members were specified. Good programming practice requires the definition of functions which use the new data type (Program 75). All these functions have been prefixed with the data type name to avoid name conflicts.[1] Misuse or failure to use the new functions cannot, however, be controlled by the compiler. The use of these functions can be recommended but not enforced. Information hiding — as required in ADT's (Sect. 9.3) — is thus only partially possible.

In C++, in addition to data members, functions can be declared *inside* the structure. These functions are used only in conjunction with the data of the structure type. Program 76 shows a structure for complex numbers consisting of a real and a imaginary part. This already looks more like an ADT, since operations on the data type are declared with tight adherence to the data specification. These functions are called "methods" or member functions (c.f. Chapter 9).

Functions *defined* within the body — the method real_part in Program 76 — are automatically inlined (Sect. 7.7). The inline keyword can be used for better readability.

Methods can be accessed like data members using a variable and a tag — the method name — separated by a "." or a "->" in the case of a pointer. In addition, a parameter list

---

[1]This is a common technique which was used in e.g. the X11 windows system for Unix.

```
void PointXY_setXY(PointXY& p, int x, int y) { p.x = x ; p.y = y; }
int  PointXY_getX(PointXY& p)                ( return p.x; }
int  PointXY_getY(PointXY& p)                ( return p.y; }
```

75

```
struct complex {                     // structure declaration
    float re,im;                     // two data members
    complex set(float,float);        // member function declaration
    float abs();                     // member function declaration
    float real_part() {return re;}   // member function definition
    float imaginary_part() {return im;}  // member function definition
};
```
76

```
complex c, *cp = &c;            // variable definition
c.set(3,3);
float f = cp->real_part();
complex c1 = c, c2 = *cp;
```
77

```
complex complex::set(float x, float y)
{
#ifndef USE_THIS
    re = x; im = y;    // will give a warning (no return value)
#else /* alternatively */
    this->re = x;      // just to give an example
    (*this).im = y;    // just to be different
    return *this;      // this is returned
#endif
}
```
78

can be given. As can be seen from Program 77, structures can be assigned as a whole; they can also be returned from functions.

Definition of methods outside the structure use the structure name followed by : :[2] and the method name (Program 78). The complete name of a variable or a function consists of the scope (mostly the structure name), the double colon, and the variable name. We now see that the type name in the enumeration definition in Sect. 4.2 fits logically into this concept (e.g. complex: : set in Program 78); the structure name prefix is a scope resolution which uniquely determines the name space where the function name has to be searched for by the compiler. Inside the methods, other methods and data members are known without explicitly mentioning the structure name. They can be accessed explicitly by the this pointer, which points to the actual object for which the method is invoked. This variable is declared and initialized by the C++ compiler in each and every (non–static) member function.[3] In some cases, the this pointer is required to access the actual object as a whole (return statement in the second implementation of the method complex: : set in Program 78).

Note also the preprocessor statement for conditional compilation depending on the existence of a defined (in terms of the preprocessor) macro in Program 78. This kind of

---

[2]c.f. Sect. 2.9

[3]The compiler implicitly prefixes all the access expressions to class members by a this-> pointer.

```
class assoc_int {        // association between integer and string
 private:                // can be omitted: classes start private
    int value;
    char * key;
 public:                 // the following defines the interface
    const char * Key() { return key; }   // read access to data
    void Key(char * k) { key = k; }      // set key
    int Value() { return value; }        // read access to data
    void set(int v, char * k);           // set value
};                                                                    (79)
```

definition is often passed to the preprocessor from the compiler command line e.g. with
CC -DUSE_THIS -c prog.C.

10.2   Class Declarations

Structures as introduced in Sect. 4.1 partially satisfy the requirements of ADT's. The primary feature that is missing is "Information Hiding". This is possible with the class declaration in C++. Variables of a class type are called *objects*.

Classes are structures with access regulations. Data members and methods can be excluded from external usage; they are then accessible only inside other methods. Three keywords are used for access regulations: The label public: introduces unrestricted parts of the class. The label private: restricts the following entries to be for internal class use only. The label protected: will be introduced in Sect. 13.2. These labels can be repeated and can occur in any order. Program 79 shows a class declaration of a so called assoc_int.[4] A key (e.g. a name) is associated with an integer (e.g. a telephone number). The data members are accessible only by the public methods.

Structures as well as unions in C++ are exactly the same as classes except for one small difference; the initial access mode for structures is public; the initial mode for classes is private. Several uses, both legal and illegal, of the class assoc_int are shown in Program 80. Making the return value of Key a const char * protects the association string from manipulation after a call to the method.

10.3   Object Construction

It would be tedious and error prone if every class or structure had a method for initialization (as in Program 75–79 the method set or ...setXY) which had to be called explicitly for every object (Program 80, 77).

---

[4]We will later see applications of this class.

```
assoc_int ai1, ai2;              // object definition
ai1.set(857894,"Paulus");        // legal use of method
ai2.set(857826,"Hornegger");     // legal use of method
ai1.value = 33;                  // error, value is private
char * n1 = ai2.key;             // error, key is private
char * n2 = ai2.Key();           // warning, constant assigned
                                 // to char *
const char * n3 = ai2.Key();     // ok
```
80

```
class assoc_int {
 private:
    int value; char * key;   // private
 public:                     // the following defines the interface
    assoc_int();             // default constructor
    assoc_int(int,char*);    // alternative constructor
    const char * Key();
    int Value();
};
```
81

```
assoc_int ai1;          // definition and call of default constructor
assoc_int ai2(10,"a"); // definition and call of second constructor
assoc_int * aip1 = new assoc_int;        // use default constructor
assoc_int * aip2 = new assoc_int(11,"b");// use second constructor
```
82

C++ introduces special methods for classes called *constructors*. These — usually over-loaded — functions share the name as their class. They are used upon definition of an object and can initialize internal and external data automatically. Syntax and usage is best seen through an example. Program 81 shows a modification of the class introduced in Program 79. The method set is now left out.

Program 82 is a modified version of Program 80. Instead of explicitly initializing the objects we use constructors. The example also shows the use of the new operator on classes. The so called "default constructor" is used when no argument list is provided. If it is not explicitly implemented, this constructor is provided by the compiler. As for overloaded functions, the choice of the appropriate constructor depends on the argument list. Program 83 shows the definition of the default constructor for this class.

Arrays of objects can be defined in a similar way to arrays of simple types (Sect. 5.1). The default constructor is called for every object in the array (Program 84). If no default constructor is defined for the class, the compiler should give an error message.

```
assoc_int::assoc_int()       // default constructor
{                            // initialize members
    value = -1; key = NULL;  // by default
}                            // values
```
83

```
assoc_int aia[10];        // definition and call of default constructor
assoc_int * aip3 = new assoc_int[11];  // default constructor 11 times
```

```
class PointXY {              // declare new data type
 private:
   int xa,ya;                // members are xa and ya
 public:
   PointXY();                // default constructor
   PointXY(const PointXY &); // reference constructor, always const arg.
   PointXY(int, int);        // third constructor
   int x();                  // read access to member xa
   int y();                  // read access to member ya
};
```

```
PointXY::PointXY() { xa = 0; ya = 1; }
PointXY::PointXY(const PointXY & r) { xa = r.xa; ya = r.ya; }
PointXY::PointXY(int i, int j) { xa = i; ya = j; }
```

It is often useful to initialize one object with the contents of another object of the same type. The *reference constructor* (copy constructor) is used for this purpose. Declaration and use is shown in Program 85 which extends Program 17. If there is no declaration of a reference constructor, the compiler will automatically create one which copies all components recursively. This constructor is used when an object is returned from a function or passed to it as an argument. Note, that it is *not* called, if the argument is passed as a reference; i.e., to avoid unnecessary copying, function arguments should be declared as constant references!

Program 86 shows the definition of the constructor methods declared in Program 85.

Constructors never have a return type. However, they can be terminated by a return statement like any other void function.

10.4 Destruction of Objects

Similar to object construction, the destruction code of an object is generated automatically by the compiler if it is not declared explicitly. The "destructor" is a special method; its name is the class name prefixed with a tilde (resembling the unary not operator, Table 4.1). A string class with destructor is shown in Program 87.

Typically, destructors release any memory which was allocated in the constructor (Program 88). Other examples can be found in the following sections.

The destructor is called on an object when this object goes out of scope (and is not static, of course). Objects created by new can be destroyed by delete. This will call

```
class string {              // declare new data type
  private:
    char * st;              // internal pointer
  public:
    string(char *);         // constructor
    string(const string &); // copy constructor
    ~string();              // destructor
};
```
                                                                    87

```
#include <string.h>
string::string(const char * s)
  { st = new char [1+strlen(s)]; strcpy(st,s); }          // allocate
string::string(const string & s)
  { st = new char [1+strlen(s.st)]; strcpy(st,s.st); } // allocate
string::~string() { delete [] st; }                     // free
```
                                                                    88

```
void fct(char * sa)
{
    string s(sa);                   // allocate string
    string *sp = new string("ab");  // constructor call
    delete sp;                      // delete using destructor
    return;                         // quit function
}                                   // s will be destroyed
```
                                                                    89

the destructor as well (Program 89). For arrays, the destructor is called automatically for every element. There is only *one* destructor per class which always has no arguments and no return type. As with constructors, a return from the destructor with a `return` statement is possible. Static objects are also deleted, when the function `exit` is called from any point in the program. This feature can be useful, for example, for files which have to do some cleanup on permanent storage: like removing temporary files or locks on devices as the program terminates.

10.5   Operators

Several operators were introduced in C for fundamental types. They all have their fixed association rules. The operators can be redefined for classes. The syntax of operator declarations is as follows:

| Syntax: | *return–type* operator *op (argument-list)* |

where user definable operators are, for example; +,*,-,=,[ ],( ), or ==.[5]

---

[5]For a complete list refer to the manual [Str91].

```
complex complex::operator= (const complex& c)   // assign complex
   {re = r.re; im = r.im; return *this;}
complex complex::operator=(double d)        // assign float
   {r = d; i = 0; return *this; }
complex complex::operator+ (const complex& c)
   {complex nc(c); nc.re += re; nc.im += im; return nc;}
complex r, q, s;    // declare
r = s;              // assign
s = q = r;          // assign twice
s = q + r;          // addition and assignment
```
90

```
complex::operator float ()   // conversion of a complex to a float
{
    assert(im==0);          // assert that it is no complex number
    return re;              // return the real part
}
```
91

Redefinition of an operator is called "operator overloading" which is one type of polymorphism (Sect. 9.7). We will not treat this topic in all details. We only give some clarifying examples for commonly used operators such as [ ], =, ( ) and leave the rest to the references. When used with care, operator overloading can facilitate programming and make programs easier to read. When misused, the results may be disastrous.[6] Operator overloading is possible only for classes.

Program 90 shows the definitions of the assignment and addition operators for the class complex (Program 85) (the declaration in the class is obvious). By passing the actual object as a return value, sequences of assignments are possible.

Other overloaded operators will be explained and applied in later sections (c.f. Chapter 15). One of them is the conversion operator explained in the next section.

10.6   User–Defined Conversion

Several conversion rules are defined for fundamental types; for example, a floating point number is truncated when it is assigned to an integer. Explicit type conversion takes place with a type cast. It can now be specified how this conversion to a given type should be performed on a user–defined data type. In order to do so, a conversion operator can be declared in a class as exemplified for the complex numbers in the implementation in Program 91. Note, that no return type is specified, since this type is known from the type the class is converted to (in this case a float).

Such type conversion can shorten expressions and in many cases be useful and simplify programming. As always, side effects have to be strictly avoided. Three examples for

---

[6]Imagine a program with + defined as multiplication on some numeric class ...

```
complex a;
float f0 = (float) a;      // C style cast
float f1 = float(a);       // conversion function
float f2 = a;              // implicit conversion
```
92

```
class A {                  // artificial example
 private:
    int a;                 // some member
 public:
    A(int i) { a = i; }    // constructor definition
};

class B {                  // some other class
 private:
    int b;                 // with some member
    A   a1, a2;            // uses the first class
 public:
    B(int, int, int);      // declares a constructor
};
```
93

```
B::B(int i, int j, int k)
    :                      // start member constructors
    a1(j),                 // constructor for first object
    a2(k)                  // constructor for second object
{
    b = i;                 // assign a value to the member
}
```
94

the invocation of the conversion function are shown in Program 92. Especially with the implicit conversion, all side effects would be disastrous on the readability of the program.

10.7 Advanced Methods and Constructors

If a class contains data members of class type as shown in Program 93, the question arises how to provide constructors for these objects.

The solution is shown in Program 94. After a colon, a list of constructor calls for member objects can be given before the *definition* of a constructor function body. The member objects are constructed before the body of the constructor function for B is executed.

It is sometimes important to know the order of member and base class construction. This order is not determined by the sequence of calls, for example in Program 94. Instead, the base classes and members are called in the order of their declaration in the class!

```
class bytevector {
 private:
    byte * row;                    // the actual data
    unsigned int size;             // number of elements
 public:
    bytevector(int);               // constructor
    byte    operator [] (int i) const; // access also for const objects
    byte & operator [] (int i);    // access as usual
};
```
95

```
static void checkit(int i, int s)        // local helper function
{
    if (i >= s) { // could use exceptions here
      fprintf(stderr,"Index %d out of range (max is %d)\n",i,s);
      exit(1);
    }
}

byte bytevector::operator [] (int i) const // access also for
                                           // const objects
{ checkit(i,size); return row[i]; }        // return byte
byte & bytevector::operator [] (int i)     // read/write access
{ checkit(i,size); return row[i]; }        // return reference
```
96

10.8   Vector Class

We now introduce a simple vector class which will reveal several new features for classes and methods. We first restrict our class to a vector of byte elements (Program 95).

In Program 95, note the following things:

1. the overloaded operator [ ]: this operator has one argument of type int. We can now access bytevector objects like arrays with an index in square brackets.

2. the const method (or a const operator): methods can be declared as const. This indicates to the compiler that the method will not change any data internal to the object. In particular, these methods are used when the object is itself a const object (Program 95).

   Since the compiler can decide a constant from a variable object, the two declarations of the operator are legal.

3. reference as return value: to allow for an indexed expression of a bytevector on the left side of an expression, we use a reference to the element as return value.

Program 96 shows the implementation of the vector access methods. The meaning of the const operators and the reference return value will be exemplified in the following.[7]

---

[7]Rather than calling exit, an exception should be raised here.

```
class bytevector {
  private
      byte * row;                           // the actual data
      unsigned int size;                    // number of elements
  public:
      bytevector(int);                      // constructor
      ~bytevector();                        // destructor
      byte   operator [] (int i) const;     // access also for
                                            // const objects
      byte & operator [] (int i);           // access as usual
      operator byte * () { return row; }
      int Size() const { return size; }
};
```
97

```
#include <assert.h>
bytevector::bytevector(int i) // constructor
{
    assert(i>0);
    size = i;
    row = new byte[i];
}
bytevector::~bytevector()        // destructor
{
    delete [] row;
}
```
98

We now extend Program 95 to a complete simple and efficient vector class. We define constructors and introduce a conversion `operator byte*` which greatly increases the efficiency of this class (Program 97). This operator method is invoked when an object (not a pointer)[8] is cast to a `byte *`.

The implementation of the constructor and destructor methods is shown in Program 98. The use of this class and its methods can be seen in Program 99.

The function `fct1` in Program 99 uses the index operator `[]` and allows assignment to vector elements, since this operator returns a reference to the indexed byte. In contrast, the function `fct3` has a constant argument. The index operator on this object uses the method for constant objects which returns a `byte` instead of a reference. Assignment and modification of the object is thereby disabled. Read access is, however, possible. The method `Size()` can be used, since it is also declared as a constant method. The vector access in `fct2` is unprotected; when the function is called in the main program, the compiler already knows the argument type of the function which is a `byte*`; the actual argument is the object `bv` which will be converted to a `byte*` using its conversion operator.

---

[8]It is a very common error to cast the pointer instead of the object itself. The compiler will think this is intentional and will not give a warning!

```
void fct1(bytevector & bv)
{
    for(int i = bv.size() - 1; i >= 0; --i ) bv[i] = 0;
}
void fct2(byte * bp, int s)
{
    for(int i = s - 1; i >= 0; --i ) bp[i] = 0;
}
void fct3(const bytevector & bv)
{
    int s = 0;
    for(int i = bv.size() - 1; i >= 0; --i ) s += bv[i];
}
main(int argc, char ** argv)
{
    bytevector bv(10);
    byte * bp = (byte *) bv;  // call operator byte *
    fct1(bv);                 // pass array by reference
    fct2(bv,bv.size());       // convert to byte * using operator
    fct2(cp,bv.size());       // equivalent
    exit(0);
}
```
99

An explicit cast to a `byte` * as in the main function body of Program 99 will also invoke the cast operator.

10.9   Class Design

We conclude this chapter with several useful hints for class design in C++. Some of them are not obvious from the language definition but are required because of compiler limitations. The goals for class design in pattern analysis applications have to be:

- efficiency (due to the time limitations) *and*
- clean design (due to general software rules and the particular difficulty of the problem).

Classes or data structures should be declared for every complex unit in the description of the problem for which you have a clear conception in mind. Internals should be hidden to provide a clear interface in a modular programming style. It is good practice to put all data members in the private section of a class and to provide read only access methods for those values which should only be changed in a controlled way. Often the same message (i.e., function name) is used for read and write access with two overloaded functions as in Program 79. However, during the class design care is needed. If you use objects for every small detail, you lose efficiency. For example, it is not useful to represent each image point by an instance of a class for pixels. The resulting image processing and analysis programs will show overheads and will not be efficient enough with such a degree of granularity.

If you split the program source for the methods of one class to several files, this can in some cases increase the time for the program to be linked. On the other hand, it can also reduce the program size.[9] Keep in the middle between high granularity (i.e., many small files) and a monolith (i.e., one huge program source file). Generally, definitions (except for inline functions) should be separated from declarations. Class, variable, and function declarations should be put into a header file (.h); definitions should be put into several modules (.C) which are independent of each other in the sense that they do not contain functions that mutually call each other.

Inline constructors for objects should in general be avoided for non–trivial construction tasks. Some compilers will generate a lot of code for each construction and the overhead of a function call will be small in comparison to the overall time for object construction.[10] The same holds for destructors.

Memory allocation and release in C++ is partially the task of the compiler which will call the destructor for automatic objects when they go out of scope. Objects allocated with the operator new have to be discarded explicitly by the user. Programs which allocate at one point (e.g., in a deeply nested function) and release memory at an other point (e.g., in another function) are often hard to understand and thus a possible source of errors. We recommend that wherever possible, the function which allocates an object with new should also release the object with `delete`.

Exercises

10.a Implement a `String` class with useful methods for substrings, modification, indexing etc. Extend Program 87 accordingly.
      Include overloaded operators (`operator+`) for assignment and concatenation. Which other operators can you think of?

10.b Implement a class for points as a modification of Program 85.
      Include overloaded operators for assignment and vector addition. Which other operators can you think of?

10.c Implement an alternative complex number class with a representation using r and ϕ (c.f. Eq. (12.10)).

10.d Extend the arithmetic operators for complex numbers. Which internal representation is better suited for multiplication?

---

[9]Think of a call of a little function in a large module that contains other functions which you will not call.

[10]Look at Program 93; what will the compiler have to generate in the case of an inline constructor?

11 Representation of Signals

Intensity based images are the most common input data structure for image processing and analysis. In practice, matrices are used for the representation of these discrete gray–level images. Each element of the two–dimensional matrix describes the gray–level of the digital image at its associated location. These "picture elements" are called *pixels*.

In this chapter we define a simple class for images. Motivated by the given examples, we introduce the concept of templates for classes in C++ and demonstrate their advantages with respect to software engineering projects. We also implement a class for speech signals using these templates.

11.1 Array Class

In chapter 5 we introduced the representation of images using two–dimensional arrays. It was explained in detail how these arrays are declared and used in C and C++ programs. The declaration of a matrix as an argument to a function requires that the fixed size of the arrays is known at compilation time. In general, it is expected that image processing modules are suitable for images of arbitrary size. A compilation for each image size is – obviously – unreasonable. Hence, other ways of dealing with images have to be found.

As was shown when the definition and implementation of the class bytevector was presented (Program 95), the use of the C++ new operator allows the dynamic allocation of storage for arbitrary arrays during the execution of programs. For the same purpose we now define a class byteArray2d. The class declaration for the abstract data type byteArray2d is designed to provide a constructor, whose arguments are the size of the two–dimensional array. The size of an array is thereby no longer required to be known during compilation. Parts of the header–file of the required class byteArray2d are shown in Program 100.

The implementation of the constructor byteArray2d(int, int) is shown in Program 101. Note that a vector is first allocated to hold the complete array in consecutive memory locations. Then, a pointer array is allocated by new and initialized to the starting positions of each row in the array in the for–loop. The internal representation of a matrix is illustrated in Figure 11.1. This example also shows that members of a fundamental type can be initialized in the same syntactic style as member objects (c.f. Sect.10.7).

```
class byteArray2d {    ·
  private:
    int xsize;                          // number of columns
    int ysize;                          // number of rows
    byte** matrix;                      // array
  public:
    byteArray2d();                      // default constructor
    byteArray2d(int, int);              // constructor
    ~byteArray2d();                     // destructor
    const byte* operator[] (int) const; // access to vector with
    byte*&      operator[] (int);       // ... index check
};
```
100

```
byteArray2d::byteArray2d(int x, int y) : xsize(x), ysize(y) {
  byte * array = new byte[x*y];    // vector of size x*y
  matrix = new byte*[y];           // generate byte matrix
  for (int i = 0; i < y; ++i)      // all rows
    matrix[i] = & (array[i*x]);    // fill in vector pointers
}
```
101

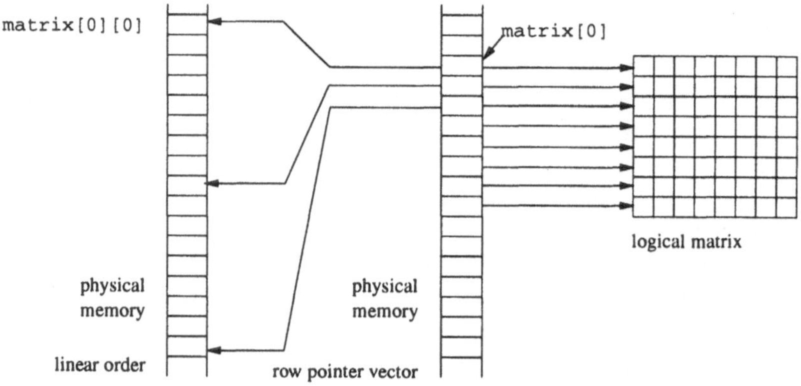

Figure 11.1 Internal representation of a two–dimensional array.

This technique allows for index checking of the first index in an array access operation (Program 102). If instead of a byte**, a vector of byte–vectors (see Program 95) is used, which provides access control, the indices can be checked for both dimensions. This idea, however, requires changes in the class bytevector. In order to allocate a variable length vector of bytevectors, the new operator has to be used. Thus, the bytevector class has to provide a default constructor. In addition, after creation with the default constructor, the actual length has to be set and the internal pointer has to be allocated. These extensions are left as an exercise (Exercise 11.a).

```
const byte * byteArray2d::operator[] (int i) const
{
  if (i > ysize)
    { fprintf(stderr,"out of bounds\n"); } // need smarter routine!
  return matrix[i];
}
```
102

```
byteArray2d::~byteArray2d()
{
  delete [] matrix[0];   // allocated by array = new byte[..]
  delete [] matrix;      // allocated by new byte*[..]
}
```
103

The destructor of this class just has to release the memory allocated in the constructor (Program 101). The memory allocated in the variable array is accessible as
matrix[0]. This is shown in Program 103.

11.2 Templates

We now have a matrix class for components of the type byte. This class is sufficient
for the representation of gray–levels in intensity images. What happens, if we need a
class of matrices with real numbers? We have to implement the class realArray2d.
The only difference between byteArray2d and realArray2d is that we have to
substitute the data type byte with float or double. It would be annoying, if we had
to program the matrix classes for different types of elements over and over again. Thus,
it would be advantageous to have the possibility of "parameterized types" (Chapter 9).
Operations like multiplication or addition are reduced to multiplications and additions of
the components which are parameterized. The arithmetic of matrices would not depend
upon the special types of the entries. Fortunately, C++ offers a feature to realize these
parameterized classes automatically. This concept is called a *template*. The syntax for
declaring a class template is

Syntax:	template < class *T* > *class–declaration*

A declared template specifies that an argument of type T will be used in the declaration of
the parameterized class immediately following the template prefix. Formally expressed,
type T is used within the declaration in exactly the same way as other types are. It does
not have to be a class; it may as well be a simple type like an int. The concrete type of
the parameter T is specified when a variable is declared. The name of the template class
followed by the type in brackets < > can be used exactly like the conventional classes.

Program 104 shows the implementation and the use of a template class for matrices. It
directly extends Program 100. The template class for matrices is used in a C++ program

```
template<class T> class Matrix {
 private:
  unsigned int xsize;              // number of columns
  unsigned int ysize;              // number of rows
  T ** matrix;                     // parameterized array
 public:
  Matrix();                        // default constructor
  Matrix(int, int);                // constructor
  ~Matrix();                       // destructor
  T* operator[] (int);             // access to vector
  void operator= (const Matrix&);  // assign matrix
  void operator= (const T& v);     // assign v to each element
  const T* operator[] (int) const; // read only access
  operator T**(){ return matrix; } // efficient access
  int SizeX()const{return xsize;}  // size information x
  int SizeY()const{return ysize;}  // size information y
};                                                            104
```

```
template <class T> Matrix<T>::Matrix(int x, int y)
{
    xsize= x; ysize= y;
    T * array = new T[x*y];        // vector of size x*y
    matrix = new T*[y];            // generate T matrix
    for (int i = 0; i < y; ++i)
       matrix[i] = & (array[i*x]); // fill in vector pointers
}
template <class T> T* Matrix<T>::operator[] (int i)
   { return matrix[i]; }
template <class T> const T* Matrix<T>::operator[] (int i) const
   { return matrix[i]; }                                      105
```

```
Matrix<int> m1(256,256);          // define a matrix of integers
Matrix<float> m2(512,256);        // define a larger matrix of floats
int c1= m1[2][100];               // access one element (secure,
float c2= m2[5][120];             // since the indices are checked)  106
```

as shown now in Program 106. The implementation of methods uses the class template as shown in Program 105. The allocation is done exactly as in Program 101.

The compiler and linker have to take care that code for every parameter type is generated. This should be transparent to the user.

11.3 Images

We now introduce image classes as the primary data structure for image processing and analysis. It quickly turns out that intensity images are not simply byte matrices. In real applications, we need further information about the image generation process. For example, it is necessary for recognition and classification purposes to know the camera geometry, i.e. the focal length or other parameters. Matrices are used as an internal representation of the image signal. Most common imaging devices use gray-level images with 256 gray levels which can be stored in one byte (see Figure 11.3 or Figure 11.2 for examples). The components of the image's byte–matrix represent intensity values.

Figure 11.2 Example images: on the left a color image (printed as gray–level image), on the right a gray–level image

Another type of signals used for three–dimensional image processing are *range images*. Each component of the image matrix no longer represents an intensity value; instead, the *distance* of the scene points with respect to a given reference plane are stored within the matrix. The matrix elements in a range image can be any of the types byte, int, float, or double. It depends only upon the discrete step–sizes chosen for the depth values. Additional information in the class range image could include the position of the reference plane or the scaling of the depth values. Figure 11.3 shows an example of a range image.[1] The depth values of the industrial part are encoded as gray–levels. The higher the gray–level, the lower is the distance of the scene point with respect to the optical sensor.

The declaration in Program 107 introduces the abstract data type GLImage for gray–level images, wherein the defined template class for matrices is used, i.e. the class

---

[1] Due to the optical measurement device used in this case, there are areas on the object for which no range value is computed (like a shadow on the left).

[2] (Ref. to Figure 11.3) Images by the Institute for Physics, University of Erlangen–Nürnberg

Figure 11.3 An example for a gray–level image (left) and the corresponding range image (right)[2]

```
class GLImage {
 private:
  float focus;           // focal length
  float aperture;        // lens aperture
  float scaling;         // pixel side relation
  char * description;    // textual information
  Matrix<byte> image;    // the pixels
 public:
  GLImage(int,int);              // constructor
  ~GLImage();                    // destructor
  int isEqual(const GLImage&);   // test equality
  // etc.
  byte * operator [] (int i) { return image[i]; } // delegation
  int SizeX() { return image.SizeX(); }
};
```

107

Matrix is a client of the abstract data type GLImage. Additionally, we have members which represent the focal length and the aperture of the camera lens as well as a scaling factor which describes pixel characteristics.[3] Later, we will enhance this class definition (Program 160).

Pixel access is simply delegated to the image array with an inline operator [] which again checks the validity of the first index. We commonly choose the origin of the image coordinate system in the right upper corner. Therefore the first index of an image matrix corresponds to the y–coordinate axis, the second index belongs to x.[4] The method isEqual tests whether two images are equal.[5]

---

[3]Pixels may be either quadratic (the rare case), or rectangular depending on the layout of the CCD. The relation of the sides is stored in the scaling factor (c.f. Exercise 1.g).

[4]This means that $f(x, y) = f_{yx} = f_{ij}$. You should try to be consistent in your programs with respect to argument orderings and variable names!

[5]This is the test for equality is a complicated topic which will not be discussed here. It is different from the test for identity (isSame).

11.4 External Data Formats

Images require a large amount of external storage due to the large number of pixels. The image in Figure 11.2 has a dimension of 511×491 which requires 250901 bytes on disk. The simplest form of storage is the so called raw format (c.f. Program 34). For asymmetric image sizes, raw format may be insufficient; the image can only be read, when the dimensions are known. How should the computer decide whether the image is 511×491 or 491×511?

Normally, various information about sizes, contents, resolution etc. is stored in the image files (e.g. in the common TIFF **T**ag **I**mage **F**ile **F**ormat, see [Poy92]). If the image elements are of a more complex data type than bytes, the external storage has to be conformant with machine dependent internal formats. Machine independent storage is essential for the exchange of images between different computer architectures. Byte order of integral data types and floating point format are the major problems that have to be dealt with. Several standards exist for data representation, either by a standard committee (ISO/ANSI/DIN, c.f. for example, [Pra95]) or as a "de–facto" standard imposed by the leading market position of some company (see also IIF e.g. in [Cla92]).

Images often contain a lot of redundancy. For that reason, image compression algorithms and strategies are of major importance. The JPEG (Joint Photographic Expert Group, [Wal90]) image compression standard and the MPEG (Motion Pictures Expert Group, [Gal91]) are commonly used for image transmission. Since the data compression using these algorithms discard information, these techniques are not always useful for image analysis. However, under appropriate parameterization, JPEG coded images can be used for image analysis and camera control in active imaging [Wal90].

The program `compress` which is distributed with most Unix systems is designed for text compression. The same holds for `gzip` which is part of the GNU project. These programs are also applicable to images without loss of information, but of course with lower compression rates than JPEG or MPEG.

An image format suitable for object–oriented programming will be introduced in Chapter 15 and Chapter 16.

11.5 Binary Images

When every pixel in an image may be only black or white, then we are talking about *binary images*. This class of images is particularly useful in many areas as the speed of computation is generally higher e.g. with respect to gray–level images.

Logically, binary images and gray–level images are different image classes, since different operations are applicable to them. However, internally, they may both use a byte matrix, since only few computers allow efficient direct bit access. Most often, the smallest addressable unit is a byte.

Figure 11.4 Gray–level image and two binary images with different thresholds

The question arises how the bipartition of gray–levels has to be selected such that an intensity image can be converted into a binary image in an *optimal* manner. We will learn about this in Chapter 20. Figure 11.4 shows a gray–level image and two binary images computed with different bipartitions.

11.6   Color Images

The human retina (c.f. Figure 1.7) has three types of color receptors called *cone* cells. This justifies that color are usually represented through the combination of the three colors red, green, and blue (RGB). An example is shown in Figure 11.5.[6] For each basic color we need a matrix. The declaration of a class `ColorImage` is shown in Program 108.[7]

The class for color images should include conversion to *color spaces* of other kinds, for instance, XYZ or HSL (see e.g. in [Wys82, Poy95]). These conversions are mappings from one three–dimensional vector to another. The transform of RGB to XYZ is a linear

---

[6]Of course, the color images are printed here as gray–levels. They are available in full color together with the course material (Appendix B).

[7]Would you prefer a matrix of a structure containing three bytes for each pixel? Discuss advantages and disadvantages!

Figure 11.5 Three color channels (red, green, blue) for image Figure 11.2

```
class ColorImage {          // Version 1
  private:
    Matrix<byte> red;        // color channel red
    Matrix<byte> green;      // color channel green
    Matrix<byte> blue;       // color channel blue
  public:
    // ...
};
```

108

transformation, i.e. a matrix multiplication. The conversion to HSL (hue, saturation, luminosity) is much more complicated and non–linear. An example of such a color transformations is given in (11.1).

$$
\begin{pmatrix} X \\ Y \\ Z \end{pmatrix} = \begin{pmatrix} 0.412 & 0.357 & 0.180 \\ 0.212 & 0.715 & 0.072 \\ 0.019 & 0.119 & 0.950 \end{pmatrix} \begin{pmatrix} R \\ G \\ B \end{pmatrix} \tag{11.1}
$$

The YUV color space is used primarily for PAL or NTSC video and has little use for digital component video [Poy95]. A non–linear conversion of intensity values is called a *gamma–correction*; it will be described in Sect. 20.6. Also, a conversion to gray–level images seems to be useful as shown in (11.2) for RGB color images.[8] Within the color space XYZ, the conversion from colors to gray–levels results from a simple projection. Indeed, the Y–channel of the XYZ color space represents the gray–level image in (11.1), i.e.,

$$
f_{i,j} = 0.212\, r_{i,j} + 0.715\, g_{i,j} + 0.072\, b_{i,j} \quad . \tag{11.2}
$$

Color images can also be created from gray level images by *pseudo coloring*. A color vector has to be generated for every gray–level. This can easily be accomplished with histogram mappings (c.f. Chapter 20).

---

[8]The image in Figure 11.2 was created from the color image in Figure 11.5 using this formula.

11.7   Subimages

Logically, image elements are accessed by the indices of the image array. In practice, however, pointers are often used which are set once and then incremented to gain speed. Therefore, it is essential for reliable programs to know something about the memory layout of images.

It is convenient, if an algorithm can be applied to a subimage, i.e. only a rectangular section of the image, without knowing about the size and offset to the enclosing image. For active vision, this is often called a "region of interest" (ROI). If we assume continuous allocation of pixels in the large image, the rows of the subimage will be split in memory as indicated in Figure 11.6.

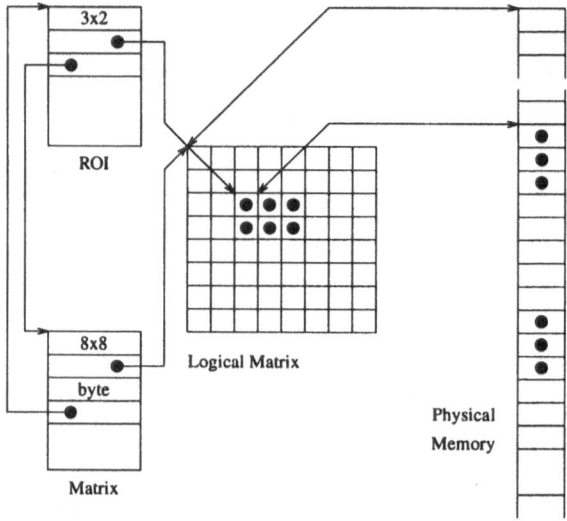

Figure 11.6 Logical and physical matrix mapped to a conventional linear storage. There exists no connected allocated storage for subimages (from [Pau92b]).

The implementation of subimages is straightforward when using the technique introduced in Program 101 (c.f. [Pau92b]). A subimage sets its line vector to the appropriate starting points in the master image. Images have to use reference counters in order to release memory correctly in the destructors.

Subimages provide a source of great performance gain in real–time image analysis, since only the relevant portion of the information has to be processed then, as proposed also by the active vision approach. For subimages to work properly, it is essential that all image operations make the only assumption that elements in the image rows are

```
extern "C" double mean(byte** image, int xs, int ys) // C-callable
{                                             // computes mean gray-value
   double res = 0;
   for (int i = ys-1; i >= 0; --i) { // first index is i / y
    byte * ptr = image[i];           // use [ ]
      for (int j = xs-1; j >= 0; --j) // second index is j /x
        res += *(ptr++);             // may use pointer
   }
   return res / (xs * ys);
}
```
109

```
template<class T> class Vector {
 private:
   unsigned int xsize;              // number of elements
   T * vec;                         // parameterized array
 public:
   Vector();                        // default constructor
   Vector(int);                     // constructor
   ~Vector();                       // destructor
   T & operator[] (int);            // access to vector
   const.T& operator[] (int) const; // read only access
   operator T*(){ return vec; }     // efficient access
   int SizeX()const{return xsize;}  // access
};
```
110

allocated consecutively. Only then it is possible to use pointer access. When skipping from one row to the next, the pointer has to be initialized again using the subimage information. This is shown in Program 109 for the computation of the mean of an image or a subimage. Implementation of subimages is left as Exercise 11.c.

11.8 Matrix Operations

We now want do to basic mathematics with matrices and vectors. First, we need a template version of Program 97 which is shown in Program 110. For linear algebra, it is useful to tag a vector as a row vector or as a column vector. We leave out this detail at this point. Using the new vector declaration we can now implement operations such as the multiplication of a matrix by a column vector or multiplication of a row vector by a matrix.

Program 111 shows a template *function* which is neither part of the class for vectors nor matrices. This function overloads the operator * for the operands Matrix and Vector. The use of this function requires that the operator * is defined on the actual type which is substituted for <T>. If this is not the case, the compiler will emit an error message.

```
template <class T>
  Vector<T> operator* (const Matrix<T>& m, const Vector<T> &v)
{
    assert(m.SizeX() == v.SizeX());            // check sizes
    Vector<T> r(m.sizeY());                    // local result vector
    for ( register short y=0; y < ysize;y++) { // loop over lines
        T s = 0;                               // sum over lines
        for( register short x=0; x < xsize; x++) // loop over columns
            s += v[x] * m[y][x];               // sum up
        r[y] = s;                              // new vector element
    }
    return v;                                  // return copy
}
```

111

```
Matrix<int> m(3,3);            // integer matrix
Vector<int> v0(3);             // integer column vector
Vector<int> v1(3) = m * v0;    // matrix times vector -> vector
Vector<int> v2(3) = 2 * v1;    // integer times vector
```

112

```
template <class T> Matrix<T> operator*(const Matrix<T>&, const Matrix<T>&);
template <class T> Vector<T> operator*(const Matrix<T>&, const Vector<T>&);
template <class T> Vector<T> operator*(const T&,         const Vector<T>&);
template <class T> T operator*(const Vector<T>&, const Vector<T>&);
```

113

Analogously we can now implement the following mathematical ideas for a scalar s, vectors $x, y \in \mathbf{R}^3$ and matrices $A, B, C \in \mathbf{R}^{3\times3}$ in a way that Program 112 is syntactically correct:

$$C = AB \tag{11.3}$$
$$y = A\,x \tag{11.4}$$
$$y = 0.12345\,x \tag{11.5}$$
$$s = x \cdot y \tag{11.6}$$

The declaration of these operations is shown in Program 113 (in the same order as for the previous mathematical equations). The implementation is left as exercises (Exercise 11.f). The multiplication of a vector by a scalar explains why the functions in Program 113 are not member functions of any class: the choice of an overloaded operator is done by the compiler from left to right in an expression, so there must be an overloaded operator for a scalar (an integer in Program 112) which obviously cannot be a member function, since integer numbers are not instances of a class.

```
class SpeechSignal;          // forward declaration
class SpeechFrame {
 private:
   SpeechSignal * signal;
   Vector<short> samples;   // sample values
 public:
   SpeechFrame (int s) : samples(s) {};
   short & operator [] (int i) { return samples[i]; }
   Time Start();            // compute start time from index in signal
};
class SpeechSignal {
 private:
   short bias;              // added to each sample value
   long duration;          // frame length in [ms]
   float rate;             // frame sampling rate
   Time  start;            // Time class to be defined
   Sequence frames;        // Sequence class to be defined!
 public:
   SpeechSignal();                     // default
   SpeechFrame & operator [] (int i);  // references Sequence
   // to be extended
};
```

114

11.9   Speech Signal Class

Not all speech processing algorithms will split the sample values into frames of equal length. However, many computations can easily be described using such vectors of samples. Using the new Vector template we now proceed to define a speech frame class SpeechFrame. Operations are delegated to the vector template class. A basic structure is given in Program 114. The speech frame references an object SpeechSignal for the representation of a whole speech signal. Similar to the image class, we include additional information to the sample values. Since we often want to use positive sample values, we provide a member bias which is added to each sample value. A time stamp marks the start of the speech signal. A member Sequence contains a linear list of speech frames, which can be updated during the existence of the speech signal in case of real–time processing. From the index in this list, the speech frame can compute its start and end times (using the method Start()). Classes for Time and Sequence are left unspecified here. A possible implementation will be shown in Chapter 15.

Data that is common to all speech frames, such as the duration, is not replicated in each object; instead, it is kept once in the referenced SpeechSignal object.

We choose a vector of short integers for the internal representation of the sample values. Thereby signals quantized with 12–16 bits can be represented. The SpeechSignal class also gives us the freedom to discard frames at all; in this case, the class will have to be extended by a representation of the sample values as a sequence, directly.

Exercises

11.a Implement a matrix template class using a vector of bytevectors (Program 95). Extend the class `Vector<T>` (Program 110) as indicated in Sect. 11.1.

11.b Write a program to convert to and from your favorite image format.

11.c Implement the concept of subimages for the image classes introduced in this chapter. Use a reference count in the image class to decide whether the destructor should release the allocated memory, or not.

11.d Implement the color transformation (11.1) using matrix multiplication by a color vector as in Program 112. Integrate a member into the vector class for row and column vectors.

11.e Compute reverse transformations for (11.3) and (11.1). Apply the transformation back and forth several times. What kind of error will you get?

11.f Extend matrix and vector operations as indicated in Sect. 11.8.

12 Fourier Transform

In the field of image processing, a sampled signal usually serves directly as input data for algorithms which extract geometric features or segmented images (Sect. 6.5, see also Chapter 21). Gray–level images, for instance, are used to compute point or line features or to extract regions of homogeneous intensity values.

In speech recognition it is necessary to derive a set of features for the sampled signal which are convenient for the subsequent processing steps. There are many different types of parameters to represent a speech signal. You can take, for example, the sample values of the speech and compute features like the zero crossing rate, the energy of the signal, or the slope at selected points [Nie90a, Rab88]. Usually features are not computed in the *spatial domain*, but in the *frequency domain* of the signal, i.e., a transform of the signal is required. Spectral features have some characteristics which are not directly evident in spatial data [Dud73]. Therefore, it has proven advantageous to do a spectral analysis of speech signals. A more detailed motivation, introduction, and definition of spectral features will follow in Chapter 23.

In the subsequent sections we will give an introduction to the computation of Fourier transforms for signals of arbitrary dimensions including both the continuous and the discrete case.[1] The famous algorithm of Cooley and Tukey [Coo65] for the fast computation of Fourier transforms will be discussed. This is, in addition to algorithms for sorting, one of the most important and most cited algorithms in computer science and engineering. Some hints for the implementation in C++ of this basic technique will be given in the final sections of this chapter as well as some new features of the C++–language, which will be applied to a class for complex numbers.

12.1 Introductory Considerations

In linear algebra it is shown that a set of linear independent vectors can be used as a basis for a vector space. Linear independency says that no vector of the basis can be expressed as a linear combination of other basis vectors. The vector space is defined by all linear combinations of available basis vectors. A well–known example is the two–dimensional

---

[1]"Home page" of Jean Baptiste Joseph Fourier (∗ March 21, 1768 - † May 16, 1830): http://capella.dur.ac.uk/doug/fourier.html

plane $\mathbf{R}^2$, where possible basis vectors are $e_1 = (1,0)^T$ and $e_2 = (0,1)^T$. All vectors $v \in \mathbf{R}^2$ can be written as a linear combination

$$v = a_1 e_1 + a_2 e_2 \quad , \tag{12.1}$$

where the coefficients $a_1, a_2 \in \mathbf{R}$. Obviously the basis vectors are not unique, but for a given set of basis vectors, all elements of the vector space can be uniquely identified by the coefficients of the linear combination. The cardinality of the basis is not necessarily finite. The vector space for polynomials, for example, is generated by the infinite set of monomials $\{x^n | n \geq 0\}$. A polynomial

$$h(x) = \sum_{k=0}^{n} h_k x^k \tag{12.2}$$

of degree n is uniquely given by its $n + 1$ coefficients $h_0, h_1, \ldots, h_n$.

An interesting question is, whether there exits a finite or infinite set of basis elements for the space of signals. Indeed, every *periodic* signal can be written as a linear combination of sine and cosine functions. Figure 12.1 shows, for example, some plots of one–dimensional functions which are sums of trigonometric functions.

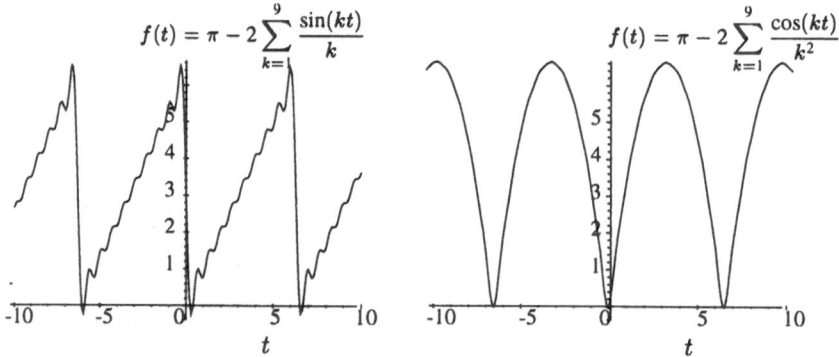

Figure 12.1 Linear combinations of trigonometric functions

12.2   Fourier Series

The basic idea of using the frequency domain of speech signals is founded on the mathematical result that an arbitrary 2π–periodic function[2] $f(t) \in \mathbf{R}$, where $t \in \mathbf{R}$, can be approximated by a — possibly infinite — Fourier series

$$f(t) = \frac{a_0}{2} + \sum_{k \geq 1} a_k \cos(kt) + b_k \sin(kt) \quad , \tag{12.3}$$

---

[2]i.e., $f(t) = f(t + 2\pi)$

i.e., a superposition of weighted sine and cosine terms. The scalar weights a_k and b_k are called the *Fourier coefficients* and can be used for the unique mathematical description of periodic functions. This cited result shows that $\{\cos(kt), \sin(kt) | k \geq 0\}$ forms a basis for the vector space of all 2π–periodic functions.

The convergence properties of this — in general infinite — sum were developed by Dirichlet and are summarized, for example, in [Bro85]. The behavior of Fourier series and the associated Fourier coefficients with respect to the symmetry properties of the periodic function $f(t)$ is remarkable and important for practical computations. The cosine function is an even function and the sine function is symmetrical to the origin of the coordinate system. This is the reason why the approximation of odd functions using (12.3) includes only summands of sine functions and analogously, even functions are superpositions of cosine terms. Thus, whenever an odd or even function is developable in a Fourier series, we know that $a_k = 0$ or $b_k = 0$, $k \geq 0$, for the involved Fourier coefficients.

It should be clear to the reader, that if a *finite* sum of sine and cosine functions approximates a function without any errors, the *continuous* function can be exactly recomputed, if the discrete values a_k and b_k of the occurring frequencies of sine and cosine terms are known. This observation constitutes the basis for the informally introduced sampling theorem of Sect.1.7. However, there are, in general, infinitely many non–zero Fourier coefficients for arbitrary, not band limited functions.

Let the function $f(t)$ be a given 2π–periodic function, which should be approximated by a Fourier series. Now the practical question arises, how can we analytically or at least numerically, compute the Fourier coefficients $a_k \in \mathbf{R}$ and $b_k \in \mathbf{R}$ for $k \geq 0$ of (12.3). Indeed, there exist closed form solutions for the computation.

For this purpose, we multiply both sides of (12.3) with $\cos(lt)$ and determine the integral over the interval $[-\pi, \pi]$ of the resulting function. Applying the orthogonality property of the trigonometric sine and cosine functions, i.e., for integer k and l, it is

$$\int_{-\pi}^{\pi} \sin(kt)\cos(lt)\,dt \;=\; 0 \quad \text{and} \tag{12.4}$$

$$\int_{-\pi}^{\pi} \sin(kt)\sin(lt)\,dt \;=\; \int_{-\pi}^{\pi} \cos(kt)\cos(lt)\,dt = \begin{cases} 0, \text{ if } & k \neq l \\ \pi, \text{ if } & k = l \end{cases}, \tag{12.5}$$

we get

$$a_k \;=\; \frac{1}{\pi}\int_{-\pi}^{\pi} f(t)\cos(kt)\,dt \quad. \tag{12.6}$$

The multiplication of equation (12.3) with $\sin(lt)$ and subsequent integration results in a similar formula for b_k, i.e.,

$$b_k = \frac{1}{\pi} \int_{-\pi}^{\pi} f(t) \sin(kt)\, dt \quad . \tag{12.7}$$

These formulas are called *Euler's formulas*.

Let us, as an example, compute the Fourier series for the step function defined by

$$f(t) = \begin{cases} 1, & \text{if } 0 \le t < \frac{\pi}{2} \\ -1, & \text{if } \frac{\pi}{2} < t < \frac{3\pi}{2} \\ 1, & \text{if } \frac{3\pi}{2} < t \le 2\pi \end{cases} \quad . \tag{12.8}$$

Due to the symmetry of this function, we conclude $b_k = 0$ for all k. The coefficients a_k are computed by the evaluation of (12.6); herein, the occurring integrals over cosine functions are fairly elementary to compute, and we get

$$a_k = \begin{cases} 0, & \text{if } k \text{ is even} \\ \frac{4}{k\pi} \sin\left(\frac{k\pi}{2}\right), & \text{otherwise} \end{cases} \quad . \tag{12.9}$$

Figure 12.2 shows the first summands of the resulting Fourier series and Figure 12.3 illustrates the superposition of these functions.[3] This example illustrates (but does not prove) the theoretical results of Dirichlet concerning the convergence properties of Fourier series, even in the case of non–smooth periodic functions.

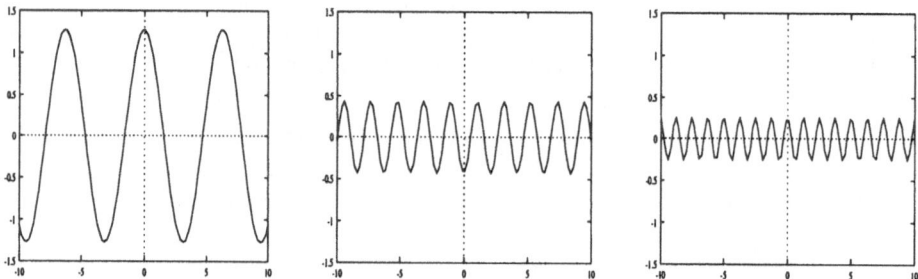

Figure 12.2 First three summands of the Fourier series for the step function defined in (12.8)

12.3   Fourier Transform

The Fourier series will now be used for the introduction and derivation of the Fourier transform. For this purpose, Fourier series will be written in complex form. By the introduction of the Eulerean formula

---

[3]The assymetrical look of the function is due to a bug in the graphical tool used for visualization.

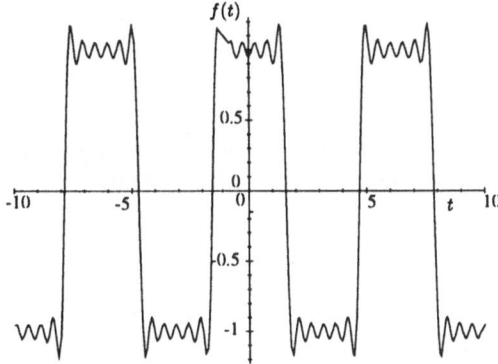

Figure 12.3 Superposition of the functions in Figure 12.2 and three further summands

$$\exp(\pm i\phi) \quad = \quad \cos\phi \pm i\sin\phi \quad , \tag{12.10}$$

where $\exp(\pm i\phi) \in C$ and i is the imaginary unit, the trigonometric functions can be written in terms of complex exponential functions, i.e.,

$$\cos(kt) \quad = \quad \frac{1}{2}(\exp(ikt) + \exp(-ikt)) \tag{12.11}$$

and

$$\sin(kt) \quad = \quad \frac{1}{2i}(\exp(ikt) - \exp(-ikt)) \quad . \tag{12.12}$$

If we put these identities into the Fourier series (12.3), we can approximate univariate, real–valued functions $f(t)$ using the infinite complex series

$$f(t) \quad = \quad \frac{1}{2\pi} \sum_{k=-\infty}^{+\infty} c_k \exp(ikt) \quad , \tag{12.13}$$

where

$$c_k = \begin{cases} \pi(a_k - i\,b_k), & \text{if } k \geq 0 \\ \pi(a_{|k|} + i\,b_{|k|}), & \text{otherwise} \end{cases} \quad . \tag{12.14}$$

The formula for computing the weights c_k of each complex summand is shown to be

$$c_k \quad = \quad \int_{-\pi}^{\pi} f(t)\exp(-ikt)\, dt \quad . \tag{12.15}$$

Obviously, even functions have no complex parts in their complex Fourier series, because there are no sine terms, i.e., $b_k = 0$ for all k.

Let us now assume that the interval of periodicity for the function $f(t)$ is infinite. The sum of (12.13) will become an integral and the coefficients c_k will result in a continuous weight function $c(k)$ with respect to the real–valued variable k, i.e.,

$$c(k) = \int_{-\infty}^{+\infty} f(t) \exp(-ikt) \, dt \quad . \tag{12.16}$$

The weight function $c(k)$ is called the *Fourier transform* of the function $f(t)$. In the following we will denote the Fourier transform of $f(t)$ by

$$F(\xi) = \int_{-\infty}^{+\infty} f(t) \exp(-i\xi t) \, dt = FT\{f\} \quad . \tag{12.17}$$

The Fourier transform of a function represents the amplitude of each frequency. For example, Figure 12.4 shows the continuous function

$$f(t) = \begin{cases} 1 & \text{if } |t| < t_0 \\ 0 & \text{otherwise} \end{cases}, \tag{12.18}$$

and the absolute values of the corresponding Fourier transform.

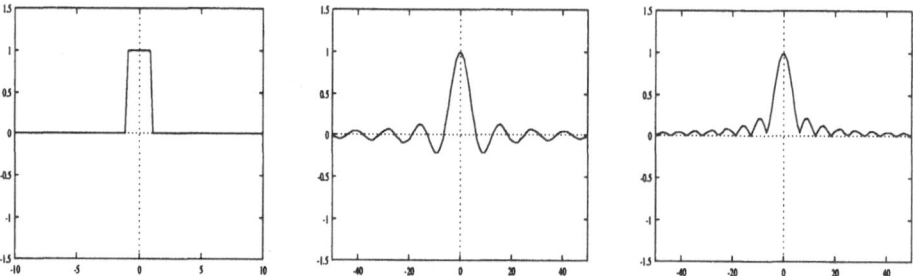

Figure 12.4 Continuous function (left), its Fourier transform (middle) and the absolute values (right)

Some useful and often needed properties of this transform are summarized in Table 12.1. The proofs are elementary and left as an exercise to the reader. The symmetry character shows that the inverse of the Fourier transform is again a Fourier transform. Thus, the computational complexity of the inverse Fourier transform is identical to the calculation of Fourier transform itself. Indeed, we have

$$f(t) = \frac{1}{2\pi} \int_{-\infty}^{+\infty} F(\xi) \exp(i\xi t) \, d\xi \quad . \tag{12.19}$$

One fundamental and the most important property of the Fourier transform is the *convolution theorem*. It states that for the function

$$h(t) = f(t) \star g(t) = \int_{-\infty}^{+\infty} f(x) \, g(t - x) \, dx \tag{12.20}$$

	spatial domain	frequency domain
scaling	$f(at)$	$\frac{1}{|a|}F(\frac{\xi}{a})$
shifting	$f(t - t_0)$	$\exp(-i\xi t_0)\,F(\xi)$
"symmetry"	$-1/(2\pi) \cdot F(t)$	$f(-\xi)$
differentiation	$d^n\,f(t)/d\,t^n$	$(i\,\xi)^n\,F(\xi)$

Table 12.1 Some properties of the Fourier transform

the Fourier transform satisfies the equation

$$H(\xi) = F(\xi)\,G(\xi) \quad , \tag{12.21}$$

since due to the shifting property of the Fourier transform we get

$$
\begin{aligned}
H(\xi) &= \int_{-\infty}^{+\infty} h(t)\exp(-i\xi t)\,dt = \int_{-\infty}^{+\infty}\int_{-\infty}^{+\infty} f(x)\,g(t-x)\,dx\,\exp(-i\xi t)\,dt \\
&= \int_{-\infty}^{+\infty} f(x)\left(\int_{-\infty}^{+\infty} g(t-x)\exp(-i\xi t)\,dt\right)\,dx \\
&= \int_{-\infty}^{+\infty} f(x)\,\exp(-i\xi x)\,G(\xi)\,dx = F(\xi)\,G(\xi) \quad . \tag{12.22}
\end{aligned}
$$

This theorem shows that the computation of the convolution of two functions can be done by the multiplication of the Fourier transforms $F(\xi)$ and $G(\xi)$ of both functions and a subsequent use of the inverse Fourier transform.

The most common application of the convolution theorem in the field of signal theory is the determination of the function $f(t)$ from equation (12.20), if $g(t)$ and $h(t)$ are known. The principle of this process is shown in Figure 12.5. Only a division is required after the transformation into the frequency domain. Without the convolution theorem, we have to solve complicated integral equation for the computation of $f(t)$. The convolution theorem is widely used in different fields of mathematics, computer science or electrical engineering. Fast multiplication algorithms for polynomials or integers [Aho74], for example, use the convolution as well as time–invariant linear systems [Nie83].

The application of the Fourier transform for speech or image processing requires some extensions in our software environment: First, all signals we can deal with are non–continuous. A discrete version of the Fourier transform and its inverse is needed (Sect. 12.4). Second, the introduction of the Fourier transform implies the necessity of complex numbers; we need an elaborated class for complex numbers, which provides methods like addition and multiplication (Sect. 12.5). Third, an extension of the one–dimensional case is required, because images represent two–dimensional signals (Sect. 12.9).

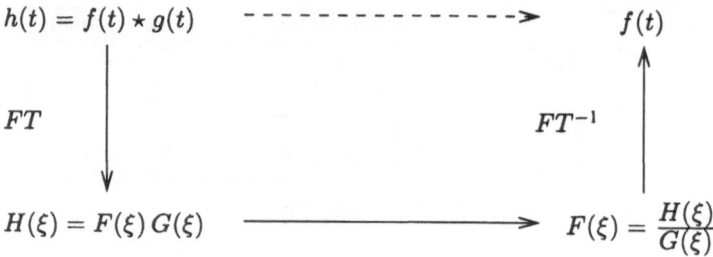

$$h(t) = f(t) \star g(t) \quad - - - - - - - - - - - - - - -> \quad f(t)$$

$$FT \qquad\qquad\qquad\qquad\qquad\qquad\qquad\qquad FT^{-1}$$

$$H(\xi) = F(\xi)\,G(\xi) \quad\longrightarrow\quad F(\xi) = \dfrac{H(\xi)}{G(\xi)}$$

Figure 12.5 Application of the convolution theorem

12.4   Discrete Fourier Transform

If we have to compute the Fourier transform of a recorded speech signal represented by the sequence of M sampling values $f_0, f_1, \ldots, f_{M-1}$, we need the discrete version of the Fourier transform. Following (12.16) we define

$$F_\nu = \sum_{t=0}^{M-1} f_t \cdot \left(\exp\left(-i2\pi\frac{\nu}{M}\right)\right)^t = \mathrm{DFT}\{f\} \quad . \tag{12.23}$$

The computation of the *discrete Fourier transform* (DFT) and its inverse can easily be done, because it is a linear transform, which thus can be written in matrix form. The discrete Fourier transform F_ν, $\nu = 0, 1, 2, \ldots, M - 1$, is a linear combination of complex numbers, which are solutions of the equation

$$x^M - 1 \;=\; 0 \tag{12.24}$$

and powers of these numbers. Let

$$m \;=\; \exp\left(-i\frac{2\pi}{M}\right) \tag{12.25}$$

and

$$m^{t\nu} \;=\; \exp\left(-i2\pi\frac{t\nu}{M}\right) \tag{12.26}$$

denote powers of the solutions of above equation. The root m is usually called the M–*th root of unity* and we know from the theory of complex numbers

$$\sum_{t=0}^{M-1} \exp\left(-i2\pi\frac{t}{M}\right) = 0 \quad . \tag{12.27}$$

Using definition (12.23) for $\nu = 0, 1, 2, \ldots, M - 1$, we get the following linear system of equations for discrete Fourier coefficients:

```
class complex {                              // structure declaration
    double r,i;                              // two data members
public:
  complex ();                                // to allow for arrays
  complex (const complex &);
  complex (const double& r, const double i = 0); // given real and img. part

  complex operator* (const complex &) const;
  complex operator+ (const complex &) const;
  complex operator- (const complex &) const;
  complex operator= (const complex &);       // assign complex number
  complex operator= (const double);          // assign real number

  const double & re() const {return r;};     // read
  const double & im() const {return i;};     // read
  double re(const double& rn) {return r = rn;}; // write
  double im(const double& in) {return i = in;}; // write

  complex power(unsigned int) const;         // compute complex power
};

inline double abs(const complex & c)         // compute absolute
{                                            // value for a
    return sqrt(c.re()*c.re()+ c.im()*c.im()); // complex number
}                                            // (magnitude)
```

115

$$
\begin{pmatrix} F_0 \\ F_1 \\ F_2 \\ \vdots \\ F_{M-1} \end{pmatrix} = \underbrace{\begin{pmatrix} 1 & 1 & 1 & \cdots & 1 \\ 1 & m & m^2 & \cdots & m^{M-1} \\ 1 & m^2 & m^4 & \cdots & m^{2(M-1)} \\ \vdots & \vdots & \vdots & \vdots & \vdots \\ 1 & m^{M-1} & m^{2(M-1)} & \cdots & m^{(M-1)^2} \end{pmatrix}}_{\boldsymbol{D_m}} \begin{pmatrix} f_0 \\ f_1 \\ f_2 \\ \vdots \\ f_{M-1} \end{pmatrix} \quad (12.28)
$$

This result shows that a straightforward implementation of the discrete Fourier transform requires one multiplication of a M–dimensional vector of sample data and a $(M \times M)$–matrix with complex components. Consequently, the complexity of the discrete Fourier transform is bounded by $\mathcal{O}(M^2)$.

12.5 Complex Number Class

For implementation purposes, we need complex numbers, operations on complex numbers, and the possibility to define matrices as well as vectors with complex components. Program 115 shows a class for complex numbers. The required multiplication of complex numbers is shown in Program 116. For the computation of the discrete Fourier

```
#include "complex.h"
complex complex::operator* (const complex& c) const      // multiply
{                                                         // two complex
    return complex(r * c.r - i * c.i, r * c.i + i * c.r); // numbers
}
```
116

```
complex complex::power(unsigned n) const  // compute the power of a
{                                         // complex number
    if (n > 1) {
        complex h = power (n/2);          // recursive call using
        return (h * h * power(n%2));      // divide and conquer-principle
    }
    if (n > 0) return *this;              // end of recursion
    else return complex(1);               // complex(1) for n == 0
}
```
117

transform, it is necessary to compute powers of complex numbers. Due to the importance of Fourier transform with respect to real–time speech recognition applications,
the computation of powers of complex numbers has to be as efficient as possible. Program 117 shows a power function which is part of the class for complex numbers. The
basic idea herein is the observation that for even exponents $n = 2n'$, the power can be
decomposed into the computation of a square and a n'–th power of the square, i.e.,

$$z^n = z^{2n'} = \left(z^2\right)^{n'} , \tag{12.29}$$

for arbitrary numbers z. Obviously, the complexity is reduced by dividing up the original
problem into smaller sub–problems. But, this *trick* does not provide the optimal way of
computing powers of complex numbers. As we have already seen in Eq. 12.10, each
complex number z can be written using the Eulerean formula, i.e.,

$$z = a + ib = \sqrt{a^2 + b^2} \exp\left(i \, \arctan(b/a)\right) , \tag{12.30}$$

where a denotes the real part of z and b the complex part. Using this identity, the power
of complex numbers reduces to the computation of a power of reals, and one additional
multiplication of reals, since

$$z^n = \left(\sqrt{a^2 + b^2}\right)^n \exp\left(i \, \arctan(b/a) \cdot n\right) . \tag{12.31}$$

The extension of the class `complex` with respect to this method is left as an exercise.
Using this power function we can computer the required M–th roots of unity in (12.28).
The complete Vandermonde matrix D_m (12.28) is computed by Program 118.

12.6 Inverse Discrete Fourier Transform

The inverse discrete Fourier transform DFT^{-1} can be computed by inverting the matrix
D_m. Due to the fact that the components of D_m are $(D_m)_{u,v} = m^{uv}$, we conclude

```
#include "Matrix.h"
void DFTM_init(Matrix<complex> & dm)
{
        complex m(cos(2 * M_PI/dm.SizeY()),     // real part
                  sin(2 * M_PI/dm.SizeX())));   // imaginary part
        for (int i = 0; i < dm.SizeY(); ++i)    // lines
          for (int j = 0; j < dm.SizeX(); ++j)  // columns
            dm[i][j]= m.power(i*j);             // compute value for element
}
```
118

$$
\begin{aligned}
(\boldsymbol{D}_m \cdot \boldsymbol{D}_{m^{-1}})_{u,v} &= \sum_{t=0}^{M-1} m^{ut} m^{-tv} \\
&= \sum_{t=0}^{M-1} \exp\left(-\frac{2\pi i}{M} \cdot t(u-v)\right) \\
&= \begin{cases} M, & \text{if } u = v \\ 0, & \text{otherwise} \end{cases}
\end{aligned}
\tag{12.32}
$$

The inverse discrete Fourier transform is thus given by a linear mapping defined by the matrix

$$
(\boldsymbol{D}_m)^{-1} = \frac{1}{M} \boldsymbol{D}_{m^{-1}} ,
\tag{12.33}
$$

where

$$
\boldsymbol{D}_{m^{-1}} = \begin{pmatrix}
1 & 1 & 1 & \cdots & 1 \\
1 & m^{-1} & m^{-2} & \cdots & m^{-(M-1)} \\
1 & m^{-2} & m^{-4} & \cdots & m^{-2(M-1)} \\
\vdots & \vdots & \vdots & \vdots & \vdots \\
1 & m^{-(M-1)} & m^{-2(M-1)} & \cdots & m^{-(M-1)^2}
\end{pmatrix}
\tag{12.34}
$$

The properties of the Fourier transform shown in Table 12.1 are also valid for its discrete version. In summary, the computation of the inverse discrete Fourier transform as well as the Fourier transform require $\mathcal{O}(M^2)$ operations of addition and multiplication. The function shown in Program 118 can be used analogously to compute $\boldsymbol{D}_m^{-1}$.

The efficiency and the numerical stability of algorithms is often influenced by the ordering and sequence of applied operations. For instance, the Horner scheme is one of the most famous examples, where the reorganization of arithmetic operations decreases the problem's computational complexity. In fact, the reorganization of mathematical operations is also useful for the computation of the Fourier transform, as we will see in Sect. 12.8.

```
Vector<complex> operator*(Matrix<complex> A, Vector<double> x)
{
    Vector<complex> r(A.SizeY());           // vector (0,0,...,0)
    for (int i = 0; i < A.SizeY(); ++i) {   // lines
        double R =0, I = 0;
        for (int j = 0; j < A.SizeX(); ++j){  // columns
            R += A[i][j].re() * x[j];       // simplified arithmetic
            I += A[i][j].im() * x[j];       // since multiplicand is
        }                                    // complex(x,0)
        r[i].re(R); r[i].im(I);             // set element
    }
    return r ;                               // return vector
}
```
119

12.7   Fourier Transforms of Speech Signals

It is time to apply the discrete Fourier transform for practical experiments. Using concepts introduced above, we can now proceed with spectral analysis of discrete speech signals. We have already implemented a class for speech signals (see Program 11.9). Using the Vandermonde matrix D_m, a discrete speech signal can be transformed into a complex vector by a simple multiplication of a matrix with a vector. This multiplication is already provided by the template classes for matrices and vectors. Speech signals, however, were represented by real numbers or integers. We could now define a conversion from vectors of doubles to vectors of complex numbers in order to use the matrix operations. Alternatively, we can define an operator for the multiplication of a complex matrix with a double vector, as shown in Program 119; this operator is not declared inside the template class and can thus make use only of the methods re() and im() providing access to the internal data.

In practice, not the complete speech signal will be transformed, but subsequent parts of it. For this purpose, the short time Fourier analysis will be introduced in Sect. 23.4. For the practical usage of the Fourier transform (possibly satisfying real–time requirements), an efficient method for DFT computations is desirable and crucial. In Program 119 we already did some improvements for efficiency reasons and did not use the operator for multiplication of a complex number by a real number. Of course, further improvements are possible for the DFT; we could, for example, omit the multiplications by the constant one which is present at various places in the matrix D_m. A highly accelerated version of the Fourier transform is introduced in the following section.

12.8 Fast Fourier Transform

We now turn to a highly efficient method for calculating the discrete Fourier transform of a given discrete signal $[f_t]_{0 \le t < M}$. For the reduction of the complexity two main principles are commonly used:

1. the *application of homomorphisms* (compare, for example, the convolution theorem for the FT), and

2. the *divide–and–conquer* principle, where the decomposition of the original problem into smaller sub–problems speeds up the computation.[4]

The divide–and–conquer principle is the basic idea that the Fast Fourier Transform (FFT) algorithm is based on. We show how a recursive decomposition of a larger Fourier transform in terms of smaller ones can be performed. The complexity of determining the discrete Fourier transform will be reduced from $\mathcal{O}(M^2)$ to $\mathcal{O}(M \log M)$ using the remarkable idea of Cooley and Tukey [Coo65].

We restrict our discussion to the fast Fourier transform of radix two. For a more general and detailed discussion of this topic we recommend the books [Aho74] and [Kro79] which emphasize the algebraic background, and the books on signal theory [Opp75] and pattern recognition [Nie83] which concentrate on implementation details and practical aspects.

The first assumption is that the number of discrete sampling values is $M = 2n$. From the previous section we know that

$$F_\nu = \sum_{t=0}^{M-1} f_t\, m^{t\nu} = \sum_{t=0}^{n-1} (f_t + f_{t+n}\, m^{\nu n}) m^{t\nu} \quad .$$

Now we define the n–th root unity $\widetilde{m} = m^2$, and take into consideration that $m^{\nu n} = 1$, if ν even, and $m^{\nu n} = -1$, if ν odd; thus we get for $0 \le u < n$ the following formulas for the values of the discrete Fourier transform divided into even and odd indices:

$$F_{2u} = \sum_{t=0}^{n-1} (f_t + f_{n+t})\, \widetilde{m}^{ut} \tag{12.35}$$

$$F_{2u+1} = \sum_{t=0}^{n-1} (f_t - f_{n+t})\, m^t\, \widetilde{m}^{ut} \quad . \tag{12.36}$$

Figure 12.6 illustrates this recursive decomposition of the DFT computation applying the symmetry properties. Solid lines indicate an addition, dashed lines subtraction. Remarkable is the permutation of the indices on the right side. We conclude that for the computation of the DFT with $M = 2n$ sampling points we have to do $2n$ operations of addition, n operations of multiplication, and finally two discrete Fourier transforms of order n. Finally, we set $M = 2^n$ and apply above idea recursively for the involved

---

[4]An example is the fast computation of powers as shown in Program 117.

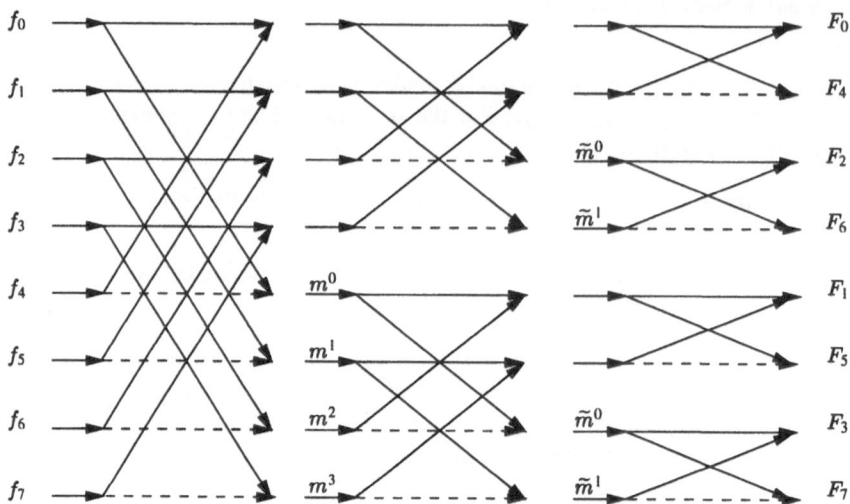

Figure 12.6 Principle of the FFT ($M = 8$)

smaller Fourier transforms. This algorithm for computing the DFT is thus bounded by $\mathcal{O}(M \log M)$ and yields an impressive decrease of the original complexity. Assume we set $M = 2^{10}$, then the Fourier transform using matrix multiplication requires 2^{20} complex multiplications. In contrast, the fast Fourier transform needs *only* $2^{10}/2 \cdot 10$ multiplications.

12.9   2–D Fourier Transform

The Fourier transform introduced so far is restricted to one–dimensional signals and can easily be extended to arbitrary dimensions. For image processing purposes the two–dimensional Fourier transform is needed. The discrete Fourier transform for 2–D signal is defined straightforward as

$$F_{\mu,\nu} = \sum_{u=0}^{N-1}\sum_{v=0}^{M-1} f_{u,v} \exp\left(-i2\pi\frac{u\mu}{N}\right)\exp\left(-i2\pi\frac{v\nu}{M}\right)$$
$$= \sum_{u=0}^{N-1}\left(\sum_{v=0}^{M-1} f_{u,v}\exp\left(-i2\pi\frac{v\nu}{M}\right)\right)\exp\left(-i2\pi\frac{u\mu}{N}\right) \quad . \tag{12.37}$$

Equation (12.37) shows that the 2–D DFT can be decomposed into two subsequent one–dimensional Fourier transforms. If $N = 2^{n'}$ and $M = 2^{n}$ the fast Fourier transform is also suitable for the 2–D case. In general, the complexity of the d–dimensional FFT is bounded by $\mathcal{O}(M^d \log M)$. The continuous version of the two–dimensional extension is obvious.

The result of the DFT applied to the image shown in Figure 12.7 is shown in Figure 12.8. The left image illustrates the real part, the middle the imaginary part, and the right one the magnitudes of the discrete Fourier transform. Herein, the DFT values are coded as gray–levels normalized to $\{0, 1, \ldots, 255\}$.

Figure 12.7   Synthetic image

Figure 12.8   Fourier transformed image (Figure 12.7): real part, imaginary part, and absolute values visualized by gray–levels

The discrete Fourier transform of an image shows the so called *spatial frequencies*. Many rapid gray–level changes mean high frequency in the direction of these changes. The typical cross in Figure 12.8 results from quantization which cuts the image into rectangular pieces. Implementation issues are discussed in Exercise 12.g.

Examples, where the discrete Fourier transform is applied to low–level image processing, are shown in Figure 12.9 and 12.10. The basic idea of filtering operations using Fourier transforms is the elimination of selected Fourier coefficients. The reduced Fourier transform is re–transformed to the spatial domain, the image, which is the filtering result. High pass filters, for instance, remove low frequencies, whereas high frequencies pass. This is important for edge detection algorithms (c.f. Chapter 14), where we look for parts of the image which show high changes in gray–levels. For smoothing signals, however, it is necessary to eliminate high frequencies of the signal. This can the done using low–pass filtering operations. The elimination of selected frequencies is easy to implement, if the Fourier transform is available. You just leave out the Fourier coefficients of the non required frequencies. Figure 12.9 shows the original image, and the results of high and low–pass filtering operations. Figure 12.10 illustrates the related 2–D Fourier transforms (magnitudes gray–level encoded). The origin of the coordinate system is the image's center.

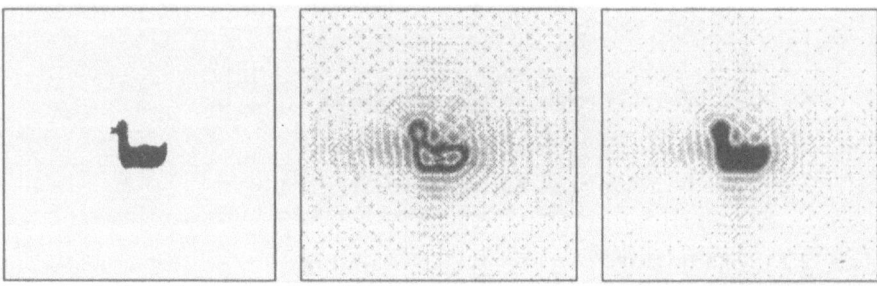

Figure 12.9 Original image, and high and low–pass filtering result

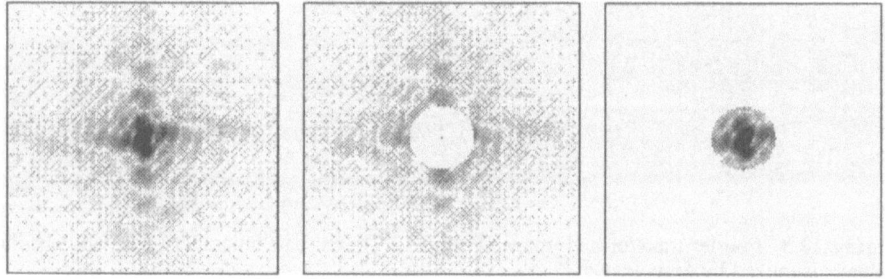

Figure 12.10 Fourier transforms of images shown in Figure 12.9

Exercises

12.a   Extend Exercise 8.f using the Fourier transform.
12.b   Proof the properties listed in Table 12.1.
12.c   Compute the Fourier transform of function (12.8).

12.d   Implement the 1–D DFT/FFT using the classes for complex numbers and the
       template classes for vectors and matrices.

12.e   Compute the Fourier transform of $[0, 1, 2, 3, 4, 5, 6, 7]$ using DFT and FFT algo-
       rithm.

12.f   Write a program which computes the Fourier transforms of gray–level and color
       images.

12.g   Find arguments, why it is not advantageous to implement the two–dimensional
       Fourier transform as two subsequent 1–D Fourier transforms. Can we use the
       functions implemented in Exercise 12.d? Do we need any extra operators for
       the matrix and vector classes?

12.h   Compute the discrete Fourier transform of the following binary image:

$$\begin{pmatrix} 1 & 1 & 1 & 1 \\ 0 & 1 & 1 & 0 \\ 0 & 1 & 1 & 0 \\ 0 & 0 & 0 & 0 \end{pmatrix}$$

12.i   The graphical visualization of the FFT induces a permutation on the indices of
       the FFT result (c.f. Figure 12.6). Use a binary representation of the incoming and
       outcoming indices and find an easy rule for describing these permutations! (Clas-
       sical variants of the resulting algorithm are discussed in [Nie83, Opp75, Pre92].
       The best version results in the *Faster Fourier Transform* which is introduced in
       [Sho91].)

12.j   Write a program for generating synthetic sound signals using Fourier series. The
       parameters of the Fourier series should be parameters of your program.

13 Inheritance for Classes

As already explained in Chapter 9, object–oriented programming is mainly character-ized by encapsulation, dynamic binding, and inheritance. The classes introduced in Chapter 11 showed implementations of ADT's and serve for the realization of encap-sulation. In this chapter we give a detailed description of the fundamental and powerful principles of inheritance and their implementation in C++. We introduce the concepts for both *simple* and *multiple inheritance*. With the use of inheritance, the real world dependency structure of objects can be mapped into a C++ class hierarchy in a natural manner.

13.1 Motivation and Syntax

The task of implementing a new function can often be simplified by inheritance of a new class from an existing class. When the new class has additional members, some additional functions, or possibly a redefinition of an already implemented function, programmers have only to define the differences in the new class with respect to the old class. Using inheritance a complete reimplementation can be avoided. Inheritance therefore makes possible high degree of code reuse.

Rectangles, for example, are a special kind of geometric shape which can be useful for object recognition purposes. Consequently, the class Rectangle is derived from the more general class Shape. Other related concepts are circles and triangles which can also be derived from the general class. Squares are a special case of rectangles and should therefore be derived from the class for rectangles.

The derivation of a class from one base class is syntactically written in the following manner:

Syntax: class *name* : [public | private] *base* { *class-members* } ;

The derivation may be repeated, i.e., a class may be derived from an already derived class as shown in the abstract Program 120.[1]

All members and methods of a superclass are inherited by the subclass. The keywords public, protected, and private control the accessibility of base class features in the derived class; these topics are discussed next.

---

[1] It is, however, illegal to have a circular sequence of derivations.

```
class A {};              // base class
class B : public  A {}; // derived with public base
class C : private B {}; // derived with private base
```
120

One syntactic difference of unions and classes with respect to inheritance is that unions can be derived from structures or classes, but nothing can be derived from unions, i.e., unions are always leaves of an inheritance tree.

13.2 Base Class Access

A class can be declared as a base class of another class either as `public`[2] or as `private`. The new keyword `protected` is introduced for class members in addition to `public` and `private` which we already saw in Sect. 10.2.

Public derivation provides the natural way of refining concepts from the general to the more specific. Private members of the base class are not accessible in the derived class. Public and protected members of the base will be public and protected members of the derived class.

Private derivation can be seen as a certain syntactic way of expressing the "part of" relation. The ideas of specialization and generalization (Sect. 9.4) do not apply here. If the base class is declared as `private`, the public and protected members of the superclass become private members of the derived class. Private derivation has a more technical application (see the examples in [Str91]). Public base classes are by far the more frequent case.

| base class | base | | base | |
members	public	private	public	private
private	no access	no access	no	no
protected	protected	private	no	no
public	public	private	yes	no
	Inside derived class		From outside	

Table 13.1 Access rules of base class members inside the derived class

These rules for accessibility are summarized in Table 13.1. The base class members get new access rights in a derived class depending on whether the base class is private or public. This is of particular importance when another class is derived from an already

---

[2]The base class can also be `protected`. This feature was added recently to the language. We just mention it and leave details to the references.

```
class A            { public: int i,j; void f(); };   // base class
class B : public A { public: int    j; };            // first derivation
class C : public B { public: int i  ; void f(); };   // second derivation

B b; C c;       // Objects      ** Artificial
b.i;            // from base A   ** example
b.j;            // B's j         ** for
c.j;            // B's j         ** demonstration
c.i;            // C's i         ** of inheritance
```

121

derived class. Also, private parts of the base class can be excluded from access by using private derivations.

As can be seen in Program 121, the same name can be used for data and function members in both the derived and base classes. The data or function accessed by default is always the closest in the inheritance hierarchy.

13.3 Construction and Destruction

The constructor of a class, which is derived from a base class, first calls the constructor of the superclass. If the base class constructor needs some arguments, then they must also be provided. Constructors are overloaded functions; the choice of the constructor depends upon the types of the constructor's arguments. The construction of class objects is done from the top down in the inheritance graph. First, the base class constructors are called, then the constructors for member variables, and finally the derived class itself.

We now outline a small hierarchy of classes for geometric objects which is graphically depicted in Figure 13.1. Inheritance is used to provide special classes with notions valid for general classes. For example, each shape has an area; this is declared in the general base class. A square is a general case of a rectangle and has a special formula for computing its area; this is defined for the class representing squares; the general interface remains the same and is inherited from the general base.

An example of a base class for geometric shapes is given in Program 122. The definition of a base constructor in a derived class is shown in Program 123; like the constructors for members, the base class constructor and its arguments are given after a colon.

The destructor of a class deletes an object from the main storage. In a hierarchy of classes, the destructor of the base class will be called after the destructor of a derived class, i.e., the execution of destructors will be in the opposite order of the constructor calls. In the destructor definition we do not have to mention the destructor of the base classes; they are called automatically (Program 123).

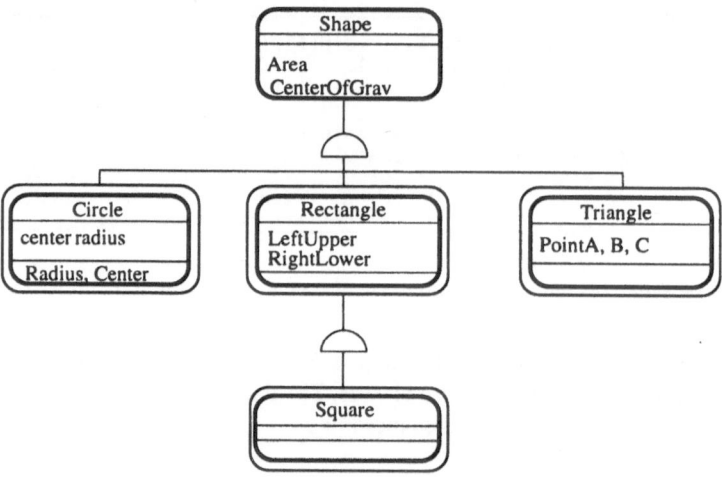

Figure 13.1 Small hierarchy of geometric shapes

```
struct Shape {            // simple base class for shapes
    Shape();              // constructor 1
    Shape(const Shape &); // constructor 2
    ~Shape();             // destructor
};
```
122

```
struct Circle : public Shape {
    Circle() : Shape() {}  // will use constructor 1 of base class
    ~Circle()          {}  // inline destructor
};
```
123

13.4   Pointer to Objects

It is necessary for pointers or references to specify the type of objects they reference. This regulation is slightly relaxed for classes which are related by public inheritance. A pointer declared to an object of a type found in a base class can point to an actual object of another type found in a derived class, if the base class is declared *public*.[3] A pointer declared as a pointer to an object of a derived class, however, cannot be set to an object of a base class; if such an assignment is required, an explicit pointer conversion has to be used. Identical rules are applicable to references to objects.

---

[3]C.f.. Exercise 13.e

```
void fct(Rectangle & r)
{   /* Shape -> Rectangle -> Square */
    Shape      * sp;        // base class pointer
    Rectangle  * rp;        // pointer to derived
    Square     * qp;        // pointer to derived from derived
    rp = &r;                // natural
    sp = &r;                // ok. every square is a rectangle
    qp = (Square*) &r;      // cast required
}
```
124

```
void fct1()
{
    Rectangle r;    // define object
    Square    s;    // define object of derived class
    fct (s);        // ok
    fct (r);        // cast in fct will be wrong!
}
```
125

```
void FctS(C & c)        // compile time binding
{                       // A -> B -> C
    A * ap = &c;        // pointer to base A*
    C * cp = &c;        // pointer to derived C*
    c.f();              // call C::f()
    ap->f();            // call A::f()
    cp->f();            // call C::f()
    cp->A::f();         // call A::f()
}
```
126

Program 124 shows pointers to objects. The cast in the last statement is required since not every rectangle object is a square. This cast can be disastrous if the object passed to fct is *not* a square (Program 125).

We now inspect the functions f() in the artificial example Program 121 with respect to pointers to objects. It is determined *at compile–time* from the pointer's type which function f() is called, similarly to the data member access in Program 121. Program 126 shows these language features. Using the scope resolution operator ::, the function to be called can be specified explicitly. Virtual functions introduced next will provide even more flexibility for member function calls.

13.5 Virtual Functions

The powerful concept of virtual functions hide the differences among facilitates the realization of dynamic binding, message passing, and polymorphism in C++. Functions can be declared virtual using the following syntax:

```
struct A           { virtual void f(); int g(); };   // base class
struct B : public A {                       int g(); };   // first derivation
struct C : public B { virtual void f(); };            // 2nd   derivation
```
127

```
void FctV(C & c)       // run time binding
{  /* A -> B -> C */
   A * ap = &c;
   C * cp = &c;
   c.f();             // call C::f()
   ap->f();           // call C::f() !!
   cp->f();           // call C::f()
   cp->A::f();        // call A::f()
}
```
128

Syntax: <u>virtual</u> *type function (arguments) ;*

If a function is declared <code>virtual</code> in the base class, a function with exactly the same name and type of arguments declared in the derived class will also be virtual even without explicit repeated specification as a virtual function. Virtual functions allow the overriding of a definition of the base class function, i.e., if a virtual function is called via pointer to an object, the function associated with the object will be invoked, no matter whether the pointer is to a base object or to the actual object.

The described override mechanism implies that virtual functions have to be declared as non static member variables. They cannot be declared as global non-member functions.

We now extend Program 121 by virtual functions to Program 127 and declare the function f() now as virtual. The function to be used is determined *at runtime* by the actual type of the object to which the method is applied. In contrast to Program 126, ap->f() now calls C::f().

A virtual function in a derived class may not redefine another return type for the same virtual function in the base class (i.e., a function with the same name and the same argument list). A virtual function in a derived class which differs from one in the base class with specification <code>const</code> is considered a different function! As outlined in Sect. 10.7, the compiler will choose the function marked <code>const</code> for constant objects.

Destructors may be declared virtual. The use and syntax of this idea is shown in Program 129. If the destructor were not virtual, the last line of the function <code>fct()</code> would not call the destructor of the derived class. Instead, due to the type of the pointer Bp only the base class destructor would be called.

```
class base                ( public: base(); virtual ~base(); )
class derv : public base ( public: derv(); virtual ~derv(); )

void fct()
{
   { base(); }              // ~base() will be called
   { derv(); }              // ~derv(), then ~base() will be called
   base * bp = new base();
   delete bp;               // ~base() will be called
   base * Bp = new derv(); // watch this!
   delete Bp;               // ~derv(), then ~base()
}                           // will be called
```
129

```
struct Shape {
   virtual void rotation() = 0; // pure virtual function
};
```
130

13.6   Abstract Classes

Many classes provide a common abstract structure where no instances of objects can exist. These abstract classes are only useful for structuring a class hierarchy. We did so already in Figure 13.1. For example, we can easily define a new class for lines derived from a common base class for geometric objects. The methods in this class depend on the concrete representation of the line and therefore must be implemented in derived classes. For each line, for instance, a method should exist, which returns the length of a line. Since the explicit representation of the line is unknown at the point when the class Line is compiled, we need a new language feature.

We can force the redefinition of a virtual function by the use of *pure virtual functions* in the class definition part. A virtual function becomes pure virtual, if the function is initialized by = 0. No other definition is allowed then.

Syntax: virtual *type function* (*arguments*) = 0;

In Program 130 the pure virtual function for the rotation of geometrical objects in general is shown. Since the class for geometric shapes is an abstract class, no instances can be generated and no concrete implementation of the method rotation is possible. No implementation of this function can be programmed. For this reason, we declare the method pure virtual. The compiler will disallow the creation of an object of the types Shape.

If the function is not declared to be pure virtual, an explicit definition of this function has to be provided (see Program 131). If inside a derived class all inherited functions are at some point of the derivation declared as no longer pure virtual, the class becomes concrete and objects can be instantiated.

```
struct Rectangle : public Shape {
   virtual void rotation();  // has to define the virtual function
};
void Rectangle::rotation() { /* ... */ }
```
131

```
class Image {
   unsigned short xsize, ysize;   // filled by the constructors
   float focus;                   // filled by the constructors
protected:                        // abstract class
   Image();                       // all methods can be used in the
   Image(int,int,float);          // derived classes
   // ops's etc.
};
```
132

```
class GrayLevelImage : public Image {
   Matrix<byte> image;                      // 256 gray levels
   // op's
};
class ColorImage : public Image {           // Version 2
   GrayLevelImage r_image, g_image, b_image; // color channels
   // op's
};
```
133

13.7 Image Class Hierarchy

In Chapter 11 we saw different classes for images. Gray–level images and color images both need the members for their size and the camera parameters. It is therefore natural to create a common base class `Image` and put all the shared information there; the information is passed to the new classes via inheritance (Program 132). Since many functions will provide interfaces for gray–level images, (e.g. filters, etc.), we now use image objects as representations for the three color channels in color images (c.f. Program 108).

The base class declares all methods as "protected"; no object of the abstract class `Image` can thus be directly created since no operations could be performed on it.

In the following chapters we will derive more new image classes from class `Image`. The class sub–tree for images is shown in Figure 13.2. These images will use elements other than byte. Therefore the image matrices are declared in the derived image classes.

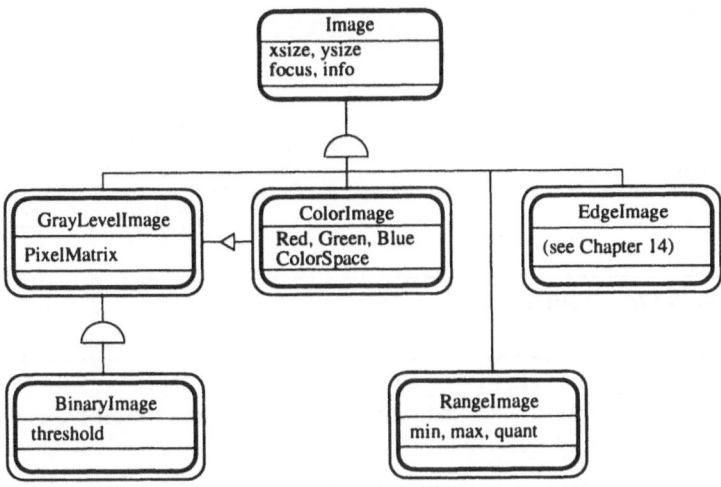

Figure 13.2 Hierarchy of image classes

13.8 Multiple Inheritance

The problems concerning multiple inheritance were already mentioned in Sect. 9.4. A class can be derived from two or more classes; each superclass can be declared public or private. Assume all super–classes have member functions with the same name. When those functions are used, they have to be disambiguated. This can be explicitly done using scope resolution, or based on different parameter lists.

Sometimes a base class is reached by more than one path in the inheritance graph. This will result in multiple instances of the base object. If this is not desired, a base class can be declared as virtual in addition to the key words public or i private. The syntax is as follows:

| Syntax: | class *name* :

    { [virtual] [public | private] *base* ,}*

    { [virtual] [public | private] *base*}+ {

       class-members };

New aspects of a given idea can be programmed by multiple inheritance. Imagine a class visible which adds display capabilities to a graphics device. The interface to graphics routines can be inherited on top via inheritance from general to specific classes

```
struct visible {
     void display();                    // all public
     visible(int color);
};
struct Rectangle: public Shape,         // first base
                  public visible {      // second base
   Rectangle() : Shape(), visible(3);   // NB: the base class construction
   ~Rectangle();                        // destructor automatically ...
};                                      // ... deletes base objects      134
```

```
class GrayLevelImg: public Image, private Matrix<byte> {   // just a try
   // ...
};                                                                        135
```

(Program 134). In the constructor definition, the constructors for all bases have to be specified.

Another more C++ specific use of multiple inheritance using private base classes can be seen in Program 135. This shows how the *has–a* relation can be implemented using private inheritance. This approach will, however, fail for the class ColorImage since there we need three instances of the matrix object. Almost always it is possible to avoid multiple inheritance, and this is generally to be recommended. The class for images, for example, was not derived from class matrix (Program 132); rather, it includes a matrix as a member and delegates important operators or methods to the matrix class by inline functions.

Casting of pointers as in Sect. 13.4 is much more complicated when multiple inheritance is used. Further information about multiple inheritance can be found in the manual [Str91]; in the following we will use single inheritance only.

13.9 Implementation Issues

The most difficult problem in object–oriented software design is the mapping of the structures and dependencies of the objects in the problem domain. First, natural dependencies of objects and classes have to be formalized. Always have in mind whether two different classes relate to each other in terms of inheritance, or whether a part–of relation (client) would be more appropriate. For example, gray–level images are represented using a matrix for the internal representation; matrix and images are not related by inheritance in the sense of specialization, however.

The goal of object–oriented software design is the development of compact, readable programs. The programs should be easy to understand and easy to modify. For users of your programs which are not interested in algorithmic details, an abstract and well documented interface should be provided. Furthermore, the algorithms have to be implemented in an efficient manner. Often it is not easy to implement algorithms efficiently and at the same time to satisfy the needs of concepts like modularity and readability. The implementor has to find a compromise among these conflicting goals.

Virtual functions are treated by the compiler in a different way from non–virtual functions according to the manual [Str91]. A function table is generated for every class having virtual functions. Virtual functions are called indirectly from this table. The table is constructed by the compiler in certain modules which define constructors. It is thus a wise idea *not* to use inline constructors since some compilers will then have to create many tables for one class instead of only one. Virtual inline functions are allowed. In many cases they will, however, not be inlined. With respect to efficiency, virtual inline functions should therefore be used carefully (c.f. Exercise 13.c).

A general guideline is that destructors should be virtual when there are virtual functions in a class.

Exercises

13.a   Extend the template class for matrices and vectors. Derive the template class from a non–template base–class holding the size and access functions to the sizes. This is generally a nice idea since the non–parameterized parts can then be completely compiled at an earlier stage of compiler processing.

13.b   Implement an abstract class for lines in C++ using the concept of pure virtual functions. Derive a class for straight line segments.

13.c   Define a class in a header file and include this file in two source files. Turn virtual on and off for some methods. Also change methods or constructors to inline. How does the code size vary? Use a makefile!

13.d   Compare direct and indirect function calls with respect to execution time on your processor.

       • Use a trivial function without arguments.

       • Use a realistic function with three arguments and a non–trivial function body.

13.e   If a cast from a derived class to a private base class were allowed, we could circumvent the access restrictions (Table 13.1). Explain why and how!

14 Edge Images

Indications exist that lines, vertices, and other features based on lines, are very important for perception [Mar80]. A typical part of image segmentation is the detection of edges (c.f. Sect. 6.5). The automatic detection of line features in images usually requires several processing stages. Edge detection operators are applied to every pixel in the image. These operators check the local neighborhood for evidence of an edge. They return a measure for the likelihood of an edge at this point of the image as well as a guess of its orientation. The result is called an "edge image" (Sect. 14.6). In Chapter 21 we will further process edge images to obtain lines. This will transform edge images into more abstract geometric objects. This chapter gives a first insight into edge detection methods in gray–level images, partially based on [Brü90].

14.1 Strategies

The basic idea behind edge detection is to localize discontinuities of the intensity function in the image. Figure 14.1 shows an artificial cross section, i.e., a one–dimensional function of an edge. Figure 14.2 shows a plot of the gray–level function in the neighborhood of an edge in a real image.

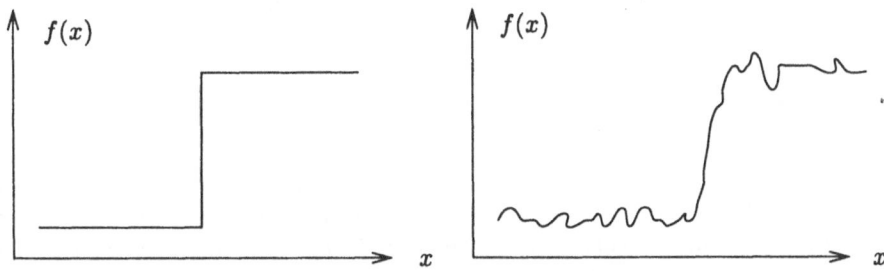

Figure 14.1 Ideal step edge (a) and real edge (b), where the x–axis is perpendicular to the edge.

Several types of edge detectors can be found in the literature:

- derivatives of the intensity function (discrete approximation),

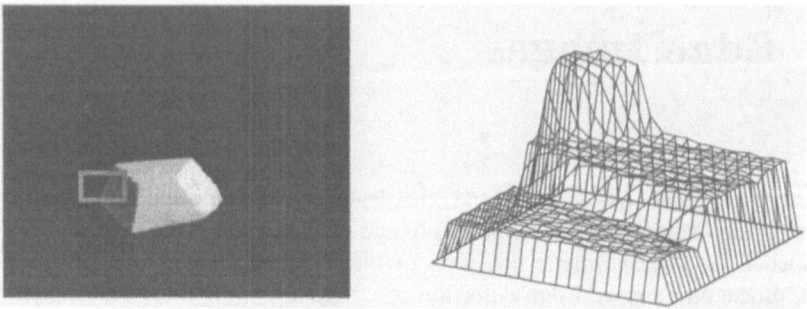

Figure 14.2 Intensity function in a real image in the neighborhood of an edge. On the left: gray–level image with marked frame (Figure 1.2); on the right: 3–D plot of the intensity in the frame.

- edge masks,
- parametric models for edges,
- combinations of the above.

The first two strategies work with local masks; the first and second derivative as well as edge masks will be treated in this chapter. The other methods, parametric models, and combined methods are dealt with in chapter 21.

In the following sections, we introduce a common edge image class which will be used for the representation of arbitrary edge operators. The resulting edge images can then be further inspected and lines can be segmented within them (Chapter 21).

14.2 Discrete Derivatives of Intensity Functions

Many approaches to edge detection are based on the idea that rapid changes and discontinuities in the gray–level function can be detected using maxima in the first derivative or zero–crossings of the second derivative. Figure 14.3 shows cross–section of step edges and the corresponding derivatives.

As described in Sect. 1.7, we assume a quantized image of a fixed size — $N \times M$ — which corresponds to an intensity function $f(x, y)$ that is defined at discrete points (i, j), where $i \in \{0, 1, \dots, N - 1\}$ and $j \in \{0, 1, \dots, M - 1\}$. The more rapidly the gray–level function changes on small changes of the location, the more likely is an edge at this location. A measure for this indication of an edge is called the *edge strength*. The direction of an edge at a certain point in the image is called the *edge orientation*. These

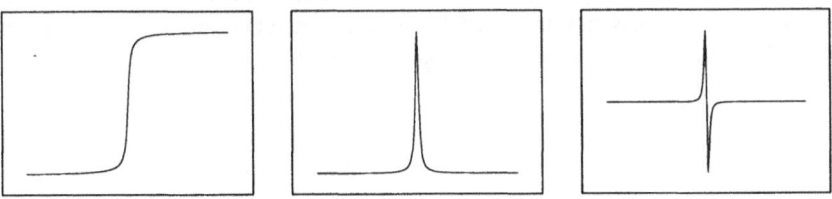

Figure 14.3 Edge (left), first derivative (center) and second derivative (right) in a cross–section.

values are computed by the discrete derivative of the intensity function which calculates the gradient of the intensity function. The *gradient* of a continuous function $f(x, y)$ is defined as the vector

$$\nabla f(x, y) \;=\; \begin{pmatrix} f_x(x, y) \\ f_y(x, y) \end{pmatrix} \;=\; \begin{pmatrix} \dfrac{\partial f(x, y)}{\partial x} \\ \dfrac{\partial f(x, y)}{\partial y} \end{pmatrix} \tag{14.1}$$

consisting of the partial derivatives of the intensity function in horizontal and vertical direction. The gradient in a position (i, j) points to the steepest ascent in its neighborhood. Discrete approximations use differences instead of differentials for the computation of f_x and f_y

$$f_x(i, j) = f(i + 1, j) - f(i, j) \quad \text{and} \quad f_y(i, j) = f(i, j + 1) - f(i, j) \tag{14.2}$$

which simply result from setting h to the smallest possible discrete value (namely one) in the well–known derivative

$$f_x(x) = \lim_{h \to 0} \frac{f(x + h) - f(x)}{h} \quad , \tag{14.3}$$

and shifting one neighbor by one to obtain a symmetric mask.

Edge strength (14.4,14.5) and *edge orientation* (14.6) can now be calculated from the gradient using vector calculus. The edge strength is computed as the length of the gradient vector. It is often convenient to use the sum of absolute values (14.5) instead of the root of the squares (14.4) since it is normally not the exact value that is important, but the value in comparison to the neighborhood.[1]

$$s \;=\; \sqrt{f_x^2 + f_y^2} \tag{14.4}$$

$$s' \;=\; |f_x| + |f_y| \tag{14.5}$$

$$r \;=\; \arctan(f_y / f_x) \tag{14.6}$$

---

[1] Approximations of the values for f_x, f_y, s', and r can thus then be calculated using integer arithmetic and without use of the square root function.

Using definition (14.6), the gradient can be computed from the orientation by a rotation of 90°. Figure 14.4 shows an image with black and white areas and the directions of the gradient along the edges, as well as the edge orientation.

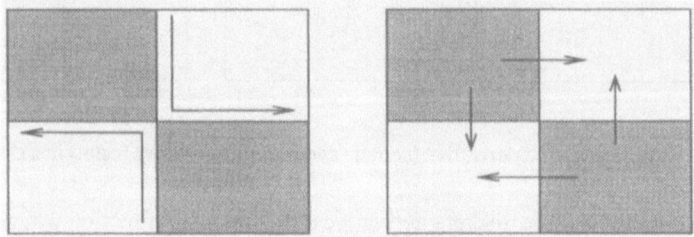

Figure 14.4 Definition of the edge orientation (left) and gradient (right)

14.3 Mask Operators

Figure 14.5 shows an interpretation of equation (14.2) as a symmetric mask. The derivative can be estimated by a discrete convolution of the image f with the mask h

$$g = f * h \tag{14.7}$$

$$g_{i,j} = \sum_{\mu=-m}^{m} \sum_{\nu=-n}^{n} h(\nu, \mu) f(i - \nu, j - \mu) \tag{14.8}$$

where h is defined in the range $i \in [-m, m], j \in [-n, n]$ (c.f. Eq. 12.20).[2] Since the distance from the central point where the derivative is estimated, is one pixel to the left and one to the right, the computation yields only half of the derivative (using Eq. 14.3). In the following, we only use the relative magnitudes of these values and can thus ignore this formal inconsistency.

Only a few pixels are taken into account when the discrete differential is computed using the simple operators in Sect. 14.2. As a consequence, these operators are very sensitive to noise. The usual cure for this problem is to apply a low–pass filter before the derivatives are calculated. Alternatively, a larger neighborhood can be taken into consideration for the computation of the derivatives, which then includes an averaging operation on several values of f_x and f_y.

Well known operators of this type are the Sobel operator [Dud73] and the Prewitt operator [Pre70], which are shown in Figure 14.6. In [Dan90] it is shown that the Sobel mask is an approximation of the first derivative.

---

[2]This means that derivatives of the intensity function can be computed with a linear filter, Chapter 19.

Figure 14.5 Masks for computation of the central differences in a point $P = (i, j)$ — marked by a circle.

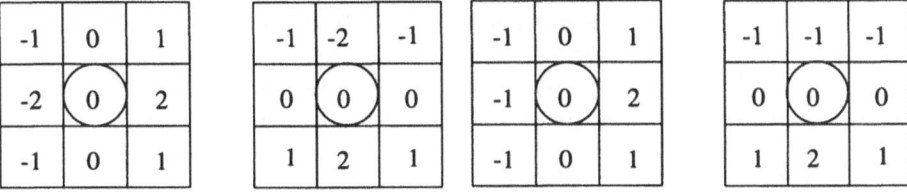

Figure 14.6 Masks for Sobel (left) and Prewitt (right) operator. Masks on the left: f_x, masks on the right: f_y. Note that these masks may be flipped with respect to other literature since we choose the origin of the coordinate system on the left top.

The more pixels that are taken into account in the computation, the lower is the sensitivity to noise. Small edges may, however, be missed by large operators. This trade–off situation is sometimes called the "uncertainty relation" of edge detection.

14.4 Discrete Directions

The application of the Sobel operator on a gray–level image yields two values: f_x and f_y. The steepest possible edge in a gray–level image is the change of 0 to 255. The values for f_x and f_y can thus be in the range of $-1024 \ldots 1024$. The edge strength will therefore be in the range of $0 \ldots 2048$ for this operator using (14.5). Other operators have similar behavior. This range can be represented using two bytes (usually a short int).

The computation of the edge direction uses the function atan2 which computes the arctan function and treats the four quadrants properly so the range of the result is $[0, 2\pi]$ instead of $[-\pi/2, \pi/2]$ for arctan. The result is a double value which now has to be quantized. 144 directions of $2.5°$ seem to be more than sufficient. This number has the advantage that directions of $5, 10, 30, 60, \ldots$ degrees can be represented as integers. 144

values can be represented in one byte (an `unsigned char` in C++). Figure 14.7 (left) shows the line directions graphically.

The function `atan2` tends to be relatively slow on most computers. Since run time efficiency is a great issue for image processing (Sect. 3.7), this computation could on the one hand be done with a table lookup. On the other hand, the following idea is introduced on [Cap91]: By only three comparisons we can determine the octant for an (x, y) value pair. As shown in Figure 14.7 (right), a value of $1 - |x/y|$ is computed in octant 1,2,5,6, which is equivalent to $1 - \cot \alpha$; the ratio $|y/x|$ is computed in octant 3,4,7,0, which is equivalent to $\tan \alpha$; these computations yield a value in the range $[0, 1]$. The absolute value will not have to be computed then, since the signs of x and y are known by that time. Finally, the octant is added to this value yielding a function which maps a point (x, y) to a value in the range from $[0, 8]$. To get the angle α from this value, we would need the arctan or arccot function. If we use a linear function $y = \frac{\pi}{4}x$ instead, we will have a maximum error of $4.1°$ [Cap91].[3] The reason why this works is simple; Figure 14.8 shows a plot of the functions for the first quadrant $y = \frac{\pi}{4}x$ and

$$y = \begin{cases} 2 - \cot x & , \quad \text{if } x > \frac{\pi}{4} \\ \tan x & , \quad \text{otherwise} \end{cases} \tag{14.9}$$

Obviously, the differences between the functions are small.

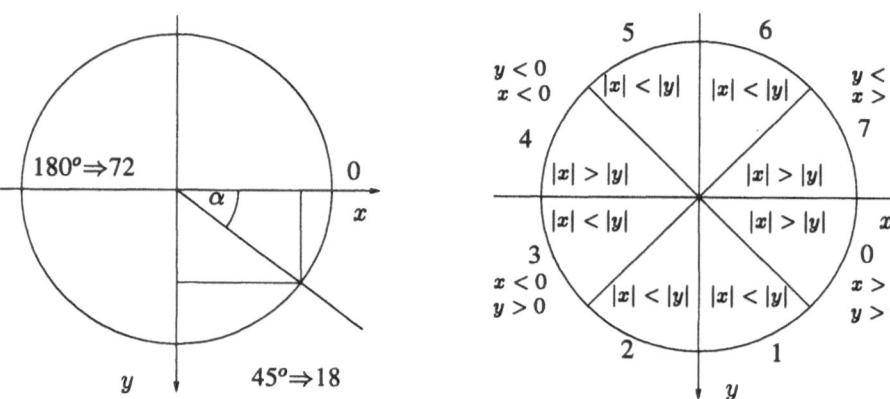

Figure 14.7   Discrete directions and quantization

---

[3]This value could also be quantized and then used for table lookup.

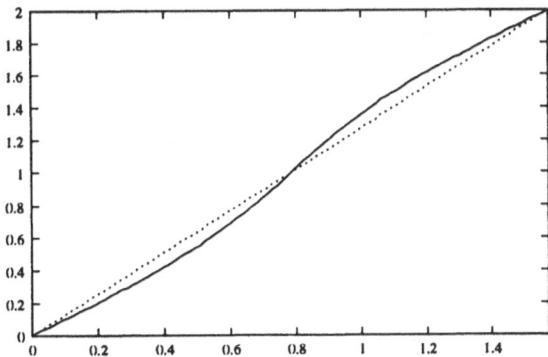

Figure 14.8 Discrete direction function

14.5   Edge Class

One implementation for edges could use a structure containing a `byte` for the edge orientation and a `short` for edge strength. Since the size of a `short` may vary between machine architectures, it is better to request exactly 16 bits using bit fields (Sect. 4.6).

In Program 136 we combine several C++ features to implement a class for edges; the macro `M_PI` which expands to the value of π is taken from `math.h`. The methods hide the internal implementation of the data structure. We define constants for the number of orientations and for the quantization unit. In Sect. 15.3 we will see how these extra global names can be avoided. Note that the structure has no name and is used directly via the structure member `fields`. Also note that the union has neither a name nor a variable associated with it: Program 137 shows the inline definition of a constructor for edges; this method uses members of the union directly. Since we do not derive this simple class from any other base class, inline construction is useful — in contrast to the hints given in Sect. 13.9.

The structure `Edge` will require four bytes in memory on most 32 bit computers even if we only ask for 24 bits;[4] we might as well use the remaining bits for further information. We will later need some features for each edge element. In Sect. 21.3 we will extend the definition and introduce other fields in the union.

---

[4]Try this on your machine with the `sizeof` operator!

```
const int    orient_num = 144;
const float orient_dunit = 360 / float(orient_num);
const float orient_runit = 2 * M_PI / float(orient_num); // M_PI from math.h
class Edge {
    union {
        unsigned int all;                  // assume 32 bit architecture
        struct {                           // need no name
            unsigned int f_strength : 16;
            unsigned int f_orient   : 8;
        } fields ;                         // use member directly
    };                                     // union has neither name nor variable
public:
    Edge()              { all = 0; }     // clear
    inline Edge(unsigned s, unsigned o); // set strength and orientation
    unsigned strength() const { return fields.f_strength; }
    // etc.
};
```
136

```
inline Edge::Edge(unsigned s, unsigned o)
{
    fields.f_strength = s;
    fields.f_orient = o;
}
```
137

```
class EdgeImage : public Image {
    Matrix<Edge> image;
    unsigned short max_s;   // maximum strength in the edge image
public:
    EdgeImage(int,int);
    Edge* operator[] (int i) { return image[i]; }
    const Edge* operator[] (int i) const { return image[i]; }
    virtual Display(DisplObj&); // explained later
    // etc.
};
```
138

14.6   Edge Images

The application of an edge operator on every pixel of a gray–level image will produce an *edge image*. Like the images classes in the previous section, edge images share the information of the class Image (Program 132) by inheritance. Edge images can thus extend the image hierarchy shown in Figure 13.2. A code fragment is shown in Program 138. The operator [ ] maps the access operation to the matrix object by delegation. Again, it turns out to be useful that the matrix operators in Program 113 were not members; matrix multiplication would make no sense for edge matrices

Since different operators create edge images with different ranges for the edge strength, an entry max_s is useful. It is, however, difficult to guarantee a consistent value for this slot, since the matrix can be accessed and changed by the operator [ ].

Visualization of edge images is shown in Figure 14.9. Edge strength is coded as gray–level;[5] orientation can be directly coded as gray–levels in the range of zero to 144 (Figure 14.9, right).

Figure 14.9 Gradient image computed with the Sobel operator on the image shown in Figure 11.2.

14.7   Robert's Cross

Edge detection using the first derivation was motivated by the differences in (14.2). An implementation using this idea will make use of the four out of eight neighbors of a given pixel. The so called *Robert's Cross* operator which also uses only four pixels (14.10) is even simpler than (14.2) and uses a smaller neighborhood.

$$f_1(i,j) = f(i,j) - f(i+1,j+1) \quad \text{and} \quad f_2(i,j) = f(i,j+1) - f(i+1,j)(14.10)$$

Since the differences are computed diagonally (as a "cross"), the values f_1 and f_2 are not the horizontal or vertical derivations, but instead they are the approximations of directional derivatives. The results of this operator are shown in Figure 14.10. This operator is very sensitive to noise but very simple to compute.

14.8   Second Derivative

Instead of searching for maximal edge strength in the first derivative of an intensity image, the zero–crossings of the second derivative can also be used. Figure 14.3 already showed this idea for continuous one–dimensional functions.

---

[5]The range of the edge–strength is histogram equalized to 256 bit, i.e., a gray–level image, using the algorithms described in Sect. 20.5.

Figure 14.10 Robert's image: strength and orientation

The second derivative can be computed by the *Laplace operator* for discrete images. The Laplace operator for continuous functions is defined by

$$\nabla^2 f(x,y) \;=\; f_{xx} + f_{yy} \quad . \tag{14.11}$$

For the discrete Laplace operator we consider the derivative operator defined by

$$D_x f(x,y) \;=\; \lim_{h \to 0} \frac{f(x+h,y) - f(x,y)}{h} \quad . \tag{14.12}$$

In the discrete case the closest we can get to zero is $h = -1$ and $h = 1$. For that reason we define the difference operators ∇_i and Δ_i by

$$\nabla_i f(i,j) \;=\; f(i+1,j) - f(i,j) \quad , \quad \text{and} \tag{14.13}$$
$$\Delta_i f(i,j) \;=\; f(i,j) - f(i-1,j) \quad . \tag{14.14}$$

The definition for ∇_j and Δ_j are analogous. The discrete Laplace operator results from the twofold application of the difference operators, i.e.,

$$\begin{aligned} \nabla^2 f(i,j) &= \nabla_i \Delta_i f(i,j) + \nabla_j \Delta_j f(i,j) \\ &= 4f(i,j) - f(i-1,j) - f(i+1,j) - f(i,j-1) - f(i,j+1). \end{aligned} \tag{14.15}$$

Three variations of this operator are shown in Figure 14.11, where the left matrix corresponds to (14.15). These operators are mostly similar, but have slightly different sensitivity to noise. Another possible definition uses larger neighborhoods, i.e.,

$$g(i,j) = \sum_{\mu,\nu} (f(\mu,\nu) - f(i,j)) \quad . \tag{14.16}$$

A major disadvantage of this operator is its sensitivity to noise as with all methods based on the discrete second derivative. Usually, the Laplace operator will detect amongst the correct edges various scattered edge points. Additionally, the definitions in Figure 14.11 and (14.16) will compute no edge direction, in contrast to the other edge operators introduced so far.

0	-1	0
-1	4	-1
0	-1	0

-1	-1	-1
-1	8	-1
-1	-1	-1

1	-2	1
-2	4	-2
1	-2	1

Figure 14.11 Mask definition for the discrete approximation of the second derivation (Laplace operator)

Various edge operators are based on Laplace operators (c.f. for example [Mar80]). Usually, the intensity image is filtered with a Gauss filter[6] in order to reduce the sensitivity of the operator to noise. The result of Laplace edge detection on the un–filtered intensity image is shown in Figure 14.12, where all negative values are mapped to gray–level zero, all positive values are mapped to 255, and values close to zero resulting from the operator are mapped to 128.

Figure 14.12 Laplace image gray–level encoded

14.9 Color Edge Operators

Edge detection is possible on color images as well as gray–level images. The differences (14.2) or the Sobel operator can be generalized for several channels. We can reorganize

---

[6]This filter will be introduced in Sect. 19.1.

the definition in Figure 14.6 as a three–fold weighted (with factor 1 or 2) sum of differences (one to the left/up subtracted from one to the right/down).

For the implementation of edge detectors we therefore need a scalar difference value for color vectors. According to [Shi87] the following distances of color pixels $f_1 = (r_1, g_1, b_1)^T$ and $f_2 = (r_2, g_2, b_2)^T$ can be used:

$$D_1(f_1, f_2) = \{(r_1 - r_2)^2 + (g_1 - g_2)^2 + (b_1 - b_2)^2\}^{\frac{1}{2}} \qquad (14.17)$$

$$D_2(f_1, f_2) = |r_1 - r_2| + |g_1 - g_2| + |b_1 - b_2| \qquad (14.18)$$

$$D_3(f_1, f_2) = \max\{|r_1 - r_2|, |g_1 - g_2|, |b_1 - b_2|\} \qquad (14.19)$$

The disadvantage for our purpose is that these distances are all positive. In order to compute the edge direction properly, we need negative values as well. One simple possibility is shown in (14.20). The different channels can be weighted with w_r, w_g, w_b; there may, however, be color vectors, for which the function D_0 will be zero although they look different to the observer.

$$D_0(f_1, f_2) = w_r(r_1 - r_2) + w_g(g_1 - g_2) + w_b(b_1 - b_2) \qquad (14.20)$$

The gradient image can now be calculated using (14.20). The resulting edge image can be further processed with the same programs as edge images resulting from gray–level images or other edge operators. The result of (14.20) on the color image in Figure 11.2 (left) is shown in Figure 14.13

Figure 14.13 Gradient image computed with the color Sobel operator on the image shown in Figure 11.2.

Exercises

14.a Show how the second derivative may be computed using equation (14.2) twice.

14.b Create a program which has an edge image as an input and creates a gray–level image as an output.

14.c Implement a program which generates a table of the 144 discrete direction values for the arctan function `atan2`. The number of directions (e.g. 144) should be a parameter of the program.

14.d Create a program which has a color image as an input and creates an edge image as an output. Use a color–Sobel operator with the difference D_0 in equation (14.20).

14.e How can edge strength and edge orientation consistently be derived from the Robert's Cross definition?

15 Class Libraries

The implementation of large software systems and class hierarchies using C++ obviously requires the development of a common class library whose implemented classes are useful, convenient, and necessary for a majority of applications. In this chapter we describe stream classes which are part of the standard C++ library supplied with the compiler and header files.

We give an overview of the NIHCL class library. This software package is in the public domain and satisfies the requirements of a general purpose C++ class library. We describe the basics in simplified form — just to enable the use of of the library or to re–implement some of the basic ideas. Details of NIHCL can be found in the book of K. Gorlen et al. [Gor90]. We discuss abstract and very general classes, which are the super classes of all classes which are implemented in the system. We introduce static class members for C++ and also survey the Standard Templates Library [Mus96].

15.1 Stream Input and Output

Input and output operations like reading or writing data from a file are necessary for many programs. In C++ we implement input and output operations on objects which are instances of user–defined classes. The syntax of the C++ programming language does not provide the facilities for input and output of built–in objects. Those operations are implemented in an object–oriented environment using so called *streams* which are part of the C++ *library* definition. The resulting function calls for I/O–operations are safer than the use of stdio, since all function calls are checked by the compiler for correct argument number and type (see below in Program 141).

The implemented classes for input and output streams are istream and ostream. Predefined global static objects are cerr, cout, and cin which are attached to standard error, standard output and standard input respectively (though can be redirected, of course). These C++ classes become available when the header file iostream.h is included. The class ostream has an overloaded operator << which writes an object to a stream. Analogously, istream provides overloaded methods >> for reading data. Program 139 shows a simple program which reads an integer and writes it to standard output. If the value of the given integer is negative, an error message will be written to standard error instead.

```
#include <iostream.h>              /* interface for streams */
main()
{
   int  i;                         // integer to be read from standard input
   cout << "Type a nonnegative integer!\n";
                                   // write to standard output
   cin >> i;                       // read i from standard input
   if (i >= 0)                     // input correct
    cout << "Your number is: " << i << "\n";
   else                            // wrong input, type error message
    cerr << "Your number is a negative integer!\n";
}
```
139

```
ostream& operator<<(ostream& strm, const Image & i)  // function which
{                                                    // outputs all
   strm << "focal length: " << f << "\n";            // information
   strm << "image size   : " << i.getxsize() << "," // attached
        << i.getysize() << "\n";                     // to image
   return strm;                                      // objects
}
```
140

```
char formatstr[] = "%d %4f\n";             // format string
fprintf(stderr, formatstr, "test", 2.0, 'a'); // no warning !!!
cout.precision(4);                         // valid until next call
cout << "abc " << 4.12345 << endl;         // endl will call flush
```
141

The definition of operators << and >> for built–in abstract data types can be extended in the following way: assume you want to write the member variables of the given class Image to stdout or some other stream. For that purpose, you have to define an operator << as shown in Program 140. As in Program 113, we use a function rather than a member.

Program 141 contrasts the stream concept to the stdio concept of traditional C.[1] The program shows function calls with too many or wrong arguments. Even the C++ compiler can not check these errors since the interpretation of the format string is a semantic information; this information may in addition not be available at compile time since the format string may be a variable defined or initialized elsewhere in the program.

The operator << can be used for the output of user–defined objects. This operator maps the arguments to the overloaded virtual function put which — depending on its arguments — stores the given data to the output stream in an appropriate format. An input function reading into an existing image object can be defined analogously.

These mechanisms have to be extended for object–oriented programming; this was one key issue of NIHCL which is introduced in the next session. We do not provide any other information about C++ streams and refer the interested reader to the manual [Str91].

---

[1] For details of the mostly obvious meaning of precision and endl we refer to [Str91].

15.2 National Institutes of Health Class Library (NIHCL)

As outlined in Sect. 9.8, Smalltalk was the most important ancestor for object–oriented programming languages. The NIHCL class hierarchy re–implements some of the Smalltalk ideas for C++ using the same identifiers for methods and classes. Figure 15.1 shows the important classes of the NIHCL–class tree which are outlined shortly in the following. This tree shows that concrete classes can exist (Set) which have derived classes, i.e. not every class having subclasses must be abstract.

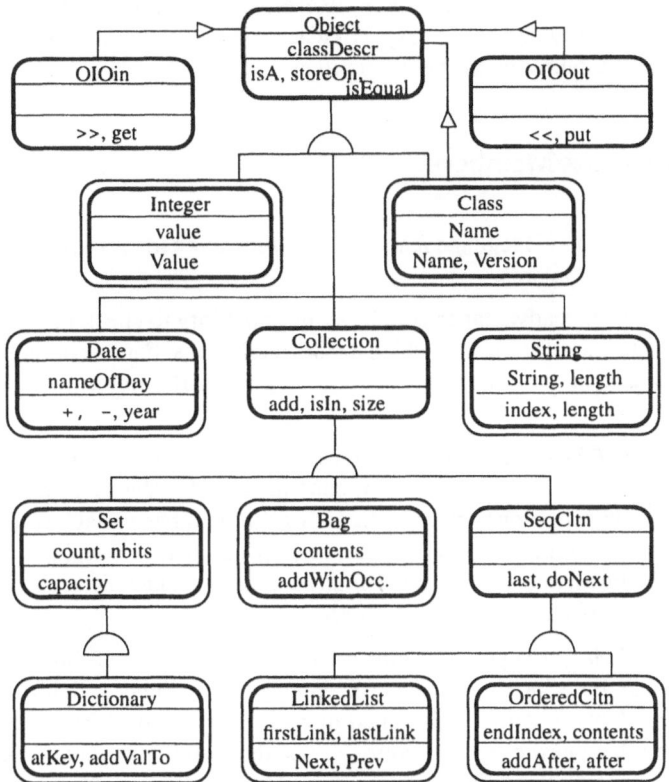

Figure 15.1 Essential classes of NIHCL. Method names are abbreviated.

Conceptually, the most general class in NIHCL is the abstract class Object.[2] This class provides the general interface by member functions which have to be implemented

---

[2]For technical reasons, a class NIHCL is put on top of the hierarchy which is not shown in Figure 15.1.

in the derived classes, where the explicit representation of an object is known. The general member functions of the class Object can be divided into three main categories: functions for identifying and testing the class of an object at runtime (like isA) functions for comparing objects (like isEqual) and finally functions for input and output operations of objects (like storeOn). A comfortable interface to input and output of objects (OIO) is provided by abstract classes (OIOin and OIOout); derived classes specify possible sources and destinations and data representation as binary or ASCII.

The implementation of a derived class of the class Object must include the declaration and definition of about 20 functions of the above mentioned three categories to be compatible with other NIHCL classes. Nevertheless, the implementation of these functions is elementary and fairly easy. NIHCL provides some macros which support the declaration and definition of these functions.

15.3 Static Class Members

We now introduce a new language feature along with some ideas of the NIHCL library and common C++ problems.

In many situations it is advantageous to have the capability to check the type of a given object, i.e. to determine the class to which the object belongs. For this purpose, Smalltalk provides a "meta class". Forthcoming versions of C++ will provide this feature as well (Sect. 26.9).

In NIHCL, a class Class is implemented, which allows access to runtime information of the involved objects. The information, contained in the class Class, is the name of the class the object belongs to, the classes of the member variables, the size of its instances, inheritance information, and the version number. A simplified version of a class Class is shown in Program 153. The structure of the class hierarchy is also stored by a pointer to a base class description object.

To ensure that all classes supply this information, a virtual member function isA() in the class Object is declared, which returns a pointer to a member variable classdesc of type Class. This function is redefined in every class derived from Object; each such class provides a new class description. Since the member variable classdesc is equal for all instances of one class it can be shared by these instances. It is not necessary that each object of the class has its own copy of this member variable. For this purpose, C++ provides the declaration of static members, where all instances of the class share those static variables; i.e. the keyword static indicates to the compiler that this member is allocated *once* for every *class* — not for every object. Such variables are called *class variables* in Smalltalk – in contrast to *object variables*. Program 142 outlines this idea in a simplified form.

```
class Class;
class Object {                       // root of the object tree
    static Class classdesc;          // once in the program
public:                              // enquire class membership
    Object();                        // default constructor
    virtual ~Object();               // virtual for all obj's
    virtual const Class* isA() const; // { return & classdesc; }
    virtual void storer(OIOout&) const; // external representation
    void storeOn(OIOout&) const;     // will call storer
    static const Class * desc();     // static function!
};
class Class : public Object { // simple version
    const Class * base;          // here: only single inheritance
    char * className;            // what's my name
    int version;                 // store my version
public:
    Class(char *, const Class *, int);
    const char * ClassName() const { return className; }
    int Version() const { return version; }
    const Class * Base() const { return base; }
};
```
142

```
Class Object::classdesc ("Object",NULL,0); // static member definition
const Class* Object::isA() const { return & classdesc; } // virtual
const Class* Object::desc()      { return & classdesc; } // static
Object::Object() {};
Object::~Object() {};
```
143

Class variables are like regular data members and obey the visibility and scoping rules. The only difference is that they exist only once and that they have to be initialized *once* in the program. Naturally, this initialization cannot be done in the constructors; instead, the variable is defined outside of all functions (Program 143). The C++ runtime system will guarantee that such objects are created before the function main starts.

Member functions, as well as member variables, can be declared static, such as the function Object::desc() in Program 142. The function definition in Program 143 looks exactly as a normal member function. However, static member functions can be called without an associated object just by the complete name consisting of the class name, scope operator, and the function name. A static member function can not be declared constant.

Every NIHCL class redefines isA and defines its own classdesc i.e. there exists exactly one class description per class. The different static variables classdesc can be accessed by the prefix e.g. Time:: (Program 144).

Since all classes which use NIHCL have to define these members and methods, and since all these definitions are textually identical, NIHCL provides macros for their definition. Again, a simplified version is shown in Program 145;[3] the real macros in NIHCL have

---

[3]Multi–line macros use a backslash to continue on the next line.

```
class Time : public Object {          // one typical example
    static Class classdesc;           // again, one object
public:                               // isA() looks similar
    virtual const Class* isA() const; // { return & classdesc; }
    static const Class * desc();      // again a static function
    Time();
};

Time::Time() {};
const Class* Time::isA() const { return & Time::classdesc; }
Class Time::classdesc ("Time",Object::desc(),0);
```

● 144

```
#define DECLARE_MEMBERS(c)                                        \
    private: static Class classdesc;                              \
    public:  static const Class * desc();                         \
    public:  static c * readFrom(OIOin&); /* not virtual */       \
    public:  virtual const Class* isA()  const;                   \
    public:  virtual const char* ClassName() const;               \
             virtual void storer(OIOout&) const;                  \
    private:
#define DEFINE_CLASS(c,b,v)                                       \
    const Class* c::isA() const { return & c::classdesc; }        \
    const Class* c::desc()      { return & c::classdesc; }        \
    const char* c::ClassName() const                              \
      { return c::classdesc.ClassName(); }                        \
    c* c::readFrom(OIOin&) { /* dummy here  */ return NULL; }  \
    Class c::classdesc(#c,b::desc(),v);
```

● 145

more parameters. The token #c expands to a string containing the macro argument c, if an ANSI preprocessor is used. The first macro is used in the class declaration. The second macro is used in the module which defines the methods. The second argument uses the static function desc() to access the class description of the base class. In cases such as Program 145, macros are required, or at least simpler than templates.

The methods readFrom and storeOn reference the OIO classes. These classes are special *streams* for input and output of objects in an object–oriented environment. The virtual function storer is called from storeOn declared in class Object. We will introduce these streams next.

15.4 Input and Output for Objects

The method readFrom() in Program 145 is declared static in the class, and can thus be called without having an object of that type. This function reads *and creates* an object.[4]

---

[4]This is a complicated problem which is described in [Gor90].

```
#include "Image.h"
main()
{
    OIOifd in(cin);                     // object's input stream
    OIOofd out(cout);                 , // object's output stream
    Object * o = Object::readFrom(in); // static readFrom
    o->storeOn(out);                   // virtual storer
    Image * i = Image::readFrom(in);   // static readFrom
    o = i;
    o->storeOn(out); // will call virtual Image::storer
}
```

146

The mechanisms for input and output in NIHCL extend the notion of streams (Sect. 15.1) and add methods for storing arbitrary objects (with storeOn resp. storer) and construction from streams. An example for the class Image is shown in Program 146 which we will further inspect now. The abstract base classes for object input OIOin and output OIOout are shown in Figure 15.1. The major difference to standard C++ streams is that these streams automatically recognize type and version of the object during a read operation and create the required objects, whereas using the streams of Sect. 15.1 an object has to be created first, before data can be read into it.

Here, we only give an overview of the interface allowing the user to store and read objects in NIHCL.[5] NIHCL uses two types of streams one of them uses binary and one uses textual representation of objects. The usage is basically the same; we describe binary storage, since images and speech data has to be stored in binary format to save space.

Objects are stored via the storeOn method which has to be defined for each class which will eventually call the method storer. Arbitrary objects can be read using readFrom; this function is defined by the DEFINE_CLASS macro. The actual code for reading has to be provided in a constructor which has an input stream as an argument.[6] Clearly, when an object is read, its base class has to be initialized as well. This is simply done by the base class constructor which is executed before the object is initialized. An example is shown in Program 147.

This automatic mechanism is not available for the opposite direction, the storage operation by the method storer. The storer method of the base class has to be explicitly called; this is done using the name of the base as a prefix. It is convenient to define a macro for the actual class name and base (Program 147); for the DEFINE_CLASS we cannot use the THIS macro since otherwise this argument would expand to "THIS" instead of the desired "Image" in the expansion of #c in Program 145.

---

[5]Again, the reader is referred to [Gor90] for details.

[6]A tricky mechanism is used to call a constructor from the readFrom function.

```
#include "OIOnih.h"                        /* input / output */
#include "Image.h"                         /* image class declaration */
#define THIS Image
#define BASE Object

DEFINE_CLASS(Image,BASE,0)                 /* cannot use THIS here */

THIS::THIS(OIOifd& strm) : BASE(strm)      // constructor from stream
{
    strm >> f >> xsize >> ysize;           // reads image sizes and focal length
}
void THIS::storer(OIOofd& strm) const      // opposite direction
{
    BASE::storer(strm);                    // write base class data
    strm << f << xsize << ysize;           // store sizes and focal length
}
```

●147

The class Object's input and output functions provide consistency checks and version control. In addition, the class name is stored; thereby, arbitrary objects can be read from a stream without exactly knowing in advance which object will be read.

Interfaces of OIO streams to the streams in Sect. 15.1 exist in NIHCL. In Sect. 16.9 we derive our own special classes for object input and output from the NIHCL classes. We will show there how to open a stream and how to close it.

15.5 NIHCL Application Classes

In this section we list useful classes that are provided by NIHCL. The classes mentioned here can also be found in Smalltalk.

Strings are frequently used structures and string manipulations on character pointers in C++ as well as C is error prone, since explicit requests and releases of memory are required. NIHCL provides handy classes for dynamic strings including access and manipulation.[7] As in Smalltalk, these classes are called String and SubString. The methods available for objects of the class String are, for example, concatenation, comparison of strings, the selection of one character of a given string, methods for determining the length of a string, etc. The class SubString supports some manipulation of parts of a string. For example, a constructor is defined for declaring a substring of a specified length of a known object of the class String. Some applications are shown in Program 148. Individual characters can be accessed by an overloaded index operator. Allocation and release of the memory for the strings is managed automatically during construction and destruction.

---

[7]Compare Program 87 and Exercise 10.a on page 120.

```
String S1="string 1";    // define and initialize
String S2("string 2");   // alternative construction
S1[7]= '2';              // index checked access
S2[7]= '1';              // runtime error
cout << S1 << "\n";      // prints "string 2"
cout << S2 << "\n";      // prints "string 1"
```
148

```
Date bdpa(9,"April",59);    // create date object
Date bdho(10,"August",67) ;
int year= bdho.year();      // select the year
Time t(bdho,                // date
       8,                   // hour
       12,                  // minute
       0);                  // second
cout << bdho - bdpa << "\n"; // difference
```
149

```
Point  p(108,67), q(123,68); // two points (x,y)
Rectangle r(p,q);            // corner points
cout << r << " " << r.area() << "\n";
```
150

NIHCL provides classes for the access and manipulation of the date and time. As in Smalltalk, the classes are called Date and Time. In these classes, the complexity of calendars is encapsulated. In application programs Time and Date objects provide arithmetical manipulations of this data. The programmer can handle these objects as if they were ordinary numbers. For instance, the date can be compared with another one or you can add some days and will get the new resulting date. Some applications are shown in Program 149.

For graphical applications, NIHCL provides classes for simple geometric objects like points or rectangles (classes Points and Rectangle). [8] For image processing applications, this small class hierarchy will not be sufficient. In Chapter 16 a class hierarchy for image processing and analysis will be described. Applications in [Gor90] include the definition of the class Line, Triangle, Circle, and the class Picture. These classes are all derived from the abstract class Shape.

Numeric data in C++ is represented as in C as standard predefined data type. No object–oriented programming is possible with these data types. NIHCL defines the classes Integer and Float which can be accessed as *objects*. Thereby, they can for example be stored on object streams. Arithmetic methods are available, operation is, however, slow in comparison to standard data types.

---

[8]Compilation of NIHCL with X11 may as well cause problems since Point, Line, etc. are defined there as well.

15.6   NIHCL Collection Classes

Common examples for frequently used data structures are linked lists, stacks, or sets. In NIHCL the general super–class `Collection` holds instances of NIHCL classes as described in the previous sections. The methods of the abstract class `Collection` are functions for comparing instances of the `Collection` class, adding objects, removing objects, converting containers, the "element of" relation, or a function for determining the cardinality of an object. The polymorphic implementation guarantees that the code is useful for a wide range of applications.

Derived classes are the already mentioned classes `Set`, `Stack`, and `LinkedList` with their customary meanings. A subclass `Bag` can contain multiple occurrences of one object, or several objects which are equal. The classes `OrderedCltn` and `SeqCltn` are used to store arbitrary objects which are either sorted by a compare function (which has to be defined for the object to be added) or by the temporal order in which they are added to the `SeqCltn`. Elements of collections can be arbitrary NIHCL objects; a method `hash` and a predicate `isEqual` has to be provided for those collections which compare for equality, comparison has to be implemented for ordered collections.

In addition to the high degree of reusability of the polymorphic container classes, they also allow the definition of recursive data structures. For example, the elements of a set can also be sets and so on. Most of the problems concerning the use of container classes are due to the fact that container classes hold pointers to objects and do not represent the objects explicitly, i.e. they hold no explicit copy of objects, only references. Therefore, the programmer should take care and pay attention to correct memory management. In particular, we must be very careful about the lifetime of the objects which are parts of containers.

Some applications of sets and collections are shown in Program 151. Elements can be added to and removed from collections. When an element is added to a set, the existing objects are compared for *equality* with the new object. The contents of s will be {"Jonathan", "Joachim"} when it is printed. The collection o will contain {"Joachim", "Jonathan", "Carola", "Joachim"}. Collection management is further enhanced by the use of a hashing function (`hash`).

An attempt to remove an element which is not in the collection is an error and will raise an exception. NIHCL also provides macros for iteration over all elements in a collection as in a loop.

Program 79 (p. 111) showed a simple class declaration of an "association" data type between a string and an integer. NIHCL provides a more elaborate version of associations using a key–object and a value–object. The `String` class is often used for the key and an arbitrary `Object` as value. For example the key can be an English word and the value object is a list of all possible German translations of this word. A collection of these associations is called a `Dictionary`, if every key occurs only once. The class name

```
Set s;                  // define an empty set
OrderedCltn o;          // objects will be sorted
String s1="Carola";     // define and initialize
String s2("Jonathan");  // other initialization
String s3= "Joachim";   // s3 and s4 will be
String s4= "Joachim";   // equal, but not the same
s.add(s1);              // add several strings
s.add(s2);              // to the set s
s.add(s3);              // here comes joe
s.add(s4);              // will have no effect
s.remove(s1);           // remove element
o.add(s3);              // now add strings
o.add(s2);              // to the ordered
o.add(s1);              // collection
o.add(s4);              // joe will go in twice!
cout << "s:" << s << endl; // print contents of s
cout << "o:" << o << endl; // print contents of o
```
151

```
Dictionary d;              // define object
String word1("time");      // some string object
String word2("date");      // another string
d.addAssoc(word1,word2);   // add to dictionary
Object * op = d.atKey(word1); // retrieve information
String s5 = *(String *) op; // must use cast
cout << d << " " << *op << endl; // print d and op
```
152

Dictionary is obvious with respect to the above example. An application is shown in Program 152. NIHCL collections may contain any object derived from Object. Even within one set, each element may have a different type. This implies that the general manipulation functions can operate only on objects. Pointers or references have to be cast *down* to the actual type, e.g. to a String as in Program 152.[9]

Multiple occurrences of the same object in a collection will be recognized upon write and only one copy will be stored. This will also be recognized, when a collection is being read in. Using this mechanism, object *references* can be stored and restored.

15.7 Memory Allocation

In order to work efficiently with NIHCL, it is necessary to know about some internal features with respect to memory management. In particular this refers to input and output as well as to collections.

Objects to be put into a container class have to be allocated either dynamically, or they will be lost after they go out of scope. Collections only keep *references* to the objects

---

[9]This may be difficult in combination with multiple inheritance. NIHCL provides some save macros for such casts.

```
Set s;                           // empty set
for (int i = 0 ; i < 10 ; ++i ) {
   Integer j(i);                 // create temporary object
   s.add(j);                     // add it to set
}                                // object will be deleted here
cout << s;                       // Chaos !
```
153

```
template <class T> Matrix<T>::operator= (const Matrix& m)
{                    // simple version, should check sizes and x = x;
   int j, xs = m.xsize, i, ys = m.ysize;
   for (i = 0; i < ys; ++i)
     for (j = 0; j < xs; ++j)
       (*this)[i][j] = m[i][j]; // index checked!
}
```
154

inside. Program 153 gives an example of a wrong allocation strategy. The set will occur empty and will possibly have references to objects which no longer exist, when it is output to `cout`: the `Integer` `j` is local to the loop and will be destroyed when the loop is finished.

Another pitfall is the required cooperation of

- copy constructor, (`THIS::THIS(const THIS&)`)
- assignment operator, (`THIS::operator= (const THIS&)()`)
- object's copy method (`THIS::deepenShallowCopy()`).

If member allocation is done incorrectly in these functions, assignment, passing as parameter to functions, etc. may on the one hand result in "tangling references", i.e., memory which is still allocated but can no longer be accessed by a pointer; on the other hand, failure in allocation can also result in disastrous effects when an object frees memory which is still referenced and required in another.

Program 154 and Program 155 shows an implementation for the matrix template declared in Program 104. Instead of the slow safe assignment (index checked), one should first check whether the matrix sizes match and then assign without index checking. The special case of assigning an object to itself has to be considered if in the operator the memory is freed, reallocated, and then assigned. Program 156 shows an application.

The implementation of the method `deepenShallowCopy()` for classes derived from NIHCL–object is described in [Gor90; p. 127–134]. The purpose of this method is to ask an object to provide a complete copy of itself. In a *deep copy* all referenced objects have to be copied as well. The method `deepenShallowCopy()` is called for all member objects and pointers recursively. What is missing in [Gor90; p. 127–134] is the case of objects having pointers to data as members which do not point to an NIHCL–object and which have to be copied. An example of how to implement this is shown in Program 157.

```
template <class T> Matrix<T>::Matrix(const Matrix& m)
{
    int j, xs = m.xsize, i, ys = m.ysize;
    T * array = new T[x*y];           // vector of size x*y
    matrix = new T*[y];               // generate byte matrix
    for (i = 0; i < ys; ++i)
        matrix[i] = & (array[i*x]);   // fill in vector pointers
    Matrix::operator= (m);            // use assignment operator
}
```
155

```
Matrix<int> A(10,10);      // 10x10 integers
Matrix<int> B(A);          // copy constructor
Matrix<int> C = A;         // also copy constructor
B = A;                     // assignment operator
```
156

```
class A : public Object {          // artificial example
    unsigned int n;                // number of elements
    int* field;                    // field[0...n-1]
  public:
    void deepenShallowCopy();
};

void A::deepenShallowCopy()
{
    int* orig = this->field;                   // save original data
    this->feld_int = new int[this->n];         // reallocate
    for (unsigned int i=0; i<this->n; i++)     // for each element
        this->field[i] = orig[i];              // replace new by old
}
```
157

A call to `shallowCopy` makes a copy using the copy constructor. It returns an object pointer which can be disposed via `delete`. This implies that copy constructor, destructor, assignment operator and copy method have to be compatible. Especially for real–time programs it is crucial that all memory allocated will be deleted by the destructor. The following rules serve as a general guideline for an allocation strategy:

- Every constructor *copies* its arguments. If the argument is a pointer, the constructor creates a copy of what the pointer references. In particular, the copy constructor makes copies of all data referenced by pointers.

- The assignment operator releases its allocated memory and then also copies the data of its operand.

- The destructor releases the memory allocated by the constructor.

This strategy has been previously applied in Program 88. The natural extension for the assignment operator is shown in Program 158. A similar strategy is used in the NIHCL class `String`.

```
string::operator= (const string &s)
{
    delete st;                          // release allocated memory
    st = new char* [strlen(s.st) + 1];  // reallocate
    strcpy(st,s.st);                    // copy to new memory
}
```
158

The next two guidelines refer to classes derived from NIHCL objects:

- Since deepCopy calls shallowCopy which in turn uses the copy constructor, the function deepenShallowCopy will be empty in most cases.

- Use the same allocation strategy as NIHCL for collections: Leave the allocation and disposal to the application programmer. Only these classes using collections will have to implement the function deepenShallowCopy.

15.8   Standard Template Library

The Standard Template Library (STL,[Mus96]) satisfies the same needs as NIHCL for general collection classes. As indicated by the name STL, templates are used instead of a hierarchy of classes. The authors claim that this design is fastest, i.e., more runtime efficient than the exhaustive use of virtual functions. Syntactically similar template interfaces are provided for implementations with different runtime characteristics; these interfaces are not related to each other by inheritance. For example, adding an element to a linked list with constant runtime uses the same syntax as adding to an indexed pointer array which in turn has constant access time.[10] STL will be distributed with the forthcoming standard C++ compiler and library. Elements of a set must all be of the same type. A new template instantiation is required for each type of elements. In contrast to NIHCL, STL provides no concept for storing and retrieving collection objects.

15.9   Templates vs. Inheritance

The beauty of object–oriented programming is strongly connected with inheritance and code reuse of abstract function definitions. Template definitions are more related to the ideas of Ada. However, this beauty is difficult to realize in C++ as could be seen in Program 152. Although the operations on a collection can mostly be implemented in an abstract way, a static type conversion by a cast is often required.

---

[10]In the implementation of ERNEST [Nie90b] we implemented similar ideas in C using the C macro preprocessor. The application programmer's interface was simple, the internal implementation rather messy.

Templates are hard to implement but often easy to use once they are implemented. Older versions of C++ compilers only poorly supported templates. Even new versions still vary in the strategy for template instantiation. Since templates can not be completely syntax–checked when they are provided by the programmer, it may be that, during template instantiation, an incorrect use may give you a *compiler error* in a piece of code which is not written by you! This may of course puzzle at least the inexperienced programmer.

We found that the use of virtual functions adds only very little runtime overhead (c.f. Sect. 17.6). A wrong decision for a hash function, however, may dramatically reduce efficiency of NIHCL. Concrete comparisons of virtual functions and direct function calls will be outlined in Sect. 17.6).

This book is mainly dedicated to the application of object–oriented programming to pattern recognition and signal processing. It is not our goal to judge which design of general purpose classes is better suited, templates or inheritance. Often, the right choice might be a mixture of both:

- The requirement of a common file interface for segmentation results is in any case simplified by NIHCL.
- Matrix objects are efficiently implemented as templates.

Exercises

15.a Implement the class `Image` using the class `Class` for runtime information about the objects.

15.b Extend the implemented classes with respect to input and output facilities using streams.

15.c Implement a `String` and `SubString` class compatible with Program 87. Carefully apply the allocation guidelines listed in Sect. 15.7.

15.d Implement a `Date` and `Time` class compatible with what you saw in Program 149.

Part III
Object–Oriented Image Processing

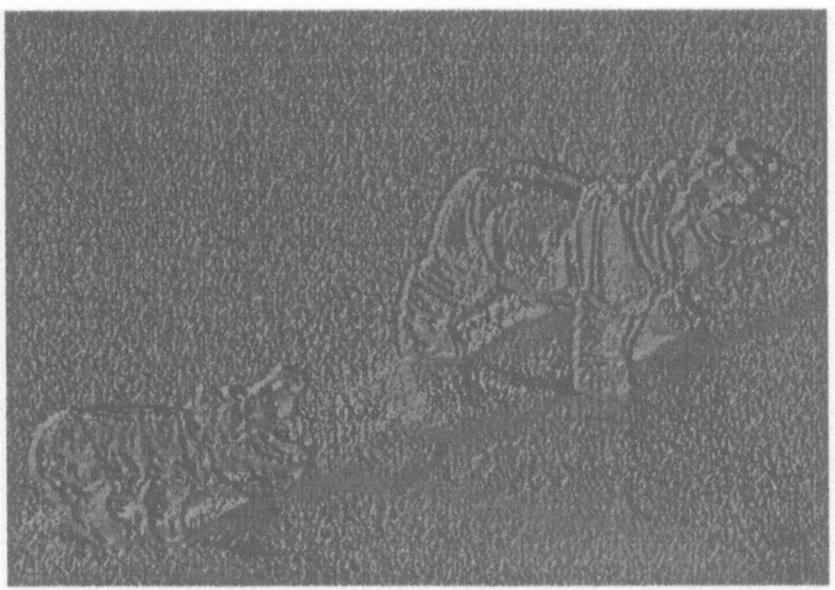

Edge orientation associated with the edge strength shown on p. 97 computed on the image on page 3.

In this part of the book we implement a simple image segmentation system using most of the object–oriented ideas introduced in Part I and Part II.

16 Hierarchy of Picture Processing Objects

The object–oriented programming system ἵππος[1] for image analysis was introduced in [Pau92b]. In this chapter we outline the ἵππος–system in general. We describe the concepts of lines, their representations as classes, and the implementation in C++ in detail. We also introduce the concept of friends in C++.

16.1 General Structure

The overall structure of ἵππος is described in [Pau92a, Pau92b, Pau92c]. The classes described in this book and in the appendix are only a trimmed down subset of the corresponding classes in the ἵππος system, with a reduced number of classes and much fewer methods. Algorithms and programs using these smaller classes can be compiled and run with very few changes in the complete system for 2–D segmentation.

The system consists of a large class tree with the top node class HipposObj (Sect. 16.2) which is directly derived from the NIHCL–class Object (Sect. 15.2). All classes required for image segmentation are derived from this class; they inherit the basic functionality for image processing.

Some other classes in ἵππος are derived from other branches of the NIHCL–tree. This is done for concepts which are not directly related to image processing. Template classes for matrices are defined and derived in a matrix–subtree The persistent storage of objects as implemented in NIHCL can be in a machine dependent binary format or in a machine independent ASCII format (Sect. 15.4). A machine independent efficient storage scheme for NIHCL and ἵππος is introduced in Sect. 16.9 using the XDR–classes.

Visualization is decoupled from algorithmic structure for all these classes by using a class for image display that interfaces with several devices. Similarly, images are input from a camera class that we will describe in Sect. 17.3.

A top level view of the ἵππος–hierarchy and the related classes is shown in Figure 16.1. The classes above the dotted line are NIHCL–classes (c.f. Figure 15.1); the classes below belong to ἵππος. On the left we show the superclasses for representation of data, on the right we depict the classes which extend NIHCL for data storage with XDR (Sect. 16.9).

---

[1] HIerarchy of Picture Processing ObjectS, c.f. Sect. 3.9

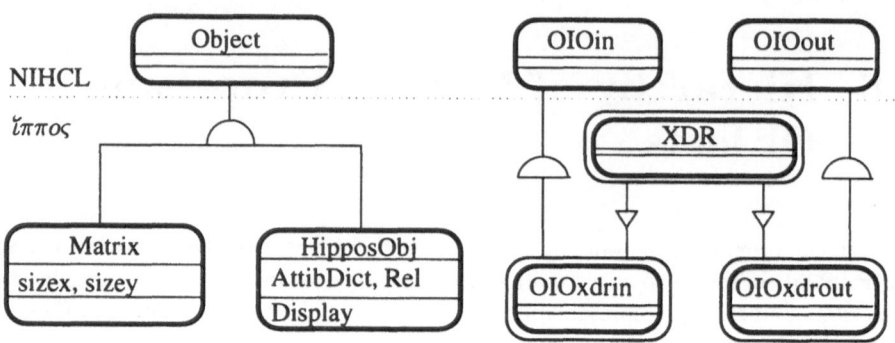

Figure 16.1 Interface of NIHCL and ἵππος

16.2 HIPPOS Object

The ἵππος tree is dedicated to the *representation* of data which is computed during image segmentation. The representation is general enough to include all known segmentation algorithms. These classes are collected in a subtree under the abstract class HipposObj. Its basic purpose is to bundle all the derived classes for image processing and analysis and to provide the basic functionality of every object of this application area (Figure 16.2). All image types are derived from the abstract Image class. The Representation subtree contains classes for the results of various line–based or region–based algorithms. Geometric objects provide a more abstract interface to these representations (Sect. 16.7). Relational objects RelObj will be needed in Sect. 16.8.

Three major features can be found in all imaging objects:

- Image processing objects usually reflect some sort of visual information. They can commonly be displayed on an appropriate graphics display.

- In order to specify a problem independent control strategy for knowledge based image analysis (Sect. 6.4), it is essential that every segmented object is attached with a judgement or quality measure (Sect.6.5).

- In addition to compiled–in members, image processing objects often have varying additional information which may be useful in one application but not required in another. An example is the mean contrast along a segmented line which may be computed by a line finding algorithm but ignored in the following steps.

These features are translated to C++ in a straightforward way. The displaying feature is taken into account by a pure virtual Display function which passes the graphics information to its argument which is another object derived from the HipposObj called a "virtual frame buffer" DisplObj (Figure 16.2). This object can be mapped to

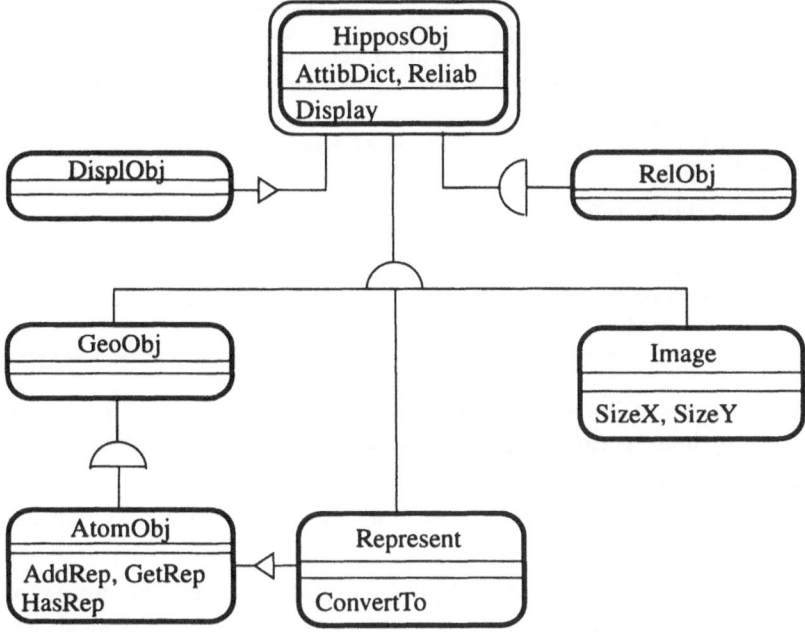

Figure 16.2 Top of image processing class hierarchy

an arbitrary physical device (Sect. 17.3).[2] The varying information on attributes is stored in an NIHCL–Dictionary with keys restricted to strings. The judgement is a floating point value that is inherited by every object in the hierarchy. A basic implementation of this class is shown in Program 159. As recommended in Sect. 15.7, we require that an object set as an attribute has to be allocated by the user. Consequently, this class will need a function deepenShallowCopy which will replace the attribute dictionary by a deep copy of itself.

16.3 Images and Matrices

Images were introduced as classes in chapter 11; this class is now integrated in the image processing hierarchy. Several classes for images are derived from a common abstract

---

[2] In the ἵππος implementation this is decoupled from the imaging objects. The display information is passed from the virtual frame buffer to a graphics server using remote procedure calls. The server then invokes the required display routines, for example, on an X11 device. This means, that the programs do not have to compile and link in any X11 routines!

```
#include "Dictionary.h"
class DisplObj;                     // need not care about it here
class HipposObj : public Object {   // abstract class, no public part
 private:
    DECLARE_MEMBERS(HipposObj)
    Dictionary * attributes;        // not always != NULL
    float judgement;
 protected:
    HipposObj(float r=0.0);
    const Dictionary & Attributes()  const;
    float              Judgement() const;
    void setAttrib(const char *, const Object *);   // add to Dictionary
    virtual int Display(DisplObj&) = 0;             // pure virtual
    void deepenShallowCopy();                       // required here
};
```
159

base class Image in ἵππος. Stereo images, range images, color images, gray–level images, binary images, edge images, etc. are available for programming together with their appropriate operations.

Subimages, as described in Sect. 11.7, are available for any image class. Stereo images may be either gray–level or color images.

Pixels are naturally stored in matrix objects. A matrix class tree was created for parametric matrix classes. Matrices with numeric elements declare mathematical operations like addition, multiplication, transposition, etc. Other matrices — e. g. those containing edge elements — only provide basic access and input–output functions. Since these matrix classes do not directly refer to image processing, they are not derived from the HipposObj. Thereby they are available to speech processing or any other non–image processing purposes without linkage of the ἵππος class library.

The abstract class Image can contain additional textual and numeric descriptions, such as the camera used and its parameters (lens, focus, aperture, exposure time, etc.). A basic definition for a gray–level image is given in Program 160.

In the first stage of segmentation, we use images and transform them to other images. The next step in segmentation (in the sense of Figure 6.5) is to detect geometric objects in a representation close to the pixel data.

16.4   Chain Code Class

The chain code representation is a common representation for lines and very close to the pixel raster data. This representation uses the start point of a line and a sequence of numbers from the interval 0 . . . 7 which indicate the next point in the line, called *links*.[3]

---

[3]Alternatively, we could use an STL template for this purpose.

```
#include <HipposObj.h>
#include <Matrix.h>
class Image : public HipposObj {   // extend as outlined in the text
 private:
   int x,y;                                 // private data
 public:
   Image (int xs,int ys) : x(xs), y(ys) {}   // set size info
   int SizeY() const { return y; }           // read size y
   int SizeX() const { return x; }           // read size x
};
class GrayLevelImage : public Image {
 private:
   DECLARE_MEMBERS(GrayLevelImage)
   Matrix<byte> img;                          // image data
 public:
   GrayLevelImage(int x,int y) : Image(x,y), img(x,y) { };
   byte* operator[] (int i) {return img[i];}
   const byte* operator[] (int i) const {return img[i];}
   virtual Display(DisplObj&);
};
```

160

This is exemplified in Figure 16.3. The information about the intensity of a line along a chain code is lost.[4]

Chain codes are very common in the first stages of image segmentation since they are a compact representation with a nice set of simple operations (c.f. Chapter 22, [Fre80]). The program in Program 27 in Sect. 4.9 is also used for chain codes (c.f. Chapter 22).

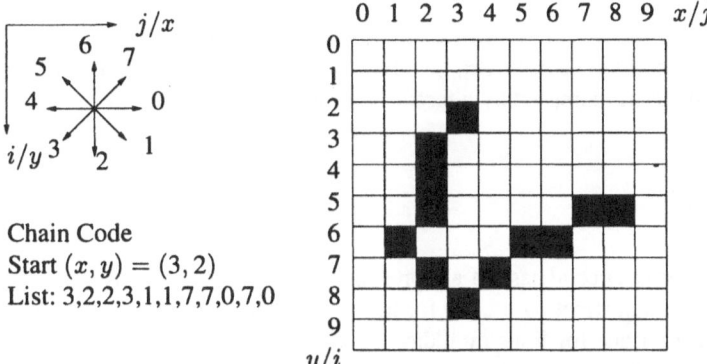

Chain Code
Start $(x, y) = (3, 2)$
List: 3,2,2,3,1,1,7,7,0,7,0

Figure 16.3 Definition of the directions in a chain code and example for a line represented by a chain code

---

[4]We will, however, record the mean intensity difference — the so called contrast — along the line in an attribute of the base class HipposObj.

```
class ChainSeq {                // no public part
  private:
    friend class Chain;         // grant access to internals
    byte * seq;                 // actual chains
    unsigned len;               // number of bytes allocated
    unsigned act;               // number of bytes used
    ~ChainSeq();                // destructor releases seq
    ChainSeq(unsigned);         // pre allocate
    ChainSeq(const ChainSeq&);
    int length() const { return len; }
    void append(byte);          // appends to the sequence seq
    byte & at(unsigned i) { return seq[i]; }        // read/write access
    byte   at(unsigned i) const { return seq[i]; }  // read access
};
```
161

For the implementation of a class for chain codes, we first introduce a helper class
ChainSeq (Program 161) to represent sequences of links. This class will be usable
only by the class Chain (Program 163) which is a friend of the class ChainSeq.
This language feature of C++ grants access to private parts of the class without any
restrictions; this permission is given only to those classes or functions which are declared
as friends.

Friends should generally be used only rarely, since they disturb modularity and data
abstraction. In this example, the contrary is the case; the dependencies are clear and
both classes can be in the same module. So this is, in effect, a useful application of the
friend concept. In general, we recommend that classes related as "friends" are declared
in the same header file, and that this feature is well documented.

The method ChainSeq::append appends a byte to the sequence. If there is no more
space available in the vector seq, i.e., len == act, then the object has to reallocate
memory with len increased by a factor (e.g., with factor 1.5).

16.5 Edges

Chain codes are a special case of a representation for lines. Other representations exist.
We introduce an abstract base class for line representations in Program 162. It contains
the general interface for lines including access to start and end, predicates for closed
lines, etc., and it separates these representations from those for regions.[5] This class
utilizes the class PointXY (Program 85, Exercise 10.b).

As will be described in Chapter 21, edges will be connected and chain codes can be extracted from an edge image. It is a useful extension for edges to add a possible successor

---

[5]In ἵππος, this class is actually separated into a class for three dimensional lines and one for lines in
two dimensions.

```
#include "PointXY.h"
class LineRep : public Represent {   // class for line representations
 private:
    DECLARE_MEMBERS(LineRep)          // required by NIHCL
    PointXY start;                    // only member
 public:
    LineRep();                        // default constructor
    LineRep(const PointXY&);          // set point
    LineRep(const LineRep&);          // copy constructor
    virtual PointXY End() const;      // must be part of derived class
    const PointXY& Start() const;     // reference to member
    int isClosed() const ;            // e.g., { return start == End(); }
    virtual double length() const;    // return length
};
```
162

```
class Chain : public LineRep {
 private:
    DECLARE_MEMBERS(Chain)
    ChainSeq chain;
 public:
    enum ChainDir { east = 0, se = 1, south = 2, sw = 3,
        west = 4, nw = 5, north = 6, ne = 7};
    static const int DefaultLen; // default chunk length for chain
    ~Chain();
    Chain();
    Chain(PointXY &, int = Chain::DefaultLen);
    Chain(const Chain &);
    int number() const { return chain.act + 1; }   // current length
    void append(byte b)   { chain.append(b); }      // extend
    void append(const Chain&);                       // concatenate
    inline byte operator[] (int) const;             // direct access to links
    virtual double length() const;                  // return length
    virtual int Display(DisplObj&);                 // show on screen
};
inline byte Chain::operator[] (int i) const {return chain.at(i); }
```
163

```
DEFINE_CLASS(Chain,LineRep,0)              // NIHCL functions
const int Chain::DefaultLen = 8;           // static member initialization
Chain::Chain() : chain(DefaultLen) {}      // default constructor
Chain::Chain(PointXY & p, int l) : LineRep(p), chain(l) {}
Chain::Chain(const Chain &c)      : LineRep(c.Start()), chain(c.chain) {}
```
164

to an edge element that points to any of its eight neighbors. This can naturally be done with a chain code, i.e., with the enumeration inside the class Chain (Program 164).

Program 164 and 165 show the implementation of some of the methods associated with chains. Note the constant static variable for the default allocation length declared in class scope.

Since we made the definition of the chain direction public, we can use it in an extended edge class (Program 166, c.f. Program 136). We also store with each element whether

```
Chain::~Chain() {}                      // all actions done in ~ChainSeq
ChainSeq::ChainSeq(unsigned l)
{
    act = 0;                            // currently no entries
    len = 1;                            // current buffer length
    seq = new byte[l];                  // allocate memory
}
ChainSeq::~ChainSeq() { delete [] seq; } // release memory
```
165

```
struct Edge {
    static const int ONUM;          // will be defined as 144
    enum edge_type { start = 0, end = 1, closed = 2 };
    unsigned int    strength : 16;
    unsigned int    orient   : 8;
    edge_type       features : 5;   // for later extension
    Chain::ChainDir succ     : 3;   // use Chain definition
};
```
166

we consider it part of an edge, part of a closed line, start or end of a line, etc. We use an enumeration data type in class scope for the symbolic description of these features. The constant class variable `Edge::ONUM` will have to be initialized as the `Chain::DefaultLen` in Program 164. [6]

16.6 Polygon Representation

A polygon is a line represented by a sequence of straight line segments. These segments can be characterized by a sequence of points. An example of a segmentation of a gray–level image into a set of polygons (a segmentation object) is shown in Figure 16.4. Polygon may be computed from a line segmentation in chain codes (c.f. Sect. 22.8). A simple algorithm for polygonal approximation is left as Exercise 16.b. Some more algorithms will be outlined in Sect. 22.8.

Polygons — like chain codes — are derived from the line representation class. A basic declaration is given in Program 167. The sequential collection (`OrderedCltn`) of NIHCL is used to store the sequence of points. For more runtime efficiency, this could be changed to an STL object without change of the user interface. [7]

---

[6]Of course, we do not derive the class `Edge` from `Object` since it would then have a virtual function table and edge images would at least double in size!

[7]If not programmed carefully, such changes may, however, severely interfere with input/output functions and external data formats, since the type of an object and version information is stored along with each object!

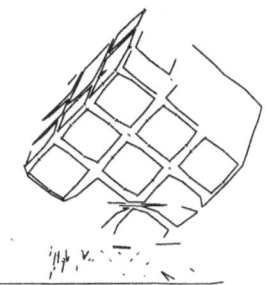

Figure 16.4 Polygon–approximation of a chain code segmented from the red channel (left) and Sobel on color image (right) of Figure 11.2 (left).

```
#include "OrderedCltn.h"
class Polygon : public LineRep {
 private:
    OrderedCltn points;           // sequence of points excluding start
 public:
    virtual double length() const; // read length (inherited)
    // ...
};
```

167

16.7 Atomic Objects

Several representations of one line in an image (or in a scene) may even exist simultaneously. For example, a chain code may be approximated by several polygons with different approximation errors. These representations are stored in an object of class AtomLine. The same holds for regions which may have several representations. An AtomLine and an AtomRegion are derived from the class GeoObj which bundles the subtree for geometric objects. The class AtomObj is introduced which separates compound objects (e.g., a collection of lines forming a rectangle) from those which contain only one instance of a given type. Compound objects are called *segmentation objects* and will be introduced in Sect. 16.8. The class hierarchy of these classes is shown in Figure 16.5.

Basic implementations of geometric objects and atomic objects are given in Program 168, 169, and 170. In Program 168 we define the abstract base class for this part of the hierarchy. Atomic objects are derived from class GeoObj; this class is abstract as well (Program 169). The method getRep will return a representation of a class indicated by the argument. If a representation is requested, which is not currently

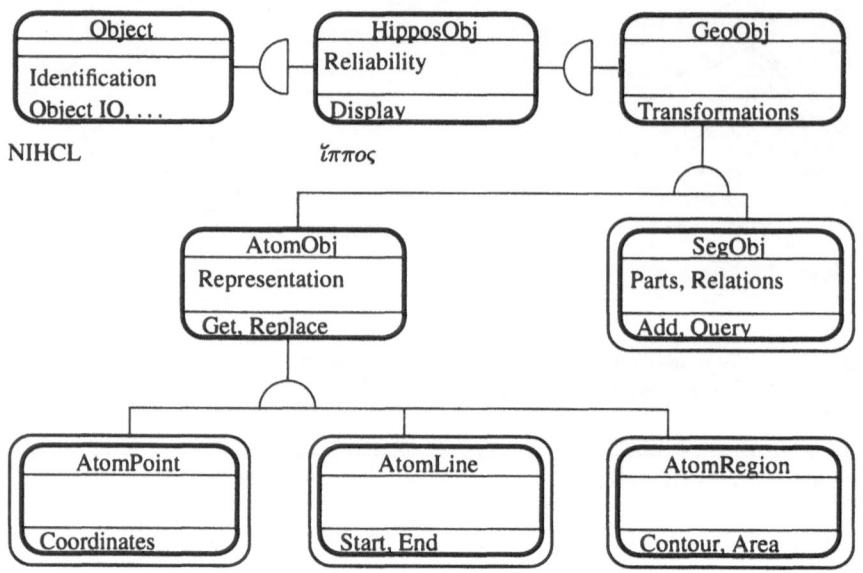

Figure 16.5 Hierarchy for geometric objects and segmentation objects

```
class GeoObj : public HipposObj {  // geometric objects
  private:
    DECLARE_MEMBERS(GeoObj)          // NIHCL functions
  protected:                         // abstract, no public parts
    GeoObj();                        // only default constructor here
    virtual int Display(DisplObj&);  // abstract interface for display
};
```

168

stored in the set of representations, a conversion method in the class `Represent` is used to produce such a representation (c.f. Figure 16.2).[8]

16.8 Segmentation Objects

It is very important to represent intermediate results of image segmentation in a common format which can be used by many segmentation programs. Generally, a so–called *segmentation object* consists of a set of parts and the relations between those parts. In most applications, these parts are geometric objects which cannot be further split,

---

[8]In the small system introduced in this book, this feature, as well as the whole class `Represent` is not further elaborated.

```
#include "Set.h"                         /* NIHCL Sets */
#include "Represent.h"
class AtomObj : public GeoObj {
 private:
   DECLARE_MEMBERS(AtomObj)
   Set representations;                  // will never be empty
 protected:
   AtomObj();                            // derived class will fill
   virtual addRep(const Represent&) = 0; // the set!
   Represent * getRep(const Class&);     // get a particular representation
   bool hasRep(const Class&) const;      // check for a representation
   void deepenShallowCopy();             // since Sets are used internally
};
```
169

```
class AtomLine : public AtomObj {
   DECLARE_MEMBERS(AtomLine)             // NIHCL functions
 public:
   AtomLine();
   AtomLine(const Represent&);
   virtual addRep(const Represent&);     // will add a
                                         // line representation
};
```
170

```
#include "Set.h"
class SegObj : public GeoObj {
   DECLARE_MEMBERS(SegObj)
   Set parts;                            // set of GeoObj (!)
   Set rels;                             // set of RelObjs
 public:
   SegObj();                             // will have emtpy sets
   void add(const GeoObj &s);            // add element to set
   virtual int Display(DisplObj&);
   void deepenShallowCopy();             // since Sets are used internally
   // etc.
};
```
171

i.e., they are atomic objects. Occasionally, segmentation objects may be recursive and include other segmentation objects, i.e., compound objects.

Segmentation results are represented in a common interface class called SegObj (Figure 16.5). Program 171 shows a basic implementation. This class is also derived from the class GeoObj and provides compound segmentation data. Parts may be added which are of the class GeoObj, i.e., either atomic objects or geometric objects. Since sets of objects of NIHCL are used, efficient functions for comparing objects have to be provided for geometric objects. Also, the function deepenShallowCopy has to be implemented to create copies of a segmentation object. As outlined in Sect. 15.7, this implies that the copy constructor creates a shallow copy of the member objects parts and rels. The same principle holds for the class AtomObj.

The very powerful SegObj class is the central class of the ἵππος system. Since segmentation objects may contain other segmentation objects, special care has to be taken that no circular structures will be created. The implementation of the method add guarantees that parts may only be included in the object if this will not create an inconsistent (i.e., cyclic) *part–of* relation. Further restrictions improve the safety of this representation scheme (see [Pau92b] for details).

Several features not shown in Program 171 are implemented in ἵππος. Parts of segmentation objects may be related in various ways to each other. For example, lines may be marked as parallel. This is represented in relations (in the mathematical sense) which we also provided as classes (see RelObj in Figure 16.1). These relational features are stored in the set rels. Vertices (see for example Figure 6.4) are special segmentation objects defined by the intersection of at least two lines.

16.9   External Representation

The NIHCL–system introduces streams for persistent objects (i.e., permanent storage of objects, Sect. 15.4). In ἵππος this concept was extended to machine independent binary storage using XDR (eXternal Data Representation, [XDR88]), which is available on almost any computer via the SUN network file system (nfs). A class XDR was introduced for this purpose. This enables a portable and highly efficient data transfer between different computer architectures.[9] All NIHCL–objects can be stored and retrieved from XDR–streams using their storeOn and readFrom methods on the derived streams. No changes are required for NIHCL.

This is a nice example of the power of virtual functions. Existing class libraries can be extended by inheritance and existing functionality can be overwritten with new virtual functions. A new class OIOxdrout is derived from the NIHCL–class OIOout. The overloaded virtual functions put declared for the NIHCL–class (Sect. 15.4) are redefined and mapped directly to the xdr functions. The method OIOxdrout::put(int i), for example, uses the xdr_int function. This derivation scheme is shown in Figure 16.1 on the right.

Without any modification or re–compilation, NIHCL–objects can now be stored to OIOxdrout–streams . . The method storeOn(OIOout&) will be used for this purpose. The same holds for the new class OIOxdrin which is derived from the NIHCL–class OIOin.

Program 172 provides a good example of object–oriented programming. The main program just reads an object, which can be of any class derived from HipposObj, and displays it using the virtual function Display. When a new class is added to the image

---

[9]including PC's.

```
#include "OIOxdr.h"
#include "HipposObj.h"
static DisplObj display;                        // local to this module
main(int argc, char **argv)
{
    OIOxdrin if(*++argv);                       // open input file
    OIOxdrin of(*++argv);                       // open output file
    HipposObj * o = HipposObj::readFrom(if);    // read arbitrary object
    o->Display(display);                        // display it
    o->storeOn(of);                             // store it
}
```

172

processing hierarchy, this program will just have to be linked again in order to know about the new possible objects and their display methods.

In an evolving programming environment, changes in classes are common. Often this requires a change, e.g., an addition, in the external representation. It is unacceptable that old external data would then have to be discarded as a result of this change. One possibility is to provide conversion routines which convert old data to the new format. A more elegant way is to extend the routines for storage and reading to handle different versions. This way, new programs will both write new data formats as well as recognize and decode old formats during read operations. Old programs will of course not be able to read the new format. Normally, old programs will either have to be re–compiled or simply re–linked, depending on the extent of the changes made. These mechanisms were incorporated into the class XDR without any changes to the underlying NIHCL mechanisms. [10]

In any modular programming system it is highly recommended that function calls will have no side effects. With respect to input and output to files, this means that no function should open a stream and write data to it, unless this is the only purpose of this function. Program 172 also shows how we recommend file input and output for image processing applications: the streams are opened and closed in the main program; file names are clearly visible to the programmer and the functions called will do the computation without further input and output. This also shows that all files will be closed properly. In most of the cases, such a structure is possible for imaging programs. This structure is consistent with the recommendation in Sect. 10.9, that memory allocation and memory release should be done in the same function, wherever possible, i.e, new and delete should occur as pairs in the source code.

---

[10]It is, however, not possible to deal with all kinds of changes in a class. For example, changes in the inheritance scheme cannot be easily masked out. Also, since the type and the version of a member variable are stored along with the data, changing the type of a member may also be difficult, i.e., programs for data conversion are sometimes required.

Exercises

16.a   Use the algorithms for line detection in Chapter 14 to fill in the classes for chain codes with data.

16.b   Invent a simple algorithm to convert a chain code into a polygon. Iterate along the chain code and approximate the current segment by a straight line. Whenever the approximation error exceeds a threshold, start a new line segment. Write a program which does this conversion from one segmentation object to another; the threshold should be given as command line argument.
We will learn more about this subject in Sect. 26.1.

16.c   Complete the definitions for the classes `Chain` and `ChainSeq` (Program 163 and 161).

16.d   Complete the switch in Program 27 for use in a chain code class.

16.e   Implement simple classes `OIOxdrin` and `OIOxdrout` to store and read arbitrary objects in a machine–independent format. Do not try to re–implement NIHCL, just provide sufficient functionality to read and write images using the same syntax as with NIHCL.

17   An Image Analysis System

In this chapter we introduce the design of the image analysis system ANIMALS (AN IMage AnaLysis System, [Pau92b]) composed of the classes which we introduced in the previous chapters. The C++ function call operator (Sect. 17.5) for classes unifies object–oriented programming and functional syntax. We present a top level program for image segmentation and use object–oriented command line syntax interpretation.

17.1   Data Flow

In Chapter 6, image segmentation was described and presented as a series of steps from the image signal to an initial symbolic description (Sect. 6.5, Figure 6.5). Every step has its own typical algorithms. The implementation of these algorithms as separate processes introduces the problem of how to connect the results. Figuratively speaking, some algorithms skip over a step in Figure 6.5, some introduce intermediate data structures and require other processes before the next step can be reached. Through this approach, the image segmentation problem can be seen as one of data flow analysis. A top view of this data flow is shown in Figure 17.1; the gray lines represent the feedback in a closed control loop for active computer vision (Sect. 6.8). Among several alternatives, algorithms suitable for the present task have to be chosen in the segmentation and analysis stage; they have to be connected in a way that will eventually lead to the symbolic description.

Ideally, models are generated from images automatically. They are stored and used as knowledge for image analysis.

17.2   Design of ANIMALS

The ANIMALS system is designed in an object–oriented way according to the data flow in Figure 17.1. Data and algorithms for image processing are organized into hierarchies. Representation of the data uses ἵππος (Chapter 16). Image analysis is mainly seen as a problem of transforming information between different levels of abstraction. Naturally, the transformations are implemented as separate processes.

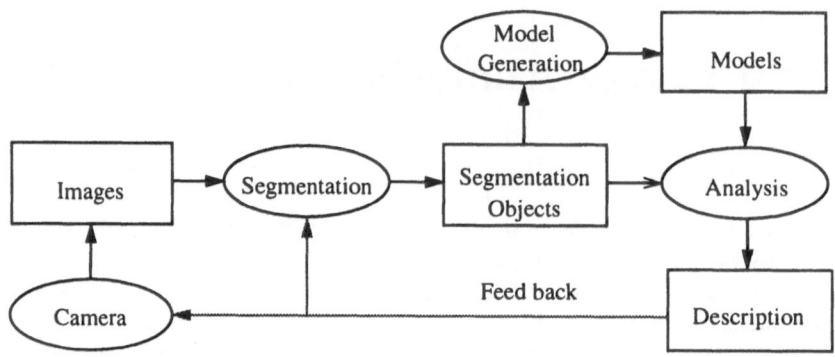

Figure 17.1 Data flow in an image analysis systems

Figure 17.2 shows the various paths from images to line segments [Pau92c]. At level
A, images are created; at level B, images are transformed; at C, edge images are
transformed; at D, segmentation objects are processed. The major data classes appearing
in this scheme are intensity images, edge images, chain codes, lines, and segmentation
objects, which were introduced in previous chapters. Edge detection leads from intensity
images (gray or color) to edge images (arrow 8). The reverse direction (arrow 9) is used
for the visualization of edge images (e.g., Figure 14.9). Line detection (Chapter 21)
leads from edge images to segmentation objects containing chain codes (arrow 11).
Visualization of segmentation objects can be done using raster images (arrow 14) or
after conversion to a graphics format (arrow 13). Often, textual descriptions of the
objects are desired (arrows 16–18).

The above transitions from one block to another can be implemented as functions,
processes or operator classes.

As indicated in Sect. 16.9, all external representations of objects is done via XDR.
The interfaces between different processing stages can thus be reduced to the objects
passed from one process to another. Since the representation is machine independent,
the processes can run on different architectures.

17.3   Display and Capture

Naturally, image processing objects will have to be displayed on a raster display. Many
different hardware solutions exist for image display. Many of them are encapsulated
by the X11 window system. However, display using dedicated frame grabber cards or
external monitors is not supported by X11. If every ἵππος–object had an interface to

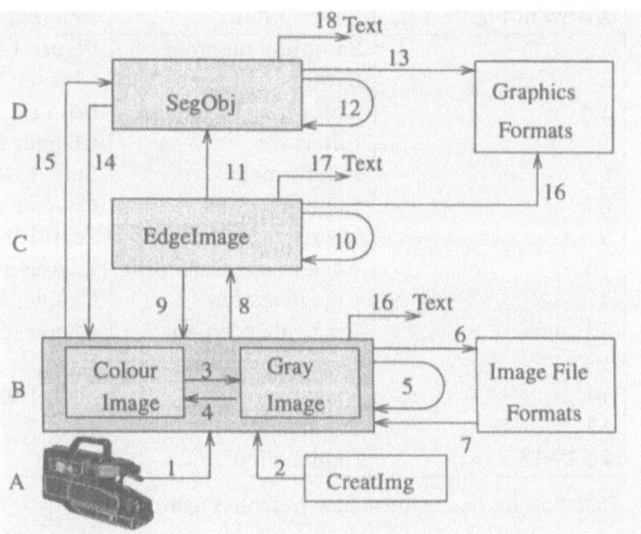

Figure 17.2 Data flow for line–based image segmentation. The arrows indicate processes that transform from one representation to another (cmp. Figure 6.5); they are explained in the text and in Table 17.1.

X11 (e.g., by a virtual method for Display in the class HipposObj, Program 159), programs would have to be linked with X11, even if no display is actually done in the program. This is due to the fact that the compiler and linker can generally not decide which virtual function will be actually called. The linker thus has to include *all* virtual functions for classes which occur in the source file, including all the virtual functions of all derived classes. Using shared libraries, i.e., dynamic linkage at runtime, the memory requirements of a program can be limited.

The solution in ἵππος could already be seen in Program 159. A class is provided for display called a *virtual frame buffer*. All display methods direct their requests to a frame grabber object. This object in turn passes the display information via remote procedure calls (RPC) to a *display server*.[1] Different servers can now act as an interface to either X11 or special frame buffer hardware.

Similarly to image display, image capturing requires interfaces to dedicated hardware which decreases portability when not handled properly. ANIMALS has a general class Camera which is specialized to the actual frame grabbing device and the connected camera. Typical parameters include the actual resolution, the image size, the input timing

---

[1]The SUN remote procedure call is used which is also based on XDR, however, this amounts only in a small storage overhead.

Arrow in Figure 17.2	Description	References
1	Sampling theorem	Figure 1.9
2	Synthetic images	Chapter 18
3,4	Color transformation	Eq. 11.2
5	Filters	Chapter 19
6,7	File formats	Sect. 11.4
8	Edge detection	Chapter 14
9	Visualization	Sect. 1.9
10	Edge image transform	Exercise 21.d
11	Line detection	Chapter 21
12	Line enhancement	Chapter 22
13	Data conversion	Exercise 17.e
14	Visualization	Sect. 1.9
15	Segmentation	—
16,17,18	Explanation	—

Table 17.1 Data flow for line segmentation (refer to Figure 17.2)

(PAL, NTSC) and the color space (Sect. 11.2). Since the data transfer has to be as fast as possible, in order to allow real–time processing, no `rpc` interface can be used here.

17.4 Geometric Distortions

We now interest ourselves in another feature of C++ classes which can simplify the interfaces for image operations. We use a low–level image operation as an example for an object–oriented implementation of operators.

A typical preprocessing step is the inversion of geometric distortions of an input image (arrow 5 in Figure 17.2). Examples may be found in [Nie90a]. An ideal (undistorted) image $s(x, y)$ is observed as $f(u, v)$, whereby the coordinates are distorted by

$$u = \Phi_1(x, y), \quad v = \Phi_2(x, y) \quad . \tag{17.1}$$

The ideal image can be computed by

$$s(x, y) = f(\Phi_1(x, y), \Phi_2(x, y)) \quad . \tag{17.2}$$

The distortion functions Φ_1, Φ_2 are usually taken from a parametric family of functions. Typical classes are polynomial, affine, or projective transformations. Φ_1 and Φ_2 may belong to the same class and differ only in the parameters. For example, Φ_1 and Φ_2 may be affine transforms $u = a_{11} x + a_{12} y + a_{13}$ and $v = a_{21} x + a_{22} y + a_{23}$.

It is convenient, if we can code (17.2) directly into the programming language:

```
s[i][j] = f[Phi1(i,j)][Phi2(i,j)];
```
                                                                                  (17.3)

The problem of reconstructing the ideal image is inherently independent of the actual distortion functions. A change in these functions should not affect the algorithm directly.

Using conventional programming languages, geometric distortions can be implemented as functions. The implementation of (17.2), for instance, will call the distortion functions via function pointers (Sect. 7.8).

Now, imagine that Φ_1 and Φ_2 belong to the same class of parametric functions, e.g., 2–D affine distortions, and differ only in their coefficients. The major problem then is to combine the function pointers with their parameter sets without duplicating code.

One might attach the parameters as a vector argument to the functions:

```
f[Phi1(i,j,a1)][Phi2(i,j,a2)];
```
                                                                                  (17.4)

However, the number of parameters for the different transformation classes are different (e.g., three parameters for the affine, six for the projective transformation). We can also find examples where the parameters differ not only in number but also in type.

17.5 Polymorphic Image Processing

Section 17.4 showed how mathematicians write down algorithms using functional syntax. The functions Φ_1 and Φ_2 in (17.2), implemented as `Phi1` and `Phi2` in (17.4) exhibit *polymorphic* behavior. Nothing is being said about the type of these functions at this point. At the time of the actual computation, they may be either affine transformations, polynomials or perspective transformations; it may as well be the case that both functions are affine transformations with different parameter sets.

This kind of semantics can be expressed by the syntax of object–oriented programming languages. It greatly simplifies programming and enables safe extensibility. If another programmer has to add radial distortions to the above mentioned transformations, the basic idea (and of course, the formula (17.2)) would not change. Neither would the (object–oriented) program.

The great advantage of polymorphic functions over conventional function pointers will now be outlined. An abstract super–class provides the general interface to geometric distortions. Special classes inherit the interface and redefine the details.

Program 173 is a simplified piece of C++ code for the declaration of three classes. The class `Dist` defines the abstract interface which is inherited by the derived classes for polynomial and affine distortion. The virtual constant operator declares an object

```
struct Dist {   // abstract class          // abstract interface
   virtual int operator() (int,int);       // apply distortion function
};
struct PolyDist: public Dist {             // polynomial distortion
   virtual int operator()(int,int);        // apply distortion function
};
class AffineDist : public PolyDist {
 private:
    double a,b,c;                // coefficients for the affine transformation
 public:
    AffineDist(int,int,int); // set a,b,c
    virtual int operator()(int,int);
};
```
173

```
#include <GrayLevelImage.h>
void correct(Dist& const Phi1, Dist& const Phi2,
        GrayLevelImage& s, GrayLevelImage& const f)
{
   for(int i = 0; i < s.SizeY(); ++i)          // all lines
     for(int j = 0; j < s.SizeX(); ++j)        // all columns
       s[i][j] = f[Phi1(i,j)][Phi2(i,j)];      // apply distortion objects
}
```
174

interface in *functional syntax*. The operator() can be used to address objects like function calls without the need of specifying a method name.

Using the code fragment, a geometric correction mapping function can be written without actually knowing which kind of transformation will be applied. Distorted image f, corrected image object s, and the two transformation objects Phi1 and Phi2 are passed to the function as arguments (Program 174).

Of course, a complete algorithm will have to take care of re–sampling, interpolation, and filtering, etc. This is left as Exercise 17.a.

The classes declare a hierarchy of *operations*; instances of these classes (objects) represent the actual (mathematical) parametric function with a fixed set of parameters. For example, an affine transformation $u = 1.1\,x + 0.9\,y$ will be an object of class AffineDist.

Two distortion objects for affine transformations *share* the code for the computation. They differ in the coefficients (a, b, c) which are bound to the object.

A conventional implementation using function pointers would either have to use a complicated mechanism for linking the coefficients to the computation, or duplicate code in order to provide two functions Phi1 and Phi2, which are textually identical, except for the coefficients of the polynomial. This may be acceptable in this (simple) case; but in general, this will decrease the maintainability of programs: in typical image processing programs, *many* simple functions are used; code duplication in several simple functions imposes the same problems on maintainability as duplications in a few complex parts.

For example, if at a later stage, someone decides that radial distortions are required, the function `correct` in the previous source code fragment will *not* have to be modified. A new class for radial distortions redefining the `operator()(int,int)` will simply be derived from the abstract base class.

An arbitrary number of transformation–objects can be created (and destroyed) during runtime. If, in the conventional solution using duplicated code, three instead of two functions are needed, the code has to be copied again, compiled, linked, etc. This also has to be done if templates are used, i.e., one further function has to be expanded from the template.

17.6 Efficiency

Sometimes people argue that object–oriented programming adds administrational over-head to the programs thereby causing a slow down in execution speed. This is not always the case, especially not in C++. Efficient image class access was described in Chapter 11. The ANIMALS system is designed to be efficient, both in storage requirements and computation time.

For example, a comparison of the execution times for a geometric distortion in an implementation in conventional C and the C++ implementation showed *no* measurable differences for affine distortions. The times were measured with `inline` virtual operators and `inline` image access operators. The conventional program used indirect function calls (via function pointer arguments) or direct function calls. In either case, the floating point arithmetic required for the evaluation of the transformation — i.e., the *real* work of the programs — by far exceeded the access and calling mechanisms. The execution times for a geometric correction using the function `correct` on an HP 735 (99 MHz, AT&T C++ 3.1) Unix workstation were around 0.2 seconds.

17.7 Command Line Options

For a program communication, organized as in Figure 17.1, several processes will have to be started from the command line. It is very useful if such programs have a common command line syntax. The functions used so far for parsing the command line were not too sophisticated. Naturally, we want to provide a command line parser as a properly encapsulated class. Such a concept is proposed in Program 175. A parser class will be used to read and analyze command line parameters. In the `Parser` class we maintain a list of all instantiated `Option` objects. Conversely, all `Option` objects require the

```
class Option;          // defined later
class Parser {
 private:
    struct OptionList { // local structure
        Option * o; OptionList * next;
        OptionList() { o = NULL; next = NULL; }
    } ;
    static OptionList start;
    static OptionList * ol;
 public:
    static void add(Option*);
    Parser(char** HelpText, int argc, char ** argv);
};

class Option {
 private:
    friend class Parser;
    char * tag;              // option identifier
    char * value;            // value on command line
    short  is_set;           // set, if option is present on command line
 public:
    Option(char * t) { tag = t; Parser::add(this); }
    operator const char * () { return value; }
    int isSet() const { return is_set; }
};
```
175

```
Parser::OptionList Parser::start;              // hook for list
Parser::OptionList* Parser::ol = &Parser::start;  // static class member

void Parser::add(Option* o)                    // add option to global
{                                              // list
    static OptionList * act = & start;
    act->o = o;
    act->next = new OptionList;                // append to linked list
    act = act->next;
}
```
176

definition of the parser class. This circular dependency is solved by an empty (forward) class declaration. Also note the local definition for the list of options OptionList.[2]

In the implementation in Program 176 we initialize the static variables and demonstrate how the linked list can be filled. The Parser object compares the arguments on the command line with the tags found in the option objects and fills in the value pointers with the appropriate strings from the command line.

The further implementation is left as Exercise 17.f. An application is shown below in Program 179. We put a much more elaborated version of this concept on the ftp site listed in Appendix B.2, including default arguments, distinction between options and arguments, abbreviations, etc.

---

[2]The ideas and original implementation are due to M. Harbeck and R. Beß.

```
#include "ipop.h"
static char * inp, *outp;          // strings
static LowPass * filter = NULL;    // filter object
static EdgeDet * edgdet = NULL;    // edge detection object
static LineDet * lindet = NULL;    // line detection object
```
177

17.8 Graphical User Interfaces

Providing a comfortable user interface with graphical tools for image analysis is a complicated matter. The system Khoros[3] has solved this problem in a brilliant way [Ras92]; data flow paths can be defined in this system, connecting a large variety of image processing operators. The system is easily extensible and main programs for user defined subroutines can be created automatically. Further research in the image understanding environment pursues this task (c.f. Sect. 6.7).

Real-time image analysis and active vision usually has to be performed without continuous user interaction. Graphical user interfaces (GUI's) are more useful for program development and for teaching. In industrial applications, in particular in real–time applications, this is less important. In ANIMALS, we can use the X11 tool which automatically creates an interface to `tcl/tk` [Ous94]. A graphical shell is put around the program which is used for argument processing in a text window and may display input and results in separate windows.[4]

17.9 Image Segmentation Program

In this section we illustrate a top down design of a program for image segmentation. The classes introduced in Part II are used for data representation. Operator classes (Sect. 17.5) are declared for image segmentation, and the actual implementation of these operators will be described in the following.

Program 177 shows the static declarations for the main module. We use pointers to operator objects which can vary upon the actual command line arguments. The classes `LowPass`, `EdgeDet`, and `LineDet` are used for image processing operations and will be filled in the following chapters. The abstract declaration is already given here in Program 178.

Program 179 shows the main program. After processing the command line, an image object is read from an XDR stream. Images for intermediate results are created with the same dimensions and the input image is filtered with a filter operator object.

---
[3]Khoros is in the public domain, c.f. Appendix B.1.
[4]We put the source code for argument processing into the public domain (c.f. Appendix B); using a tcl/tk script, a GUI can be created automatically from the output of these argument objects.

```
#include <GrayLevelImage.h>
#include <EdgeImage.h>
#include <SegObj.h>

class IP_OP : public Object { };          // general image operator class
struct Filter: public IP_OP {             // abstract class for filters
   virtual void operator() (const GrayLevelImage&,GrayLevelImage&) = 0;
};
struct LowPass : public Filter {};        // abstract low-pass filter
struct EdgeDet: public IP_OP {            // abstract class for edge detection
   virtual void operator() (const GrayLevelImage&,EdgeImage&) = 0;
};
struct LineDet : public IP_OP {           // Line detection algorithm
   virtual void operator() (const EdgeImage&, SegObj&) = 0;
};
```
178

```
#include "OIOxdr.h"
static char rcsid[] = "RCSINFO";
static char * HelpText [] = { "This program ....", rcsid, NULL };
main(int argc, char  **argv)
{
   Option inp  ("input");          // input file option
   Option outp ("output");         // output file option
   Parser p(HelpText,argc,argv);   // command line interpretation

   OIOxdrin  f_in(inp);            // input  stream
   OIOxdrout f_out(outp);          // output stream
   GrayLevelImage * f = GrayLevelImage::readFrom(f_in);
   GrayLevelImage   g (f->SizeX(),f->SizeY());
   EdgeImage        h (f->SizeX(),f->SizeY());

   (*filter)(*f,g);                // low-pass filter on input
   (*edgdet)(g,h);                 // detect edge elements
   SegObj s;                       // to hold the results
   (*lindet)(h,s);                 // connect edge elements
   s.storeOn(f_out);               // store on stream
   return(0);                      // close files, clean up, exit
}
```
179

As in Program 174, we do not exactly specify which operator will actually be used; we use a pointer to an operator class which during runtime can point to some object of its derived classes.

Edges detected in the filtered image are stored in an edge image. An edge detection object can be implemented, for instance, using algorithms of Chapter 14. Edge elements are combined to lines and stored in a segmentation object. The operator object for this purpose may be based on the methods discussed in Chapter 14 and will be extended in Program 186.

The program fragments in Program 177–179 can be combined and extended with the classes introduced in next chapters, to produce a nice, powerful, and easy–to–change image segmentation program.

Exercises

17.a   The following essential parts are missing in Program 173:

- the parameters for the polynomial mapping,
- constructors (setting the parameters),
- definition of the virtual functions (basically straightforward).

Complete the example!

17.b   Extend Program 174 to handle interpolation.

17.c   Implement a method `storeOn` which handles revision numbers. Extend your class by one new member and increment the revision. Decode the revision upon reading the data and enable your new program to read old data, for which the new member will be initialized with a default value.

17.d   Implement a class for image input from your frame grabber card. This should hide all hardware details — as in the case of speech input in Program 51.

17.e   Write a function that prints straight line segments in a graphics format you are familiar with (e.g., PostScript, xfig, etc.). Select lines from a segmentation object (`SegObj`) and write them to a file using your new routine.

17.f   Complete the implementation of the class `Parser` in Program 175.

18 Synthetic Signals and Images

When testing new algorithms, it is often useful to start experiments using synthetic data for which the result of the processing is known (c.f. Sect.3.2). Image synthesis is part of computer graphics (c.f. Sect. 1.1), and also the generation of realistic speech signals using text input is an area of research. In this chapter we mostly establish regular patterns or global features which are useful in pattern recognition for testing low–level algorithms.

Many algorithms in the field of low–level image and speech processing are concerned with noise reduction in the data (c.f. Chapter 19). These techniques are often based on assumptions about special noise distributions. For the experimental evaluation of algorithms, it is useful to have synthetic image generators for different noise effects, i.e., special distributions of noisy pixels.

In the following sections we describe some algorithms for synthetic image and sound generation. We describe how to create *magic 3–D* images and conclude the chapter with a special case of synthetic texture images.

18.1 Synthetic Sound

For the evaluation of the correctness of programs, it is often useful to have an undisturbed input signal with well–known features. In Exercise 12.j we already saw a simple version of a sound generating program. This should now be extended to allow for various tests. In addition to the frequency, we need to set the loudness of the sound. Also, rectangular and triangular signals can be generated.[1]

If we want to create a sound signal consisting of overlayed components, in general, we have several choices. We can either create a program with lots of arguments for the various parameters of the corresponding Fourier series; or, we can interactively ask for the signals to be generated; or, we can create a set of tools for the composition of sound files.

The last choice has several advantages. Imagine, you want to test your large program, and you need some sound pattern in order to verify the correctness of the behavior of your code. You simply write a sequence of sound generation commands in your makefile, compose the outputs, and then run your program on them. This way, you

---

[1]Listen to them on your sound device!

will not even have to record in your notes which signal is in which file, since this can easily be seen from your `makefile`.

The required tools are programs for sound generation, a program which takes an arbitrary number of input files and creates an output signal which contains an additive superposition of the input files,[2] and a program which modifies the amplitude of a given input signal.

18.2   Geometric Patterns

Similarly to periodic sound signals, images of two–dimensional geometric objects with known position and shape are often used to test image processing methods. In contrast to computer graphics, usually no realistic image is necessary. Instead, lines, points, circles, and rectangles — either filled or the outline only — have to be positioned in the synthetic image. Lattices of variable width or chess board patterns are also frequently used, for instance, to check edge detectors. Some examples are shown in Figure 18.1. One such example was already used in Figure 12.7 to demonstrate and test the Fourier transform.

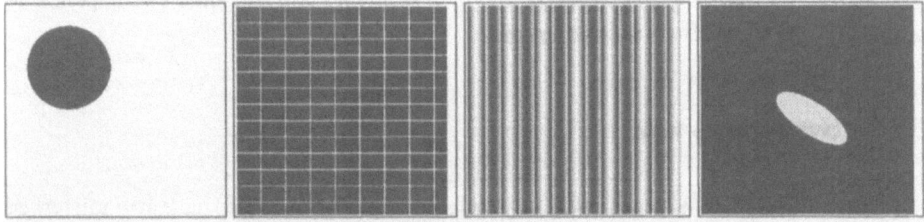

Figure 18.1   Examples for synthetic images

As in Sect. 18.1, these objects are simply created by a set of functions. For the combination of several images to a new one, additional and appropriate tools are required. Common combinations are image addition, exclusive *or*, bit wise and logical *and* and *or*, and multiplication of an image with a factor to reduce or increase intensity. Also, the combination of three gray–level images to a color image can be a nice tool. All operations require modulo arithmetics due to the quantization involved.

---

[2]The input signals do not have to be combined with addition; there exist cases where a convolution of one with the other makes sense. Also, multiplication can be used in some cases.

```
#include <Matrix.h>
#include <Options.h>

#define ImageOps(fn,op)              /* function definition macro */  \
  static void image_##fn (Matrix<byte> & out,         /* result   */  \
                 Matrix<byte> const & in1,             /* operand 1 */  \
                 Matrix<byte> const & in2) {           /* operand 2 */  \
   for (int i = 0; i < in1.SizeY(); ++i)                                \
     for (int j = 0; j < in1.SizeX(); ++j) {                           \
        int r = int(in1[i][j]) op int(in2[i][j]);                      \
        out[i][j] = (r<0) ? 0 : ((r>255) ? 255 : r); /* clip result */  \
     }                                                                  \
  }                                                                     \
  Option opt_##fn(#fn);                /* command line option */       \

ImageOps (add,+)    ImageOps (sub,-)       // define functions for
ImageOps (mul,*)    ImageOps (div,/)       // the binary operators
ImageOps (bor,|)    ImageOps (band,&)      // + - * / | &
ImageOps (lor,||)   ImageOps (land,&&)     // || && ^ %
ImageOps (xor,^)    ImageOps (mod,%)
```

180

18.3   Examples in C++

In Program 180 we show a macro that defines functions for binary operations on images.[3] Each macro expansion creates a function for image addition, multiplication, etc. In Program 180 we pass one part of the function name as the first argument to the macro and an operator as the second argument. The function name results from a concatenation of image_ and the first argument; a command line option (c.f. Sect. 17.7) is created by the concatenation of opt_ and the same argument; the argument is passed to the command line option constructor as a string. Such tricks with macros are not possible with templates. A similar macro now can be defined for unary operations. The functions clip values greater than 255 and less than 0.

Together with the geometric patterns generated in Sect. 18.2 we can now create, for example, a circular mask and *and* it to an image, to mask out only the image portion inside the circle.

18.4   Pixel Noise

Many disturbances in real images are often due to pixel noise. Let us assume that statistically each n–th pixel is disturbed by noise, i.e. every pixel will be disturbed by noise with probability $1/n$ [Pra91].

---

[3]Note that comments are written in C notation since cpp may otherwise confuse comments and the trailing backslash.

We use a program which generates a homogeneous black or white gray–level image as in Sect. 18.2. and add in average to each n–th pixel a uniformly distributed gray–level from the interval $[a, b]$ using modulo arithmetics. In the implementation, the parameters n, a and b are initialized by default values, and the user has the possibility to adjust these parameters during the function call. In Figure 18.2 examples are shown for three different choices of parameters.

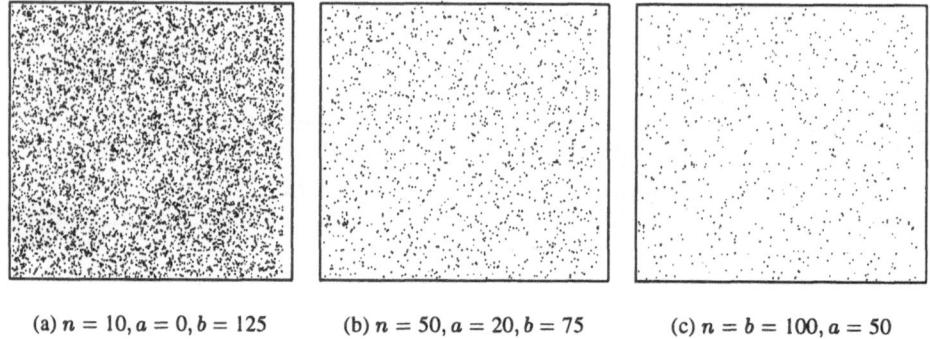

(a) $n = 10, a = 0, b = 125$ (b) $n = 50, a = 20, b = 75$ (c) $n = b = 100, a = 50$

Figure 18.2   Examples of pixel noise for different parameter values

18.5   Gaussian Noise

Gaussian noise is often assumed to be an adequate modeling of real noise effects occurring in images recorded by CCD cameras or other sensors. For generating normally distributed gray–levels with the mean zero and a variance of one, the famous and fairly tricky algorithm of G. E. P. Box, M. E. Muller, and G. Marsglia can be used [Knu73, Joh87]. The described method is based on two $[0, 1]$ uniformly distributed random numbers u_1 and u_2. Using both numbers we introduce the following transformation of random variables:

$$v_1 = 2u_1 - 1 \quad , \tag{18.1}$$
$$v_2 = 2u_2 - 1 \quad , \quad \text{and} \tag{18.2}$$
$$s = v_1^2 + v_2^2 \quad . \tag{18.3}$$

If the value of s is greater or equal to one, the algorithm starts again with the computation of both uniformly distributed random numbers u_1 and u_2. Otherwise, it can be shown that the random variable

$$X = v_1 \sqrt{\frac{-2 \ln s}{s}} \tag{18.4}$$

underlies a normal distribution using the algebra of random variables [Spr79]. Using this idea we are able to create a sound signal of Gaussian noise or a noisy image (Figure 18.3 left).

Figure 18.3 Examples of Gaussian (left) and Salt–and–Pepper noise (middle) and combination of both (right)

18.6 Salt–and–Pepper Noise

A special type of noise is the *salt–and–pepper noise*. Each pixel in the gray–level image takes one value from a set of two values $\{a, b\}$. These values appear with the same probability of $1/2$ (c.f. Figure 18.3 middle). For the implementation of a function which generates salt–and–pepper noise, the gray–levels a and b are parameters of the function call. We can also apply the same idea to sound signals and use the same random generators for both tasks.

The rightmost image in Figure 18.3 is created by a combination of synthetic images introduced so far using the functions discussed in Sect. 18.3: first, a filled circle is created (c.f. Figure 18.1). Two images are created using the algorithms for Gaussian and salt–and–pepper noise, respectively. The circle image is combined with the Gaussian noise by a bitwise *and* as in the function which is created by the macro expansion ImageOps(and,&) in Program 180, creating an image A. Subtracting each pixel value from the constant 255 inverts the circle image. Again, a bitwise *and* creates an image B containing the data to be filled into the circle. A pixelwise *or* using ImageOps(or,|) of A and B creates the image in Figure 18.3 (right).

18.7   2–D Views of 3–D Polyhedral Objects

Figure 18.4 shows different views of a polyhedral object. Synthetic views of polyhedral objects can be used in model–based image analysis when 3–D models are used and the recognition of such objects has to be verified in the image. A projection of the model to the estimated position is performed and the matches are then inspected. To this effect, we outline three steps to implement a program for the generation of synthetic views of 3–D objects, where we do not care about hidden lines or occluded parts of the object.

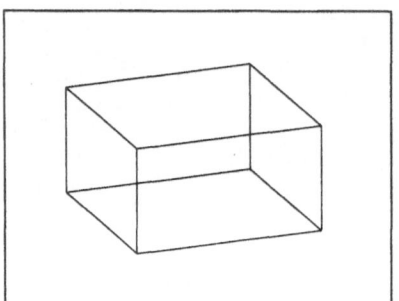 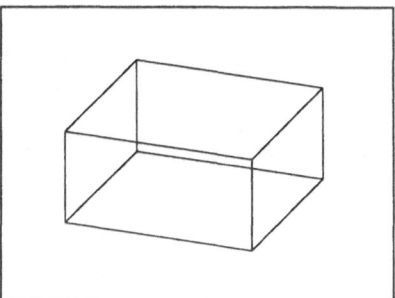

Figure 18.4   Different views of a polyhedral object

First, we write a program which creates a synthetic white image including black points at specified locations. The coordinates of three–dimensional points and their gray–level in the projection are parameters of the function call, as well as the transformation from the 3–D world coordinates to the 2–D image plane. The transformation consists of a 3–D rotation, a 3–D translation, and a projection. There exist various types of 3–D rotations. It depends on the given application which mathematical representation is appropriate [Kan90]. From a mathematical point of view, the easiest way is to multiply rotations around the axes of the world coordinate system.

The columns of the rotation matrix R_{ϕ_x} which rotates 3–D points around the x–axis by the angle ϕ_x are defined by the images of the three unit vectors. Obviously, a rotation around the x–axis does not change the vector $(1, 0, 0)^T$, but the vector $(0, 1, 0)^T$ is transformed to $(0, \cos \phi, -\sin \phi)^T$ and the vector $(0, 0, 1)^T$ to $(0, \sin \phi_x, \cos \phi_x)^T$ (c.f. Figure 18.5). The resulting matrix is thus

$$R_{\phi_x} = \begin{pmatrix} 1 & 0 & 0 \\ 0 & \cos \phi_x & \sin \phi_x \\ 0 & -\sin \phi_x & \cos \phi_x \end{pmatrix} \tag{18.5}$$

The matrices R_{ϕ_y} and R_{ϕ_z} are computed in a similar manner, and the complete rotation R is therefore

$$R = R_{\phi_x} R_{\phi_y} R_{\phi_z} \quad . \tag{18.6}$$

The projection onto the 2–D image plane of a rotated and translated 3–D point can be done using several mappings. The perspective and the orthographic projection have already been discussed in Chapter 1. Therefore, the remaining problem is the construction

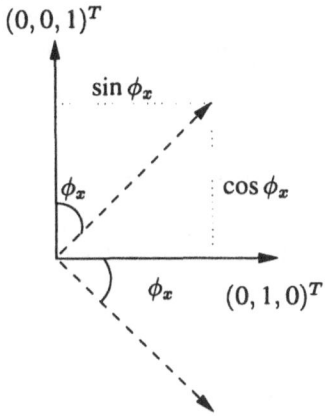

Figure 18.5 Rotation of unit vectors spanning the 3–D space

of digital straight lines which are defined by pairs of 2–D points. The easiest way of computing digital lines is to compute the analytical form of the corresponding straight lines, i.e., the 2–D coordinates (x, y) have to satisfy

$$y \;=\; m\,x + t \quad .$$
(18.7)

The digital points can be computed using the closest digital points in the image grid. The results are usually not convincing and computationally expensive. A more efficient algorithm to compute digital lines is the method attributed to Bresenham, which requires only integer arithmetics. This is a standard algorithm in the field of computer graphics, and is therefore not discussed here [Bre87].

18.8   Single Stereo Images

Recently, *single stereo images* (SIS) have become very popular. They look very mysterious on the first glance. Nevertheless, the idea those images are based on is fairly simple. Humans have two eyes. If someone looks at a point in the three–dimensional space, this point can be seen by each eye — if no occlusion occurs. The projection of this point on an image plane along the eye's ray causes a separate two–dimensional point for each eye. In autostereograms the corresponding points are elements of *one* image and get the same gray–level. Figure 18.6 (left) shows the geometrical relations. Since we have similar triangles, the distance between both projected points is

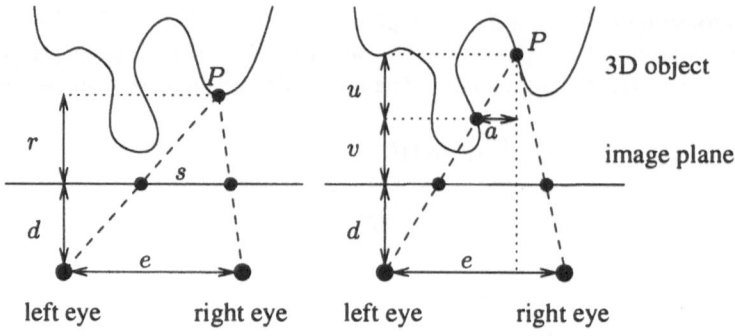

Figure 18.6 One 3–D point gets two points in the image plane (left); hidden point removal (right)

$$s = \frac{r \cdot e}{r + d} \quad . \tag{18.8}$$

If a range image is used as input data, formula (18.8) yields for each 3–D surface point the corresponding coordinates of the two–dimensional image points.

Technically speaking, it is incorrect to plot a stereo pair into the image plane which corresponds to a 3–D point on the object, being visible to one eye only, Figure 18.6 (right). If we do so, we will get ambiguities close to depth steps in the range values. Let (x_l, y_l) and (x_p, y_p) the 2–D coordinates of the left eye and the object point P. The distance u is computed by

$$u = \frac{a \cdot (d + r)}{|x_p - x_l|} \quad , \tag{18.9}$$

where $r = u + v$ is the depth value known from the range image. This equation can be used to decide, whether a point is visible by both eyes by comparing u and the corresponding range value for all admissible values of a. If the range value exceeds or is equal to $v = r - u$, the ray is intercepted and thus the point is not visible.

The geometric relationships needed for the implementation of a SIS generator can easily be derived. We can then compute the corresponding points for each of the range values. These correspondences are visualized by the assignment of identical gray–levels to each pair of pixels. The gray–levels necessary for coloring can be taken from a random image (see Sect.18.4). Figure 18.7 shows an example of an automatically generated SIS.[4]

---

[4]Generated by a program of Maja Gerkšič originally for the workshop proceedings of [Pav94].

Figure 18.7 Example of a single stereo image. To get the 3–D effect, the image has to be scaled such that the center of the two black boxes on the top are in a distance of 1.5cm.

18.9 Textures

Natural objects often have a structure which looks regular when seen from a large distance and irregular in a close–up view. Imagine, for example, an image of a corn field or a carpet on the floor. This kind of structure is called *texture* in computer graphics and image processing.

In [Kle95; p. 45–48] a simple algorithm for texture generation is described. Given parameters a_{lu}, a_u, a_{ru}, and a_l, with values from the interval $[-50, 50]$, and a parameter $n \in [50, 200]$, we create an $M \times N$ gray–level image f with G gray–levels. We define $H := (G - 1)/2$. The gray–values of the image are computed sequentially line by line as shown in the structogram in Figure 18.8. Let Z be a uniformly distributed random variable in the range $[0, G - 1]$. The function $r(x, y)$ creates noise with uniform distribution by

$$r(x,y) = (Z - H)\frac{n}{100} \qquad\qquad (18.10)$$

Create simple texture
$\forall x, \forall y : f(x,y) = 0$
FOR $y \in [2 \ldots N - 1]$
FOR $x \in [2 \ldots M - 1]$
$q :=$ $f(x-1,y-1) - 0.01Ha_{lu} + f(x,y-1) - 0.01Ha_u +$ $f(x+1,y-1) - 0.01Ha_{ru} + f(x-1,y) - 0.01Ha_l + r(x,y)$
$p := \begin{cases} H+q, & \text{if } 0 \le H+q \le G-1 \\ 0, & \text{if } H+q < 0 \\ G-1, & \text{otherwise} \end{cases}$
$f(x,y) := \min\{H + p, G - 1\}$

Figure 18.8 Simple texture generation

Examples of synthetic images generated using this technique and natural textures are shown in Figure 18.9.

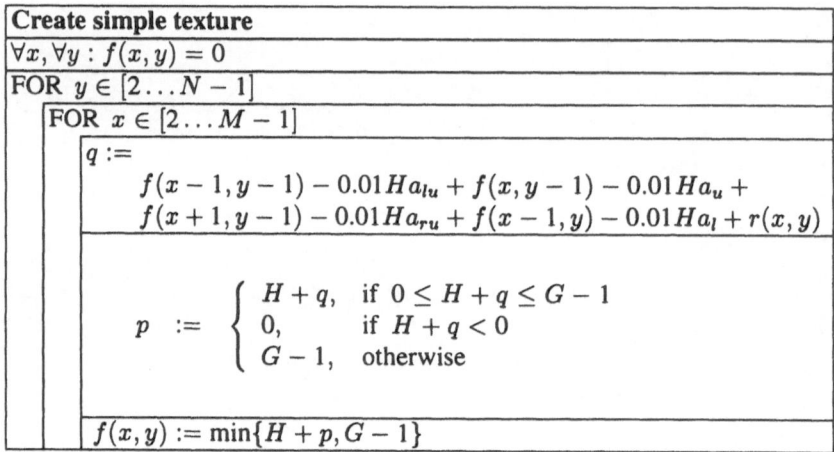

Figure 18.9 Example of synthetic (left, middle) and natural textures (fabric, right)

Exercises

18.a   Use the functions in Sect. 18.4 and build a program `CreateImage` where options allow the generation of different noisy images with different parameters.

18.b   Generate a synthetic range image of a polyhedral object.

18.c   Write a program which reads a range image, a noise image, and computes an autostereogram.

18.d   Implement a class which allows the generation of speech signals representing parameterized trigonometrical functions. The class should also provide methods for additive superposition and other operations on these speech signals.

18.e   Using the algorithms given in Sect. 18.9, extend your main program to create textured images.

18.f   Extend Program 180 to a complete program which reads images and does arithmetic on the pixels.

18.g   Extend Exercise 18.f to color images.

18.h   Use the textual description of the algorithm in Sect. 18.5 for an implementation of a random number generator for normally distributed numbers with mean zero and variance one. Use this function to generate a Gaussian image where the mean gray–level is determined by the parameter m. The variance can be modified by choosing different quantization steps of the continuous density function.

19 Filtering and Smoothing Signals

Filters and operators used for smoothing signals are fundamental parts of the preprocessing stage. In Sect. 12.9 we already showed how the Fourier transform can be used to filter a signal. Filters, in general, can be designed for two different domains: the frequency and the spatial–domain. In the following sections we will filter images in the spatial domain, rather than using the spectral domain.

In chapter 18 we implemented some algorithms for generating noisy signals. Noise in images or other signals used for pattern recognition purposes is an undesirable effect and has to be reduced or eliminated, as far as possible. The reduction of noise can be realized by the smoothing of patterns. Many different approaches for smoothing and filtering signals can be found in the literature. The following sections will briefly introduce some basic algorithms which are useful for images as well as speech. We describe the more complicated case of two–dimensional signals; the simpler version for one–dimensional signals can easily be derived from the examples.

Beside the elimination of noise, digital filters are also used for emphasizing interesting parts in an image, such as regions or edges. For getting higher continuity in digital signals, smoothing operators are used.

In the first chapter we introduced and discussed the problems of how digital images can be computed out of analog signals. The quantization of intensity values induces noise effects which can be measured by the signal to noise ratio (Eq. 8.31). The following sections describe filters which reduce noise and smooth an image. One section is dedicated to the problem of how to magnify an image to double size using linear reconstruction techniques.

At the end of this chapter, we extend the hierarchy of image operator classes which we started to implement in Sect. 17.5.

19.1 Linear Filters

A filter is called *linear* if it can be expressed by the convolution of a signal with a mask, and the filtering operation is a linear transform from signals to signals. In the case of speech signals represented as vectors, the mask is a 1–D vector. In contrast, images are represented as matrices. The mask is thus a small matrix often also called a window. In the following we will discuss some elementary linear filters; another, more complicated linear filter, which mathematically characterizes the human speech production, is introduced in Sect. 23.7.

Mean–filtering is a very simple and obvious linear smoothing technique. A current pixel gray–level or value in a time–ordered signal is set to the mean of neighboring sample data. In image processing applications the neighborhood is usually defined by a quadratic 3×3 or 5×5 mask. For time ordered signals the mean is computed using some predecessors or successors of the current position. For an $n \times n$ *mean–filter*, the matrix of size $n \times n$ to convolve with is:

$$\frac{1}{n^2} \begin{pmatrix} 1 & 1 & \dots & 1 \\ 1 & 1 & \dots & 1 \\ \vdots & \vdots & \ddots & \vdots \\ 1 & 1 & \dots & 1 \end{pmatrix}. \qquad (19.1)$$

It should be mentioned that this filter smears the signal values. Images will blur and edge detection is made more difficult as a result of its use. The detection of homogeneous regions, however, is simplified if this filtering operation is used. In practice, mean–filters are easily implemented and the runtime depends on the image size and grows linearly in proportion to this measure. The runtime of an efficient implementation is approximately independent of the size of a given neighborhood. At the end of this chapter we list a simple implementation of this filter.

Figure 19.1 Mean–filter (left) and Gaussian–filter on quadratic subimage (right) of Figure 11.2

Each gray–level in the defined neighborhood is weighted with the same value in the case of the mean–filter (c.f. Eq. (19.1)). It is a reasonable assumption that increasing the distance should imply a decrease in weights. In the case of *Gaussian–filters* these weights are defined using the Gaussian density function (c.f. Sect. 8.3). A digitized version for a 3×3 neighborhood[1] is, for example,

---

[1] Assuming quadratic pixels.

$$\frac{1}{16} \begin{pmatrix} 1 & 2 & 1 \\ 2 & 4 & 2 \\ 1 & 2 & 1 \end{pmatrix}. \tag{19.2}$$

Of course, this filter is linear as well. Figure 19.1 shows examples for images filtered by mean and Gaussian filters.

Filters, which eliminate rough changes in intensity values and smooth the original signal, remove high frequencies. For that reason, these filters are called *low–pass filters*.

19.2 Rank Order Operations

The general algorithms for rank order operations first require the definition of a neighborhood of the current pixel. Here we use masks of quadratic shape; in general, arbitrary neighborhoods are possible. All gray–levels of the N neighbored pixels $f_1, f_2, \ldots, f_N$ are ordered using the „$\leq$"–relation of real numbers. If the new pixel value is the gray–level of the pixel $f_{\lfloor N/2 \rfloor}$ in the middle of this ordering, we get the so–called *median–filter*.

If we take the minimum f_1 of these ordered values, we get the *erosion–filter*. *Dilatation* is the filter which results from the maximum value f_N. In general, filters which use ordered sequences of its neighbored signal values (such as the examples in Figure 19.2) are elements of the class of *morphological operations*. One more such operation is the morphological edge detector $f_N - f_1$. Morphological operations provide very important tools for compute vision and image analysis. There exists a theoretical framework for morphological operations and their use for high–level computer vision, which cannot be introduced here. For interested readers, we strongly recommend [Ser88].

The rank order operations are fairly easy to implement. The runtime of these algorithms depends linearly on the image size.

The edge preserving character of the median–filter justifies its popularity. If a high signal–to–noise ratio is given, it is recommended to give median–filters priority over other filters (c.f. for example [Mac81]). A lot of research is being done to weight the advantages and disadvantages of this non–linear filter [Bov87, Chi83]. In [Yam81] it is shown that in images with the presence of convex or concave ramp edges and impulsive noise, median filtering will improve edge detection results.

In [Luo94] the median–filter is extended to a corner preserving filter operation called the *smoothed median filter*. The basic idea of this algorithm is a graduated application of median filtering. The 5 × 5 mask is divided into four differing stripes (see Figure 19.3). For each subset of included pixels (1–4) the classical median is computed. The final pixel value of the center of the 5 × 5 mask is computed by the median of the four resulting values of the prior median operations. It can be shown that the described smoothed median filter also suppresses Gaussian noise.

Figure 19.2 Median–filter (left), erosion (middle), and dilation (right)

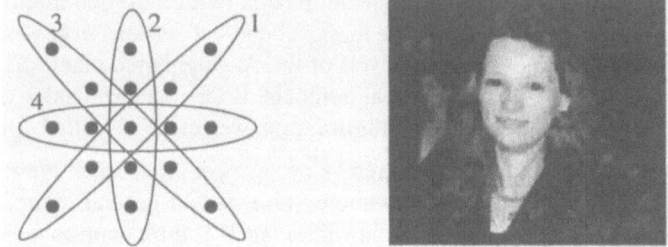

Figure 19.3 Four elliptic masks (1–4) where the median is separately applied (left); result of smoothed–median filtering (right)

19.3   Edge Preserving Smoothing

Another method which is also based on computing the mean of neighbored pixels for smoothing purposes is explained in this section. The selection of pixels for averaging is done by the use of a special technique based on statistical principles. The algorithm suggested in [Nag79] uses for each pixel P nine different 5×5 masks; three of them are shown in Figure 19.4. The pixels in the environment of P with a distinguishing mark are used for the following computations. The symmetrical use of 19.4 (a) and (b) results in eight different masks. Each of these masks include seven points for the calculation of the new gray–level. The contrast mask (c) includes nine elements for the following computations. For each mask we compute the variance (8.9). The mask with the lowest variance is selected. The central pixel P gets the mean value of all points marked in this mask. An example of the result of this filter is shown in 19.5.

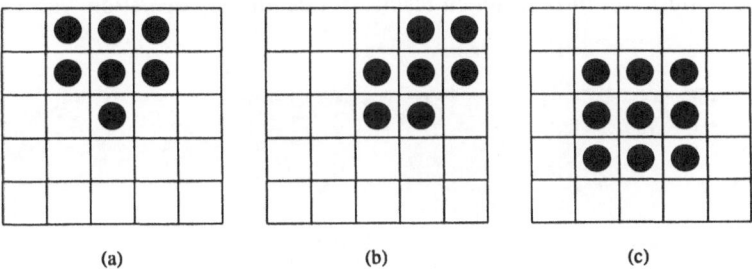

Figure 19.4 Masks for edge preserving smoothing

Figure 19.5 Edge Preserving Filtering

19.4   *K* Nearest Neighbor Averaging

The filter of *K Nearest Neighbor Averaging* [Dav78] is an additional edge preserving filter which can be used iteratively. Let P be a pixel from an array with N points. Take K points out of this array which are closest to the gray–value of the image point P, including P itself. Assign the mean of these points to the pixel P. With a growing value of K, this filter converges to the mean–filter, the reduction of noise grows and the complete image blurs.

It is suggested to use $N = 9$ and $K = 6$ [Dav78]. In this case you take eight neighbors of P and determine the five nearest gray–levels. The mean of the gray–levels of P and the five additional points is assigned to the new intensity of P.

In [Brü90] it is shown that this filter is very powerful. The computation time and the result of smoothing depends on the number of iterations. The runtime increases linearly with the image size. From previous experience it is known that three iterations yield satisfiable results.

Figure 19.6 illustrates three different results of this filtering operation with varying K values.

Figure 19.6 Examples for K−nearest neighbor filtering with $K = 2, 5, 9$

19.5   Conditional Average Filter

Another iteratively applicable filter is suggested in [Pra80] and is called *Conditional Average Filter*. In a 5×5 mask around the central pixel P we compute the mean of all pixels whose difference in the gray−level with the intensity of P is lower or equal to a given threshold θ. The gray−level of P is assigned to this value. The problem of this algorithm is obviously the selection of the threshold θ which is picture dependent. In [Brü90], the threshold θ is computed by $\theta = \alpha \cdot G_{\text{max}}$, where $\alpha \in [0, 1]$ and G_{max} is the maximum gray−level of the image. The best results were made choosing $\alpha = 0.1$. The advantage of conditional averaging is that edges, where the change in gray−levels exceeds θ, are not blurred. Regions, where gray−levels differ with a difference lower or equal to θ, are smoothed. In practice, this filter eliminates weak edges. Therefore, even an adaptive selection of the threshold should be used with caution. Compare the images shown in Figure 19.7, which are computed using different thresholds. Herein, various levels of the smoothing property are illustrated.

The sorting of gray−levels is not necessary, therefore the runtime of conditional average filters is in general lower than the one in Sect. 19.4.

19.6   Linear Reconstruction

Often it is required to change the size of an image (c.f. Figure 19.8). Image resizing requires filter applications. For size reduction we have to apply a low−pass filter in order to fulfill the sampling theorem. Here we show a simple method for image magnification

Figure 19.7 Conditional average for different thresholds ($\theta = 100, 150, 200$)

based on linear reconstruction, i.e. the gray–levels of new pixels are linear combinations of gray–levels of neighbored image points.

To get double size of the image we successively decompose the image into 2×2 squares

$$
\begin{array}{ll}
f_{i,j} & f_{i,j+1} \\
f_{i+1,j} & f_{i+1,j+1}
\end{array}
$$

and compute the gray–levels of five additional points a, b, c, d, and e using linear interpolation between the gray–levels. For that purpose, two gray–levels are connected by a straight line, and the missing value results from the function value of the straight line at the required image point. If the considered point is in the middle of two points, a simple mean computation of gray–levels allows the estimation of the missing value. For instance, if the gray–level of a in

$$
\begin{array}{lll}
f_{i,j} & a & f_{i,j+1} \\
b & c & d \\
f_{i+1,j} & e & f_{i+1,j+1}
\end{array}
$$

has to be computed, we get

$$
a = \frac{f_{i,j} + f_{i,j+1}}{2} \ . \tag{19.3}
$$

The implementation is left as Exercise 19.f.

19.7 Elimination of Noisy Image Rows

Most commercial CCD cameras do not record scenes line by line, but sample first the odd and then the even lines of the image. If we have moving objects in the scene we can observe the so called *interlace effect*.[2] Assume the sampling of each line takes t_s

---

[2]Most video cameras capture first a *half frame* consisting of the odd numbered lines, than the second half frame using even numbered lines. These frames capture data at different moments of time which may be a problem, when objects in the scene are moving.

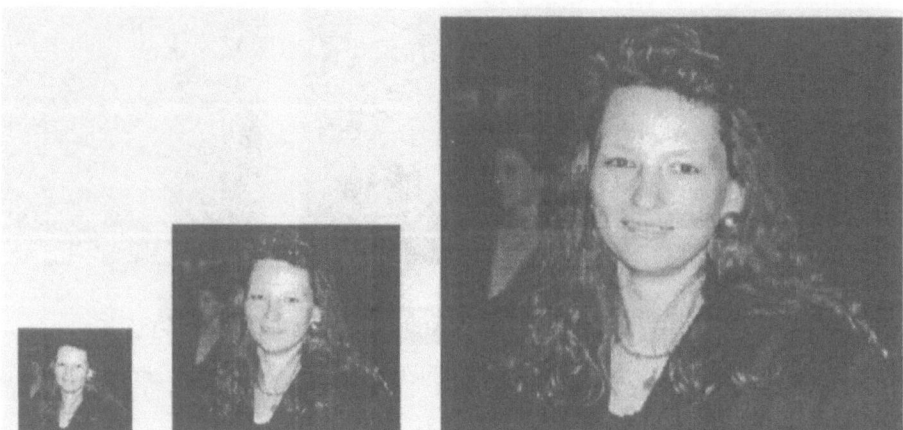

Figure 19.8 Examples for enlargements

ms time. When we start at time t at the first line of the image, the record of the second line will be $n\,t_s$ ms later, where $2n$ represents the number of lines of the CCD chip. Consequently, a moving object can change its position in $n\,t_s$ ms, and the odd and even image rows are shifted. This shift can be computed analytically, if the technical data of the CCD chip and the speed of the moving object are known. In practice, there is nothing known a priori about the moving object. Therefore, we have to find another – more convenient – approach to remove interlace effects. In practice, it is sometimes sufficient to cancel rows with even numbers and to double each odd numbered row although this violates the sampling theorem.

If rows of the image do not include the moving object we have no interlace and therefore nothing to change. One possible approach to locate and remove interlace effects in the image is the use of statistical methods. Based on the experience that the transition of one row to its successor does not include high rapidity of gray–levels, using a correlation coefficient we can decide whether one row is corrupted by interlacing or some other kind of noise. If the test is positive, we have to reduce this disturbance.

Let $f_{i,j}$ ($0 \leq i < M$, and $0 \leq j < N$) be the gray–levels of the given image. We take the covariance $\sigma_{r,r+1}$ of two successive rows r and $r + 1$

$$\sigma_{r,r+1} \;=\; \frac{1}{N}\sum_{k=0}^{N-1}(f_{r,k} - \mu_r)(f_{r+1,k} - \mu_{r+1}) \quad , \tag{19.4}$$

where μ_r and μ_{r+1} are the means of gray–levels of the actual rows. The correlation coefficient

$$\rho_{r,r+1} \;=\; \frac{\sigma_{r,r+1}}{\sqrt{\sigma_{r,r}\sigma_{r+1,r+1}}} \tag{19.5}$$

yields the following decision rule for two rows: If $|\rho_{r,r+1}| > \theta$, where θ is a threshold value, we will do no changes. Otherwise, we say both rows are not similar, consequently we have to smooth the transition from row r to $r + 1$. This can be done by copying r to $r + 1$ or by averaging two rows.

19.8 Resolution Hierarchies

The runtime behavior of many algorithms, for example, filtering, edge detection, or region segmentation, depends on the size of the processed image. For some applications one does not need maximal image resolution. In active vision, for instance, one of the main principles is selectivity of the algorithms in resolution. This can lead to a lower computation time needed, for example, in real–time image processing. Another example is some edge detection algorithm which first searches for edges on a low resolution image, and then takes these edges as an initial edge estimation for another search at a higher resolution. In this way, a more precise result can be obtained, stepwise.

The representation of an image at several resolutions leads to *image pyramids* (which look like the pyramid in Figure 19.8, although it is computed differently). An image pyramid is a series of images $f_k(i, j)$, where $0 < k < n$, and $0 \leq i, j < 2^n$. Herein, n is given by the size of the original image. The pyramid is created by a bottom up approach. Formally, the image $f_k(i, j)$ is computed from $f_{k+1}(i, j)$ applying

$$f_k(i, j) = \text{reduce } (f_{k+1}(i, j)) \quad . \tag{19.6}$$

Herein, the function reduce($\cdot$) is called the *generating function*. For each reduced image both the resolution and the sample density decreased. One simple form of the function reduce($\cdot$) is defined by

$$\text{reduce}(f_{k+1}(i, j)) = \sum_{m=a}^{b} \sum_{n=c}^{d} w(m, n) f_{k+1}(2i + m, 2j + n) \quad , \tag{19.7}$$

where $w(m, n) \in \mathbf{R}$ is a weighting function and a, b, c, d are integers. A simple version of $w(m, n)$ and the integral constants is given by $w(m, n) = \frac{1}{4}, a = c = 0$, and $b = d = 1$. In this case, the pyramid is generated by an averaging process.

There exist many variations in the way, the next lower resolution has to be computed. One possible approach is to use another weighting function or another type of function reduce($\cdot$), for example, a local maximum, minimum or morphological function.

One special case of a pyramid is the so called *Gaussian pyramid* [Bur83]:

$$a = c = -2, b = d = 2, w(m, n) = \hat{w}(m)\hat{w}(n) \tag{19.8}$$

with

$$\hat{w}(0) = \alpha \tag{19.9}$$

$$\hat{w}(-1) = \hat{w}(1) = \frac{1}{4} \tag{19.10}$$

```
class Mean: public LowPass {          // mean filter as a special case
  private:
    int xs, ys;                       // size of the filter mask
  public:
    Mean(int sizeh, int sizev) : xs(sizeh/2), ys(sizev/2) {}
    virtual void operator() (const GrayLevelImage&,GrayLevelImage&) ;
};
class GaussFilter: public LowPass {   // gauss filter as a special case
    double sigma;                     // parameters of the gaussian
    double * mask;                    // filter mask
  public:
    GaussFilter (double s);
    virtual void operator() (const GrayLevelImage&,GrayLevelImage&) ;
};
```

181

$$\hat{w}(-2) \ = \ \hat{w}(2) \ = \ \frac{1}{4} - \frac{\alpha}{2} \ . \tag{19.11}$$

The Gaussian pyramid results in a sequence of images. Each computed image represents a low–pass filtered copy of its predecessor in the given hierarchy. In [Bur83] it is shown that the Gaussian pyramid construction generates images with a band limit one octave lower than their predecessors. Thus, the pre–conditions of the sampling theorem are valid. The implementation is left as Exercise 19.g.

19.9 Image Operator Hierarchy

Using the function call operator as introduced in Sect. 17.5, we implement a hierarchy of operator classes which declares an interface even for future extensions by inheritance.

Program 181 extends Program 178 and declares the interface to filter operations which transform one gray–level image into another. A simple implementation of a mean filter which also works at the border of images is given in Program 182.

Note, that we do not declare the operator() to be const, since in future (derived) classes we might want to record temporary values inside the class during computation of the operation. This is possible only for a non–constant function. A virtual operator() is different from operator() const, i.e., the declaration will *hide* the inherited virtual function. This would most likely be a source of errors, or at least cause confusion for the programmers.

Exercises

19.a In Chapter 18 several noise generators were described. Write a program which admits the addition of noise of a special type to a given image. Verify by exper-

```
void Mean::operator() (const GrayLevelImage& in, GrayLevelImage& out)
{
  for (int i = 0 ; i < in.getysize(); ++i)              // all image lines
    for (int j = 0 ; j < in.getxsize(); ++j) {          // all image columns
      int r = 0, c = 0;                                 // temporary values
      for (int k = -1* ys ; k <= ys ; ++k) {            // all mask lines
        for (int l = -1 * xs ; l <= xs; ++l) {          // all mask columns
          if ((i + k < 0) || (i + k >= in.getysize()) || // works also
              (j + l < 0) || (j + l >= in.getxsize())))  // at borders
            continue;                                   // use only valid indices
          ++c; r += in[i][j]; }                         // sum up and count
      }
      out [i][j] = r / c; // store mean in output;  c always >= 1 !
    }
}
```
182

iments the characteristics of introduced filter operations – like the suppression of Gaussian noise by the use of smoothed median filtering.

19.b   Write a program which visualizes the difference of two filtered images. Explain the observation if you use the difference image of erosion and dilatation.

19.c   The idea of smoothed median filtering is a subsequent application of the median filter to different sets of pixels. Use this idea to develop other hybrid filters using other types than median operations. Which object–oriented programming techniques provide useful tools for realizing this kind of *polymorphism*? Do as many experiments as you like and formalize the observed results of your filters.

19.d   Implement a class hierarchy for filters as declared in Program 181.

19.e   Show that the total number M of pixels of a Gaussian pyramid is bounded by

$$M < \frac{4}{3}N^2 \quad , \tag{19.12}$$

where the first image has a resolution of $N \times N$ and a decreasing factor of two per stage.

19.f   Implement a function doubleSize which magnifies the input image using the sketched technique. Discuss different strategies for the computation of the non–unique gray–level c.

Use your program and magnify an arbitrary image iteratively. Which effects are observable? Is it possible that images shown in Figure 19.8 are computed using the above method?

19.g   For this exercise a class image pyramid for images has to be implemented. Start with an abstract base class, which contains methods for computing a weighting function, a generating function, and methods to select special resolutions of the pyramid elements. Take into consideration that several image types are possible, for example, binary images, gray–level images or edge images. Derive a concrete class and then implement the special form of a Gaussian pyramid for a GrayLevelImage.

20 Histogram Algorithms

Histograms were already introduced in Chapter 8. In the following sections we will
define several useful image preprocessing steps using histograms. Each algorithm can
easily be implemented and tested applying the implementation of a class *Histogram*.
In addition to standard methods working on gray–level images, we also introduce two
color image algorithms based on histograms.

20.1 Discriminant and Least Squares Threshold

Histograms are conventionally used for computing a binary image $[b_{i,j}]_{1\leq i\leq N,1\leq j\leq M}$
from a given gray–level image $[f_{i,j}]_{1\leq i\leq N,1\leq j\leq M}$. Binary images reduce input data and
they are often applied for separating an object from its background. The *binarization* is
usually done by a threshold operation which is defined by

$$b_{i,j} = \begin{cases} 0 & \text{, if } f_{i,j} \leq \theta \\ 1 & \text{, otherwise} \end{cases} \qquad (20.1)$$

A suitable value θ for binarization can be found by creating a gray–level histogram.
If the background and the observed object have considerably different gray–levels,
then both regions can be separated by looking at relative frequencies in the histogram.
This distinguishing of an object from its background produces what is known as a
bimodal histogram: the gray–levels for object and background pixels will have the
highest relative frequencies, other gray–levels will be weighted by lower probabilities.
The threshold, which divides up the pixels into object and background image points, is
assumed to be between the maxima found within the histogram. Figure 20.1 shows two
examples of binarization. The threshold was computed using the minimum between the
two maxima of gray–levels in the (smoothed) bimodal histogram. The second binary
image should show a lab scene (c.f. Figure 20.2), but it is totally black. This is due to the
fact that this fairly complex scene does not satisfy the condition that only foreground
and background intensities occur. The associated histogram is not bimodal such that the
suggested method necessarily fails.

This holds for many gray–level images. The technique based on bimodal histograms is
not applicable generally, because foreground and background usually have more than
just the two extrema in the histogram. Methods other than valley–seeking are required
for the determination of the threshold. A promising approach to solve this problem is to

Figure 20.1 Binary image created from Figure 14.2 (left) and from Figure 11.2 (black image on the right) with bimodal histogram analysis

use some statistical information about the gray–levels and formalizing an optimization problem for the separation of two classes, i.e. object and background pixels.

As in the above case a threshold θ has to be computed. We define the values of admissible gray–levels by $g_1, g_2, \ldots, g_L$. The discrete probability for each gray–level in a given image can be easily determined by a gray–level histogram. Let $f_{i,j}$ be the gray–level at the image point (i, j). The probability p_ν that the image point (i, j) has the gray–level g_ν is the relative frequency

$$p(f_{i,j} = g_\nu) = p_\nu := \frac{|\text{image points with gray–level } g_\nu|}{|\text{image points}|} \quad . \tag{20.2}$$

The bipartition of all gray–levels is done using a threshold $\theta = g_l$, where $l \in \{1, 2, \ldots, L\}$. Let $^l\Omega_1$ and $^l\Omega_2$ be the disjoint sets of gray–levels induced by a given threshold value g_l, i.e.

$$^l\Omega_1 = \{f_{i,j} ; f_{i,j} \le g_l\} \quad \text{and} \quad ^l\Omega_2 = \{f_{i,j} ; f_{i,j} > g_l\} \quad . \tag{20.3}$$

Using this notation, the probability that an image point lies in one of the above classes is

$$p(^l\Omega_1) = \sum_{\nu=1}^{l} p_\nu \quad \text{and} \quad p(^l\Omega_2) = 1 - p(^l\Omega_1) \quad . \tag{20.4}$$

The threshold θ is expected to satisfy the following properties:

1. $p(^l\Omega_1)$ and $p(^l\Omega_2)$ should not be equal to zero, and
2. the absolute difference of means for the gray–levels appearing in Ω_1 and Ω_2 should be as large as possible.

A criterion which takes into account these requirements is the objective function

$$J_l = p(^l\Omega_1)\, p(^l\Omega_2) \cdot \left(\sum_{\nu=1}^{l} \frac{p_\nu g_\nu}{p(^l\Omega_1)} - \sum_{\nu=l+1}^{L} \frac{p_\nu g_\nu}{p(^l\Omega_2)} \right)^2 \quad , \tag{20.5}$$

which has to be maximized with respect to the gray–level index l:

$$l = \underset{l'}{\mathrm{argmax}} \; J_{l'} \quad .\tag{20.6}$$

Thus, the computation of $\theta = g_l$ using the introduced *discriminant analysis* is bound by L evaluations of J_l. An example for a binary image computed using the threshold computed by (20.6) is shown in Figure 20.2. More details concerning this technique can be found in [Nie83].

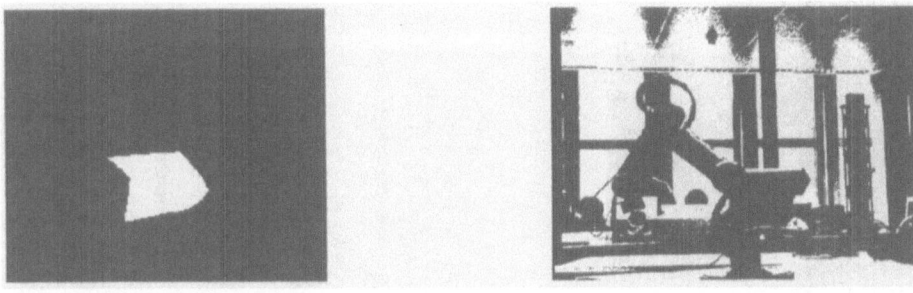

Figure 20.2 Binary image created from Figure 14.2 (left) and from Figure 11.2 (right) with discriminant analysis

20.2 Histogram Entropy Thresholding

We will now define an alternative algorithm for threshold determination using the entropy concept (c.f. Chapter 8). Let p_ν $(0 \le \nu < L)$ the discrete probabilities for observing the gray–level g_ν. Now, we search for a bipartition (20.3) of the set of gray–levels. Let θ be the threshold value g_l and let us assume that this threshold induces two distributions for the following sets of formal random variables

$$A_l = \left\{ \frac{p_1}{\sum_{\nu=1}^{l} p_\nu}, \frac{p_2}{\sum_{\nu=1}^{l} p_\nu}, \cdots, \frac{p_l}{\sum_{\nu=1}^{l} p_\nu} \right\} \quad ,\tag{20.7}$$

$$B_l = \left\{ \frac{p_{l+1}}{1 - \sum_{\nu=1}^{l} p_\nu}, \frac{p_{l+2}}{1 - \sum_{\nu=1}^{l} p_\nu}, \cdots, \frac{p_L}{1 - \sum_{\nu=1}^{l} p_\nu} \right\} \quad .\tag{20.8}$$

For each set, the entropy (8.29) can be computed as

$$H(A_l) = -\sum_{\mu=1}^{l} \frac{p_\mu}{\sum_{\nu=1}^{l} p_\nu} \log \frac{p_\mu}{\sum_{\nu=1}^{l} p_\nu}\tag{20.9}$$

and

$$H(B_l) = -\sum_{\mu=l+1}^{L} \frac{p_\mu}{1 - \sum_{\nu=1}^{l} p_\nu} \log \frac{p_\mu}{1 - \sum_{\nu=1}^{l} p_\nu}.\tag{20.10}$$

The optimal threshold for binarization results from the entropy maximization of the complete image, i.e. the sum of the entropy of the distributions A_l and B_l. The index of the discriminating gray–level $g_l = \theta$ is computed, solving the optimization task

$$l \;=\; \operatorname*{argmax}_{l'} \left(H(A_{l'}) + H(B_{l'}) \right). \tag{20.11}$$

Here again, the complexity for computing the required threshold θ is bounded by the number of gray–levels L. An application of this threshold for binarization is visualized in Figure 20.3.

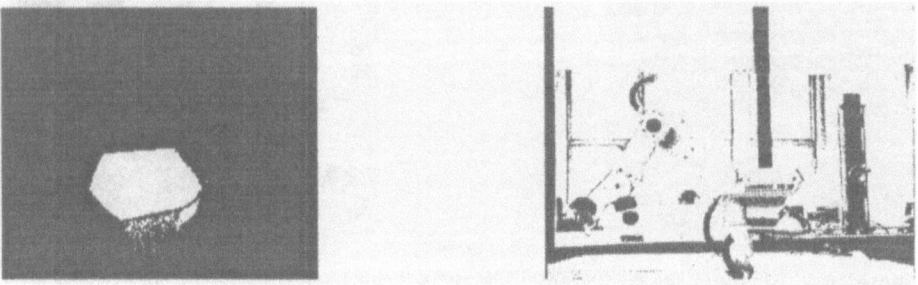

Figure 20.3 Binary image created from Figure 14.2 (left) and from Figure 11.2 (right) with entropy analysis

20.3 Multi–thresholding

If more than one object is superimposed to a homogeneous background such that the gray–level histogram has multiple maxima, the histogram is multimodal. The image should be decomposed into regions with different gray–levels. Each object and the background get uniform, but different gray–levels.

A straightforward approach for the computation of the set of thresholds can be done by the optimization of the following multivariate function, which is an obvious generalization of the entropy method of the previous section:

$$\Psi(l_1, l_2, \ldots, l_k) \;=\; \log \left(\sum_{\nu=1}^{l_1} p_\nu \right) + \log \left(\sum_{\nu=l_1+1}^{l_2} p_\nu \right) + \ldots + \log \left(\sum_{\nu=l_k+1}^{L} p_\nu \right)$$

$$- \frac{\sum_{\nu=1}^{l_1} p_\nu \log p_\nu}{\sum_{\nu=1}^{l_1} p_\nu} - \frac{\sum_{\nu=l_1+1}^{l_2} p_\nu \log p_\nu}{\sum_{\nu=l_1+1}^{l_2} p_\nu} - \ldots - \frac{\sum_{\nu=l_k+1}^{L} p_\nu \log p_\nu}{\sum_{\nu=l_k+1}^{L} p_\nu} \tag{20.12}$$

where the number k of different gray–levels must be known a priori. We simply sum up the entropies of the partition and maximize this sum. The set of thresholds is computed by solving the following discrete optimization problem:

$$(l_1, l_2, \ldots, l_k) \quad = \quad \underset{(l'_1, l'_2, \ldots, l'_k)}{\mathrm{argmax}} \quad \Psi(l'_1, l'_2, \ldots, l'_k) \quad . \tag{20.13}$$

A simple and non–sophisticated implementation will do a recursive maximization of objective function (20.12) with respect to the unknown parameters $l_1, l_2, \ldots, l_k$. Figure 20.4 shows examples for multi–thresholding.

Figure 20.4 Images created from Figure 11.2 using multi–thresholding ($k = 5, 10, 15$)

20.4 Global Histogram Equalization

Normally, the distribution of range values is an a priori unknown. One possible way to get information about the underlying statistics of the gray–levels of an image is the computation of the relative frequency of possible values in the observed sample. Histograms render possible graphical representations of these frequencies. The discrete distribution of these quantities is shown in an empirical distribution by adding the relative frequencies successively from left to right. Figure 8.1 shows a gray–level image, the computed histogram of gray–levels, and the associated discrete empirical distribution.

The transform of histograms is quite easy. A frequently used technique in the preprocessing phase of image analysis systems is gray–level scaling using histograms and the associated discrete distributions. In this connection, the discrete or continuous distribution is adapted to a special distribution – for example, uniform distribution – with the help of a distortion function. For this, the y–axis is divided up into equidistant intervals and reflected to the x–axis. In Figure 20.5 all gray–levels in the interval $[x_0, x_1[$ are mapped to the new value 2. In Figure 20.6 the result of the described linearization is shown, including the gray–level image, the distribution, and the resulting histogram. The distribution is not exactly linear, but the differences in the gray–level frequencies are considerable compared to Figure 8.1.

Practically established transformations based on histograms are the linear or logarithmic representation of speech signals with eight bits, which are given with twelve bit. In image processing, the distortion of gray–levels is used e.g. to raise the contrast of a picture. A higher contrast of the image causes the visual impression that the image is more suitable for automatic processing. Indeed, the histogram linearization does not increase

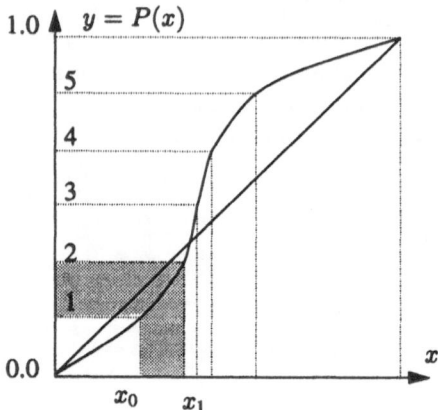

Figure 20.5 Linearization of discrete distributions

the information of an image. If programs work well on linearized images and yield no or bad results for the original ones, it shows that the implementation depends on hard encoded thresholds which expect higher contrasts. Well implemented and robust image processing operators usually do not show such dependencies.

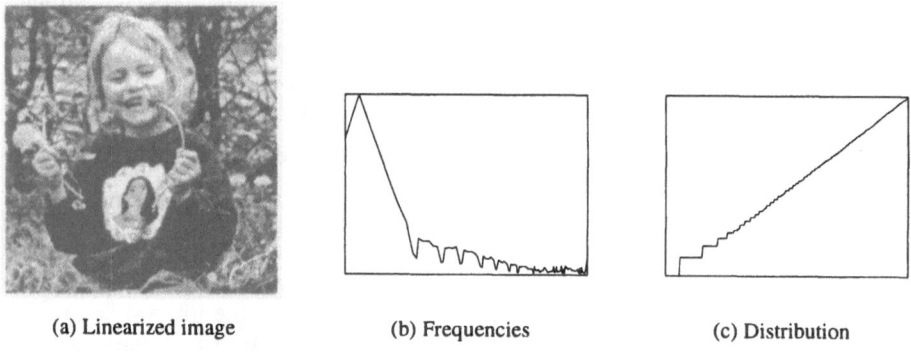

(a) Linearized image   (b) Frequencies   (c) Distribution

Figure 20.6 Results of linearization on image in Figure 8.1

20.5   Local Histogram Equalization

The principle of local histogram linearization is to use a window of size $M \times M$ instead of the complete image. The transformation of the central pixel in the window is found by equalizing the histogram of the local window. The discrete density function p_ν is defined by the relative frequencies of each gray–level g_ν in the mask. The discrete distribution function is known to be

$$P(g_l) \ = \ \sum_{\nu=1}^{l} p_\nu \ . \tag{20.14}$$

Due to the small window size, the histogram equalization transformation T over the given window, which maps gray–levels to gray–levels, is now approximated by

$$T(f_{i,j}) \ = \ \lfloor g_{max} P(f_{i,j}) \rfloor \tag{20.15}$$

for the central pixel at the point (i, j). Herein g_{max} is the maximal gray–level of the considered window. After this transform the gray–levels of the considered window are uniformly distributed and elements of $\{1, 2, \ldots, g_{max}\}$. This result is based on the fact that the random variable $x = P(f)$ is uniformly distributed, where $P(f)$ denotes an arbitrary cumulative distribution for gray–levels f. This is true, because the cumulative density $P_x(x)$ of the random variable $x \in [0, 1]$ is monotonic and thus holds

$$P_x(x) \ = \ p(P(f) \le x) = p(f \le P^{-1}(x)) = P(P^{-1}(x)) = x \ . \tag{20.16}$$

In Figure 20.7 you can find an example for local histogram equalization.

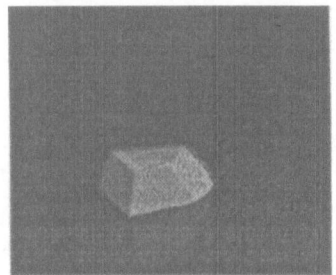 

Figure 20.7 Result of local histogram equalization on Figure 14.2 (left) and Figure 11.2 (right) with window size 5×5

20.6 Look up Table Transformation

The transformation of gray–levels via histograms is often used as a preprocessing step. Another transform of gray–levels g can be defined by a function $f(g) \in \{0, 1, \ldots, 255\}$, for instance, a univariate polynomial.

Two functions $f_1(g)$ and $f_2(g)$ in Figure 20.8 describe the assignment of each gray–level of the original image (g–axis) to the new value. The distortion in this example is based on a polygon or a third order polynomial

$$f(g) \;=\; \sum_{i=0}^{3} f_i \, g^i \tag{20.17}$$

which is determined by four points $(0, a)$, (b, c), (d, e), and $(255, f)$.

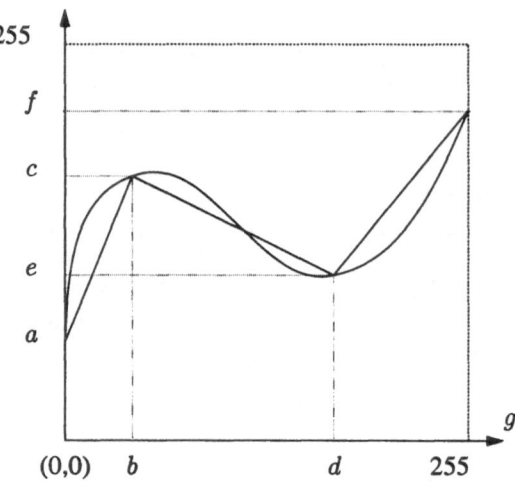

Figure 20.8 Correction of gray–levels

The computation of the coefficients can be done by solving the system of linear equations:

$$
\begin{aligned}
a &= f_0, & (20.18) \\
c &= f_0 + f_1\, b + f_2\, b^2 + f_3\, b^3, & (20.19) \\
e &= f_0 + f_1\, d + f_2\, d^2 + f_3\, d^3, \text{ and} & (20.20) \\
f &= f_0 + 255 f_1 + 255^2 f_2 + 255^3 f_3 . & (20.21)
\end{aligned}
$$

A solution of the parameters is given in Appendix C.1. Those symbolic computations are usually done by computer algebra systems like MAPLE, Mathematica or Axiom. An application of this technique is shown in Figure 20.9.

The introduced look up table transform can be defined by arbitrary functions and is, of course, not restricted to polynomials. This transformation is generally called *gamma correction*.

Figure 20.9 Result of a look up table transform with polyline ($a = 50, b = 70, c = 90, d = 144, e = 200, f = 100$) on Figure 14.2 (left) and Figure 11.2 (right)

```
class Histogram {                           // class for 1-D histograms
  Vector<int> bins;                         // absolute frequencies
  long nelem;                               // number of entries
 public:
  Histogram(int);                           // number of bins
  Histogram(const Histogram &);             // copy constructor
  void smooth(void);                        // smooth the histogram
  double operator[] (int i) const;          // relative frequency of occurrence i
  void addto(int i, int v = 1);             // advance bin i to a value v
  long at(int i) const;                     // return bin i

};
int bimodal_threshold(const Histogram&);        // minimum between two maxima
int least_square_threshold(const Histogram&);   // least square method
int max_entropy_threshold(const Histogram&);    // entropy method
```
183

```
double Histogram::operator[] (int i) const {return bins[i]/(1.0*nelem); }
Histogram::addto(int i, int v) { nelem a=v; bins[i] += v; }
Histogram::Histogram(int nb)  : bins(nb) { nelem = 0; }
```
184

20.7 Histogram Class

The previous sections show that there are a lot of operations on histograms which can naturally be implemented as a class Histogram. The concrete representation and computation of histograms is hidden from its users. A suitable header file for this class is given below (Program 183). The internal representation of a histogram is based on a vector of integers, i.e. Vector<int>. The index represents the current gray-level and the associated entry the number of occurring in the given image.

The detailed implementation of each method is easily done by applying the explanations given so far. One example is shown in Program 184.

20.8 Color Quantization

Histogram equalization was used to create images with linear distribution of gray–levels. A somewhat similar principle is used in the so called *median cut algorithm* for color images [Hec82]. The general aim here is the reduction of the number of possible color vectors (e.g. in RGB). For example, one wants to represent an image with 256 color instead of the maximally possible 2^{24} color combinations. The basic idea is that each of the coded color values should occur approximately with the same frequency in the new image.

The procedure is as follows: initially, all colors of a color look up table are combined in a so called *box*. This box is then recursively partitioned until the desired number of boxes (each representing a new color) is reached. For that purpose, inside each box we choose the one of the three coordinate directions for which the color values vary the most, i.e., for which the difference of the minimal and maximal value or the statistical variance is maximal. The vectors in the box are sorted in ascending order for this coordinate. The median of this list is used to split the box into two new boxes which again are subject to the same procedure. Therein, all color vectors inside a box are represented by their mean vector. This is a special case of a so called *vector quantization* which encodes a cluster of vectors by one representative vector (c.f. Sect.s:classifier:ooa).

An example of this algorithm on a color image (here printed as gray–level image) is shown in Figure 20.10.[1] Alternative color quantization algorithms use simple modifications of standard vector quantization methods which are widely used in speech processing and coding [Fuk90]. Another highly efficient algorithm for color quantization, which applies similar statistical criterions for clustering, can be found, for instance, in [Wu91]; herein the reduction of color is optimized through a linear search process.

20.9 Histogram Back–Projection

Another algorithm primarily used with color histograms is the so called *histogram back–projection algorithm* [Swa91]. This algorithm can localize a known object in a scene based on its color appearance. For that purpose we need histograms which are represented by a sequence of relative frequencies of color values. Since the color spaces are large, we define so called *bins* which combine several possible color values. For instance, in the histogram $H = [H_k]_{k=1...K}$, H_k represents the probability to observe a color value of the k-th bin. We are free to choose an appropriate value for the number of bins K; for example, we can split the usual RGB color space from 2^{24} possible values into $K = 512$ bins of size $8 \times 8 \times 8$.

---

[1] Of course, the images are printed here as gray–level images. On the slides (Sect. B.4) you can see them in full color!

Figure 20.10 Median cut algorithm applied to the image in Figure 11.4 left with 128, 64, and 8 output colors

For the object o to be localized, we first need an image from which we compute the histogram $T = [T_k]_{k=1...K}$. Then we try to find this object in a scene s for which we again compute a histogram $H = [T_k]_{k=1...K}$. The algorithm uses the following definitions:

- ratio histogram $R = [R_k]_{k=1...K}$ with $R_k := \min\{\frac{T_k}{H_k}, 1\}$

- $h(c)$ maps each color vector c to color–bin in the histogram

- a mask $D_r = [1]_{1 \le i,j < r}$ representing the size of the object, or some other mask D_r describing the shape of the object at size r

The algorithm is shown in Figure 20.11. This simple and fast idea can be similarly applied to 2–D or 3–D histograms in various color spaces or components, such as RGB, UV, or H. Examples are shown in Figure 20.12.

Given: image histogram H, Wanted: object position (i_t, j_t)
Compute color histogram T
FOR Each bin $k \in \{1, \dots, K\}$
$\quad R_j = \min\{\frac{H_k}{T_k}, 1\}$
FOR All positions (i, j) in the image
$\quad A_{i,j} := R_{h(c_{i,j})}$, where $c_{i,j}$ denotes the color vector at position (i, j)
$B := D_r \star A$, where $\star$ denotes convolution
$(i_t, j_t) := \mathrm{argmax}_{i,j}(B_{i,j})$

Figure 20.11 Histogram back–projection algorithm

Figure 20.12 shows an example object on the left, a scene in the center and the back–projection in the UV color space on the right. The red part of the object is clearly visible.

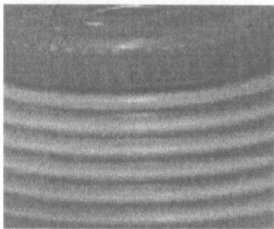  

Figure 20.12 Histogram back–projection examples from [May96]

Exercises

20.a Implement a complete class `Histogram`. The methods should include all algorithms described so far, i.e. smoothing, global histogram linearization, and local histogram equalization.

20.b Write utilities for the visualization of histograms and the discrete distribution function of gray–levels.

20.c Proof that (20.5) is equivalent to

$$J_l = \frac{p(^l\Omega_1)\sum_{\nu=1}^{L}g_\nu p_\nu - \sum_{\nu=1}^{l}g_\nu p_\nu}{p(^l\Omega_1)(1-p(^l\Omega_1))}. \tag{20.22}$$

20.d Generalize the least square threshold technique (Sect. 20.1) for solving the multi–threshold problem (Sect. 20.3).

20.e Show that the multi–threshold computation is bounded by $\binom{L+k-1}{k}$ evaluations of $\Psi(l_1, l_2, \ldots, l_k)$.

20.f Extend Exercise 14.b such that you use histogram equalization to transform the edge strength to 256 gray–levels.

20.g Do you think it is useful to apply global histogram equalization for the binarization of images? Why?

20.h Why is the function in Figure 20.6 (right) not exactly linear?

20.i Find ten differences between the pictures in Figure 20.10!

21 Edges and Lines

Various principles for pre–processing methods which create edge images from gray–level images could be seen in Chapter 14. As already outlined in Sect. 14.1, further algorithms for edge detection and line segmentation exist. Some of them will be introduced in this chapter. Especially some line detection algorithms which are based on connecting edge elements will be discussed. The optimal line detector for a given edge image depends upon the image data and on the subsequent processing steps. There is, in general, no way of defining an universally optimal method for line segmentation. Which type of segmentation algorithm has to be used depends on the given application. Under certain assumptions, however, an optimal detector can be defined (Sect. 21.9).

21.1 More Edge Detectors

The masks in Sect. 14.3 and 14.8 were used to compute discrete derivatives of bivariate intensity functions by the convolution of image functions and masks.

Another approach to edge detection is the application of several edge masks which represent typical shapes or directions of edges; a convolution of the image function with these masks will yield a large response if an edge of the expected form and direction is present at the actual position in the image. Figure 21.1 shows four elementary masks of size 3 × 3 which define the *Robinson operator* [Rob77]. For every pixel of the image, all four masks are applied; the greatest response is used as the edge strength. The four masks represent edge directions of 0, 45, 90, and 135 degrees. The sign of the response can be used to extend the directions to the range 180...360 degrees. Figure 21.2 shows one result of this operator.

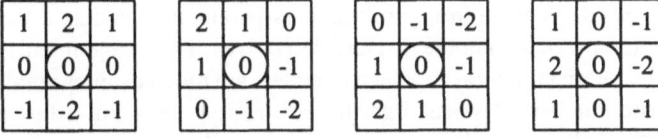

Figure 21.1 Mask definition for the Robinson operator.

Another operator, which also allows the computation of edge strength and edge orientation, is introduced in [Nev80]. It uses six masks of size 5 × 5 which detect twelve

Figure 21.2 Robinson image: strength and orientation

orientations; three masks are shown in Figure 21.3, the others result from a rotation by 90 degrees and from a mirrored version of the masks. The relatively large masks will smooth the image implicitly; the operator is thus less sensitive to small changes in the image intensities than, for example, the Robinson–operator. The result of the Nevatia/Babu operator is shown in Figure 21.4. Further operators of this type are, for example, by Prewitt [Pre70] and Ritter [Rit86].

100	100	100	100	100
100	100	100	100	100
0	0	0	0	0
-100	-100	-100	-100	-100
-100	-100	-100	-100	-100

100	100	100	100	100
100	100	100	78	-32
100	92	0	-92	-100
32	-78	-100	-100	-100
-100	-100	-100	-100	-100

100	100	100	-32	-100
100	100	92	-78	-100
100	100	0	-100	-100
100	78	-92	-100	-100
100	32	-100	-100	-100

0°   30°   60°

Figure 21.3 Mask definition according to Nevatia and Babu

Another type of edge detection algorithms uses parametric models for edges instead of mask operators, which compute discrete derivatives. The image intensity function is compared to the model function and the parameters are tuned to an optimal fit according to an error criterion. The classical algorithm of this type was published by Hückel in [Hue73]. Such methods are, however, computationally expensive and used only for special applications.

Several other ideas for edge detection have been published and tested. Indeed, many applications take advantage of edge detectors which operate in the frequency domain using the 2–D Fourier transform. High frequencies correspond to sharp edges in the

Figure 21.4 Nevatia and Babu image: strength and orientation

spatial domain. In general, edges can be found using a high–pass filter [Ros82]. A detailed discussion of these algorithms is out of the scope of this book.

Statistical classification principles can also be used for edge detection (e.g., in [Kun87, Hau84, Hua88, Har88]). So–called *multi scale algorithms* use different spatial resolutions for edge detection (e.g., [Mar80, Ekl82, Ber87]).

21.2 Edge Thinning

Due to the presence of noise in an image, most edge detectors will erroneously indicate a possible edge at many points. In addition, edges in the images are normally neither ideal step edges (Figure 14.1) nor roof edges (i.e., edge profiles looking like the roof of a house) but instead are blurred or disturbed due to sensor and quantization noise. Edge operators will thus find many false edges in the neighborhood of a real edge. Therefore, real edges appear smeared. Edge operators like the Sobel operator (Sect. 14.3) will create two edges in the edge image — even for an ideal step edge in the intensity image.

In order to facilitate the connection of edge points to lines, it is useful to eliminate some edge points after edge detection. Three algorithms will be presented in the following. They transform an edge image into a new edge image (arrow 10 in Figure 17.2). The actual position (i, j) in the edge image will be called the point P. We compute the following values which can be directly mapped to the members in the class Edge and EdgeImage:

- $f(P)$ the gray–value at point P,
- $s(P)$ the edge strength at point P,
- $r(P)$ the edge orientation at point P, and
- $S_{max} = \max_P s(P)$ the maximal edge strength in the image.

The simplest method for reduction of weak edge elements is to use a global threshold. All edges with strength below the threshold will be removed, i.e., their edge strength will be set to zero. Usually, this method is too simple. Thresholds have to be chosen differently for every image in order to get reasonably good results. A slightly better technique is to use a threshold relative to maximum edge strength in the image:

$$s'(P) := \left\{ \begin{array}{ll} s(P) & , \quad \text{if } s(P) > \gamma \cdot S_{\max} \\ 0 & , \quad \text{otherwise} \end{array} \right. \tag{21.1}$$

The parameter γ can be set globally for an image. Since this method uses the maximal edge strength, it can be applied to an edge image no matter which edge operator was used to create it.[1] The result of this operation is shown in Figure 21.5.

 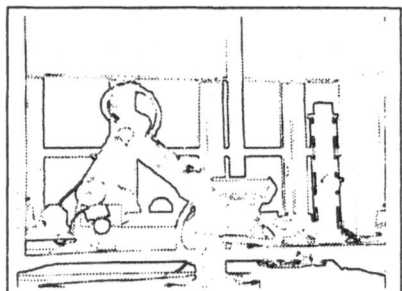

Figure 21.5 Thresholded image of Figure 11.2. On the left: threshold of 10 %, on the right: threshold of 20% (images inverted)

The algorithms for **Non–Maxima Suppression (NMS)** use the local context of an edge position for edge thinning. Preferably those edge points are taken into consideration which are close to the edge gradient, i.e., in an orthogonal direction to the edge orientation. If these neighbors have the same orientation as the actual point, they will most likely belong to the same edge in the intensity image. The goal is now to select the *best* among these points and to suppress others. An edge point is simply removed if its strength is smaller than those of its neighbors having the same orientation.

A two–phase implementation is proposed in [Nev80]: the edge image is scanned, and an internal label image is created of the same size. For every edge element P the neighbors N_L and N_R (Figure 21.6) are located. The following conditions are tested, where S_{th} is an appropriate lower threshold for the edge strength and 30° delimits the maximum difference in angle of the orientation:

- $s(P) \geq s(N_L)$ and $s(P) \geq s(N_R)$,

---

[1]Remember, the edge strength in an edge image is not normalized. Different operators will have completely different ranges of the edge strength!

- $(|r(P) - r(N_L)| \bmod 180°) < 30°$, and $(|r(P) - r(N_R)| \bmod 180°) < 30°$, and
- $s(P) > S_{\text{th}}$.

If all three conditions are true, P is marked in a label field of the same size as the input image, and N_L and N_R are marked as *excluded*.

The label image is then scanned; a new edge image is created; all edge elements marked in the label image which are not simultaneously excluded will be included in the output image. The result of NMS is shown in Figure 21.7.

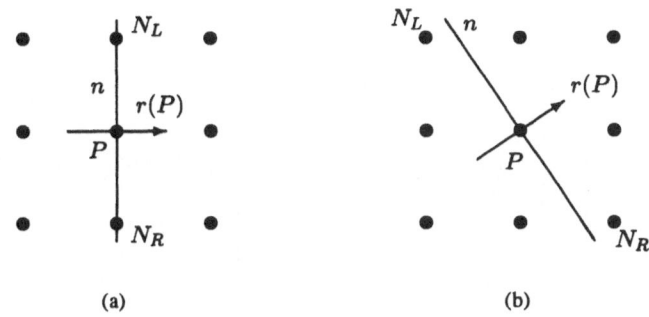

(a)   (b)

Figure 21.6 Edge thinning according to Nevatia/Babu

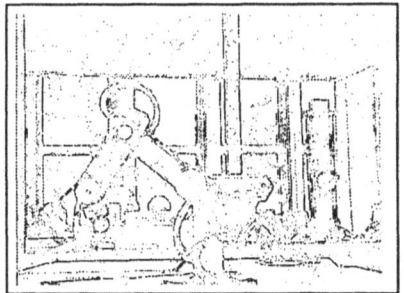 

Figure 21.7 NMS image Figure 11.2. Left: threshold 10%, right: threshold 20% (images inverted for visualization)

The Non–Maxima–Absorption (NMA) is also an iterative edge thinning method. Rather than eliminating some edge elements — as in the previous methods — the idea here is to shift edge strength from the smaller edge elements to the bigger ones. The basic ground rules are:

- if the edge strength in P is the biggest of the three, then $\alpha \cdot (s(N_L) + s(N_R))$ of the strength of its neighbors is added to P;

- if the edge strength in P is the smallest of the three, then it will be reduced by $2 \cdot \alpha \cdot s(P)$;

- if P has one neighbor P^+ with a larger strength, and another one P^- with a smaller strength value, then the strength of P will be reduced by $\alpha \cdot s(P^+)$ and increased by $\alpha \cdot s(P^-)$.

This will be done only if the orientations are similar. A difference in edge orientation of ≤ 30 degrees turns out to be a feasible value. The result of this method is shown in Figure 21.8.

Figure 21.8 NMA image Figure 11.2. Left: threshold 10%, right: threshold 20%

The implementation of the class Edge as shown in (Program 166) is efficient with respect to storage and computation time. Some bits of the storage layout, however, were unused. In Table 21.1 we list several flag values which can be associated with an edge element and which can be stored in the remaining storage space of an Edge object.

is_closed	if start is equal to end
is_start	starts a line
is_end	ends a line (successor field is valid)
is_edge	is an edge (no matter whether strength is high)
is_vertex	several lines meet here

Table 21.1 Flags for structure edge

These new features will be used in next sections. Program 185 shows how they are incorporated in the class for edges (Program 136). Special care has to be taken to the

```
struct Edge {
   static const int ONUM;           // constants in class-scope
   static const float odunit, const float orunit;
   union {                          // anonymous union
     unsigned int all;
     struct {
       unsigned int f_strength : 16;
       unsigned int f_orient   : 8;
       unsigned int successor  : 3; // chain code
       unsigned int is_closed  : 1; // see table
       unsigned int is_start   : 1; // see table
       unsigned int is_end     : 1; // see table
       unsigned int is_edge    : 1; // see table
       unsigned int is_vertex  : 1; // see table
     } fields ;
   };
   Edge() { all = 0; }     // clear
   // etc.
};
```
185

```
struct Sobel: public EdgeDet {       // Sobel operator as a special case
   virtual void operator() (const GrayLevelImage&,EdgeImage&) ;
};
struct Prewitt : public EdgeDet {    // Prewitt edge operator
   virtual void operator() (const GrayLevelImage&,EdgeImage&) ;
};
```
186

external representation of edge objects. The order of bit fields is machine dependent; thus, the value of all may not be used for external storage.[2]

A simple implementation of the Sobel operator (Sect. 14.3) and the Prewitt operator (Sect. 21.1) using this edge class is declared in Program 186 and implemented in Program 187. As already mentioned in Sect. 14.2, a simplified version of the arctan function could be used in the auxiliary function geto in Program 187.

21.3 Line Detection

After edge detection with one of the various operators, edge thinning, edge elements may still be isolated or scattered in space. In order to detect continuous lines, these edge elements have to be connected and gaps have to be closed. Groups of edge elements are connected to lines.

The input to line detection algorithms is an edge image (EdgeImage); the output is a set of lines which is represented by a segmentation object. Different line detection

---

[2]That means that the method storeOn has to code the flags into an integer value using bit operations; then, xdr_int can be used, c.f. Sect. 16.9.

```
const int Edge::ONUM = 144;                  // discretization for angle

static int geto(int fx, int fy)              // get orientation from x and y
{
 return (((fx==0) && (fy==0)) ? Edge::ONUM+1 :
         int((M_PI+ atan2(fy,fx)) / Edge::ONUM));
}

int Sobel::operator() (const GrayLevelImage& in,EdgeImage& out)
{
  for (int i = 1 ; i < in.getysize()-1; ++i) {          // rows
    for (int j = 1 ; j < in.getxsize()-1; ++j) {        // columns
      int fx= -in[i-1][j-1] - 2*in[i][j-1] - in[i+1][j-1]   // horizontal
            + in[i-1][j+1] + 2*in[i][j+1] + in[i+1][j+1];   //
      int fy= -in[i-1][j-1] - 2*in[i-1][j] - in[i-1][j+1]   // vertical
            + in[i+1][j-1] + 2*in[i+1][j] + in[i+1][j+1];
      out [i][j].strength = int(sqrt(fx*fx + fy*fy));    // convert
      out [i][j].orient   = geto(fy,fx);                 // gradient
    }                                                     // to angle
  }                                                       // and strength
  return 0;                                               // always o.k.
};
```
187

```
struct Hystline : public LineDet {    // hysteresis line detection
   virtual void operator() (const EdgeImage&, SegObj&) ;
};
```
188

algorithms create different line representations. The most basic result is a segmentation object (SegObj) consisting of lines represented as chain codes (Chain). Some algorithms (e.g., the Hough transform, Sect. 21.7) will compute straight line segments without going through the chain code representation.

Segmentation objects are used as common interface data structures representing all possible results of image segmentation. No matter whether the line segmentation algorithms compute straight line segments — as in the Hough transform (Sect. 21.7) —, or chain codes, as in the following algorithm, the representation should still look similar in order to facilitate further processing (arrow 12 in Figure 17.2, e.g. post–processing of chain codes in Chapter 22).

Segmentation objects form a shell around Sets of NIHCL and guarantee that no inconsistencies occur in the representation (Sect. 16.8). The sets in NIHCL will only record *references* to the objects in the set, i.e., they will not create a copy of them. It is thus essential to allocate a new line object for each line detected and to add this to the segmentation object. A code fragment is shown in Program 189. This program again extends the operator definitions in Program 178 and declares an operator for line detection in Program 188.

For simple line detection based on edge images, we now compute three additional values for each element of the edge image:

```
Chain * follow(Edge ** ei, int i, int j)
{
    Chain * cp = new Chain(j,i);  // (x,y) coordinates
    // ----------------------
    // TO BE FILLED IN HERE:
    // follow the edge, append to cp
    // ----------------------
    return cp;
}
void LineDet::operator() (const EdgeImage& e, SegObj& s)
{                                              // hysteresis line detection
    for(int i = ei.getsizey()-1; i >= 0; --i)    // rows
      for(int j = ei.getsizey()-1; j >= 0; --j) {  // columns
        Edge* e = & ei[i][j];                    // for fast access
        if (e->strength > threshold)             // allocate and
            s.add(*new AtomLine(follow(ei,i,j)));  // insert new line
      }                                          // into segmentation
}                                                // result
```

189

- We number all the lines found in the image. The first number is a label for the line which the edge element belongs to. A temporary label field is needed for this purpose (a matrix of integers).

- The second value is a chain code number pointing from the actual edge element to the potential successor. The edge class was already extended for that reason (Sect. 21.2).

- The flag field in the edge class will contain information about features of the edge as indicated in Table 21.1.

The so–called *local connectivity analysis* can be used to connect edge elements to lines. The neighborhood of an edge element is searched for potential line elements.

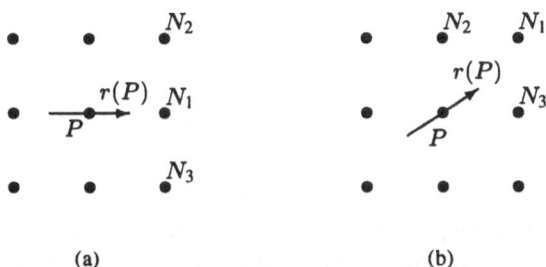

(a)   (b)

Figure 21.9 Neighborhood for line following [Nev80].

Nevatia and Babu [Nev80] propose a parallel and a sequential component for the algorithm. In the parallel part (Figure 21.10), we inspect a 8–neighborhood of each edge point. As shown in Figure 21.9, three points N_1, N_2 and N_3 will be used, which are closest to the inspected edge direction $r(P)$ of the actual point P. The successor of P is selected from these points based on the most similar edge direction $r(P)$. If more than one point have similar directions, the one with the highest edge strength will be chosen. If all three neighbors show similar directions and strengths, the point closest to the edge direction — in Figure 21.9 this is always called N_1 — of pixel P is chosen. This direction is recorded as a chain code in the field `successor`.

In the next (serial) step, all marked edge points will be grouped to lines (Figure 21.11). The image is scanned line by line to find potential start points for lines. If the edge strength at the actual position exceeds a given threshold and if the actual point does not yet belong to another line, it is marked as a start point of a new line; a new line label is created. Using the successor field, the line is then tracked through the image until the path reaches a position with an edge strength which is too low, or a position which belongs to another line already. All these points are marked with the same line label. The lines, represented as chain code objects, are added to a segmentation object which is the final result of the line detection algorithm. Since this algorithm tries to combine *all* edge points to lines, it is essential to apply line thinning before line tracking.

21.4   Hysteresis Thresholds

The use of larger contexts for edge localization may enhance the recognition, but also increases the computational complexity of the problem. Instead of considering small neighborhoods for edge detection, the whole context along the line can be important for line detection.

Two thresholds for the edge strength are used in the so–called *hysteresis algorithm*: an upper limit θ_o and a lower threshold θ_l. These parameters are coupled by a factor β according to

$$\theta_l = \beta\,\theta_o \quad .\tag{21.2}$$

Good results can be obtained with β in the range of 0.3 to 0.5. Experimental evaluation in [Brü90] showed that the choice of β is not critical for the result. A default value of $\beta = 0.33$ is reasonable.

After an edge thinning step, all those positions in the edge image which have an edge strength higher than θ_o are chosen as candidates for a start of a line. Each start point is tracked in both directions — along the edge orientation and in the opposite direction. Candidates for successors are selected as illustrated in Figure 21.9.

In order to be accepted as a line element, a candidate has to fulfill three conditions:

- the edge strength has to be greater than the lower threshold θ_l,

Search for edge point P_{act} which does not belong to any segment.				
Assign to P_{act}: new number *SegNum* and label "has no predecessor".				
	IF	P_{act} has a successor $c(P_{act})$		
	THEN	Choose point P_N which is successor of P_{act} reachable by $c(P_{act})$.		
	ELSE	**Try to jump over gaps of one pixel** (Sect. 21.5)		
		Compute potential successors $N_i \in \{N_1, N_2, N_3\}$ of P_{act}, and for all N_i the potential successors N_{i1}, N_{i2} and N_{i3} (Figure 21.9).		
		Search for the first point N_{ij}, where $i, j \in \{1, 2, 3\}$ and: $(\|r(N_i) - r(P_{act})\| \bmod 180°) < 30$ degrees $\wedge$ $(\|r(N_{ij}) - r(N_i)\| \bmod 180°) < 30$ degrees $\wedge$ chain code element $c(N_{ij})$ (i.e., there exists a successor of N_{ij}).		
		IF	N_{ij} is found (i.e., closing of gaps succeeded)	
		THEN	Connect (P_{act}) and N_i. Let next point P_N be N_{ij}.	
		ELSE	No successor P_N of P_{act} is found (end of segment).	
	IF	Successor P_N of P_{act} is found		
	THEN	IF	P_N has already a segment numberS_N	
		THEN	IF	S_N is equal to *SegNum*
			THEN	P_{act} is labeled by "end cycle". Label P_N "start cycle".
			End of segment is reached.	
		ELSE	P_N gets actual segment number *SegNum*.	
			Let P_N be the new actual point P_{act}.	
UNTIL End of segment is reached..				
UNTIL Each edge point has a segment number (i.e., all image points are traversed).				
Label segments with new numbers (Figure 21.11).				

Figure 21.10 Parallel part of line following algorithm according to [Nev80].

- the orientation in the actual position P must be similar to the candidate's orientation, and
- the candidate may not be member of another line.

If more than one candidate fulfill all three conditions, the one with the highest edge strength is chosen. This can happen only in two cases. Either these candidates belong to the same line and have not been eliminated by the edge thinning phase. Such points should not be used as members of other lines: their edge strength is reduced to a value below the lower limit θ_o. If on the other hand these candidates belong to different lines, their edge strength will be increased to $\theta_l(1 + \epsilon)$, where $\epsilon = 0.01$. This is illustrated in Figure 21.12–21.14.

New number for each segment:
Let new segment number *NewSegNum* = 0.
FOR All points P_a with the label "has no predecessor" or "start cycle"
Increment *NewSegNum*.
Choose successor of P_a as next point P_N reachable by $c(P_a)$.
Set the segment number of P_N to *NewSegNum*.
Let P_N be the new actual point P_a.
UNTIL There exists no successor of P_a (i.e., $c(P_a)$ has no value $\vee$ P_a is labeled by "end cycle").

Figure 21.11 Serial part of line following algorithm according to [Nev80] cont.

Search for one edge point P without a segment number, where the edge strength $s(P)$ is greater than the upper threshold θ_o. Call this point P_{act} and assign to this point the not yet used segment number *SegNum*.
Search forward
Set the actual point P_{act} to the start point P.
Search backward
UNTIL All edge points are processed (i.e., traverse the whole image).

Figure 21.12 Line following with the hysteresis algorithm (1) [Brü90]

21.5 Closing of Gaps

After the lines have been followed as outlined above, an attempt can be made to close small gaps which result from errors or noise in the edge image. The goal of this step is to combine lines which are separated by few (here: up to two) pixels.

For each line found in the image, the end is inspected and the points shown in Figure 21.15 are searched for possible start or end points of another line. The positions will be visited in the order given by the numbers. The points are shown for an edge orientation of $r(P) = 0^o$ in Figure 21.15 (a) and for $r(P) = 45^o$ in Figure 21.15 (b).

Similar neighbor masks can be used for other directions. It is useful if the implementation of chain codes has a method for gluing one chain to another (function append (const Chain&) in Program 163).

Usually, small segments are discarded in a final processing step, e.g., all those chain codes shorter than three pixels.

Search forward			
Compute possible successors $N_i \in \{N_1, N_2, N_3\}$ of P_{act} of the direction $r(P_{act})$ (Figure 21.9).			
Compute successor N_i, where: $s(N_i) > \theta_l \ \wedge \ (\|r(N_i) - r(P_{act})\| \mod° 180) <$ 30 degrees $\wedge \ \{N_i$ has no segment number $\vee \ N_i = P$ (= start point of the segment)$\}$.			
IF	Successor N_i was found		
THEN	IF	One point is P (start point of the line)	
	THEN	A cyclic period is found. Connect P_{act} and P. The start and end of the segment is reached.	
	ELSE	Let N be the candiate with maximum $s(N_i)$. Connect N and P_{act}. Let N be the actual point P_{act}. Let N be the temporary end point P_e.	
	Reduce the set of non processed candidates $s(N_i)$ to $\theta_l + \epsilon$.		
ELSE	End of segment is reached.		
UNTIL	End of segment is reached.		

Figure 21.13 Line following with the hysteresis algorithm (2) [Brü90]

Search backward			
Determine potential predecessors $V_i \in \{V_1, V_2, V_3\}$ of P_{act} with the orientation $r(P_{act}) + 180$ degrees according to Figure 21.9.			
Compute the predecessor V_i, where: $s(V_i) > \theta_l \ \wedge \ (\|r(V_i) - r(P_{act})\| \mod 180°) <$ 30 degrees $\wedge \ \{V_i$ has no segment number $\vee \ V_i = P_e$ (= end point of the segment)$\}$.			
IF	Predecessor V_i is found		
THEN	IF	One of the candidates is P_e (end point of the line)	
	THEN	Cyclic period is found. Connect P and P_{act}. The start point of the segment is reached.	
	ELSE	Let V be the candidate with maximum $s(V_i)$. Connect V and P_{act}. Let V be the actual point P_{act}.	
	Reduce the set of non processed points $s(V_i)$ to $\theta_l + \epsilon$.		
ELSE	Start of the segment is reached.		
UNTIL	Start of the segment is reached.		

Figure 21.14 Line following with the hysteresis algorithm (3) [Brü90]

21.6 Zero–Crossings in Laplace–Images

The Laplace operator (Sect. 14.8) will generate an edge image with zero–crossings corresponding to lines in the intensity image. These have to be located. Since we have to deal with images, zero–crossings of a two–dimensional function have to be found.

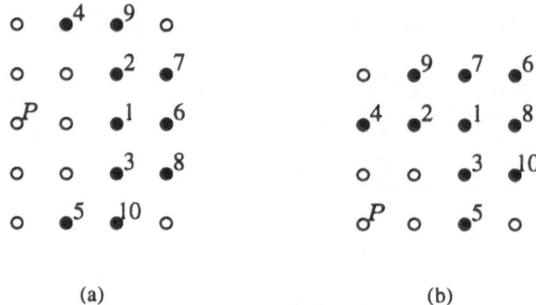

(a)   (b)

Figure 21.15 Points which will be inspected for gap closing.

0	0	0	0	10		.	.	.	.	.
0	0	0	20	30		.	0	-40	20	.
0	0	20	30	0		.	-40	20	80	.
0	20	30	0	0		.	20	80	-60	.
20	30	0	0	0		.	80	-60	0	.
30	0	0	0	0		.	.	.	.	.

Figure 21.16 Image and Laplacian image

Figure 21.16 shows an ideal diagonal edge and the corresponding response of the operator (using Figure 14.11, left). One simple algorithm is to locate horizontal and vertical zero–crossings and to mark these points as edges. A heuristic search for tracking these points and generating lines is described in [Mar76].

Another method is to search the neighborhood of a pixel for zero crossings of the same direction (either negative to positive, or vice versa) and connect these points by a chain coded line.

We can also trace the borders of areas in the Laplace image which are defined by the property that they contain only negative values or only positive values. An algorithm for this idea will be introduced in Sect. 22.4.

21.7   Hough Transform

The application of the *Hough transform* [Hou62] is one example of an algorithm which generates straight line segments without intermediate chain code representation [Bal82].

The very general idea behind the Hough transform is to express features in a parameterized form; we will use this idea below in the special case where the features to be detected are straight lines which will be computed directly from the edge image. The signal, associated with parameters, is transformed to the *parameter space*. If a feature, for instance, is uniquely defined by a parameter vector, the feature is mapped to a point in the parameter space, and a set of features is mapped to a set of points in the parameter space. The parameter space is digitized and quantized and called an *accumulator array*. Occurrences of features are recorded in the accumulator, i.e., all features indicating an object at a certain position increment the value at the corresponding parameter *position* in the parameter space. Local maxima in the accumulator are used as an indication of the frequency of this feature in the image.

This rather theoretical idea can be applied to the detection of straight lines.[3] The lines are expressed in a two–dimensional parameter space by their orientation α and the distance d of the line to the origin (see Figure 21.17 (left)). This representation is preferred to the common description as $y = ax + b$ which parametrizes the line by (a, b), since the values for (α, d) are in a finite range for images of a known size, whereas m is infinite for lines parallel to the y axis. We use an edge image (EdgeImage) as input and create a segmentation object (SegObj) as output containing straight lines (which have to be represented as objects; in ἵππος this is done in a class StrLineSeg[4]).

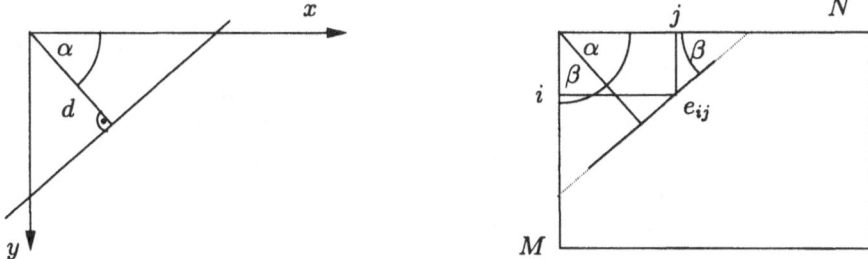

Figure 21.17 A straight line and its parameters d and α of the accumulator array

Assume an input edge image $\boldsymbol{E} = [e_{ij}]_{i=1\ldots M, j=1\ldots N}$ of size $M \times N$. A temporary integer array called the *accumulator* $\boldsymbol{A}$ of dimension $2\sqrt{M^2 + N^2} \times 144$ — this is twice the maximum distance of a line in the image to the origin times the quantized orientation — is initialized to zero.

---

[3]A nice implementation can be found in
http://www.lut.fi/dep/tite/XHoughtool/xhoughtool.html.
    [4]The implementation is left as an exercise (21.e).

```
inline int dist(int dmax, int y, int x, int o)
{  // sin_tab and cos_tab include values of sine and cosine functions
    return dmax + (int)(x*sin_tab[o]+y*cos_tab[o]);   // add offset to sin/cos!
}
void hough(Edge** E, int sizex, int sizey)
{
    const int M = int(1+sqrt(sizex*sizex+sizey*sizey);
    const int N = Edge::OrientNumb;
    Matrix<int> A(N, 2 * M) = 0;                              // accumulator
    for(int i = sizey-1; i >= 0; --i)
      for(int j = sizex-1; j >= 0; --j) {
        Edge* e = & E[i][j];
        int alpha = int(e->orient + (360.0 / N * 90)) % N;   // general !
        if (e->orient < Edge::OrientNumb)
          A[dist(M,i,j,e->orient)][alpha] += e->strength;
      }
}
```

190

For each edge element e_{ij} in the edge image we calculate the parameters of a line that possibly passes through this point $P = (i, j)$. The parameter α is computed from $90° - \beta$, where β is the line orientation $r(P)$. From geometrical considerations which can be derived from Figure 21.17 (right), the distance d turns out to $d = i \cos \beta + j \sin \beta$. Since this can result in a negative value for d, we add the maximal value for d to shift the range to positive values and use an accumulator array of the required size.

The two values α and d are used as indices in the accumulator $A[\alpha][d]$ which is incremented by the edge strength $s(P)$. Maximal values in the accumulator are then used as indication of a straight line in the input image. Program 190 shows the core of the transform algorithm in C++. Since the angle `alpha` is an integer in the range $0 \ldots 144$, we can use a table for the sine and cosine computations to speed up computation. Program 190 also shows how the implementation can be kept independent of the quantization for the angle (see the line for the computation of `alpha`).

Some problems in the implementation are the difficulty to find maxima in the accumulator and the fact that non–connected straight lines in the input image create *one* value resp. cluster in the accumulator. After such a maximum has been found, the *edge image* has to be inspected, and start and end of one or several lines have to be found.

An example for lines detected with the Hough transform is shown in Figure 21.18. This result was created with a slightly different implementation where the accumulator was incremented by one for all possible edge directions at those positions exceeding a certain edge threshold.

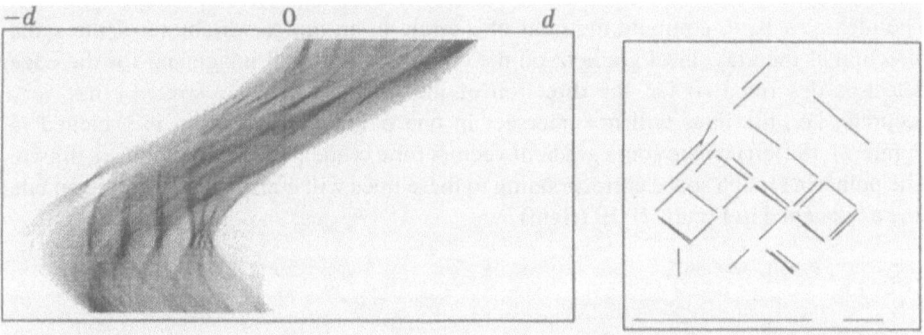

Figure 21.18 Hough accumulator (left) and result of straight line detection with the Hough–Transform of Figure 11.2

21.8 Circle Detection

The idea of the Hough transform can be used to detect objects which can be described as parametric curves with more than two parameters. Some restrictions have to be imposed on the parameter space in order to reduce the effort for searching in the accumulator. This way, circles or ellipses [Bal82, Ill87, Hor93a] can be detected.

For the detection of a single circle in an image, we can avoid computationally expansive search in a three–dimensional (x_c, y_c, r) accumulator array which would be induced by the parametric circle description

$$(x - x_c)^2 + (y - y_c)^2 = r^2 \quad . \tag{21.3}$$

In a two–step procedure we proceed as follows: we first search for the centers of possible circles using a Hough transform; then we search for the circle itself in the edge image, where we use the estimated centers and inspect circles with increasing radius around them. The detection of the center is based on the following relation which uses a line representation as $y = ax + b$:

For all straight lines $g_i : y = a_i x + b_i$ which intersect in one point $\boldsymbol{x} = (x_c, y_c)^{\mathrm{T}}$ we can associate points (a_i, b_i) in a Hough space. These points are all elements of one line in the Hough space.

To prove this, we realize that all lines g_i fulfill the condition

$$y = a_i(x - x_c) + y_c = a_i x + (y_c - a_i x_c) \quad .$$

The associated points for the lines g_i in the Hough space are $(a_i, y_c - a_i x_c)$. These points lie on the line $b_i = -a_i x_c + y_c$ in the Hough space.[5]

---

[5]This relation reveals the duality principle for this line representation as $y = a_i x + b_i$, where a point in Hough space corresponds to a line in the image, and vice versa.

The idea now is, to compute the radii of a circle in an image which are of the same direction as the gray–level gradient on the circle. For a digital image and for the edge detectors described so far, the direction of the gradient will, however, be not very accurate, i.e., the lines will not intersect in one point. This situation is sketched in Figure 21.19 (left) where some gradient vectors for a crudely digitized circle are drawn. The points in Hough space corresponding to these lines will consequently not lie on one line as sketched in Figure 21.19 (right).

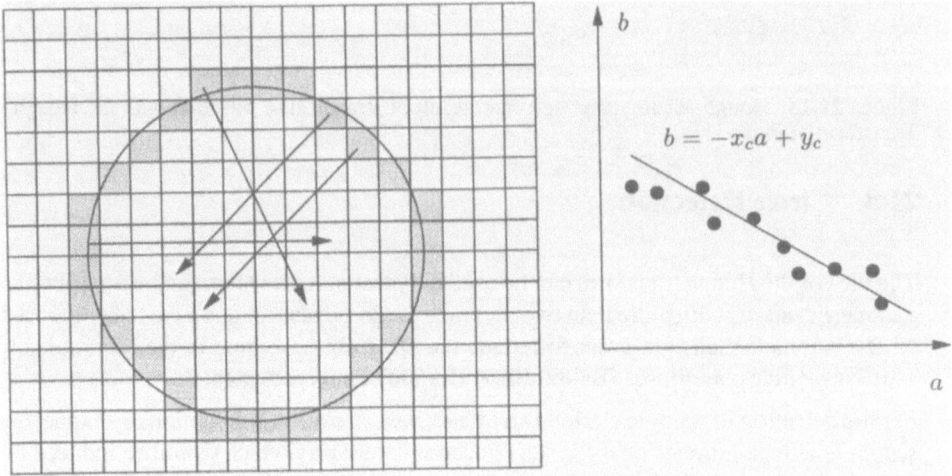

Figure 21.19 Detection of a circle's center with Hough transform

For the line in the Hough space $b = -x_c a + y_c$ which will be used to localize the center of the circle $(x_c, y_c)^T$, we have to solve a system of linear equations $b_i = -x_c a_i + y_c$ which result from the computations for the gradients in the circle image. Depending on the number of equations used, this system of equations will not be solvable. A recursive and efficient way to find an approximation of the solution is due to Levinson (c.f. [Nie83; p. 99]), but this method will not be introduced here. Instead, we follow a elementary algebraic approach and use the *pseudo–inverse matrix* of the linear system of equations above. The minimization of the mean square error for the computation of prediction coefficients can be interpreted in a geometrical manner. We rewrite the system of N equations in the form $b = A x$ as

$$b = \begin{pmatrix} -a_1 & 1 \\ -a_2 & 1 \\ \cdots & 1 \\ -a_N & 1 \end{pmatrix} \begin{pmatrix} x_c \\ y_c \end{pmatrix} . \tag{21.4}$$

The matrix A defines a mapping from $\mathbf{R}^2$ to $\mathbf{R}^N$. More general, we can use this approach to solve any system of linear equations for M unknowns based on N observations;

$A \in \mathbf{R}^{N \times M}$ then defines a mapping from $\mathbf{R}^M$ to $\mathbf{R}^N$. If there exists no vector $x = (x_1, x_2, \ldots, x_M)^T$ which satisfies equation (21.4), we conclude that the vector $b = (b_1, b_2, \ldots, b_N)^T$ of sample data is not element of the range of matrix A. The range

$$\text{im}(A) = \{v \mid v = Aw, \quad w \in \mathbf{R}^M\} \subseteq \mathbf{R}^N \tag{21.5}$$

is a sub–vector space of $\mathbf{R}^N$. The minimization of the mean square error is thus equivalent to solving the system of linear equations

$$A x = P b \,, \tag{21.6}$$

where $P b$ is the orthogonal projection of b onto the sub–space for the range of matrix A (Figure 21.20). The orthogonal projection coincides with

$$(A x - b) A v = 0 \tag{21.7}$$

for all $v \in \mathbf{R}^M$, which is equivalent to

$$(A^T A x - A^T b) v = 0 \,. \tag{21.8}$$

Since (21.8) has to be valid for all vectors v of the domain of matrix A, we conclude that the best parameter vector x with respect to criterion (21.4) can be computed by solving (21.9). Therefore, we multiply both sides of equation (21.7) by the transposed matrix A^T from the left, and get the closed form solution

$$\begin{pmatrix} x_1 \\ x_2 \\ x_3 \\ \vdots \\ x_M \end{pmatrix} = \left(A^T A \right)^{-1} A^T \begin{pmatrix} b_1 \\ b_2 \\ b_3 \\ \vdots \\ b_M \end{pmatrix} \,. \tag{21.9}$$

The matrix $A^+ = \left(A^T A \right)^{-1} A^T$ is the *pseudo–inverse* of A.[6]

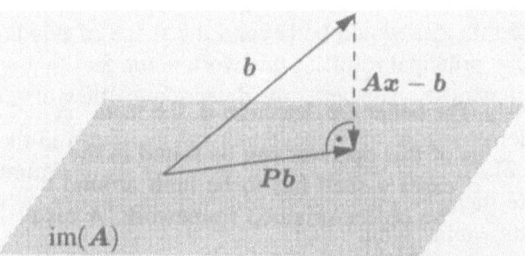

Figure 21.20 Orthogonal projection on the range of matrix A

To conclude our search for circles in the image, we estimate a line from a set of approximatively co–linear points in the accumulator and thereby get the position of the

---

[6]See also Exercise 21.h.

circle's center. We then test various radii around this center and try to optimize the fit of the circle using a criterion which takes into account the edge strength on the circle and the size of the circle. One such choice is to sum up the edge strength on the circle for all those points which have an edge orientation close to the tangent and to divide the sum by the radius. The maximal response is used to determine the final circle.

21.9   Optimal Line Detection

Figure 21.21   Canny image: strength and orientation and final (inverted) result

Canny introduced an algorithm for line detection in [Can86] which optimizes the following criteria for the detection lines based on step edges (c.f. Figure 14.1) in images:

- *detection,*
- *localization*, and
- *uniqueness.*

This algorithm combines Gaussian–filtering, edge detection, edge thinning, and line detection to an optimal solution for a given type of edges. A complete mathematical description of this idea would be beyond the scope of this book, see [Can86, Nie90a] for details. One principal result of this work is the fact that we cannot maximize these criteria simultaneously. The better the detection is, the worse the localization will be.

Various implementations of this operator can be found in the public domain software (c.f. Sect. B.2). In most cases a shell has to be built around these routines in order to incorporate them into the object–oriented framework. A result of the Canny edge detection is shown in Figure 21.21.

Although Canny showed the principally optimal solution for edge detection (under certain assumptions), the research still continued. The Deriche–Filter [Der91, Der90] and the *operator of Shen and Castan* [She86, She88] also use Gaussian–filters and combined edge detection; the major advantage in comparison to the Canny operator is the more efficient implementation.

Exercises

21.a   Which discrete values for the orientation (Sect. 4.6) will be appropriate for the
masks in Sect. 21.1?

21.b   Estimate minimal, maximal, and *normal* edge strength for the various edge
operators.

21.c   Implement a fast and machine independent storage routine for the edge elements
(Program 185).

21.d   Convert an edge image to a gray–level image using the edge strength. Normalize
it to 256 gray–values using histogram equalization.

21.e   Implement a class `StrLineSeg` for straight line segments. Derive it from the
class `LineRep2D`.

21.f   Get public domain versions of various edge detectors and adapt them to your
object–oriented system. Use external C functions (Sect. 7.4) and encapsulate the
functions without modifying them (if possible).

21.g   Proof the correctness of distance computation in Program 190!

21.h   For the matrix A in (21.4), prove that

$$(A^\mathrm{T} A)^{-1} = \frac{1}{N \sum\limits_{i=1}^{N} a_i^2 - (\sum\limits_{i=1}^{N} a_i)^2} \begin{pmatrix} N & \sum\limits_{i=1}^{N} a_i \\ -\sum\limits_{i=1}^{N} a_i & -\sum\limits_{i=1}^{N} a_i^2 \end{pmatrix} . \quad (21.10)$$

21.i   We could try to localize a circle in an image by just computing the mean of all
intersections of lines shown in Figure 21.19 (left). Why is the Hough transform
more robust?

22 Chain Codes

A suitable and often used representation for lines is the *chain code* (Chapter 16, Figure 16.3). The basic principles of chain codes were already introduced in Sect. 16.4. In this chapter we describe some additional methods briefly. Some of the described algorithms are suggested in [Fre80, Zam91].

22.1 Smoothing

Chain codes created by line detection algorithms are often twisted, disturbed by noise, and have indentations. We need a method in the class for chain codes which smoothes lines represented as chain codes, and still preserves as much information as possible.

Let S_1 and S_2 be two subsequent directions in the given chain code. In Table 22.1 (from [Zam91; p. 21]) rules are summarized which can be used for smoothing chain codes. For that purpose, we define $m = \min(S_1, S_2)$ and $M = \max(S_1, S_2)$. The arithmetic, i.e., addition, is done modulo 8. The smoothing procedure has to be repeated until there is no change of the chain code. Figure 22.1 shows an example.

$M - m$	m	new direction
0	—	no change
1	—	no change
2	odd	$m + 1, m + 1$
2	even	$m + 1$
3	odd	$m + 1$
3	even	$m + 1$
4	—	delete m and M
5	odd	$m - 1$
5	even	$m - 2$
6	odd	$m - 1, m - 1$
6	even	$m - 1$
7	—	no change

Table 22.1 Rules for smoothing chain codes

Figure 22.1 Original chain code (left) and smoothed line (right).

A slightly more complex smoothing algorithm is proposed in [Hu97]; the iterative algorithm eliminates repetitive small variations while an error measure computed with respect to the original curve is below a given threshold.

22.2 Digital Linear Lines

Due to the fact that chain codes have only eight discrete directions, straight lines in the image have to be approximated by these discrete steps. The process of drawing straight lines characterized by two points, i.e., the start and the end point, was already an exercise (Exercise 18.b). We can now use this function and implement a constructor for a chain code of a straight line, where the start and end points are given arguments. Furthermore, a boolean function has to be implemented which returns true if a given chain code represents a straight line and false otherwise. The decision criteria for a straight line are specified as follows:

(a) The whole chain code includes only two different directions, S_1 and S_2, where the following constraint has to be valid: $|S_1 - S_2| \equiv 1 \bmod 8$.

(b) The direction which is less often element of the chain code always has the other direction as predecessor and successor in the sequence of directions.

(c) S_1 and S_2 must be *homogeneously distributed* over the complete chain code.

The conditions (a) and (b) are easily checked. The homogeneity can be computed using the following recursive procedure: let the direction, which is more often part of the chain code, be denoted by S. We compute from the given chain code a new formal chain code where the directions are the number of directly subsequent elements of the direction S. We check for this formal chain code conditions (a), (b), (c) until convergence.

In a statistical framework, the term *homogeneously distributed* indicates uniformly distributed directions, i.e., $p(S_1) = p(S_2) = 1/2$. Figure 22.2 shows that this constraint is not sufficient to define straight line elements. The changes in directions of subsequent chain elements are also assumed to be uniformly distributed. We need a method which tests hypotheses on distributions and give some measure for reliability.

The χ^2–*test* allows the decision to which extend you can believe hypotheses for observed relative frequencies. Let us assume we have n random variables $X_1, X_2, \ldots X_n$, where $X_i \in \{1, 2, \ldots, k\}$, and let $p_1, p_2, \ldots, p_k$ denote the discrete probabilities over the domain $\{1, 2, \ldots, k\}$, i.e., these probabilities define a histogram. Our hypothesis is that

$$p(X_j = i) \quad = \quad p_i \quad , \tag{22.1}$$

where $j \in \{1, 2, \ldots, n\}$ and $i \in \{1, 2, \ldots, k\}$. The basic random variable related to the test is the so–called *Pearson statistic* T which is defined for n observations by

$$T_n = \sum_{i=1}^{k} \frac{(N^{(i)} - np_i)^2}{np_i} \quad ; \qquad (22.2)$$

herein $N^{(i)}$ denotes the number of observed random variables X_j which satisfy $X_j = i$. We define α to be the so called level of the test, and compute the probability $p(T \geq s)$ for which we demand that $p(T \geq s) \leq \alpha$. The value

$$t(\alpha) = \operatorname*{argmin}_{s} \{p(T \geq s) \leq \alpha; s\} \qquad (22.3)$$

is the basic measure of the test. We accept the hypothesis, if the experimental value T_n holds $T_n \leq t(\alpha)$, otherwise it is rejected. The discrete probability $p(T \geq s)$ is defined by a χ^2–distribution with $k - 1$ degrees of freedom [And58]. For an infinite number of observations we have

$$\lim_{n \to \infty} p(T_n \geq s) = \frac{1}{2^{k/2}\Gamma(k/2)} \int_0^s y^{(k-1)/2} \exp(y/2) \, dy \quad . \qquad (22.4)$$

The Gamma–function is defined by

$$\Gamma(x) = \int_0^\infty \exp(-t) \, t^{x-1} \, dt \quad . \qquad (22.5)$$

This distribution is used to approximate $p(T_n \geq s)$ for a given set of observations. The implementation of the χ^2–test requires the distribution (22.4) for various k. The code for the χ^2–test and the required probability distribution can be found in look–up tables [Bro85] or in [Pre92].[1]

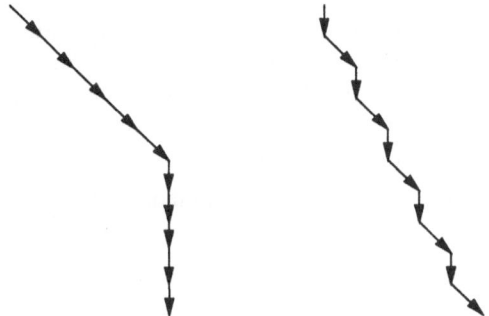

Figure 22.2 Uniformly distributed chain code directions

22.3 Neighborhood

Rectangular or quadratic tessellation of digital images and the definition of different types of chain codes induce the problem of how to define a neighborhood of a pixel and

---

[1]c.f. http://cfatab.harvard.edu/nr/bookc.html

the directions of the chain code. A pixel (i, j) is usually considered closer to $(i + 1, j)$ than to $(i + 1, j + 1)$. Two alternatives can be chosen for those pixels which are assumed to be directly adjacent to (i, j):

- *4–connectivity*, for which the four pixels

$$\{(i + 1, j), (i - 1, j), (i, j + 1), (i, j - 1)\} \tag{22.6}$$

  are used, and

- *8–connectivity*, for which eight pixels are used, namely the 4–connected pixels and the set

$$\{(i - 1, j - 1), (i + 1, j - 1), (i - 1, j + 1), (i + 1, j + 1)\} \quad . \tag{22.7}$$

Figure 22.3 Neighborhood of a pixel: 4–connectivity (left) and 8–connectivity (right)

The neighborhood definitions are visualized in Figure 22.3. Both versions have advantages and drawbacks, when sets of similar pixels are searched in segmentation, which should result in a connected region. Imagine, for example, a chess board; if we define that each of the eight neighbors of a pixel is adjacent to it, all white fields are connected — as well as all black fields.

In the next section we need this notion of a neighborhood to trace lines.

22.4   Contours in Binary Images

In [Nie74] a simple algorithm for contour tracking in binary images is presented. Assuming that the object is white and the background is black, the following rules are used to create a line around an object:

1. after three consecutive turns in the same direction, turn to the other and ignore the following rules
2. turn left if you are on a white pixel
3. turn right if you are on a black pixel

The foreground (white) is regarded as 4–connected her. The background is 8–connected. An example is shown in Figure 22.4. Binary regions which can be used for this algorithm can simply be computed by the threshold algorithms of Chapter 20.

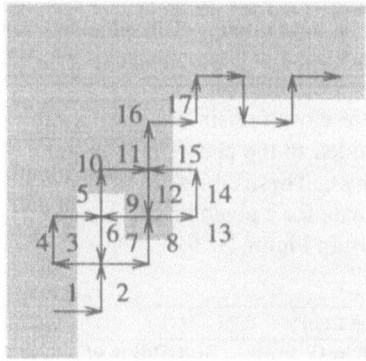

Figure 22.4 Contour following algorithm

Using this algorithm, we can complete line detection using the Laplace operator. We apply the operator and create an image which has three values as in Figure 14.12: the image will be 0 for negative results, it will be 128 wherever the operator results in 0, and will be 255 for the positive case. We can now detect lines when we trace the borders of these regions. The results will, however, be satisfying only if some extra filtering is done on the input image.

22.5 Length, Area, and Similarity

In Program 163 we introduced the class Chain but did not show many methods for it. The length of a chain coded line can be computed using the simple formula

$$l = a + b \cdot \sqrt{2} \quad , \tag{22.8}$$

where a is the number of even– and b the number of odd–valued links in the given chain corresponding to the 4–neighborhood and the 8–neighborhood in Sect. 22.3. An implementation of the method length which was declared in Program 163, is shown in Program 191. This definition is too simple in real applications: Think, for example, of a chain code $[(0, 0)020202020202]$; more effort has to be put into the implementation of the method length() to treat such special cases correctly. Some problems of twisted chain codes can be solved by smoothing techniques described in the previous section.

```
#include <math.h>
double Chain::length() const                    // return length
{
    int a=0, b=0;                               // two counters
    for (int i = chain.act -1; i >= 0; --i)     // iterate along chain
        if (chain.seq[i] & 0x01) ++a; else ++b; // check even/odd link
    return M_SQRT2 * a + b;                      // compute length
}
```

The area enclosed by a closed chain code can simply be computed. We assume two tables which can be added to the class chain as static members; one is called x_next and one is called y_next. These tables are of size eight and contain the differences for the x and the y coordinate for a given link (e.g, x_next [3] =-1 and y_next [3] =1). The algorithm is shown in Figure 22.5.

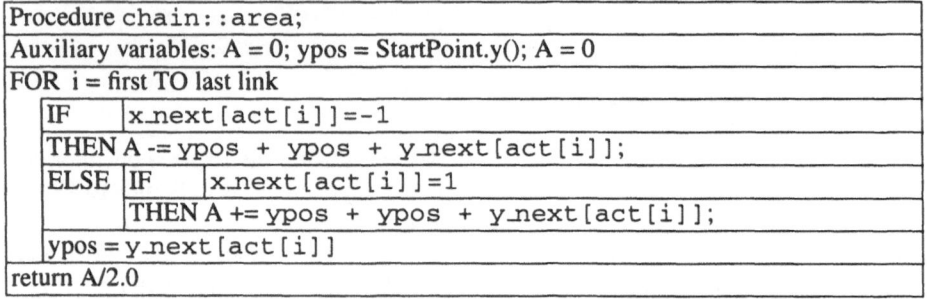

Procedure chain::area;		
Auxiliary variables: A = 0; ypos = StartPoint.y(); A = 0		
FOR i = first TO last link		
IF	x_next[act[i]]=-1	
THEN A -= ypos + ypos + y_next[act[i]];		
ELSE	IF	x_next[act[i]]=1
	THEN A += ypos + ypos + y_next[act[i]];	
ypos = y_next[act[i]]		
return A/2.0		

Figure 22.5 Structogram for computation of area from a closed chain code

For the classification of objects based on lines, like e.g. classification based on shapes, it is often necessary to match chain codes. Of course, the lines will not fit exactly, when real images are used. Therefore, we need a similarity measure for chain codes. For that purpose compute the absolute area A included by two lines. We assume that the area equals the number of enclosed pixels and the start and end points of each chain code are connected by virtual lines. Let l_1 and l_2 be the length of both lines. A measure for similarity is defined by

$$d = 2 A (l_1 + l_2) \quad . \tag{22.9}$$

Using the length computed in (22.8) we can easily implement this measure.

22.6   Intersections

A line can have intersections with itself. For example, the digit 8 is written with one intersected line. We have to extend the class for chain codes by a method which computes the set of intersections of one chain code.

A method for the determination of intersections of two chains is also required. For that purpose, we determine the bounding rectangle for each chain. Obviously, any intersections of both chains will lie in the common area of these two bounding rectangles. If there exist no intersections, the two chains are disjunctive. For the intersection areas of the bounding boxes we proceed recursively as follows: we discard the portions of the chain codes lying outside, and for the remaining parts we compute the bounding rectangles, again. This process is repeated until all intersections are found or it is established that no intersection exists.

22.7   Rotation

It is often useful to provide geometric objects with methods for geometric transformations. Such methods can be added as an abstract interface to the class GeoObj in Sect. 16.7. In this section we inspect rotations and translations for chain codes. The translation is trivial; only the start point has to be moved. For that reason, it is useful to provide point objects with an additional method which translates the point for this purpose (c.f. Program 85). Even the rotation by multiples of 45° or 90° is fairly easy. The directions can be modified using modulo summation. Arbitrary rotations, however, will cause distortions. The chain must be treated as a curve and thus rotated, re–quantized as well as re–coded considering the underlying image lattice (c.f. Figure 22.6). Let the center of rotation be the starting point of the actual chain. A simple implementation proceeds as follows:

1. Rotate each element of the image grid belonging to the given line using the induced rotation matrix (use a modified version of the method already discussed in Sect. 18.7 for that purpose!).

2. Compute for each of the eight chain code directions the difference in horizontal and vertical direction taking into account the rotation angle.

3. Move along the chain and compute the new sequence of directions by the minimization of distances induced by the floating point and discrete coordinates.

An example for rotation and re–quantization is illustrated in Figure 22.6.

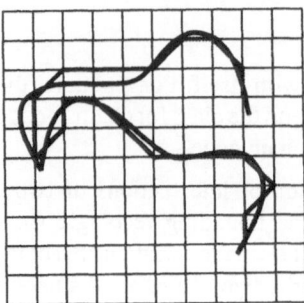

Figure 22.6 Illustration of a line, the rotation of the line (40°) and the corresponding chain codes

22.8 Conversion

A data reduction of chain code representations results from a polygonal approximation of lines by using straight line segments. The computation of the needed straight line segments can be formalized as an optimization problem: the approximation error should be below a given threshold; whereas, the number of line segments should be as minimal as possible. This principle was proposed in [Ram72]. Some algorithms for the conversion of chain codes to polygons are proposed in [Hu97].

For the judgment of the quality of the approximation a distance measure between straight lines and a chain code element is needed. One suitable measure was defined in Sect. 22.5. In the current case, we have the constraint that both the chain code and the polygonal approximation begin and end up in identical points.

A more sophisticated solution of this problem is the so called *split algorithm*. The basic idea of this approach is due to a recursive division of the line segment into smaller segments. The decomposition of one segment stops, if the linear segment approximates the curved segment with an appropriate error. An example for polygonal approximations of line segments was already shown in Figure 16.4.

22.9 Corners of Chain Codes

The basic problem of segmenting a digital line into a sequence of segments is to identify the locations where the line has to be split. Usually, *corners* (i.e., small segments on the line of high curvature) are used. Corners can be detected basically in two ways: either in the image directly, or after line segmentation. We only treat the second case in the following which transforms a segmentation object into a new one. We show how to compute measures for curvatures using discrete lines.

For the computation of the curvature in the point p_m on the line represented as a parametric curve $c(t)$, two points p_l and p_r are used. These points are chosen such that the path along the line from p_l to p_m is equal to the path p_m to p_r; this length is a parameter k of the algorithm. The distance H between p_m and the middle point p_c of a secant through two points p_l and p_r is an appropriate measure for the curvature in the point p_m. Alternative curvature parameters are the length of h (c.f. Figure 22.7 for definitions), the angle ϕ, the sum $s_l + s_r$, or the area of triangle $p_l p_r p_m$ [Ros71]. These ideas can be used to get curvature measures for discrete lines.

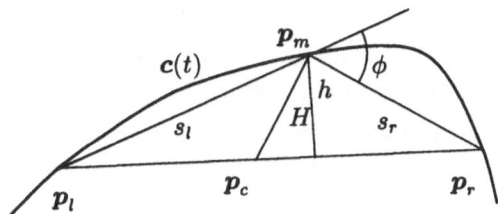

Figure 22.7 Corner detection on continuous line

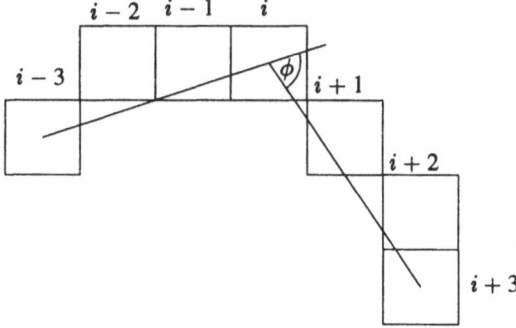

Figure 22.8 Corner detection on chain codes

For each chain coded discrete line resulting from line following, line is inspected using various values of k, where k is the number of links in the discrete case. The maximum value is chosen as a measure a corner. In [Har96] it is shown that for discrete lines H is more appropriate to detect corners close to each other, than ϕ. Figure 22.8 shows this computation for the case $k = 3$. In order to access links left and right of the point currently inspected, it is useful to have the access operator [ ] which was defined in Program 163.

Exercises

22.a Implement the contour tracking algorithm described in Sect. 22.4. Represent the resulting line as a chain code.

22.b Images of animals such as shown in Figure 22.9 should be recognized and distinguished in gray–level images. Assume a homogeneous black background and let $\Omega_1, \Omega_2, \Omega_3$ and Ω_4 be the associated pattern classes.

    (a) Binarize the images using a threshold detection algorithm.

    (b) Compute the closed contour–line for each object from a given gray–level image using the algorithm in Sect. 22.4.

    (c) Write programs for the determination of features like the area, length of the contour, or moments using the algorithm in Sect. 22.5.

    We will later continue with this problem in Exercise 24.c.

22.c Give a proof that the algorithm in Sect. 22.1 terminates after a finite number of iterations. Write a program for the visualization of chain codes, i.e., generate a synthetic image which shows the (set of) chain codes. Describe the smoothing effects!

22.d Implement a boolean function for Sect. 22.2 and check whether your straight lines generated in Exercise 18.b fulfill this criterion.

22.e Implement the similarity measure of Sect. 22.5 as a method in your class. Test this distance function using several examples and discuss your results.

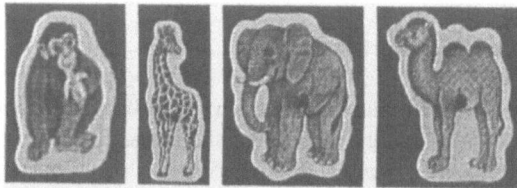

Figure 22.9 Animals

Part IV
Speech and Pattern Analysis

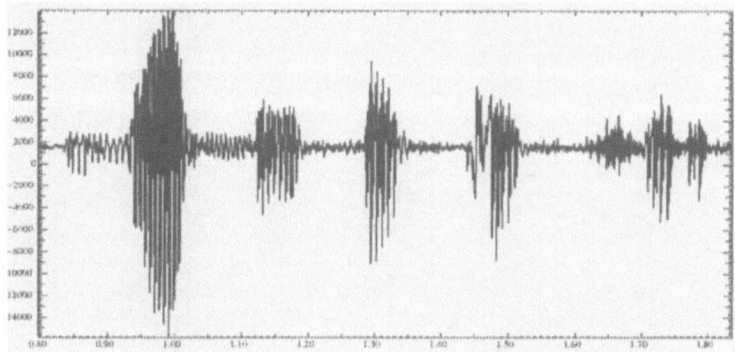

Sound signal: "This is a picture" spoken by D. Paulus

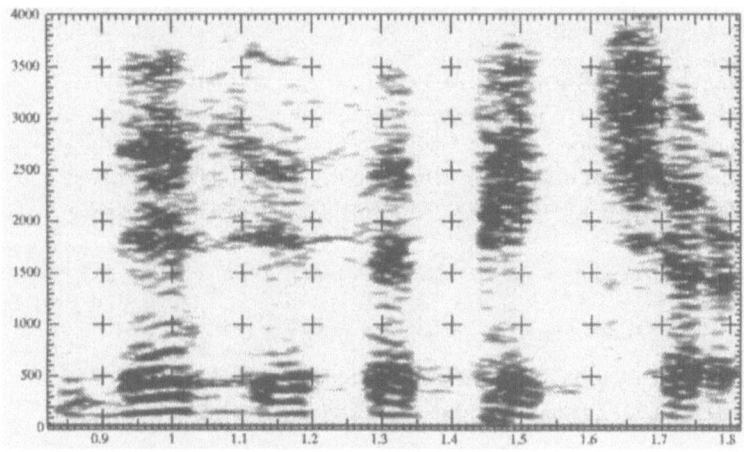

Corresponding spectrogram

In this part of the book we will describe a system for pattern classification. We will show several applications of spectral features and applied statistics.

23 Spatial and Spectral Features

The goal of pattern analysis, in general, is to transform signals into symbolic descriptions [Dud73, Nie90a, Pen86]. For simple classification problems this corresponds to the computation of a class number for an observed signal (c.f. Figure 6.1). Since the amount of data is too high, if images or speech signals are used directly, the signals are transformed into lower dimensional vectors, so called *features*. Features retain all the information needed for pattern recognition. For image and speech recognition, it is necessary to have a set of features which are, for example, appropriate for the subsequent classification of objects, of single words or for the identification of speakers. The following sections introduce several types of features which can be applied to solve selected classification problems in the fields of image and speech processing.

23.1 Different Types of Features

A variety of parameters can be used to represent digital signals. You can take, for instance, differences between gray–levels or the waveform of speech signals. Features like the zero crossing rate, the energy of the signal or first derivatives (average slopes) might be computed [Nie90a, Rab88]. In particular, for speech recognition applications it has proven to be advantageous that features are not computed in the spatial domain,[1] but in the frequency domain of the signal (c.f. Chapter 12). Features of the frequency domain show some characteristics like the fundamental frequency or the perceptual equivalent, the pitch, which are not directly evident in spatial data. Features of the frequency domain often provide a higher discriminating power [Dud73].

The task of the system and the classification strategy influence the choice of useful features. If we have to implement a speaker independent speech recognition system, features have to be used which are significant for words and which can be detected within speech signals produced by arbitrary speakers [ST95]. In contrast, identification of speakers requires features which characterize the speaker [Fal95, Gis94]; herein, the recognition of spoken words is of minor interest. The same holds for topic spotting applications [War97], where the system has to recognize the topic of utterances and not the sequence of words. Similar decisions have to be made for image analysis. The identification of people based on their video images, for example, requires features that

---

[1]In speech processing the spatial domain is usually called temporal domain. Here we simply use "spatial domain" for both cases, image and speech processing.

are invariant with respect to movements of their faces, i.e., invariants under geometric transformations and distortions. In contrast, for gripping objects and pose estimation we need features which include information on the object's position and orientation in the world coordinate system.

It should be obvious that speech and image features of the mentioned examples will differ from each other extremely. Up to these days, there exists no unified mathematical framework which allows the (efficient) computation of features from an arbitrary signal, which are optimal with respect to a pre–defined recognition task. In general, in pattern recognition theory it is distinguished between heuristic and analytical methods for the computation of features [Nie83]. Heuristic methods apply well–known mathematical methods for signal to feature transforms, like the Fourier transform (c.f. Chapter 12) or orthographic projections into sub–spaces (c.f. Sect. 21.8). The experience and the computed recognition rates justify their use. Analytically computed features usually result from problem specific derivations. The given pattern recognition problem is formalized as an optimization task based on a well–defined objective function. For instance, features are computed by maximization of the recognition rate for a given classifier [Nie83].

The following sections will give an introduction to the computation of heuristic features like the short time Fourier transform. Methods for the calculation of spatial and frequency features for speech signals and images are discussed. The treatment of analytical techniques for feature extraction and selection methods to get the best elements of a set of features are left out here; these methods are much more difficult than heuristic methods. For interested readers, we recommend [Jai97, Nie83, Rip96, Sch92, The89].

23.2 Frames and Blocks

The computation of only one feature for a given signal seems difficult and inadequate. One and the same spoken work might have varying duration or an utterance is a sequence of completely different words. Multiple object scenes show unknown number of objects, and therefore feature vectors of constant dimensions cannot be expected. These simple examples make clear that the decomposition of signals into smaller units is essential. The subdivision here, however, is done in a systematic way, i.e., in contrast to those methods introduced in Chapter 14, no explicit segmentation will be done. Without considering any knowledge about the spoken words or the objects shown in a scene, sensor signals are divided up into short intervals of equal length or size.

In the case of speech signals, these intervals are called *frames* or *windows*. The length of frames has to be large enough to keep characteristic information about the speech signal, which is necessary for solving the recognition problem successfully. It is expected that the frequencies of the digital time signal does not vary too much within the chosen frame, i.e., the frame should be relatively small. The length of the window should at least include two periods of the glottis (c.f. Figure 23.14). In fact, the frame size depends on the application and the system design should adapt the balance between resolution in time and in frequency. In general, short frames induce high resolutions in time, but low resolution in frequencies. For increasing window size, the resolution in time decreases and the frequency resolution increases. In speech recognition, for instance, the windows have an average duration of 10–20 ms and they may overlap [Nie90a, ST95]. For topic spotting, however, frame sizes of 80 ms haven proven to be more appropriate [War97], since this corresponds to the average duration of phonems.

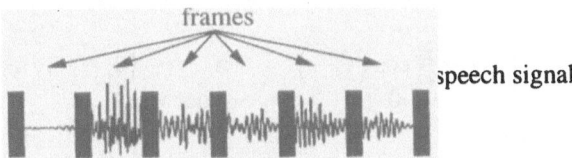

Figure 23.1 Decomposition of speech signals into frames

Also images can be partitioned into smaller subimages or *blocks* (Figure 23.2) which usually have quadratic size; commonly used window sizes are 3×3 or 5×5 [Bal82, Xu96]. The partitioning of images is not as common as for speech signals. Nevertheless, there exist some low– and high–level vision applications which make use of window functions. For instance, JPEG image coding (c.f. Chapter 11) requires a partition into blocks of size 8×8. For high–level vision, the use of blocks is mainly restricted to the computation and use of resolution hierarchies (Sect. 19.8). Further examples are stereo or object tracking algorithms which are based on block matching techniques, where blocks correspond to subimages [Kir90, Pos90].

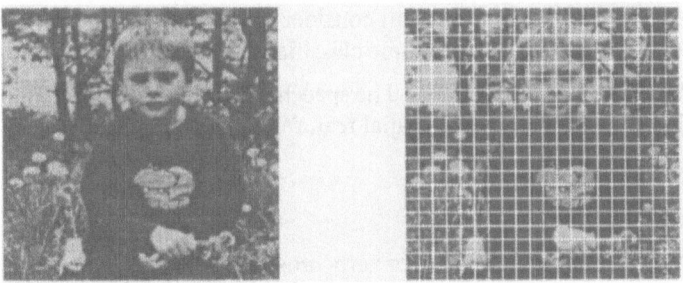

Figure 23.2 Decomposition of images into blocks

Mathematically, the decomposition of a sequence $[f_t]_{t\geq 0}$ of sample data into frames is done by multiplying the original signal with a window function w_τ. The components of the new signal $[f_t^{(\tau)}]_{t\geq 0}$ are defined by

$$f_t^{(\tau)} = w_{\tau-t} f_t \quad . \tag{23.1}$$

There exist different types of window functions which are applied in practice. The easiest one is the rectangle window function given by

$$w_\tau = \begin{cases} 1 & , \quad \text{if } \tau \in \{0, 1, \ldots, M-1\} \\ 0 & , \quad \text{otherwise} \end{cases} \quad . \tag{23.2}$$

The parameter M controls the window size. More often used functions are the Hamming window

$$w_\tau = \begin{cases} \frac{27}{50} - \frac{23}{50}\cos\left(\frac{2\pi\tau}{M-1}\right) & , \quad \text{if } \tau \in \{0, 1, \ldots, M-1\} \\ 0 & , \quad \text{otherwise} \end{cases} \tag{23.3}$$

and the Hann window

$$w_\tau = \begin{cases} \frac{1}{2} - \frac{1}{2}\cos\left(\frac{2\pi\tau}{M-1}\right) & , \quad \text{if } \tau \in \{0, 1, \ldots, M-1\} \\ 0 & , \quad \text{otherwise} \end{cases} \quad . \tag{23.4}$$

The introduced window functions allow the transform of speech signals into single frames of length M. Both the Hamming and the Hann weighting window functions attach smaller weights to samples at right and left sides of windows. This reduces noise effects in the computed feature sequences [ST95]. The extension of window functions to compute blocks for 2–D signals is straightforward and left to the reader.

23.3 Spatial Features

Spatial features result from the sample values without transforming the signal into the frequency or other domains. The algorithms for feature detection work on the quantized signal directly. In the following we will consider some selected sets of spatial features, which are appropriate for solving simple classification tasks.

Let $[f_t]_{t\geq 0}$ be a discrete speech signal. The speech signal is decomposed into a sequence of frames. For each frame, several spatial features can be computed:

- the zero–crossing rate,
- the autocorrelation,
- the sequence of average slopes for zero–crossings,
- the short time energy.

Dependent on the utterance, the zero–crossing rate of speech signals varies. Vowels like the "a" show a lower frequency of zero–crossings than the the spoken letter "s" (Figure 23.3). Thus, the zero–crossing rate seems to be an appropriate feature for discriminating voiced and unvoiced. The zero–crossing frequency threshold for the classification of voiceless and voiced signals is 1000 Hz for male and 1500 Hz for female speakers. Many systems also apply the *autocorrelation*

$$c_\nu^{(\tau)} = \sum_{t=-\infty}^{+\infty} f_t^{(\tau)} f_{t+\nu}^{(\tau)} \tag{23.5}$$

to identify voiced and voiceless parts [ST95].

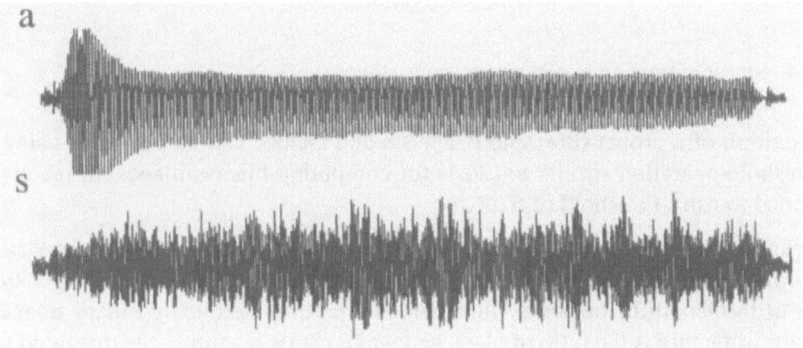

Figure 23.3 Speech signals corresponding to the utterances "a" (upper) and "s" (lower)

Another appropriate feature, which is associated with zero–crossings, is the average slope of the speech signal at those points where the speech signal intersects the time axis. The computation of slopes for a given neighborhood is usually done by linear regression introduced in Sect. 21.8. The principle of slope computation is illustrated in Figure 23.4.

For many applications in speech recognition, the system records signals all the time, but the recognition module should only start working, if somebody speaks to the system. The classification of speech and silence is required for that reason, and it can be done by using the short time energy. The energy of the complete signal is defined by

$$E = \sum_{t=-\infty}^{+\infty} f_t^2 \quad , \tag{23.6}$$

but usually frames are considered instead of the complete utterance. For single frames we get the *short time energy* by

$$E^{(\tau)} = \sum_{t=0}^{M-1} \left(f_t^{(\tau)} \right)^2 = \sum_{t=0}^{M-1} w_{\tau-t}^2 f_t^2 \quad . \tag{23.7}$$

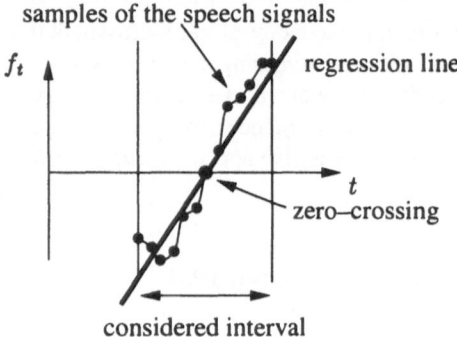

Figure 23.4 Linear regression to compute average slopes

By the definition of a proper threshold θ, speech and silence can be classified using a simple threshold operation similar to (20.1) for computing binary images. In practice, it is suggested to use a threshold of 5 dB.[2]

Binary images are often the first step towards spatial features for computer vision purposes. Many classification systems in image processing apply features like the area of objects or the length of boundary lines which are computed using binary images. Another type of feature is the ratio of black and white pixels or simply the threshold for binarization, which is usually computed using operations on histograms (Chapter 20). Not only the threshold for binarization, but also the relative frequencies of single gray–levels, the number of maxima or the shape in general are features derived from histograms and used for for solving many problems of practical relevance [Jäh93, Jai90, Pit93]. Averaging techniques based on gray–level images are especially useful for solving simple classification problems. Examples for averaging methods are the computation of means μ and variances σ^2 of sample values in a frame (c.f. Sect. 8.3). A measure for the smoothness of the signal is the *relative smoothness* which is defined by

$$s \; = \; 1 - \frac{1}{1 + \sigma^2} \qquad\qquad (23.8)$$

and computed for each considered block. The relative smoothness allows, for instance, the classification of textures (c.f. Chapter 18). The value of s vanishes for blocks of constant intensity, and it is close to one for rough textures with varying gray–levels.

The mean and variance are powerful features for the classification of objects, where no rigorous changes in gray–levels of the test images and illumination conditions occur. Features computed by averaging techniques are approximately invariant with respect to

---

[2]This threshold, of course, depends on your recording device and varies.

2–D rotations and translations of objects.[3] Other features for texture identification are the gray–level matrix, or other statistical measure, which characterize the distribution of gray–levels [Nie90a]. Other spatial features are based on edge images instead of gray-level or binary images. Features are defined by the major edge direction, the average edge strength, the variance of edge strength or the zero–crossing rate using the second derivatives computed by the Laplace mask (c.f. Chapter 14).

23.4 Short Time Fourier Analysis and Spectral Features

The computation of the energy (23.6) or the Fourier transform for complete signals is not useful, because changes of the spectrum within the signal include a high degree of information. Therefore, the integrand of the signal's Fourier transform is weighted by window functions which were introduced in Sect. 23.2. Instead of transforming the complete signal, we compute the Fourier transform frame by frame. In order to use the FFT (Sect. 12.4), it is useful and advantageous to have a frame length M which is a power of two (e.g., M=256 samples).

The discrete Fourier transform of this weighted signal is

$$F_\nu^{(\tau)} = \sum_{t=0}^{M-1} f_t^{(\tau)} \exp\left(\frac{-2\pi i\nu\tau}{M}\right) = \sum_{t=0}^{M-1} w_{\tau-t} f_t \exp\left(\frac{-2\pi i\nu\tau}{M}\right) \quad . (23.9)$$

Since the window function fades out most of the signal, this transform is called the *short time Fourier transform*.

The computation of the short time Fourier transform proceeds as follows: the speech signal is transformed into a sequence of frames. For each frame the discrete Fourier transform yields a sequence of Fourier coefficients $[F_\nu^{(\tau)}]_{\nu\geq 0}$, where $F_\nu^{(\tau)} \in C$. These coefficients or subsets of these coefficients can be used as features. Instead of using these coefficients directly, the absolute values of these complex numbers are used. This is advantageous, because we are more familiar with real than with complex numbers; the main reason, however, is due to the fact that absolute values are invariant with respect to translations of the signal. The phase of the signal does not influence these features, because due to the shifting property of Fourier transforms, the translation corresponds to a multiplication by $\exp(-2\pi i\nu m/M)$, and we know that $|\exp(-2\pi i\nu m/M)| = 1$ such that:

$$|F_\nu^{(\tau)} \exp\left(\frac{-2\pi i\nu m}{M}\right)| = |F_\nu^{(\tau)}| \quad . \tag{23.10}$$

The absolute values $[|F_\nu^{(\tau)}|]_{\nu\geq 0}$, for instance, result in the power spectrum of the speech signal, which provides appropriate features for speech processing. Figures 23.6, 23.7,

---

[3]From a theoretically point of view this is not correct, but in practice averaged features show sufficient invariance with respect to different types of transforms.

Figure 23.5 Speech signal of the utterance: "this is one word"

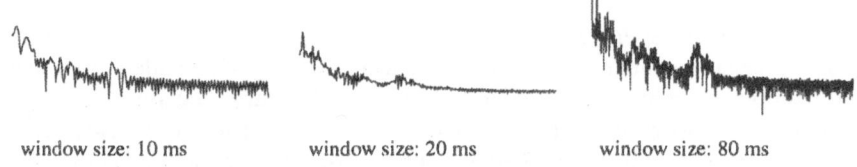

window size: 10 ms   window size: 20 ms   window size: 80 ms

Figure 23.6 Logarithmic spectrum using rectangular windows of varying size

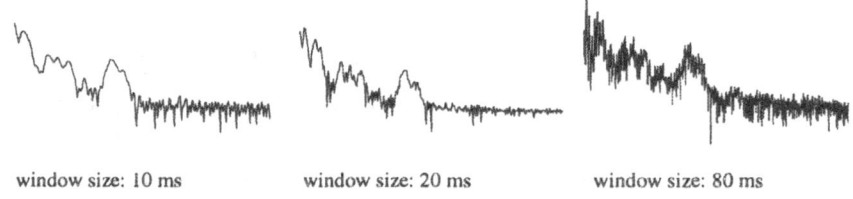

window size: 10 ms   window size: 20 ms   window size: 80 ms

Figure 23.7 Logarithmic spectrum using Hamming windows of varying size

and 23.8 show examples of logarithmic spectra $[\log |F_\nu^{(\tau)}|]_{\nu \geq 0}$ with different window functions and varying frame size corresponding to the speech signal of the utterance "this is one word" (Figure 23.5). Each frame of the speech signal can be associated with a spectrum. An utterance thus induces a sequence of spectra, like those shown so far.

There is a way from sound back to images. Image generation and visualization methods can be applied for the construction of *spectrograms*. Spectrograms allow the illustration of all frames' spectra in a single image. For each pixel in the image, the row is determined by the frequency $|F_\nu|$ (or its logarithm), the column is determined by the time. The intensity or color values are related to the the real values $|F_\nu|$ or $\log |F_\nu|$ of the related frequency in the sound signal. For that reason, a mapping has to be defined which assigns real values to discrete pixel values. The frequency analysis of each individual frame in the speech signal is done using the short time Fourier transform, and defines one column of the synthetic image. For simplicity, we compute the absolute values of

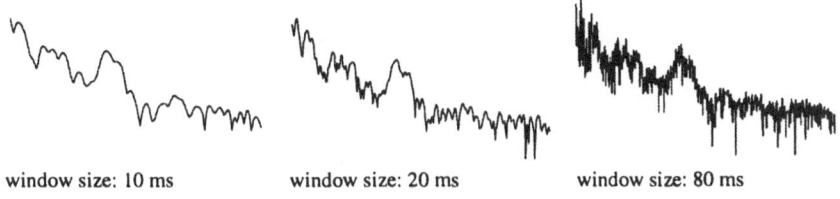

window size: 10 ms   window size: 20 ms   window size: 80 ms

Figure 23.8 Logarithmic spectrum using Hann windows of varying size

Fourier coefficients from sample values and scale the resulting floating point numbers to 256 gray values or colors. These 256 values now correspond to a column in the image. An example of a spectrogram corresponding to the complete utterance of Figure 23.5 is shown in Figure 23.9. Spectrograms are distinguished with respect to the chosen frame size. *Narrow band* spectrograms resolve harmonics and blur temporal details, and *wide band* spectrograms resolve temporal details, but loose line frequency details. Figure 23.9 shows an example of a narrow band spectrogram, and illustrates the wide band spectrogram of the same utterance.[4]

The idea of the short time Fourier transform can also be applied to image processing. The image is decomposed into blocks, and the Fourier transform can be done on each block separately. Figure 23.9 (left) shows an example of a synthetic interferogram; such pictures result, for instance, from the superposition of a holographic image with its optical image [Ost91]. For the analysis of this image, it is useful to compute the Fourier transform for each 64×64 window. The absolute values of the result are visualized in Figure 23.9 (right). For JPEG, 8×8 subimages are converted to the spectral domain by the discrete cosine–transform (Sect. 12.2), and then processed further.

It is well–known that you can get the information about the shape of a signal using primarily relative phases. Obviously, the absolute phases cannot be responsible for shapes, since shapes change with translations. The absolute phase, however, is eliminated, whenever the magnitudes of the Fourier coefficients are considered (c.f. (23.10)). A well established feature which can be used for shape classification is the *bispectrum.*. We restrict the following discussion to bispectra of 1–D signals; 2–D generalizations are left to the reader. The bispectrum of a discrete signal $[f_t^{(\tau)}]_{t=0,...,M-1}$ is defined by the bivariate discrete function

$$B_{\nu_1,\nu_2}^{(\tau)} = F_{\nu_1}^{(\tau)} F_{\nu_2}^{(\tau)} F_{-\nu_1-\nu_2}^{(\tau)} \ , \tag{23.11}$$

wherein $[F_\nu^{(\tau)}]_{\nu=0,...,M-1}$ denotes the discrete Fourier transform of $[f_t^{(\tau)}]_{\tau=0,...,M-1}$. It can be shown that the bispectrum is uniquely defined in the interval defined by

$$0 \le \nu_1 \le \nu_2 \le \nu_1 + \nu_2 \le 1 \ . \tag{23.12}$$

---

[4]There is a nice URL where you can find information on "Seeing with your ears": http://home.pi.net/%7Emeijerpb/javoice.htm

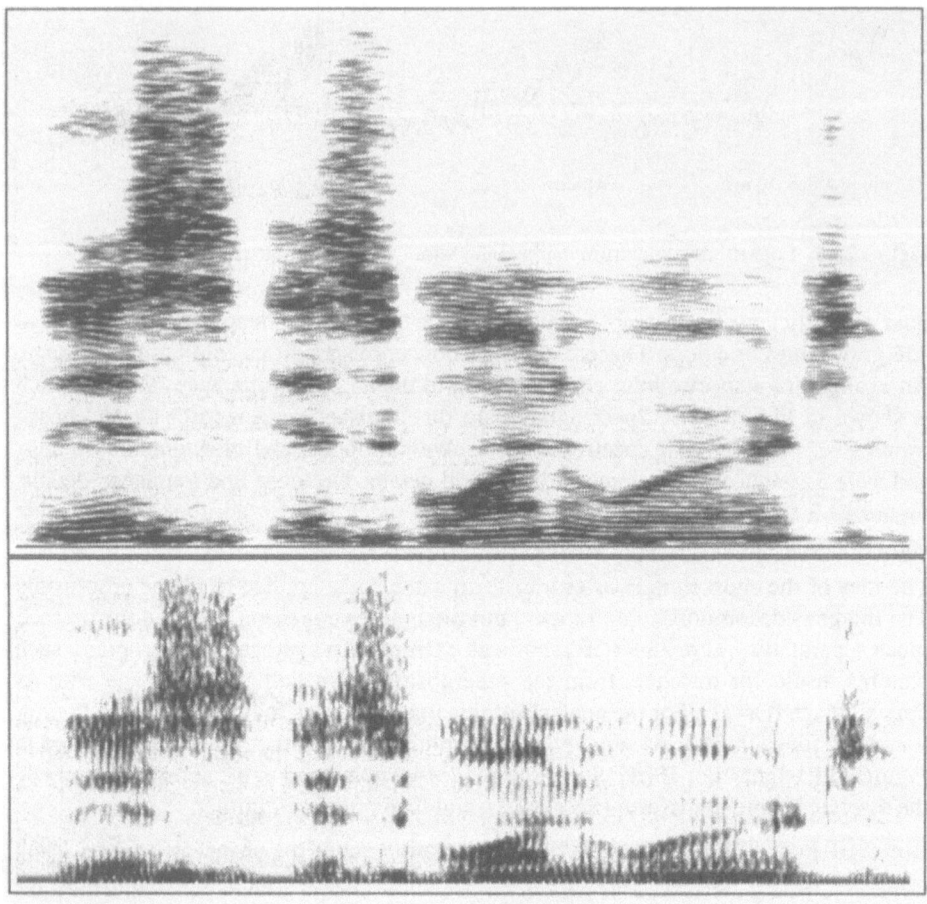

Figure 23.9 Narrow band (top) and wide band (bottom) spectrogram of the utterance: "this is one word"

The bispectrum is commonly applied to define invariants for one–dimensional signals. For object recognition purposes, for instance, the authors of [Cha91, Cha92] show that the bispectrum can be used to define features which do not change with respect to translations, adding a constant to sample values, and scaling. These bispectral invariants are successfully applied to solve 2–D object recognition problems using images including single objects and homogeneous background.

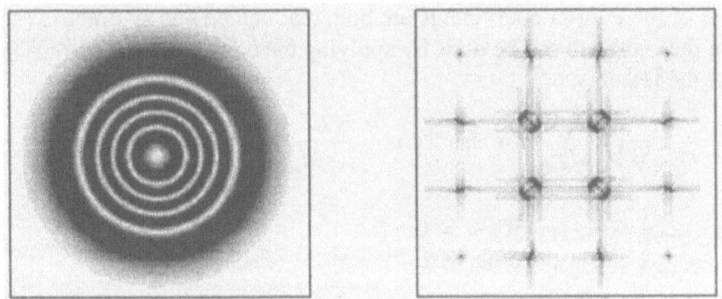

Figure 23.10 Synthetic image and its spectrum using a 64 × 64 window

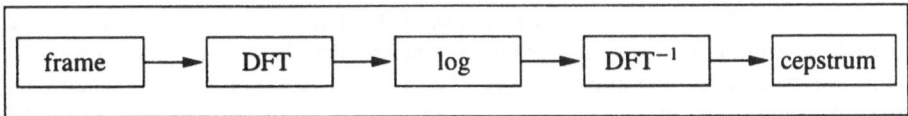

Figure 23.11 Computation of cepstral features

23.5 Cepstral Features

Another fundamental spectral feature for speech processing applications is the so–called *cepstrum*. The components $c_\nu^{(\tau)}$ of the complex cepstrum $c^{(\tau)} = (c_0^{(\tau)}, c_1^{(\tau)}, \ldots, c_{M-1}^{(\tau)})^T$ are defined by

$$c_\nu{}^{(\tau)} = \frac{1}{M} \sum_{\nu'=0}^{M-1} (\log F_{\nu'}^{(\tau)}) \exp\left(\frac{2\pi i \nu \nu'}{M}\right) \quad ; \tag{23.13}$$

these features are usually applied for the classification of phonemes. Due to the fact that the Fourier transform produces complex results, it is necessary to compute the complex logarithm, which is defined by

$$\log z = \log |z| + i \arg(z) \quad , \tag{23.14}$$

where $z = \mathrm{re}(z) + i\,\mathrm{im}(z)$, $\arg(z) = \mathrm{im}(z)/\mathrm{re}(z)$, and $\mathrm{re}(z), \mathrm{im}(z) \in \mathbf{R}$. The real valued (and more practical) cepstrum $^r c_\nu{}^{(\tau)}$ uses the absolute values instead of complex numbers and is thus defined by

$$^r c_\nu{}^{(\tau)} = \frac{1}{M} \sum_{\nu'=0}^{M-1} (\log |F_{\nu'}^{(\tau)}|) \exp\left(\frac{2\pi i \nu \nu'}{M}\right) \quad ; \tag{23.15}$$

obviously it avoids the evaluation of the complex logarithm. Due to the fact that the magnitudes of the Fourier coefficients are both real valued and symmetric (!), the computation of the cepstrum can be done by applying the cosine–transform (c.f. Sect. 12.2), and we get the features:

$$
{}^r c_\nu^{(\tau)} \;=\; \frac{s(\nu)}{\sqrt{M}} \sum_{\nu'=0}^{M/2-1} \log |F_{\nu'}^{(\tau)}| \cos \frac{\nu\,\pi(2\nu'+1)}{M} \quad, \tag{23.16}
$$

where

$$
s(\nu) \;=\; \left\{ \begin{array}{ll} \sqrt{2} & , \quad \text{if} \quad \nu = 0 \quad, \\ 2 & , \quad \text{otherwise} \quad. \end{array} \right. \tag{23.17}
$$

A closer look to the definition of the cepstrum shows that the cepstrum is indeed a spectral analysis of the spectrum. The mathematical modeling of Fant's source filter theory [ST95] allows a systematical derivation of the spectrum and is omitted here. In fact, cepstral features allow the decomposition of the signal into independent components concerning stimulation and impulse response of the human vocal tract. A low–passed filtered cepstrum eliminates the excitation, whereas the characteristics of resonances remain in the features. A more detailed and deeper discussion of different spectral and cepstral features, and their use for speech recognition applications can be found in [Hua90, Nie90a]. Nevertheless, the following sections summarize some further important features applied in pattern recognition, omitting physiological and mathematical details.

23.6 Mel Spectral and Cepstral Features

Many researchers in the field of physiology and speech processing have tried to determine the type of frequency analysis performed by the human ear. Speech signals are received by humans as pressure variations. The real frequencies are mapped to activities of the basilar membrane. Empirical studies have shown that this mapping is a non–linear frequency transform. Indeed, the human ear resolves frequencies in different ways: the higher the frequency of speech signals, the lower the resolution. This empirical result has lead to the definition of scales for frequencies based on human perception capabilities. The dependency of human resolution and real frequencies was determined by experiments, where humans had to listen to sound of varying frequencies. They had to describe the change in perception, like high frequency, half as high frequency etc. Using these empirical data, the linear frequency axis (f) is converted into a *Mel scale* (f_{mel}) applying the transform [Fan73]

$$
f_{\text{mel}} \;=\; 2595 \log \left(1 + \frac{f}{700\,\text{Hz}} \right) \quad. \tag{23.18}
$$

The graph of this mapping is illustrated in Figure 23.12.

With respect to this observation, we have to consider modified definitions of the originally introduced spectrum and cepstrum. The *Mel spectrum* results in a weighted

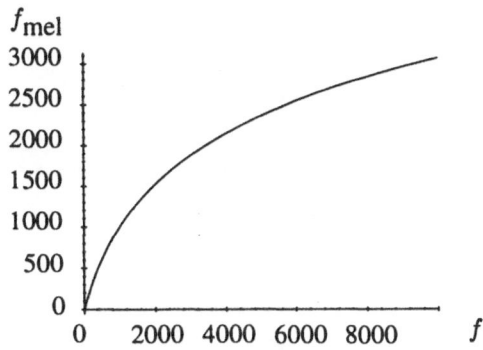

Figure 23.12 Mel scale

version of the original spectrum. The basic idea is to define discrete filters $[h_t^{(k)}]_{t \geq 0}$, $k = \{0, 1, \ldots, K - 1\}$, which operate on the discrete signal $[f_t^{(\tau)}]_{t \geq 0}$. Examples of three different triangular discrete filters are illustrated in Figure 23.13. The resulting signal $[g_t^{(k,\tau)}]_{t \geq 0}$ is defined by

$$g_t^{(k,\tau)} = \sum_\mu f_\mu^{(\tau)} h_{t-\mu}^{(k)} \quad . \tag{23.19}$$

Obviously, the operation in (23.19) is a discrete convolution of $[f_t^{(\tau)}]_{t \geq 0}$ and $[h_t^{(k)}]_{t \geq 0}$. Therefore, the Fourier transforms $F_\nu^{(\tau)}$, $G_\nu^{(\tau,k)}$, and $H_\nu^{(k)}$ satisfy (convolution theorem, c.f. Sect. 12.3)

$$G_\nu^{(\tau,k)} = F_\nu^{(\tau)} H_\nu^{(k)} \quad . \tag{23.20}$$

Using this equation, the Mel spectrum is simply defined by

$$\text{MFC}^{(\tau,k)} = \sum_{\nu=0}^{M-1} (H_\nu^{(k)})^2 (F_\nu^{(\tau)})^2 \quad , \tag{23.21}$$

and the *Mel cepstrum* is analogously

$$\text{MFCC}_\nu^{(\tau)} = \sum_{k=0}^{K-1} \log |\text{MFC}^{(\tau,k)}| \cos \frac{\nu \pi (2k + 3)}{2K} \quad . \tag{23.22}$$

The 25 linear filters, which are commonly used for computing Mel spectra and Mel cepstra, are based on seven triangle shaped functions with $f_1 = 150$ Hz, $f_2 = 200$ Hz, $f_3 = 250$ Hz, $\ldots$, $f_7 = 450$ Hz. The width of each triangle is 100 Hz. Furthermore, each octave between 500 Hz and 4000 Hz[5] includes six filters, where the filters start and end at the frequencies of their neighbors [ST95].

---

[5]i.e., 500 Hz — 1000 Hz, 1000 Hz — 2000 Hz, and 2000 Hz — 4000 Hz

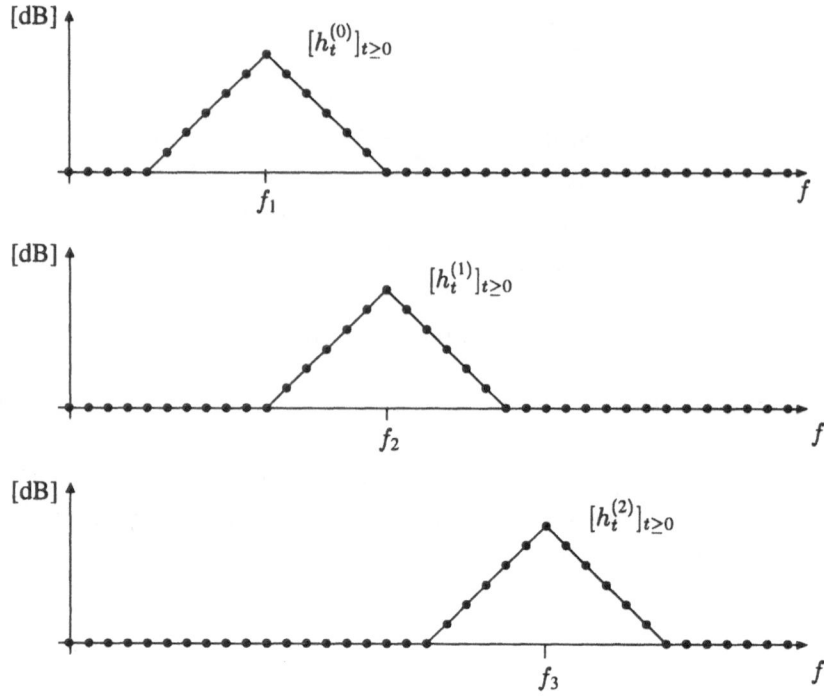

Figure 23.13 Three filters for the computation of the Mel cepstrum

23.7   Linear Predictive Coding

Speech recognition algorithms apply combinations of spatial, spectral, and cepstral features, to construct features, and to improve the recognition results. The crucial point of speech recognition algorithms and the associated features is that researchers look for suitable mathematical models. These models should consider both the speech production and the speech perception of human beings, because for pattern analysis it is useful to know about the principles of speech generation and about speech reception. In this sense, speech analysis is more complex than computer vision, which simulates only the human *sensor* (the eye, Figure 1.7). The human sensor — the ear — was already shown in Figure 1.3, and the perception as well as the resolution of frequencies was empirically studied, and is modeled within the Mel scale. In Figure 23.14, we see the anatomy of the human speech generation system. All speech signals are produced by air streaming from the lungs through the *vocal tract* including throat and mouth. Consequently, the characteristics of the vocal tract influence speech signals. The average length of the adult male vocal tract is 17 cm, and the diameter varies up to 2.5 cm. If voiced speech

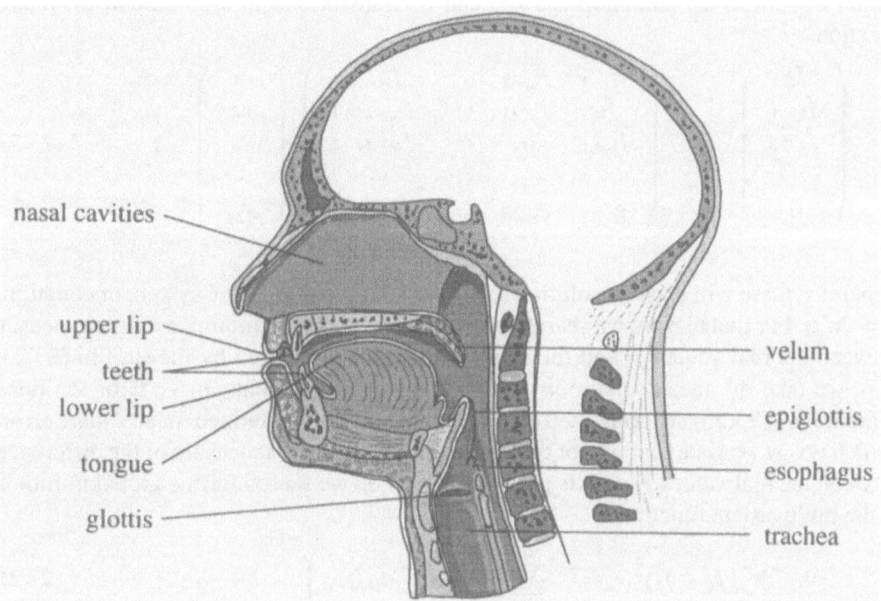

Figure 23.14 Speech production: the vocal tract

is produced, the vocal folds are caused to vibrate. The vibration frequency is the so–called *pitch frequency*. The pitch frequency of an adult speaker is in the range of 50 to 500 Hz. Children or women have higher pitch frequencies than male speakers, because the vocal folds are shorter. In a physical sense, the vocal tract forms a tube which is characterized by its resonances, the so–called *formants*. Since humans show differences in the structure of the vocal tract (length, diameters, resonances, etc.), the influence of the tube on the speech signal is not significant for recognition purposes and should be eliminated. Linear predictive coding (LPC) provides a complete model for speech production, and it analyzes the speech signal such that the characteristic effects of the vocal tract and its formants can be separated from the excitation. The process of removing the formants is called *inverse filtering*, whereas the remaining signal is called the *residue*.

Without introducing mathematical details and results from signal theory, the basic idea of LPC is that each discrete value f_t of the speech signal $[f_t]_{t\geq 0}$ has to be represented by a linear combination

$$f_t = \sum_{\mu=1}^{M} a_\mu f_{t-\mu} \tag{23.23}$$

of M predecessors $f_{t-1}, f_{t-2}, \ldots, f_{t-M}$. For all samples f_t, $t_0 \leq t \leq t_1$, of a given frame, this linear combination (23.23) can be transformed into an equivalent matrix equation

$$
\begin{pmatrix} f_{t_0} \\ f_{t_0+1} \\ f_{t_0+2} \\ \vdots \\ \hat{f}_{t_1} \end{pmatrix} = \underbrace{\begin{pmatrix} f_{t_0-1} & f_{t_0-2} & \cdots & f_{t_0-M} \\ f_{t_0} & f_{t_0-1} & \cdots & f_{t_0-M+1} \\ f_{t_0+1} & f_{t_0} & \cdots & f_{t_0-M+2} \\ \vdots & \vdots & \vdots & \vdots \\ f_{t_1-1} & f_{t_1-2} & \cdots & f_{t_1} - M \end{pmatrix}}_{M \in \mathbf{R}^{(t_1-t_0) \times M}} \begin{pmatrix} a_1 \\ a_2 \\ a_3 \\ \vdots \\ a_M \end{pmatrix} . \tag{23.24}
$$

Generally, there will exist no solution $a = (a_1, a_2, \ldots, a_M)^T$ of the system of equations, $f = Ma$. For that reason, we search for parameters a which minimize an error measure between the real values f_t and their approximations $\hat{f}_t$ defined by the sum in (23.23). Here we take the mean square error. The predictor coefficients $a_\mu \in \mathbf{R}$ of the linear combination (23.23) are computed by minimizing the parameterized mean square error ϵ (which is a M–variate function of the vector a). This error is a measure of the differences between the real values f_t and its predictions $\hat{f}_t$, i.e., we search for the global minimum of the multivariate function

$$
\epsilon = \sum_{t=t_0}^{t_1} (f_t - \hat{f}_t)^2 = \sum_{t=t_0}^{t_1} \left(f_t - \sum_{\mu=1}^{M} a_\mu f_{t-\mu} \right)^2 . \tag{23.25}
$$

The optimization of (23.25) can be done using the gradient and the zero–crossings of the gradient vector with respect to the variables $a_1, a_2, \ldots, a_M$. The partial derivatives are

$$
\frac{\partial \epsilon}{\partial a_\nu} = -2 \cdot \sum_{t=t_0}^{t_1} \left(f_t - \sum_{\mu=1}^{M} a_\mu f_{t-\mu} \right) \cdot f_{t-\nu} , \tag{23.26}
$$

for $1 \leq \nu \leq M$, and we get M linear equations

$$
\sum_{\mu=1}^{M} a_\mu \sum_{t=t_0}^{t_1} f_{t-\mu} f_{t-\nu} = - \sum_{t=t_0}^{t_1} f_t f_{t-\nu} , \tag{23.27}
$$

wherein the computation of the autocorrelation (c.f. (23.5)) is required. A recursive and efficient way to solve this system of linear equations is due to Levinson (c.f. [Nie83], p. 99), but this method will not be introduced here. Instead, we use the pseudo–inverse matrix, which was already introduced in Sect. 21.8, and get

$$
\begin{pmatrix} a_1 \\ a_2 \\ a_3 \\ \vdots \\ a_M \end{pmatrix} = M^+ \begin{pmatrix} f_{t_0} \\ f_{t_0+1} \\ f_{t_0+2} \\ \vdots \\ f_{t_1} \end{pmatrix} , \tag{23.28}
$$

where $M^+ = \left(M^T M \right)^{-1} M^T$ is the pseudo–inverse of M.

One common problem associated with linear prediction is the question, how many predecessors of f_t should be considered in the linear combination. Experimental evaluations have shown that the sampling frequency, measured in kHz, plus 4 or 5 is an appropriate number of prediction coefficients ([Nie83], p. 100). This general rule allows an appropriate computation of residues.

The practical use of LPC coefficients is multifarious. They are used for speech encoding, speech synthesis, and speech recognition. Of course, for different speech signals we get different prediction coefficients. The vector of LPC coefficients can thus serve as a feature vector for discriminating signals of different classes. In addition to the coefficient vector a, usually the mean–square error (23.25) is also used as an component of the feature vector [Nie83, Nie90a].

The discussion so far is restricted to one–dimensional signals. Of course, linear prediction is also applied for image processing, especially for texture modeling [Mao92]. A suitable neighborhood $[f_{i,j}]_{n_0 \leq i \leq n_1, m_0 \leq j \leq m_1}$ is chosen and gray–levels of the image are expressed by linear combinations of their neighbors, i.e.,

$$f_{i,j} = \sum_{\substack{\mu=n_0 \\ i \neq \mu}}^{n_1} \sum_{\substack{\nu=m_0 \\ j \neq \nu}}^{m_1} a_{\mu,\nu} f_{i-\mu,j-\nu} \quad . \tag{23.29}$$

The computation of the coefficient matrix $(a_{\mu,\nu})_{\mu,\nu}$ is done analogously to the one–dimensional case. We have to minimize the mean square error of the prediction:

$$\epsilon = \sum_{i,j} (f_{i,j} - \hat{f}_{i,j})^2 \quad . \tag{23.30}$$

The resulting matrix of coefficients can be used as image features and can be applied for the comparison or classification of textures or images.

23.8 Model Spectrum and Cepstrum

Most speech recognition system use two types of cepstral features. On the one hand DFT cepstral features are applied as introduced in Sect. 23.5 and Sect. 23.6, where the Fourier transform is directly operating on the speech signal. The LPC coefficients a can be used to compute the *model spectrum* (or *LPC spectrum*), which is the discrete Fourier transform of the computed prediction coefficients a.

The model spectrum is a smoothed version of the Fourier transform of the original signal. The maxima of the model spectrum indicate the formants and are discriminating features for vowels ([Nie83], p. 108). Figure 23.15 shows the model spectrum using a varying number of prediction coefficients. The smoothing property is illustrated in Figure 23.16. Cepstral coefficients corresponding to the LPC coefficients are widely used in speech recognition.

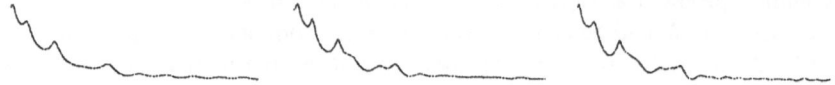

Figure 23.15 Logarithmic model spectrum using Hamming windows (duration 10 ms) and 20, 30 and 40 prediction coefficients

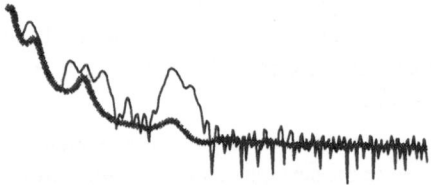

Figure 23.16 Logarithmic spectrum and logarithmic model spectrum (20 prediction coefficients) using Hamming windows (duration 10 ms)

The model spectrum can be used to compute the *model cepstrum*. For that purpose, the magnitude of Fourier coefficients related to the model spectrum are the input components of a discrete Fourier transform. A nice theoretical result shows that the model cepstrum can be computed without an explicit Fourier transform. The required recursive formulas are omitted and can be found in [ST95]. In general, the cepstral features resulting from LPC coefficients represent the characteristics of the vocal tract and excitation separately. The advantages of the model cepstrum are that higher order coefficients encode the excitation coefficients, whereas the lower ones include the characteristic properties of the vocal tract.

23.9   Implementation Issues

The computation of the pseudo–inverse in Sect. 23.7 requires matrix inversion and multiplication. All these operations were already introduced and implemented in our template class for matrices. Thus, the computation of LPC coefficients is easy and straightforward.

The regression line in Figure 23.4 could as well be computed using the pseudo–inverse. A more efficient and easier solution was shown in Exercise 21.h.

This chapter treats many features and methods to compute them. Obviously, features for speech and image processing purposes are different from each other. A very general view on speech classification is shown in Figure 23.17. The features denoted by c_i vary greatly between applications: they may be sequences of scalars, sequences of vectors,

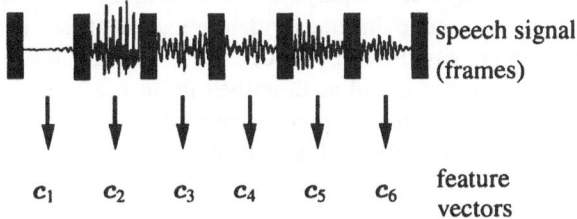

Figure 23.17 Decomposition of speech signals into frames, and the associated sequence of features

```
#include "Object.h"
class RandomVariable : public Object {} ; // to be refined
class Feature : public Object {
 public :
  virtual double operator- (const Feature&) const = 0;   // distance function
  virtual operator RandomVariable () const = 0;
};
```
192

sequences of feature sequences, matrices, sets of matrices and others. With respect to implementation issues, classifiers should work with arbitrary features. They should be independent from the concrete representation as much as possible. For that reason, we define an abstract class for features to be used for classification purposes (Program 192). As we will see in Chapter 24, it is most useful to have a distance function in order to compare two features; this is implemented in Program 192 as a pure virtual operator. For the implementation of a classification we will now have to derive our own class for features from this abstract base class; in this derived class we can have any combination of the numeric feature values which were introduced in this chapter. Our derived class will have to define a distance function which is dependent on the particular classifier and on the application.

For statistical classification it is often useful to convert a feature to a random variable. We also provide a conversion for this purpose and outline how this can be declared in Program 192.

Exercises

23.a   Typical features of a speech signal are the zero–crossings and the slopes of the univariate function in those points. Write a program which computes all zero–crossings of a given speech signal. Implement the calculation of the slope for a zero–crossing. For that purpose define a neighborhood of discrete sample values and use the pseudo–inverse for determination of the slope.

23.b   Use the signals created in Sect. 18.1. Overlay them with noise created in Sect. 18.5 using a tool as described in Sect. 18.1. Create an image object of appropriate size and compute the spectrum.

23.c   A one–dimensional signal is defined by

t	0	1	2	3	4	5
f_t	2	6	1	-4	-3	0

Compute the coefficients a_1 and a_2 of the linear prediction and use the result for the determination of f_6.

23.d   Implement a function which computes the LPC prediction coefficients for each sample of a given frame of the speech signal. Use the Gauss elimination procedure for solving the occurring system of linear equations. Now apply your algorithm for speech encoding and send the resynthetisized signal to your soundcard.

24 Numerical Pattern Classification

Numerical pattern classification deals with the problem of assigning feature vectors c to a class Ω_κ of the available classes $\Omega = \{\Omega_1, \Omega_2, \ldots, \Omega_K\}$. The features are computed from (noisy) sensor data, like images or speech signals. We postulate that signals can be associated with features which allow the classification, i.e., features of different classes should be different and separated from each other. Features belonging to the same class are thus expected to occupy a compact area of the feature space [Nie90a].

Let us assume that the numerical feature c is a d–dimensional, real valued vector. Thus a classifier is mathematically defined by the discrete mapping

$$\zeta : \begin{cases} \mathbf{R}^d & \to & \{1, 2, \ldots, K\} \\ c & \mapsto & \kappa \end{cases} \tag{24.1}$$

which assigns a class index κ to each feature vector c. The assignment ζ is the so–called *decision function*.[1]

In speech recognition, for instance, this function might map a speech signal to a single word of a given lexicon or into a sentence with its semantics. Other examples, where it is not important to understand *what* is said, are the identification of languages or the classification of persons using speech signals. The classifier assigns a language class or a person's name to each speech signal,

Special types of classification problems, which are used in image processing, were already discussed in Sect. 20.1. The computation of binary images requires the classification of each pixel. We have to decide for each element of the gray–level image, whether it is part of the back– or foreground. In this case, the classification rule is defined by a simple threshold operation. The multi–thresholding algorithm (c.f. Sect. 20.3) applies another classifier which assigns pixels to more than two classes. More common and far more complicated applications of pattern classifiers than preprocessing are the identification and localization of objects shown in a given scene. The classification rule for binarization is easily derived from fairly elementary arguments using histograms and relative frequencies; the classification of speech or image signals, in general, requires more complicated and sophisticated decision rules.

Several numerical classifiers are introduced and discussed in the following sections. The reader will get a brief and illustrative introduction to classification theory and a proper insight into various classifiers without extensive mathematical expositions. For detailed theoretical considerations, we strongly recommend [Dev96, Nie83, Sch92, The89].

---

[1] In the following text we use *decision function* and *decision rule* for ζ.

24.1   General Notes on Classifiers

Before we start with various definitions of the decision function ζ, we have to explain some basic concepts of classification theory.

Figure 6.1 has introduced the common structure of simple pattern classification systems, where the classification module requires the definition of an appropriate decision function ζ. The classification rule depends on the considered problem domain. A general decision procedure which solves all classification problems within the given feature space seems impossible. The construction of classifiers basically uses observable data and takes experience and domain knowledge (not necessarily of experts) into consideration. Using these sources of information, a general decision rule is computed which also allows the classification of features which were not part of the sample data. The process of constructing a decision rule using a set of samples is usually called the *learning stage* (or *training*) and the generalization property of classifiers. In pattern recognition theory there is a differentiation between two types of learning: if the classes of sample elements are known, we call it *supervised learning*. Otherwise the learning stage is *unsupervised*. Both approaches can be used to create a classifier automatically.

A common problem is the judgement of classifiers and the development of measures for the quality of classifiers. Obvious and most applied criteria are the probability of misclassification or the concrete recognition rate for predefined sample sets. Standard test beds and benchmark data for pattern recognition are, for instance, the U.S. Postal Service database [Vap96], the Computer Vision Test Images,[2] the ECVnet Benchmarking[3] or the speech data of the North American Business Corpus. In general, the optimality of classifiers depends on the chosen criteria. If, for example, a classifier provides the lowest probability for misclassification and the computational complexity prohibits its practical use, we will not denote this decision procedure to be optimal for real world applications. For that reason, classifiers are often judged by the produced costs of the decision rule. Correct, false, and rejected classifications may cause different costs. The expected costs of a decision function might be considered as an appropriate measure for the implemented classifier. A classifier, for instance, which decides, whether a person is allowed to enter a high security zone, will cause lower costs if an authorized person is rejected, than allowing access for an unauthorized person. Nevertheless, in the following we define the best classifier by the minimization of the error probability. It can be shown that this classifier is equal to the classifier using a cost function which weights correct decisions with zero and misclassifications with one. The error probability p_B of this optimal classifier is the so–called *Bayesian error probability*. The major problem is the computation of a decision rule which results in an optimal classifier.

---

[2]c.f. http://www.cs.cmu.edu/~cil/v-images.html
[3]c.f. http://peipa.essex.ac.uk/benchmark

```
struct Sample : public Object {  // auxiliary class
  int classnumber;               // ordered pair for labeled
  Feature * feature;             // sample
};

class Classifier : public Object {
 private:
  int number_of_classes; // dimension
  int has_reject_class;  // if 1, classes range from 0...number_of_classes
  int trained;           // if 1, classifier is ready to do classification
 public:
  virtual int classify(const Feature & f) const = 0;
  virtual void train(const Bag&);    // supply trainings 'set'
};
```
193

Different types of decision rules result in classifiers with various properties. It is interesting from the theoretical point of view to compare different classifiers with respect to several characteristics. In particular, the relationship between the considered and the optimal classifier is of highest importance. Another significant property of classifiers is the consistency of their decision rules. A discrimination rule is called *consistent*, if an increase of the sample data size implies the approximation of the Bayesian error p_B.

24.2 Design of Classifiers

The design of classifiers is based on the fundamental assumption that feature vectors of the same class have a small distance with respect to a suitably defined distance function. This measure might be a geometric distance function (e.g., the Euclidean distance), some probability measure (e.g., a posteriori probability) or others. The very general structure of a classifier in C++ is shown in Program 193. A function which gets a reference to a feature computes the class number, and is a pure virtual function of the abstract class Classifier. Various ideas for the implementation of this function are considered in the following.

Training a classifier can be defined by a method train which accepts as an argument a Bag, i.e., an unsorted collection of samples which each may occur several times in the collsection. The class Sample is derived from Object, so objects of this class can be added to the Bag.[4] For supervised learning, this collection will consist of pairs which associate a feature with a class number. We introduce an auxiliary class for this purpose. For unsupervised learning, this set will consist of features. The derived classes will have to define the learning procedures.

A classifier defines and induces a partition of the feature space. Each subset is associated with a class. This partition is automatically computed in the case of threshold operations

---

[4]Only NIHCL–objects are allowed as elements of collections, c.f. Sect. 15.6.

(c.f. Sect. 20.3). The same holds for the quantization of signals, where a continuous signal is mapped to a discrete value. Methods which compute a partition of a vector space without knowing the assignment function ζ are called vector quantization methods. For one–dimensional vectors, there exist closed form solutions. For higher dimensional vectors, there is no analytical solution available [Nie83]. A simple example of vector quantization was discussed in Sect. 20.8, where the number of different color vectors was reduced.

24.3 Linear Discriminants

The discussion of linear discriminants is first restricted to two classes, i.e., we deal only with binary classes Ω_1 and Ω_2. This simplifies the understanding of linear classifiers, and allows an easier and clearer insight into basic concepts.

Linear functions can be used to define hyperplanes. The idea of linear discriminants is to split the feature space by such a hyperplane into two half-spaces. Each of these half-spaces represents the area of a single class.

For a formal definition, we set $c = (c_1, c_2, \ldots, c_d)^T \in \mathbf{R}^d$ to be the observed, d–dimensional feature vector. A linear discriminant classifier applies the decision rule

$$\zeta(c) = \begin{cases} 1, & \text{if } q(c) > 0 \\ 2, & \text{otherwise} \end{cases}, \tag{24.2}$$

where the *splitting function*

$$q(c) = q_0 + \sum_{i=1}^{d} q_i\, c_i = q_0 + (q_1, q_2, \ldots, q_d) \cdot (c_1, c_2, \ldots, c_d)^T, \tag{24.3}$$

and $q_i \in \mathbf{R}$. This decision rule is easily implemented and the computational complexity of the decision process is linear in d.

Figure 24.1 and 24.2 illustrate linear discriminants for one– and two–dimensional features. Boxes are samples belonging to one class, circles to the other. In the 1–D case, (24.2) defines a single point in the feature space, the *splitting point*. The linear function $q(c)$ reduces here to $q(c) = q_0$. This classifier corresponds to the decision rule applied for binarization, where we computed a threshold θ for discrimination. In case of 2–D feature vectors, the classifier is defined by (24.2) and the induced partition of the feature space is characterized by a single 2–D line (c.f. Figure 24.2), the *splitting line*. It should be clear that misclassification can occur, whereas the optimal classifier in this case will define the splitting curve, which is not necessarily linear, such that the number of misclassifications is minimal. The given 2–D example shows two misclassifications.

If the components of the feature vector are discrete and defined on a finite domain, i.e., $c \in \{1, 2, \ldots, n\}^d$ the computation of the optimal classifier corresponds to a discrete

Figure 24.1 Two classes in a one–dimensional feature space

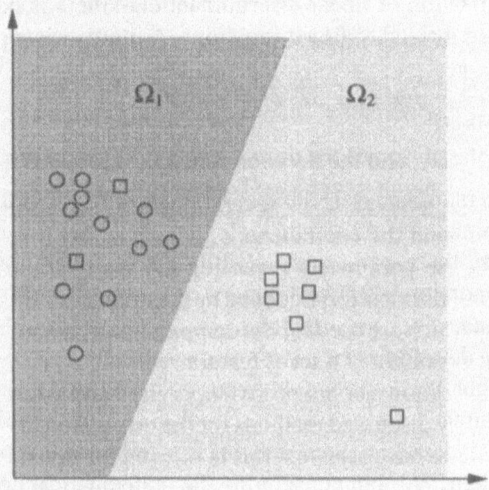

Figure 24.2 Two classes in a two–dimensional feature space

optimization problem. In general, the exhaustive search over all possible linear classifiers is bounded by the total number of $2\binom{n}{d}$ different linear discriminants.[5]

Now we extend the decision rule (24.2) such that multiple class problems can be treated. For that purpose, we introduce two linear functions $q_1(c)$ and $q_2(c)$, one for each class Ω_1 and Ω_2, where $q_\lambda(c) = q_{\lambda,0} + \sum_{i=1}^{d} q_{\lambda,i}\, c_i$. Let the splitting function be defined by $\tilde{q}_1(c) := q_1(c) - q_2(c)$. For a given feature vector c we decide for class Ω_1, if $\tilde{q}_1(c) > 0$, i.e., in this case we have $q_1(c) > q_2(c)$. Analogously, we can define $\tilde{q}_2(c) := q_2(c) - q_1(c)$, and decide for Ω_2, if $\tilde{q}_2(c) > 0$ resp. $q_2(c) > q_1(c)$. This observation motivates the following definition for the multiple class decision rule of linear classifiers:

$$\zeta(c) \;=\; \underset{\lambda}{\mathrm{argmax}}\; \tilde{q}_\lambda(c) \;=\; \underset{\lambda}{\mathrm{argmax}}\; \left(\tilde{q}_{\lambda,0} + \sum_{i=1}^{d} \tilde{q}_{\lambda,i} c_i \right) , \tag{24.4}$$

---

[5]Check this!

where $\tilde{q}_\lambda$ denotes the *splitting polynomial* of class Ω_λ. Thus, we associate with each class Ω_λ a linear function, and decide for the class with the highest function value for a given feature vector c. Obviously, the geometric interpretation and visualization of splitting functions for $k > 2$ is not as simple as for $k = 1, 2$ [Sch77].

24.4 Polynomial Classifiers

An obvious generalization of linear discriminant classifiers is possible, if multivariate polynomials are used instead of linear functions. A multivariate polynomial

$$q_\lambda(c) \quad = \quad \sum_{i_1,i_2,\ldots,i_d=1}^{m} q_{\lambda,i_1,i_2,\ldots,i_d}\, c_1^{i_1}\, c_2^{i_2} \cdot \ldots \cdot c_d^{i_d} \quad , \qquad (24.5)$$

is attached to each class Ω_λ, and the decision rule (24.4) remains unchanged.

Polynomial classifiers, in general, show several degrees of freedom: the degree of the multivariate polynomial and the coefficients $q_{\lambda,i_1,i_2,\ldots,i_d} \in \mathbf{R}$. It is a highly non–trivial problem to optimize these parameters regarding the recognition rate. The degree of discriminating polynomials is a priori bounded by the number of free coefficients and the available training data, which are used for the computation of these unknown parameters. Usually, the training data consist of a set of feature vectors $\{c_1, c_2, \ldots, c_N\}$. The classes of these features might be known or unknown (supervised and unsupervised learning). In Sect. 20.1 we have already discussed methods for the estimation of the splitting point for image binarization, and we have seen that this is — even for this restricted classification task — a hard problem. Without considering the mathematical details, the computation of the coefficients and determination of discriminating polynomials can be solved, for instance, by linear programming methods, like the simplex algorithm (c.f. [Sch77]), stochastic approximation [Nie83], or in some cases even by closed form solutions [Nie83]. The introduction and discussion of the required mathematical framework is not in the scope of this book. We recommend [Nie83, Sch77] for more details. Nevertheless, the general implementation of a classifier in an object–oriented framework can provide possible extension slots for such ideas, as we show in the following.

In the next section, we choose density functions and discrete probability mass functions instead of polynomials for discrimination. In contrast to polynomials, we already know (partially) how to compute free parameters of statistical measures. In Chapter 8 we have discussed the calculation of relative frequencies and maximum likelihood methods to estimate parameters of probability density functions.

24.5 Bayesian Classifiers

The statistical characterization of classes requires both the a priori probability $p(\Omega_\kappa)$ and the probability density function $p(c|\Omega_\kappa)$ of each class $\Omega_\kappa \in \Omega$.

The discrete value $p(\Omega_\kappa)$ denotes the probability to observe the class Ω_κ without taking the observed feature vector into consideration. If, for instance, all classes appear with the same probability, we have $p(\Omega_\kappa) = p(\Omega_\lambda)$ for $\kappa, \lambda \in \{1, 2, \ldots, K\}$. In most practical applications, pattern classes have different a priori probabilities. Words of a language, for example, have different a priori probabilities. In an arbitrary text, an auxiliary verb like "is" appears more probable than the word "beer". If we have to classify a gastric ulcer in an image with respect to malignity, we know that benign ulcers have a higher a priori probability. This a priori knowledge should influence decision finding.

The class–specific density $p(c|\Omega_\kappa)$ is a measure for the probability to observe feature vector c if the pattern class Ω_κ is present. This density might be, for instance, a Gaussian density function (c.f. Sect. 8.3) or, in the case of discrete features, a histogram (c.f. Chapter 20). The a posteriori probability

$$p(\Omega_\kappa|c) \quad = \quad \frac{p(\Omega_\kappa)\, p(c|\Omega_\kappa)}{p(c)} \quad = \quad \frac{p(\Omega_\kappa)\, p(c|\Omega_\kappa)}{\sum\limits_{k=1}^{K} p(\Omega_\kappa)\, p(c|\Omega_\kappa)} \quad . \tag{24.6}$$

summarizes the probability that the class Ω_κ is present, if the feature vector c is observed. This discrete measure is the basic component of the Bayesian classifier and its decision rule.

For an observed feature vector c, the Bayesian classifier chooses the class with the highest a posteriori probability, i.e., the class index is computed by

$$\zeta(c) \quad = \quad \underset{\lambda}{\operatorname{argmax}}\, p(\Omega_\lambda|c) \quad = \quad \underset{\lambda}{\operatorname{argmax}}\, p(\Omega_\lambda)\, p(c|\Omega_\lambda) \quad . \tag{24.7}$$

The principle of Bayesian classifiers is illustrated in Figure 24.3. The second part of this equation holds, since the class index for the maximum of the a posteriori probability does not depend on the scaling factor $1/p(c)$. Thus the result of the optimization is independent of the denominator $p(c)$.

The above equation also shows that, in the case of uniformly distributed classes ($p(\Omega_\kappa) = p(\Omega_\lambda)$ for all classes), the Bayesian decision rule (24.7) reduces to the maximum likelihood decision, i.e.,

$$\begin{aligned}
\zeta(c) \quad &= \quad \underset{\lambda}{\operatorname{argmax}}\, p(\Omega_\lambda|c) \quad = \quad \underset{\lambda}{\operatorname{argmax}}\, p(\Omega_\lambda)\, p(c|\Omega_\lambda) \\
&= \quad \underset{\lambda}{\operatorname{argmax}}\, p(c|\Omega_\lambda). \tag{24.8}
\end{aligned}$$

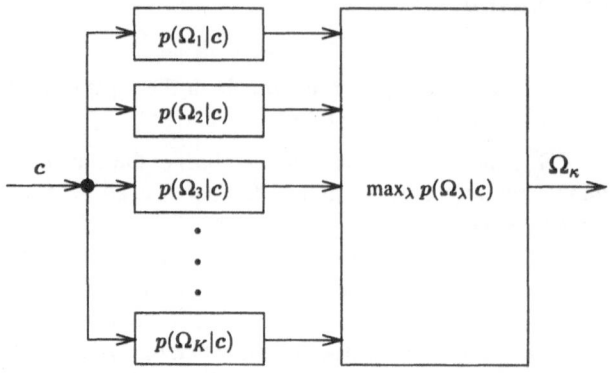

Figure 24.3 The principle of the Bayesian classifier

24.6 Properties of Bayesian Classifiers

The error probability of Bayesian classifiers is denoted by p_B, and it is well–known that this probability is a lower bound for misclassifications of all classifiers. If we choose the cost function, which weights a correct decision by zero and a wrong decision by one, no classifier will produce lower costs than the Bayesian classifier [Nie83]. Consequently, the design goal of all classifiers has to be the approximation of the Bayesian classifier. Many comparative studies show that statistical classifiers can be approximated by polynomial classifiers with similar reliability [Nie83, Sch92, Set91, Sch77, Gel94]. Experimental comparisons, for example, of polynomial and statistical classifiers for character recognition show similar recognition rates [Nie83]. Thus, for the solution of many practical problems, reliable classifiers exist which do not depend on statistics. Non–statistical classifiers are usually applied for practical reasons, especially in those cases where the available feature vectors are not normally distributed and the parametric density is unknown. This already points out the most important task concerning Bayesian classifiers: the determination of statistical properties of pattern classes.

The a priori probabilities $p(\Omega_\kappa)$, $1 \leq \kappa \leq K$, are easily computed via relative frequencies and classified sample data. Even if the sample data are not classified, incomplete data estimation techniques are required [Hor94, Hor96a, Tan93] which can deal with this unsupervised learning problem.

The modeling of probability density functions of features is more difficult. Dependent on their representation, we distinguish between parametric and non–parametric statistical classifiers in pattern recognition theory. We will not introduce these types of classifiers theoretically, but show the difference by two examples.

A non–parametric classifier applies discrete probabilities for decision finding. We have already introduced histograms. In general, histograms characterize discrete probabilities, which can be applied for statistical classification directly. Histograms for the probabilistic modeling of features and a priori probabilities can be estimated using discrete observations (c.f. Chapter 8). Figure 24.4 shows the a priori probabilities (left) and the class specific probabilities of features (middle, right) for two classes. If a scalar

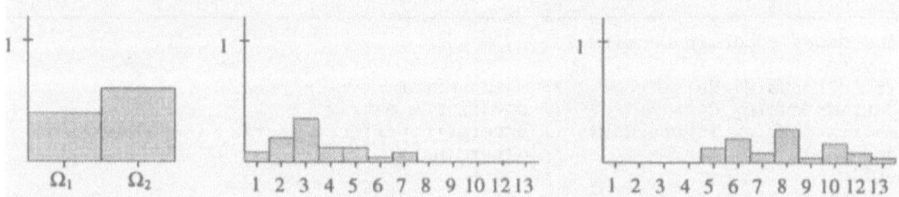

Figure 24.4 A priori probabilities (left), probabilities of scalar discrete features corresponding to class Ω_1 (middle), and class Ω_2 (right)

feature $c \in \{1, 2, \ldots, 13\}$ has to be assigned to a class, the a priori probability $p(\Omega_\kappa)$ results from the left histogram, and the probabilities $p(c|\Omega_\kappa)$ for each class are computed using the middle histogram for Ω_1 and the right one for Ω_2.

If the features underlie a parametric distribution, parametric densities instead of histograms can be used for classification. We consider the most commonly used parametric density concerning statistical classification: the Gaussian probability density function (c.f. Sect. 8.3). If d–dimensional feature vectors of a class are normally distributed, each class $\Omega_\kappa \in \Omega$ and its corresponding features can be characterized by the multivariate Gaussian density function

$$p(c|\Omega_\kappa) = \frac{1}{\sqrt{|\det 2\pi \Sigma_\kappa|}} \exp\left(-\frac{(c - \mu_\kappa)^T \Sigma_\kappa^{-1}(c - \mu_\kappa)}{2}\right) \quad . \tag{24.9}$$

The parameters of this probability density, the mean vector μ_κ and the covariance matrix Σ_κ, can be estimated applying the maximum likelihood method discussed in Chapter 8, presupposing that classes of sample data are known. If the training samples are not classified, again incomplete data estimation algorithms have to be applied [Red84]. As a consequence, it is not the histograms that have to be stored, but the parameters of the densities, i.e., μ_κ and Σ_κ. This shows the low storage requirements of parametric Bayesian classifiers.

A density function is a mathematical function satisfying several properties (c.f. Chapter 8). For this reason, we introduce an abstract class `Density` for probability density functions, which is shown in Program 194. This class includes pure virtual functions for the evaluation of densities for given random variables. The derived class for Gaussian

```
class Density : public Object {         // abstract interface
 public:                                // all data to be defined in
  Density(void);                        // derived classes
  virtual ~Density(void);
  virtual double probability(const RandomVariable& X) const = 0;
  virtual double log_probability(const RandomVariable& X) const;
};
```

194

```
class Gauss : public Density {
 private:
  Vector<double> Mu;          // mean vector
  Matrix<double> Cov;         // covariance matrix
  Matrix<double> InverseCov;  // inverse covariance matrix
  double         Det;         // determinant
 public:
  Gauss(void);
  Gauss(int order);
  Gauss(const Gauss & g);
  Gauss(const Vector<double> & mu, const Matrix<double> & cov);
  virtual ~Gauss(void);
  const Vector<double> & mean(void) const;
  const Matrix<double> & covariance(void) const;
  const Matrix<double> & inverse_covariance(void) const;
  const double determinant(void) const;
  void estimateParameters(const Bag & trs);   // training 'set'
  virtual double probability(const RandomVariable & X) const;
  virtual double log_probability(const RandomVariable & X) const;
};
```

195

densities provide a concrete implementation of these pure virtual methods (c.f. Program 195) and for parameter estimation from a 'set' of samples, where the samples are again provided in a class Bag.

24.7 From Bayesian to Geometric Classifiers

Using specialization, the Bayesian classifier, which uses normally distributed features, can be reduced to a simple classifier which uses Euclidean distances for decision making. For simplicity, we consider only two classes Ω_1 and Ω_2. The discrete a priori probabilities $p(\Omega_1)$ and $p(\Omega_2)$ as well as the Gaussian densities $p(c|\Omega_1)$ and $p(c|\Omega_2)$ are assumed to be known. In this situation the Bayesian classifier decides for class Ω_1, if

$$p(\Omega_1)p(c|\Omega_1) > p(\Omega_2)\,p(c|\Omega_2) \quad . \tag{24.10}$$

Now we specialize this decision rule by

$$p(\Omega_1) = p(\Omega_2) , \quad \text{and} \quad \Sigma_1 = \Sigma_2 = \Sigma , \tag{24.11}$$

and get the discriminant

$$(c - \mu_1)^T \Sigma^{-1}(c - \mu_1) < (c - \mu_2)^T \Sigma^{-1}(c - \mu_2) \quad . \tag{24.12}$$

If we additionally assume that the covariance matrix Σ is the identity matrix, the classification is based on the inequality

$$(c - \mu_1)^T(c - \mu_1) \quad < \quad (c - \mu_2)^T(c - \mu_2) \quad , \tag{24.13}$$

i.e., this decision rule compares the quadratic Euclidean distances

$$||c - \mu_1||^2 \quad < \quad ||c - \mu_2||^2 \quad , \tag{24.14}$$

between feature and mean vectors, i.e., class centers.

The above specialization has shown that statistical classifiers result in a simple distance measure for restricted statistical assumptions. The minimum distance classifier with respect to class dependent mean vectors is optimal, if the used feature vectors are normally distributed with covariance matrices Σ which are the identity matrix.

Classifiers based on parametric densities show the disadvantage that a parametric distribution of used feature vectors must be known. This causes some problems, especially for features which are not normally distributed. In general, there exist three possibilities to verify a density assumption:

1. the distribution of features is known by construction,

2. the hypothesized parametric density is proven by statistical tests or

3. the recognition rate of the resulting classifier suggests the correctness.

The use of the Euclidean distance to one reference vector — the mean vector of each class — motivates the introduction of nearest neighbor classifiers. Instead of computing mean vectors for each class and using a distance measure to mean vectors for discrimination, we utilize all observed feature vectors of the training set for reference. The resulting classifier is the nearest neighbor classifier.

24.8 Nearest Neighbor Classifier

The nearest neighbor classifier requires a set of classified sample data, i.e., for each element c_i of $C = \{c_1, c_2, \ldots, c_n\}$ the class $\zeta(c_i)$ number is known. For a new feature vector, the class is chosen that points to the reference vector with the closest distance to the new vector. Thus, the decision rule is defined by

$$\zeta(c) \quad = \quad \underset{\zeta(c_i)}{\mathrm{argmin}} \quad \{||c - c_i|| \mid i = 1, 2, \ldots, n\} \quad . \tag{24.15}$$

This simple decision rule shows several degrees of freedom: the number of reference vectors and the choice of the distance measure. The distance function is not predefined, and the performance of the classifier will depend on the chosen metric. Two possible distance measures are the Euclidean distance or the city block metric. If the number of reference vectors is n, the complexity of the suggested nearest neighbor classifier is linear in n and thus bounded by $\mathcal{O}(n)$.

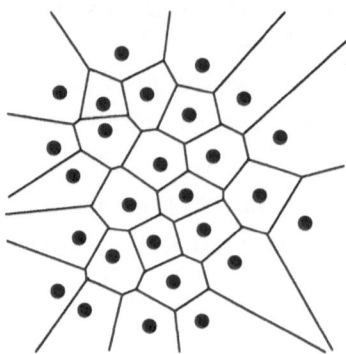

Figure 24.5 Voronoi diagram with 27 two–dimensional reference vectors

The nearest neighbor decision rule is very simple and used for many applications. Without any knowledge about pattern recognition or decision theory, the most obvious classifier applies the nearest neighbor decision rule. Depending on the training data, the nearest neighbor classifier induces a partition of the feature space. Every feature of the feature space is assigned to the class of the closest training feature. The set of points whose nearest neighbor is c_i is called the Voronoi cell of c_i. Figure 24.5 shows the set of Voronoi cells induced by 27 two–dimensional feature vectors. Obviously, these cells result in a partition of the feature space, the Voronoi partition. The theory shows that the nearest neighbor classifier yields a suitable approximation of the distribution of features, if no concrete density functions are available [Fuk90].

The success of this classifier strongly depends on the chosen reference patterns. It is a theoretically proven and well–known result that the nearest neighbor classifier is consistent and the error probability p_{NN} satisfies the following fundamental inequality

$$p_B \leq p_{NN} \leq 2p_B \quad , \tag{24.16}$$

presupposing that an infinite sample set is available. In addition to experimental tests which prove the reliability of classifiers, this relation to the optimal Bayesian classifier justifies the practical use of nearest neighbor classifiers.

There exist various modifications of the nearest neighbor classifier. An obvious extension can be done by introduction of the k–nearest neighbor decision rule, which we already applied in the case of edge thinning (c.f. Sect. 21.2). Instead of looking for the closest reference vector, we decide for that class, which is the class of the majority of the k nearest neighbors. The probability of misclassifications for the k–nearest neighbor classifier converges against the Bayesian error probability with increasing training data. Compared to the nearest neighbor classifier, the suggested modification, in general, leads to more reliable decisions.

The computational complexity and the storage requirements of nearest neighbor classifiers are influenced by the size of reference data sets. Storing n reference vectors and applying the k–nearest neighbor decision rule, classification time is bounded by $\mathcal{O}(k\,n)$, if naive comparisons are done. This time complexity can be decreased to $\mathcal{O}(k\,\log n)$ if an approximated version of the nearest neighbor classifier is used [Ary94]. This classifier returns the nearest neighbor with a relative error margin. The more reference patterns are available, the higher are the storage requirements and the needed comparisons for decision finding. However, less reference patterns induce a lower recognition rate. During the design stage of a classification system applying the nearest neighbor decision rule, the engineer should take these properties into consideration.

24.9 Implementation of Classifiers

The implementation of classifiers, which we give in the following, is restricted to the explicit encoding of decision rules and the management of reference patterns, density functions or discriminating functions. The decision rule depends on the features used and the chosen classifier. Since the distance measure for the nearest neighbor classifier, for instance, can be any metric (Euclidean distance measure, city block metric or others), an implementation should leave the choice of the actual measure. This is the reason why we declared the virtual `operator-` in Program 192.

Figure 24.6 suggests a class hierarchy for different types of classifiers. An abstract base class provides the pure virtual function `classify` (c.f. Program 193), which assigns features (objects of the class `Feature`) to classes. The derived classes implement the concrete decision rule of selected classifiers. For example, the maximum a posteriori decision is programmed for Bayesian classifiers or nearest neighbor classification rule is implemented, if no density functions or parametric discriminating functions are available.

Assume, objects of an class `Density` defined in Program 194 are defined and represent the density functions associated with each class. Concrete classes might be a Gaussian density as in Figure 24.6 or any other probability density function like Poisson distributions. If the class definition of Bayesian classifiers provides a method for evaluating a posteriori probabilities, the Bayesian classifier is implemented as shown in Program 196. and Program 197.

More density classes will be shown in Chapter 25.

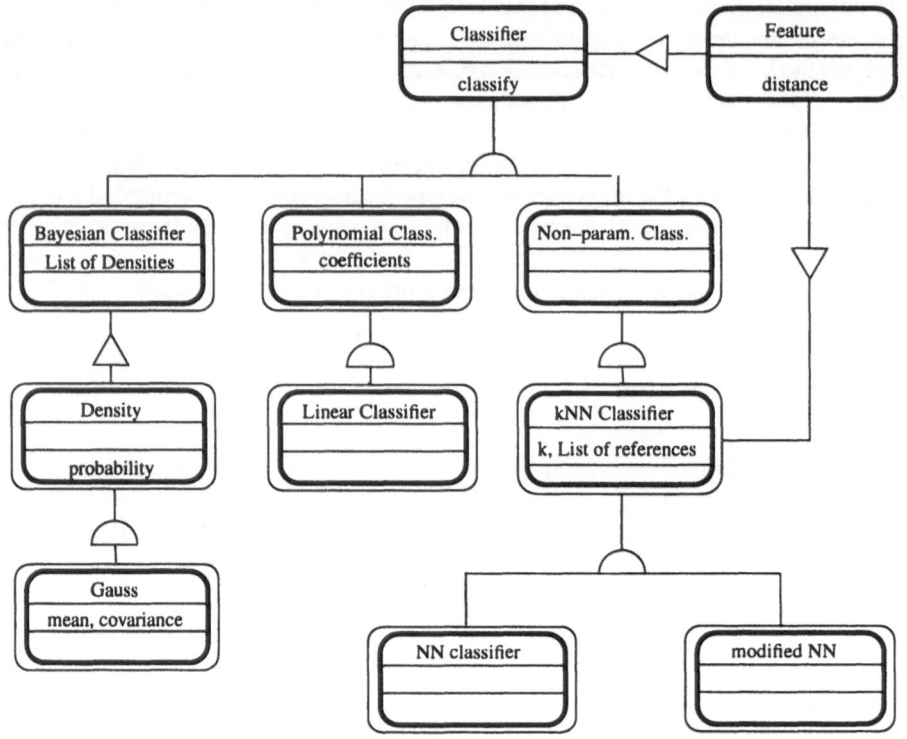

Figure 24.6 Class hierarchy for classifiers and features

Exercises

24.a Determine a threshold θ such that the optimal classifier will apply the decision
rule

$$\zeta(c) \quad = \quad \left\{ \begin{array}{ll} 2 & , \text{ if } p(c\,|\,\Omega_1)/p(c\,|\,\Omega_2) > \theta \\ 1 & , \text{ otherwise} \end{array} \right. \tag{24.17}$$

for the discrimination of two classes.

24.b Let the set of 2–D vectors

$$\left\{ \begin{pmatrix} 2 \\ 3 \end{pmatrix}, \begin{pmatrix} 3 \\ 3 \end{pmatrix}, \begin{pmatrix} 1 \\ 2 \end{pmatrix}, \begin{pmatrix} 1 \\ 6 \end{pmatrix}, \begin{pmatrix} 5 \\ 5 \end{pmatrix}, \begin{pmatrix} 5 \\ 1 \end{pmatrix} \right\}$$

represent the reference data for a nearest neighbor classifier. Implement a graphical tool which computes the Voronoi diagram! Compute the areas for class Ω_1
and Ω_2 if the following bipartition is valid:

```
class Bayesian_Classifier : public Classifier {
private:
    Vector<Density*> densities;   // list of class densities
    Vector<double>   a_priori;    // a priori probabilities
public:
    virtual int classify(const Feature & f) const;  // classification interface
    virtual void train(const Bag&);                  // Bayesian training

    double prior(int k) const       { return a_priori[k]; }
    void   prior(int k, double d)   { a_priori[k] = d; }
    const Density& dens(int k) const { return *(densities[k]); }
};
```

196

```
int Bayesian_Classifier::classify(const Feature & f) const
{
    int    index= -1;
    double max  =  0;
    for (int i= 0; i< densities.SizeX(); i++) {
     double a_posteriori= prior(i) * dens(i).probability(f);
     if (max< a_posteriori) { max  = a_posteriori; index= i; }
    }
    return index+1;   // classes range from 1 to nuber_of_classes
}
```

197

$$\text{features assigned to } \Omega_1 \quad : \quad \left\{ \begin{pmatrix} 2 \\ 3 \end{pmatrix}, \begin{pmatrix} 3 \\ 3 \end{pmatrix}, \begin{pmatrix} 1 \\ 2 \end{pmatrix} \right\}$$

$$\text{features assigned to } \Omega_2 \quad : \quad \left\{ \begin{pmatrix} 1 \\ 6 \end{pmatrix}, \begin{pmatrix} 5 \\ 5 \end{pmatrix}, \begin{pmatrix} 5 \\ 1 \end{pmatrix} \right\}$$

24.c We now proceed with the animal recognition problem in Exercise 22.b. Now define for each object a reference pattern r_λ and classify an observed object characterized by f using the decision rule

$$\kappa = \min_\lambda \|r_\lambda - f\|, \tag{24.18}$$

where κ is the computed class number and $\|.\|$ denotes the Euclidean distance of vectors.

Capture a sufficiently large sample of images such as the ones shown in Figure 22.9 and test your classifier.

24.d Extend the class hierarchy shown in Figure 24.6 for histograms.

25 Speech Recognition

Speaker independent recognition, analysis, and understanding of utterances of spoken language is much more complicated than the classification of simple patterns: with each simple pattern a feature vector of known dimension can be computed, and decision rules introduced in Chapter 24 can be applied to solve the classification task. As it was already shown, speech signals are decomposed into frames. Thus, each speech signal is associated with a *sequence* of features. The number of sequence elements depends on the duration of the utterance and varies for each signal. Obviously, the simple application of the Bayesian classifier or the nearest neighbor decision rule, as defined for single feature vectors, is not possible. Extensions of these decision procedures are required, even for the implementation of a single word recognition system.

This chapter introduces algorithms for solving the classification problem in the presence of feature sets and feature sequences of varying cardinality. In the first part we motivate classification in speech recognition, discuss several problems we have to deal with, and introduce the mathematical notation. We explain the dynamic time warping (DTW) algorithm for the comparison of feature sequences with missing correspondences of single features. Motivated by some disadvantages of DTW, a basic statistical technique for the classification of speech signals using mixtures of densities and hidden Markov models (HMM) is explained, considering both automatic training and classification algorithms. This chapter concludes with a discussion of different types of hidden Markov models and an object–oriented implementation.

25.1 Classification of Speech Signals

Speech signals can induce several types of classification problems with increasing complexity. Generally, we distinguish between single word recognition, recognition of a sequence of words, and speech understanding, where the word sequence and its meaning are required [Nie90a, Rab93, ST95]. Here the discussion is restricted to single word recognition problems. For that purpose, each speech signal is transformed into a sequence of features (c.f. Chapter 23).

The decision rule maps a feature sequence to a class index κ of class Ω_κ, i.e.,

$$\zeta : [c_k]_{k=1,2,\ldots,m} \mapsto \kappa \quad . \tag{25.1}$$

Figure 25.1 shows the general structure of a single word recognition system: the utterance is decomposed into frames, features are computed, and the recognition has to be done using the resulting sequence of features. Independent of the speaker and the duration

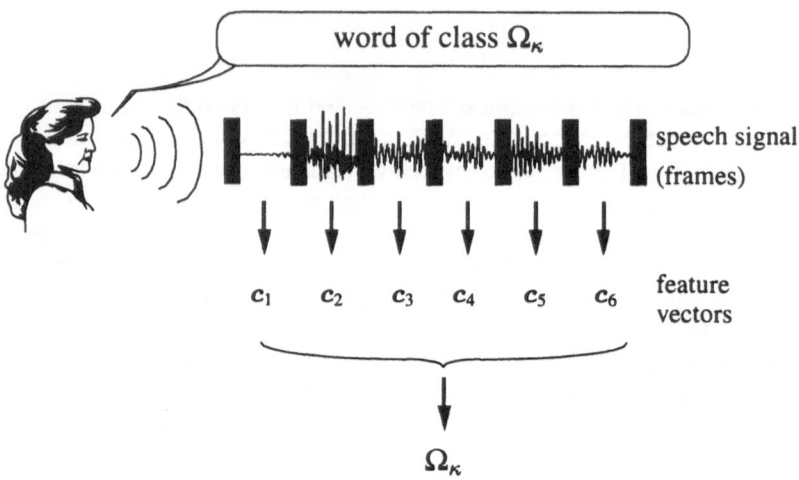

Figure 25.1   Single word recognition (according to [You96])

of an utterance, the classification of this speech signal should be possible, although speech signals differ considerably between speakers (Figure 25.2). The energy of the speech signal as well as the chosen microphone should not influence the class decision. Thus, the classifiers have to deal with variations both in the feature vectors' values and in the number of features. These observations suggest the use of statistical methods for recognition. The following sections introduce statistical principles for modeling. Starting with dynamic time warping and geometrically based methods, we introduce a general, unified, and new statistical framework.

25.2   Dynamic Time Warping

The classification of speech signals can be done by the comparison of input signals with prototypes of different pattern classes. If a distance measure suitable for the comparison of sequences is available, the nearest neighbor decision rule can be applied. We decide for that class which the nearest reference pattern belongs to (nearest neighbor classifier, Sect. 24.8). For classification purposes, we can use sample values, spectral features, cepstral features, zero–crossings of the speech signal, LPC coefficients or sequences of any other types of features [Nie83]. The easiest way to obtain a similarity measure for

speaker no. 1

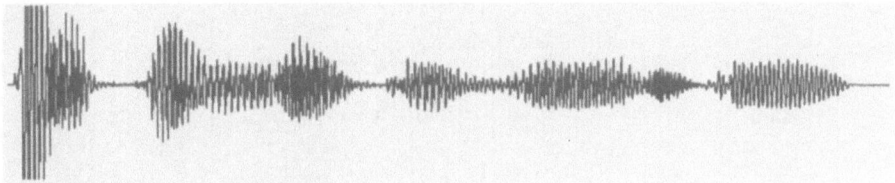

speaker no. 2

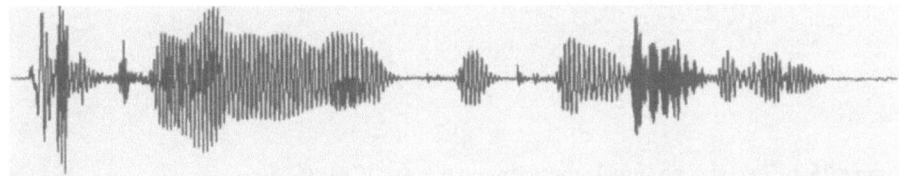

speaker no. 3

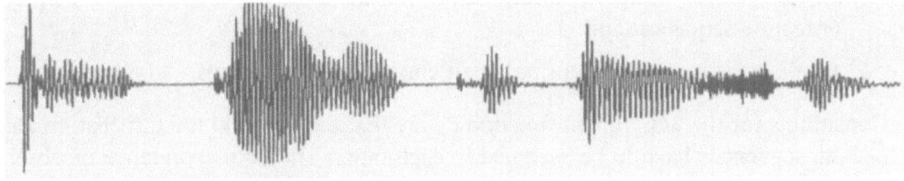

Figure 25.2 The utterance "pattern recognition" of three different speakers

time signals is through the computation of the features' distances along corresponding time and accumulation. This simple distance measure is practically prohibited [Nie83]: depending on the speed of speaking, speech signals can be stretched or compressed, and the induced distortion of the speech signal is supposed to be non–linear. Vowels, like the "o" of the word "word" can be stretched in different manner, whereas the duration of "d" is approximately constant. Figure 25.3 shows two speech signals for the word "word" with different durations. This example shows that a non–linear mapping ζ_λ from the feature sequence $[c_k]_{k=1,2,\ldots,m}$ resulting from the speech signal to the prototype sequence of class Ω_λ, i.e., $[c_{\lambda,l}]_{l=1,2,\ldots,n_\lambda}$, is required. The *assignment function* ζ_λ relates the observed and reference features. The accuracy of the complete distance between reference pattern and the observed signal significantly increases through the use of a non–linear mapping ζ_λ, which minimizes the effects of stretching and compressing. The non–linear mapping has to be computed during the classification stage and — unfortunately — increases the complexity of classification. The distance measure is thus characterized by two fundamental components:

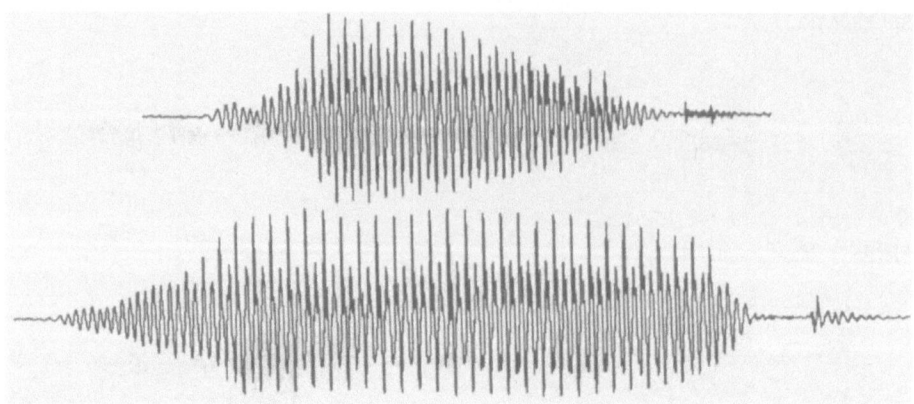

Figure 25.3 Two speech signals representing the word "word"

1. the (non–linear) assignment function ζ_λ for the reference and the observed pattern or feature sequence, and

2. the distance measure for a single pair corresponding features.

Constraints for the assignment function ζ_λ are that the first and the last feature values of both sequences have to be assigned to each other. The correspondence of observed features and the reference pattern starts from left to right, and ends with the assignment of the last feature c_m of the observation. The index of the reference sequence in the t–th step of this assignment procedure is defined by $i(t)$ and the corresponding index of the other sequence is $j(t)$. Thus, a pair $(i(t), j(t))$ denotes the correspondence of $c_{\lambda,i(t)}$ and $c_{j(t)}$. The resulting sequence of completely matched pairs is denoted by the sequence of corresponding indices

$$S = [(i(1), j(1)), (i(2), j(2)), \ldots, (i(m), j(m))] \quad . \tag{25.2}$$

The assignment of features can be illustrated by a graph, and the computation of the best assignment corresponds to a graph search problem. The pair $(i(t), j(t))$ defines a node of a graph. The path ${}^tS = ((i(1), j(1)), (i(2), j(2)), \ldots, (i(t), j(t)))$ defines a sequence of vertices and edges of this graph. The weight of the path is the sum of single distances of corresponding features. Figure 25.4 shows a graph and the path associated with the assignment

$$S \quad = \quad [(1, 1), (1, 2), (1, 3), (2, 4), (3, 5), (4, 6), \ldots, (13, 19)] \quad . \tag{25.3}$$

If the constraints for the assignment of the first and last features are considered, the total number of possible assignments is $11^{17} = 5054470284992293771$. A first reduction of assignments is enforced by the constraint of monotonic increasing indices, i.e., for all t we have

$$i(t) \le i(t+1) \quad \text{and} \quad j(t) \le j(t+1) \quad . \tag{25.4}$$

Using this inequality, we have *only* $\binom{11+17-1}{17} = 13123110$ paths to check for the minimum distance.[1] The complexity of this search procedure further can be reduced. For that reason, we take a closer look at the distance measure and its properties.

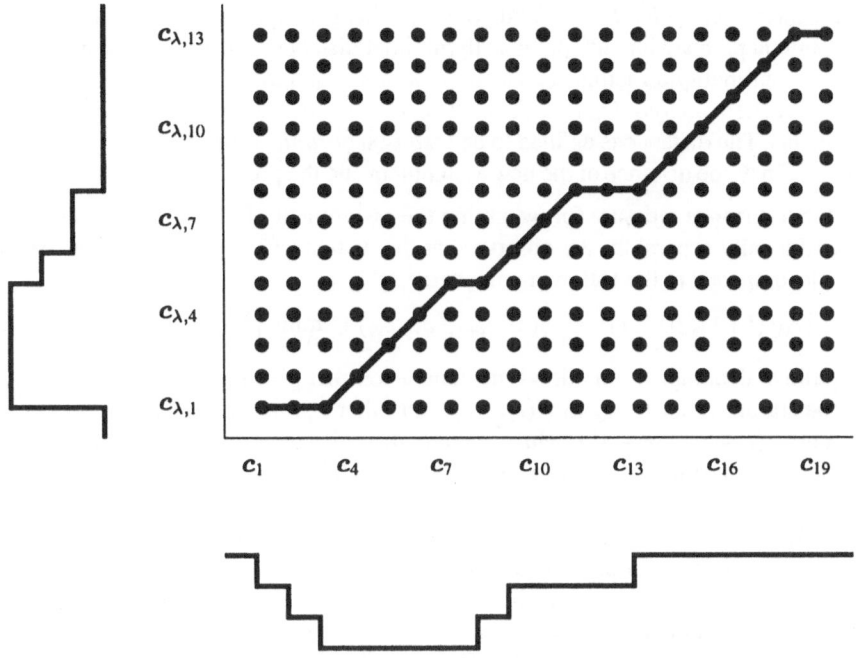

Figure 25.4 Assignment of features: a graph search problem

The optimization problem is the minimization of the accumulated distance D_λ for the matching of observed and reference sequences, i.e.,

$$D_\lambda = \min_S \sum_{t=1}^{m} d(c_{\lambda,i(t)}, c_{j(t)}) \quad , \tag{25.5}$$

where $d(c_{\lambda,i(t)}, c_{j(t)})$ denotes a suitable distance measure, like, for example, the Euclidean distance. The minimization runs over all possible assignments (i.e., paths of the graph) between the observation and the reference. If all combinations without any constraints are considered, the complexity of this optimization is bounded by $\mathcal{O}(n_\lambda^m)$; the monotonicity constraint (25.4) for indices reduces the complexity to $\mathcal{O}\left(\binom{n_\lambda+m-1}{m}\right)$.

---

[1]Prove this!

An efficient algorithm for the computation of the optimal sequence S^* of index pairs, which minimizes the distance D_λ, results from the application of the *dynamic programming* technique [Big89]. Dynamic programming is well–known in discrete mathematics and indeed supports the efficiency in computing the non–linear mapping between two sequences of features we are looking for. The basic idea is a recursive decomposition of the given optimization problem. The use of a recursive procedure is possible, if *Bellman's principle of optimality* is valid [Bel67]. This principle states that all sub–paths of the optimal path are already paths with minimal distances. Distance measures which satisfy the optimality principle are usually monotonic and locally separable. A distance measure is called *monotonic*, if the distance increases monotonically with the number of assignments. The distance is defined to be *locally separable*, if the distance is computed from the sum of the distance of the new assignment and the previously assigned features.

Indeed, our distance measure for weighting the assignment of sequences is both monotonic and locally separable. We observe that the distance (25.5) of the $(t + 1)$–st step can be decomposed in the following manner:

$$^{t+1}D_\lambda(i(t+1), j(t+1)) = d(c_{\lambda,i(t+1)}, c_{j(t+1)}) + \min_{i(t),j(t)} \left\{ {}^t D_\lambda(i(t), j(t)) \right\} . \quad (25.6)$$

This additive decomposition allows the conclusion that given an optimal path $S^*_{i(t),j(t)}$ from the staring point $(1, 1)$ to $(i(t), j(t))$, all other optimal paths for the successive index pair $(i(t + 1), j(t + 1))$, which include the pair $(i(t), j(t))$, enclose the optimal path $S^*_{i(t),j(t)}$ as a sub–path. Consequently, the search for the optimal path S^* does not require the evaluation of all possible paths from $(1, 1)$ to $(i(t + 1), j(t + 1))$ including $(i(t), j(t))$, but only one. Using this observation, the combinatorial search space is drastically reduced and only the best assignments for a subsequence ending up in a special pair $(i(t), j(t))$ have to be stored. Figure 25.5 shows the principle of the assignment procedure which computes the minimum distance between the observed and the reference sequence. The complexity is obviously bounded by $\mathcal{O}(mn_\lambda^2)$. The description also shows that the name dynamic programming is rather misleading, and it is better considered as a recursive optimization method.

Input: Sequences $c_1, c_2, \ldots, c_m$ and $c_{\lambda,1}, c_{\lambda,2}, \ldots, c_{\lambda,n_\lambda}$		
$D_\lambda(1, 1) = d(c_{\lambda,1}, c_1)$		
FOR $j = 1$ to m		
	FOR $i = 1$ to n_λ	
		$D_\lambda(i, j) = d(c_{\lambda,i}, c_j) + \min\limits_{i' \leq i, j' \in \{j-1, j\}} \{D_\lambda(i', j'); \ i \neq i' \text{ or } j \neq j'\}$
Output: $D_\lambda(n_\lambda, m)$		

Figure 25.5 Dynamic programming approach

In speech recognition applications the set of corresponding indices is usually restricted to special types of index pairs. For single word recognition, for instance, the constraint

$$(i(t), j(t)) \quad = \quad \left\{ \begin{array}{l} (i(t-1), j(t-1)+1) \\ (i(t-1)+1, j(t-1+1)) \\ (i(t-1)+1, j(t-1)) \end{array} \right. \tag{25.7}$$

defines a suitable reduction of admissible indices, if prototype and spoken word do not differ too much in duration. If this neighborhood function (25.7) is used in Figure 25.5, then the complexity of the dynamic time programming approach reduces to $\mathcal{O}(mn_\lambda)$. This modified algorithm is called *dynamic time warping*, and widely used in (simple) speech recognition applications.

If minimum distances D_λ, $\lambda = 1, 2, \ldots, K$, are computed between a given speech signal and the reference signals of classes Ω_λ, $1 \leq \lambda \leq K$, the classification can be done applying the nearest neighbor decision rule (Sect. 24.8); we decide for that class which shows the minimum distance, i.e.,

$$\zeta([c_k]_{1 \leq k \leq m}) \quad = \quad \kappa \quad = \quad \underset{\lambda}{\operatorname{argmin}} \, D_\lambda \quad . \tag{25.8}$$

An object–oriented implementation of the dynamic time warping algorithm should be as general as possible. The theoretical discussion motivates several basic requirements for an implementation of the dynamic programming approach:

- Without neglecting the generality of dynamic programming, above discussion was restricted to the comparison of feature vectors. Of course, the dynamic programming approach also works for sequences of arbitrary features. The classifier has to be implemented for general sequences of features. The features have to belong to the class Feature which was already introduced in Chapter 23.

- The dynamic programming algorithm requires a distance measure for the comparison of single features. It should not be restricted to the Euclidean distance measure. The concrete implementation of the distance measure is not required for the implementation of the algorithm shown in Figure 25.5. If the distance function is a virtual function, dynamic linkage cares for the right implementation dependent on the chosen features.

- It is expected that the dynamic programming module can be extended to use restrictions for the considered neighborhood, for instance, defined by (25.7).

Dynamic programming approaches are not only restricted to speech recognition, but have many applications in pattern recognition [Hor93b, Moo79, Ney84, Yam91] and operation research [Bel67, Big89]. Prospective examples for image processing applications are line following algorithms [Bal82, Pit93] or the classification of contours [Bal82]. All in all, dynamic programming is a powerful tool for the classification of patterns, especially speech signals [Nie90a]. The success of speech recognition systems, however, is not based on this technique. Statistical methods applying several types of stochastic automata are more established for recognition purposes. The advantages of statistical approaches for solving classification problems are manysided:

1. Statistical approaches can deal with uncertainties in a natural manner.

2. The classifier is trainable (c.f. Sect. 8.4); a sufficient set of training samples is used to adopt the free parameters by mathematical estimation techniques.

3. Prior knowledge can be explicitly modeled (c.f. Sect. 24.5).

4. The application of the maximum a posteriori decision rule (c.f. Sect. 24.5) leads to an optimal classification system with respect to the probability of misclassifications.

The design of statistical classifiers, in general, requires the solution of several problems: an appropriate statistical model for pattern classes has to be defined (*structure of models*), and the parameters of these models have to be estimated using a set of training samples (*parameter estimation*). The following sections introduce mixtures and hidden Markov models as well as related learning algorithms based on the dynamic programming approach discussed in this section. These models form the fundamental concepts of most modern speech recognition, analysis, and dialog systems [Nie90a, Rab93, ST95].

25.3 Mixture Densities

The dynamic programming approach requires both the computation of an appropriate reference sequence (prototype) and the definition of a distance measure for comparing single features. The most challenging problem is the automatic construction of reference patterns based on a set of sample data. Instead of one single reference utterance, some kind of *mean feature sequence* has to be computed, i.e., we implicitly incorporate statistical information. In a general probabilistic framework, however, the distance measure is induced by probability density functions. For that reason, we associate with each feature $c_{\lambda,l}$ of the reference sequence $[c_{\lambda,l}]_{l=1,2,...,n_\lambda}$ a parametric density function, i.e., $p(c|a_{\lambda,l})$. For instance, this could be a Gaussian density where the parameter $a_{\lambda,l}$ includes the mean vector $\mu_{\lambda,l}$ and the covariance matrix $\Sigma_{\lambda,l}$ of the considered reference vector $c_{\lambda,l}$. The reference is thus related to a sequence of probability density functions, i.e., $[p(c|a_{\lambda,l})]_{l=1,2,...,n_\lambda}$. The densities are identified by their parameters $[a_{\lambda,l}]_{l=1,2,...,n_\lambda}$.

Using the sequence of densities for classification instead of features and the Euclidean distance, for example, this concept allows the definition of prototypes which take the probabilistic behavior of features into consideration. The length n_λ of prototype sequences, however, remains constant and cannot be varied (up to now). If the densities (i.e., parameters $a_{\lambda,l}$) are known, the algorithm sketched in Figure 25.5 can be applied for statistical classification purposes with minor changes:

The distance $d(c_{\lambda,i(t)}, c_{j(t)})$ used in (25.5) is simply substituted by the conditional probability density $p(c_{j(t)}|a_{\lambda,i(t)})$, instead of the sum we use the product, and the minimization moves to a maximization, i.e.,

$$P_\lambda = \max_S \prod_{t=1}^{m} p(c_{j(t)}|a_{\lambda,i(t)}) \quad , \tag{25.9}$$

where S is defined by (25.2). Figure 25.6 summarizes and illustrates the major changes concerning geometric and probabilistic methods for pattern classification. Herein, however, we still need an explicit mapping of observed and prototype features.

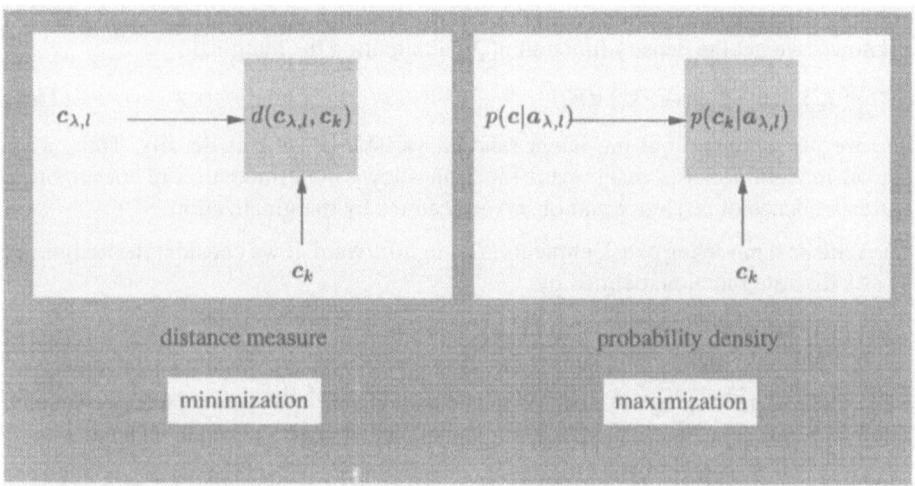

Figure 25.6 From geometric distance measures to density functions

If the prior probabilities $p(\Omega_1)$, $p(\Omega_2)$, $\ldots$, $p(\Omega_K)$ of pattern classes are known, the dynamic programming approach combined with the probabilistic modeling of single features allows the implementation of a Bayesian classifier which applies the maximum a posteriori decision rule:

$$
\begin{aligned}
\zeta([c_k]_{k=1,2,\ldots,m}) &= \operatorname*{argmax}_{\lambda} p(\Omega_\lambda|[c_k]_{k=1,2,\ldots,m}) \\
&= \operatorname*{argmax}_{\lambda} p(\Omega_\lambda)p([c_k]_{k=1,2,\ldots,m}|[a_{\lambda,l}]_{l=1,2,\ldots,n_\lambda}) \quad , \tag{25.10}
\end{aligned}
$$

where the fundamental difference between P_λ and $p([c_k]_{k=1,2,\ldots,m}|[a_{\lambda,l}]_{l=1,2,\ldots,n_\lambda})$ is that the second does not include the *optimal* assignment. Neither the concrete mathematical structure of the probability density function $p([c_k]_{k=1,2,\ldots,m}|[a_{\lambda,l}]_{l=1,2,\ldots,n_\lambda})$, nor the automatic computation of the involved parameters are obvious, yet. The generation of each reference pattern, which is required for the dynamic time warping approach, can be done using one sample or by averaging techniques based on a set of training patterns. For that purpose, the mean vectors of observed features are computed, wherein the assignment of features also can be done by the introduced dynamic time warping approach.

If statistical models are used, the parameters $a_{\lambda,l}$, $l = 1, 2, \ldots, n_\lambda$ have to be estimated, which include more statistical information on features than mean vectors. Usually, the assignment between observed features and reference densities is unknown and non–available for parameter estimation. Of course, we can compute the *most probable* assignment using dynamic programming, but if any errors occur within the assignment process, the estimated parameters are influenced. From a theoretical point of view, the statistical modeling of the assignment function would be nice. We recall that marginals allow the elimination of random variables: If, for instance, the density function $p(X, Y)$ is known, we get the density function $p(X)$ computing the marginal

$$p(X) \;=\; \int p(X, Y)\, dY \;\; , \tag{25.11}$$

i.e., we just integrate out the latent random variable Y of this density. Thus, a statistical modeling of the assignment function allows the elimination of the unknown correspondence of reference and observed features by marginalization.

The statistical modeling of assignments is straightforward, if we consider the assignment ζ_λ as a discrete function, defined by

$$\zeta_\lambda : \left\{ \begin{array}{ccc} \{c_1, c_2, \ldots, c_m\} & \to & \{1, 2, \ldots, n_\lambda\} \\ c_k & \mapsto & l_k \end{array} \right. \;\; . \tag{25.12}$$

Each observed feature c_k is assigned to the index l_k of the corresponding reference feature. Therefore, with each assignment ζ_λ, we can associate a unique vector

$$\zeta_\lambda \;=\; \begin{pmatrix} \zeta_\lambda(c_1) \\ \zeta_\lambda(c_2) \\ \vdots \\ \zeta_\lambda(c_m) \end{pmatrix} \;\; , \tag{25.13}$$

which is the so–called *assignment vector*. This vector can be considered as a *random vector* related to a probability mass function $p(\zeta_\lambda)$ which holds

$$\sum_{\zeta_\lambda} p(\zeta_\lambda) \;=\; 1 \;\; . \tag{25.14}$$

Figure 25.7, for example, shows an assignment which induces the random vector

$$\zeta_\lambda = (1, 1, 3, 1, 4, 4, 5)^T \;\; . \tag{25.15}$$

The defined assignment vector can be used to get the density for an observed sequence of features by the following marginal:

$$\begin{aligned} p([c_k]_{k=1,2,\ldots,m} | [a_{\lambda,l}]_{l=1,2,\ldots,n_\lambda}) \;\; &= \;\; \sum_{\zeta_\lambda} p([c_k]_{k=1,2,\ldots,m}, \zeta_\lambda | [a_{\lambda,l}]_{l=1,2,\ldots,n_\lambda}) \\ &= \;\; \sum_{\zeta_\lambda} p(\zeta_\lambda)\, p([c_k]_{k=1,2,\ldots,m} | \zeta_\lambda, [a_{\lambda,l}]_{l=1,2,\ldots,n_\lambda}) \;\; . \end{aligned} \tag{25.16}$$

For a known assignment vector ζ_λ we make use of definition (25.12) and the product density in (25.9) for a given assignment. Thus, we obtain the factorization

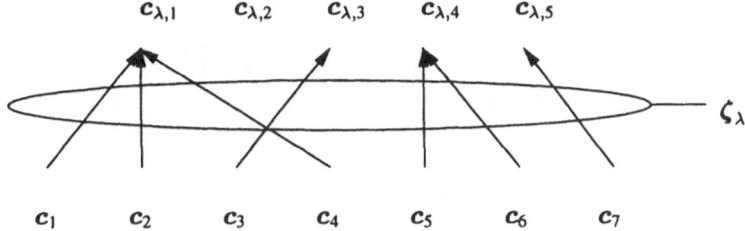

Figure 25.7 Assignment of observed and reference features

$$p([c_k]_{k=1,2,\ldots,m} | \zeta_\lambda, [a_{\lambda,l}]_{l=1,2,\ldots,n_\lambda}) \;=\; \prod_{k=1}^{m} p(c_k | a_{\lambda,\zeta_\lambda(c_k)}) \quad , \tag{25.17}$$

and therefore

$$p([c_k]_{k=1,2,\ldots,m} | [a_{\lambda,l}]_{l=1,2,\ldots,n_\lambda}) \;=\; \sum_{\zeta_\lambda} p(\zeta_\lambda) \prod_{k=1}^{m} p(c_k | a_{\lambda,\zeta_\lambda(c_k)}) \quad . \tag{25.18}$$

The evaluation of this sum requires at least $\mathcal{O}(mn_\lambda^m)$ multiplications and additions. There is no obvious advantage compared to a direct search for an optimal assignment. If we introduce, however, independency assumptions, the complexity can be reduced drastically.

Let us assume statistically independent assignments, i.e., all components of the random vector ζ_λ are pairwise statistically independent, then we obtain the factorization

$$p(\zeta_\lambda) \;=\; \prod_{k=1}^{m} p(\zeta_\lambda(c_k) = l_k) \tag{25.19}$$

for the discrete probability of the assignment vector. It is little *tricky* to show[2] that the multiple sum in (25.18) reduces to a product of single sums:

$$p([c_k]_{k=1,2,\ldots,m} | [a_{\lambda,l}]_{l=1,2,\ldots,n_\lambda}) \;=\; \prod_{k=1}^{m} \sum_{l=1}^{n_\lambda} p(\zeta_\lambda(c_k) = l)\, p(c_k | a_{\lambda,l}) \quad . \tag{25.20}$$

The density function for an observation is a product of m *mixture densities*. Mixture densities are linear combinations of density functions, where the coefficients hold the probability constraint, i.e., sum up to one (c.f. Appendix C.2). This fundamental result shows that statistically independent assignments reduce the original exponential complexity of the original marginal density evaluations (25.18) to $\mathcal{O}(mn_\lambda)$.

To summarize the sequence of conclusions and facts we have seen so far in this section, we now know how to use dynamic programming ideas to derive and implement a Bayesian approach for the classification of feature sequences.

---

[2]c.f. Appendix C.3

Figure 25.8 The handwritten word *minimum*

The efficiency of density evaluation crucially depends on the independency assumption. Assignments are considered independent from each other. In many applications, however, the consideration of context leads to essential improvements of classification results. Standard examples are speech recognition in general or — concerning image processing applications — the recognition of handwritten characters. Figure 25.8 shows the handwritten word *minimum*. The classification of single letters is even for the human being difficult. Nobody can decide which part of the word represents "m", "n" or "i". Only the consideration of context allows the correct recognition of this word.

This simple example shows that context is useful and sometimes necessary for classification. For that reason, we will give up the assumption of statistically independent assignments as stated in this section, and introduce dependent assignments of bounded order. Generally we will conclude the (expected) ground rule: *the higher the dependencies, the higher the complexity of involved algorithms*. There is a remarkable trade–off between recognition rates, dependency assumptions, and computational complexities.

25.4 Hidden Markov Models

One established stochastic modeling approach for speech recognition purposes, which consider context, are *hidden Markov models* (HMMs) [Bau67, Rab88, Rab93]. HMMs are an extension of finite automata with respect to stochastic transitions and probabilistic output generation. Hidden Markov models, however, also result from (25.18) directly, if some specializations in (25.16) or if some generalizations in (25.20) are considered — like the assumption of first order dependencies of assignments. The discrete probability for assignments is therefore factorized to

$$p(\zeta_\lambda) = p(\zeta_\lambda(c_1) = l_1) \prod_{k=2}^{m} p(\zeta_\lambda(c_k) = l_k | \zeta_\lambda(c_{k-1}) = l_{k-1}) \quad . \tag{25.21}$$

An obvious way of computing $p([c_k]_{k=1,2,...,m} | [a_{\lambda,l}]_{l=1,2,...,n_\lambda})$ is the use of the marginal density over all possible assignments, i.e., we obtain the probability density function

$$p([c_k]_{k=1,2,...,m} | [a_{\lambda,l}]_{l=1,2,...,n_\lambda}) = \sum_{\zeta_\lambda} p(\zeta_\lambda) \prod_{k=1}^{m} p(c_k | a_{\lambda,\zeta_\lambda(c_k)}) \quad . \tag{25.22}$$

If we consider (25.21), then the marginal (25.22) is expressed as

$$p([c_k]_{k=1,2,\dots,m}|[a_{\lambda,l}]_{l=1,2,\dots,n_\lambda})$$
$$= \sum_{l_1=1}^{n_\lambda} \cdots \sum_{l_m=1}^{n_\lambda} p(\zeta_\lambda(c_1)=l_1) \prod_{k=2}^{m} p(\zeta_\lambda(c_k)=l_k|\zeta_\lambda(c_{k-1})=l_{k-1}) \prod_{k=1}^{m} p(c_k|a_{\lambda,l_k}) \quad (25.23)$$

where we sum over all m–dimensional assignment vectors $(l_1, l_2, \dots, l_m)^T$, $l_k = 1, 2, \dots, n_\lambda$. The evaluation of (25.23) requires an exponentially bounded number of additions and multiplications. In case of pairwise statistically independent assignments, this complexity was reduced to $\mathcal{O}(mn_\lambda)$. In fact, a *tricky* re–organization of summations and products also leads to an efficient evaluation algorithm of polynomial complexity for first order dependencies. For that purpose, we define the *forward variable*

$$\alpha_{t,l_t} = p([c_k]_{k=1,2,\dots,t}, \zeta_\lambda(c_t)=l_t \mid [a_{\lambda,l}]_{l=1,2,\dots,n_\lambda}) \quad (25.24)$$

to be the probability density of observing the first t features $c_1, c_2, \dots, c_t$, where the t–th feature is assigned to c_{λ,l_t} resp. its associated density $p(c|a_{\lambda,l_t})$. Using the forward variable, we can recursively define

$$\alpha_{t+1,l_{t+1}} = \left(\sum_{l=1}^{n_\lambda} \alpha_{t,l_t}\, p(\zeta_\lambda(c_{t+1})=l_{t+1}|\zeta_\lambda(c_t)=l_t) \right) p(c_{t+1}|a_{\lambda,l_{t+1}}) \quad (25.25)$$

to assign the $(t+1)$–st feature to the l_{t+1}–th density. Since this probability does not depend on the assignment of the t–th feature, we use the marginal over all assignments. The value of the forward variables $\alpha_{1,1}, \alpha_{1,2}, \dots, \alpha_{1,n_\lambda}$ for the first feature is obviously

$$\alpha_{1,l_1} = p(\zeta_\lambda(c_1)=l_1)\, p(c_1|a_{\lambda,l_1}) \quad , \quad (25.26)$$

such that we get finally the marginal

$$p([c_k]_{k=1,2,\dots,m}|[a_{\lambda,l}]_{l=1,2,\dots,n_\lambda}) = \sum_{l_m=1}^{n_\lambda} \alpha_{m,l_m} \quad . \quad (25.27)$$

The evaluation of (25.27) is bounded by $\mathcal{O}(mn_\lambda^2)$. Figure 25.9 summarizes the suggested iterative evaluation of marginals. The algorithm is widely used in the literature; it is the so–called *forward algorithm*.

By a further specialization of (25.23), we can reduce the introduced formalism to the standard hidden Markov modeling scheme. Hidden Markov models, in general, are extensions of finite stochastic automata. A hidden Markov model associated with a pattern class Ω_λ is characterized by:

- a set of states $S = \{S_1, S_2, \dots, S_{n_\lambda}\}$,
- initial state distribution $\pi_1, \pi_2, \dots, \pi_{n_\lambda}$
- transition probabilities a_{l_{k-1},l_k} which denote the discrete probability to change from state $S_{l_{k-1}}$ to S_{l_k},
- output symbols o_k, and
- output density functions $p(o|a_{\lambda,l})$, $l = 1, 2, \dots, n_\lambda$.

input: $[c_k]_{k=1,2,\ldots,m}$
FOR $l = 1$ to n_λ
$\alpha_{1,l} = p(\zeta_\lambda(c_1) = l)\, p(c_1 \vert a_{\lambda,l})$
FOR $t = 2$ to m
FOR $l' = 1$ to n_λ
compute
$\alpha_{t+1,l'} = \left(\sum\limits_{l=1}^{n_\lambda} \alpha_{t,l}\, p(\zeta_\lambda(c_{t+1}) = l' \vert \zeta_\lambda(c_t) = l) \right) p(c_{t+1} \vert a_{\lambda,l'})$
output: $\sum\limits_{l=1}^{n_\lambda} \alpha_{m,l}$

Figure 25.9 Forward algorithm

Using this definition, we conclude

$$0 \leq \pi_l, a_{l_{k-1}, l_k} \leq 1 \quad , \tag{25.28}$$

and

$$\sum_{l=1}^{n_\lambda} \pi_l \;=\; 1 \quad \text{and} \quad \sum_{l_k=1}^{n_\lambda} a_{l_k-1, l_k} = 1 \quad . \tag{25.29}$$

We now denote the observed features $[c_k]_{k=1,2,\ldots,m}$ by $[o_k]_{k=1,2,\ldots,m}$, and set for all k

$$p(\zeta_\lambda(o_k) = l) \;=\; \pi_l \quad , \quad \text{and} \tag{25.30}$$

$$p(\zeta_\lambda(o_k) = l_k \vert \zeta_\lambda(o_{k-1}) = l_{k-1}) \;=\; a_{l_{k-1}, l_k} \quad . \tag{25.31}$$

These equations map our former formalism to the HMM notation, and allow the following interpretation: we associate with each speech signal a sequence, i.e., an ordered list, of features. This sequence is assumed to be produced by the hidden Markov model. The statistical model generates a sequence of output symbols, guided by transition and output probabilities. Each observable symbol o_k is emitted in a state S_{l_k} of the automaton with a certain probability $p(o_k \vert a_{\lambda,l_k})$. A measure for a sequence of observed features is therefore the probability for this ordered set of features to be an output sequence of a given HMM.

The term *hidden Markov model* originates from the fact that for an observable sequence of output symbols, it is unknown which state sequence caused this. The structure may, however, be known, e.g., the number of states is defined and some transitions might be impossible ($a_{l_{k-1}, l_k} = 0$). The gray box in Figure 25.10 shows one example for a HMM with three states. The emission probabilities are left out in the figure.

During the training phase of an HMM, the initial state distribution, the transition probabilities, and the output density functions (or their parameters) have to be estimated. There exist various techniques for computing statistical parameters from a set of observable training samples. In the case of HMM, we compute the parameters such that for all observed learning sequences the likelihood function is maximized. This parameter estimation procedure has to be unsupervised, because it is not known which state sequences have generated the observable output symbols (Figure 25.10). Thus, we have to use parameter estimation techniques which can deal with such a type of incomplete data (c.f. Sect. 25.7). A direct ML estimation seems unfeasable due to the high dimensionality of the parameter space.

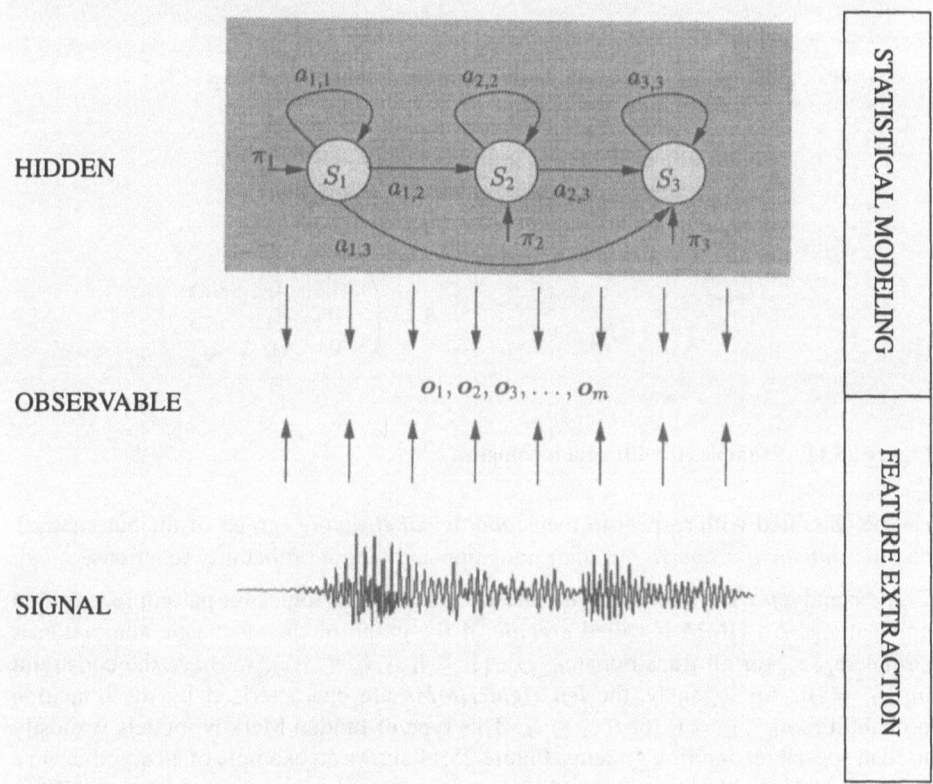

Figure 25.10 The hidden statistical processes and an observable feature sequence for parameter estimation

25.5 Topological and Statistical Variations

Before we start with the discussion of parameter estimation techniques and the computation of training formulas, we discuss different types of HMMs. HMMs, in general,

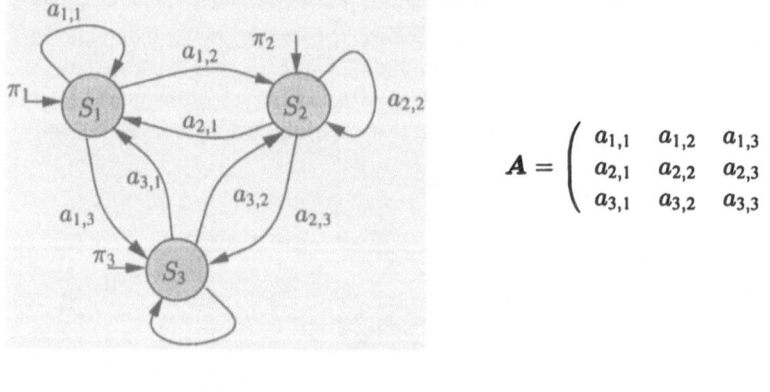

$$A = \begin{pmatrix} a_{1,1} & a_{1,2} & a_{1,3} \\ a_{2,1} & a_{2,2} & a_{2,3} \\ a_{3,1} & a_{3,2} & a_{3,3} \end{pmatrix}$$

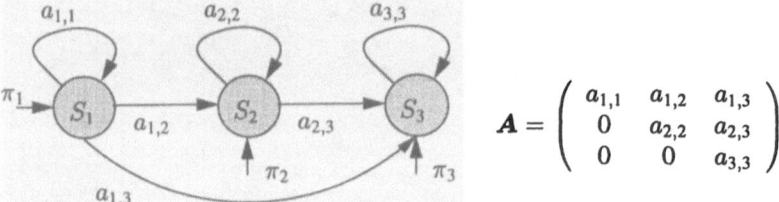

$$A = \begin{pmatrix} a_{1,1} & a_{1,2} & a_{1,3} \\ 0 & a_{2,2} & a_{2,3} \\ 0 & 0 & a_{3,3} \end{pmatrix}$$

Figure 25.11 Examples for different topologies

can be classified with respect to their *topological structure* (graph of the automaton), and the *statistical properties* of their transition and output probability functions.

Ergodic and *left right HMMs* are the most important topologies for pattern recognition applications. An HMM is called *ergodic*, if the graph of the stochastic automaton is complete, i.e., for all transitions a_{l_{k-1},l_k}, $(1 \leq l_{k-1}, l_k \leq n_\lambda)$, we have the constraint $a_{l_{k-1},l_k} \neq 0$. Analogously, the *left right HMMs* are characterized by the transition probabilities $a_{l_{k-1},l_k} = 0$ for $l_{k-1} \leq l_k$. This type of hidden Markov models is mostly used in speech recognition systems. Figure 25.11 shows an example of an ergodic and a left right HMM with the corresponding transition matrices. Again, output probabilities are omitted in the illustration.

Not only the graphical structure of HMMs allows the introduction of different types. Also the statistical properties of Markov models induce the definition of various models. An HMM is called *discrete*, if the emission probabilities of all states are discrete and we observe discrete random variables. In those cases, the emission probabilities can be represented using relative frequencies, i.e., histograms. The training of discrete HMMs corresponds therefore to the estimation of discrete input, transition, and output probabilities.

In case of continuous emission density functions, we call the resulting HMM *continuous*. For example, the parametric Gaussian density function (8.6) can be used for modeling the output densities.

There exist various other types of hidden Markov models which are successfully applied to speech recognition applications: stationary and non–stationary HMMs [Hor96a, He91], semi–continuous HMMs (SCHMM, [Rab93, ST95]), feature transform HMMs (FTHMM, [Sch95]) or generalized HMMs [Hor96a].

25.6   Generalized Hidden Markov Models

So far we have introduced statistical modeling schemes for discrete assignments. The complexity of density evaluations for observed feature sequences was reduced by considering independencies. We got mixtures of densities for pairwise independent assignments, and hidden Markov models for dependencies of first order. The related evaluation algorithms are bounded by $\mathcal{O}(mn_\lambda)$ for products of mixtures, and $\mathcal{O}(mn_\lambda^2)$ for HMMs using the forward algorithm.

By increasing the dependencies to g–th order, it can be shown that the complexity of these generalized hidden Markov models is bounded by $\mathcal{O}(mn_\lambda^{g+1})$ using a generalized version of the forward algorithm. A detailed derivation of generalized HMMs and related algorithms is omitted here and can be found in [Hor96a].

In the following, we consider the involved parameter estimation techniques which are required for automatic training purposes.

25.7   Incomplete Data Estimation

Modeling schemes including statistical properties of features should be generated of a set including representative training samples. The manual and painstaking construction of stochastic models should be avoided and computers should learn the appearance of features in speech signals automatically. The ultimate goal is that different speakers provide sample data, and the recognition system learns the presented patterns on its own — without any manual support. Therefore, the available training set should be sufficient for generalizations. The software should be able to classify patterns which are not elements of the training set.

We consider the parameter estimation problems related to statistical models introduced in previous sections. It was already mentioned that main problems are the incompleteness of available training data, and the infeasibility of a direct ML estimation due to the high dimension of the search space. The basic idea of the *Expectation Maximization algorithm* (EM algorithm) [Dem77] is the augmentation of the observable data with latent data to simplify the parameter estimation algorithm. In most applications this technique reduces complicated, high–dimensional optimization problems to a series of independent simpler maximizations. In an informal and colloquial manner we describe the available information for parameter estimation by the difference

observed information = complete information − missing information   .

This simple equation induces the *missing information principle*, since there exists a one–to–one translation into a statistical framework. Let us assume that the observable random variables are denoted by denoted by X and the missing random variables are Y. If the associated densities are parameterized with respect to B, we have (c.f. (8.26))

$$p(X, Y|B) = p(X|B) \, p(Y|X, B) \quad , \tag{25.32}$$

and therefore we get the fraction

$$p(X|B) = \frac{p(X, Y|B)}{p(Y|X, B)} \quad . \tag{25.33}$$

Taking the logarithm on both sides, we obtain an information theoretic formalization of the above difference

$$(- \log p(X|B)) = (- \log p(X, Y|B)) - (- \log p(Y|X, B)) \quad , \tag{25.34}$$

because due to definition (8.28) in Sect. 8.8, we have

$$I(X|B) = - \log p(X|B) \tag{25.35}$$

$$I(X, Y|B) = - \log p(X, Y|B) \quad , \quad \text{and} \tag{25.36}$$

$$I(Y|X, B) = - \log p(Y|X, B) \tag{25.37}$$

— the *observed*, the *complete*, and the *missing information*.

Equation (25.34) leads to an iterative method for incomplete data estimation. Let us assume $\widehat{B}^{(i)}$ and $\widehat{B}^{(i+1)}$ are estimates of the parameter B of the i–th and $(i + 1)$–st iterations. We consider (25.34) in the $(i + 1)$–st iteration, multiply both sides by $p(Y|X, \widehat{B}^{(i)})$, and integrate out the missing component Y. These operations lead to the *key–equation* of the EM algorithm [Dem77]

$$L(\widehat{B}^{(i+1)}|\widehat{B}^{(i)}) = Q(\widehat{B}^{(i+1)}|\widehat{B}^{(i)}) - H(\widehat{B}^{(i+1)}|\widehat{B}^{(i)}) \quad , \tag{25.38}$$

where

$$L(\widehat{B}^{(i+1)}|\widehat{B}^{(i)}) = \int p(Y|X, \widehat{B}^{(i)}) \log p(X|\widehat{B}^{(i+1)}) \, dY \quad , \tag{25.39}$$

$$Q(\widehat{B}^{(i+1)}|\widehat{B}^{(i)}) = \int p(Y|X, \widehat{B}^{(i)}) \log p(X, Y|\widehat{B}^{(i+1)}) \, dY \quad , \tag{25.40}$$

and

$$H(\widehat{B}^{(i+1)}|\widehat{B}^{(i)}) = \int p(Y|X, \widehat{B}^{(i)}) \log p(Y|X, \widehat{B}^{(i+1)}) \, dY \quad . \tag{25.41}$$

For the left side of the key–equation (25.38), we obtain

$$\int p(\boldsymbol{Y}|\boldsymbol{X},\widehat{\boldsymbol{B}}^{(i)}) \log p(\boldsymbol{X}|\widehat{\boldsymbol{B}}^{(i+1)}) \, d\boldsymbol{Y} \quad =$$

$$= \int \left(\log p(\boldsymbol{X}|\widehat{\boldsymbol{B}}^{(i+1)}) \right) p(\boldsymbol{Y}|\boldsymbol{X},\widehat{\boldsymbol{B}}^{(i)}) \, d\boldsymbol{Y}$$

$$= \log p(\boldsymbol{X}|\widehat{\boldsymbol{B}}^{(i+1)}) \underbrace{\int p(\boldsymbol{Y}|\boldsymbol{X},\widehat{\boldsymbol{B}}^{(i)}) \, d\boldsymbol{Y}}_{= 1} = \log p(\boldsymbol{X}|\widehat{\boldsymbol{B}}^{(i+1)}) \; ; \quad (25.42)$$

this is exactly the log likelihood function.

Changes in the parameter set $\widehat{\boldsymbol{B}}^{(i+1)}$ induce a decrease of $H(\widehat{\boldsymbol{B}}^{(i+1)}|\widehat{\boldsymbol{B}}^{(i)})$, thus an increase of the *Kullback–Leibler statistics* $Q(\widehat{\boldsymbol{B}}^{(i+1)}|\widehat{\boldsymbol{B}}^{(i)})$ causes a reduction of the *conditional entropy* $H(\widehat{\boldsymbol{B}}^{(i+1)}|\widehat{\boldsymbol{B}}^{(i)})$. Indeed, the following inequality holds for the introduced H–function (c.f. Appendix C.4):

$$H(\widehat{\boldsymbol{B}}^{(i+1)}|\widehat{\boldsymbol{B}}^{(i)}) \leq H(\widehat{\boldsymbol{B}}^{(i)}|\widehat{\boldsymbol{B}}^{(i)}) \; ; \quad (25.43)$$

This result shows that a maximum likelihood estimation can be *simulated* by an iterative maximization of the Kullback Leibler statistics $Q(\widehat{\boldsymbol{B}}^{(i+1)}|\widehat{\boldsymbol{B}}^{(i)})$, which is also called the Q–function. The final success of the EM iterations crucially depends on the initial estimate $\widehat{\boldsymbol{B}}^{(0)}$, because the EM algorithm is a local optimization technique and provides a linear convergence behavior [Wu83]. The already mentioned advantage of EM iterations instead of a straightforward ML estimation is that in most applications dealing with missing data, the search space splits into independent lower dimensional sub–spaces. Furthermore, due to its iterative nature the storage requirements remain constant. An impressive application of the introduced parameter estimation technique will be discussed in the following subsection.

25.8 Learning from Multiple Observations

Sample data for mixtures and HMMs are usually sequences of features. Let us assume, we have N training sequences which are denoted by

$$\{^{\varrho}\boldsymbol{C} \; ; \; \varrho = 1, 2, \dots, N\} \quad = \quad \{[^{\varrho}c_k]_{k=1,2,\dots,^{\varrho}m} \; ; \; \varrho = 1, 2, \dots, N\} \quad , \quad (25.44)$$

where $^{\varrho}m$ denotes the number of sequence elements of the ϱ–th observation. Due to the fact that the assignment function ζ_λ, which maps observed features to reference elements, is not part of the training set, we have to deal with an incomplete data estimation problem. The estimation of mixture and HMM parameters has to be done by applying the EM algorithm. However, the EM–algorithm described so far is based on a single observation sequence, i.e., $\boldsymbol{X} = [c_k]_{k=1,2,\dots,m}$ instead of the training set

$$\{^{\varrho}\boldsymbol{X} \; ; \; \varrho = 1, 2, \dots, N\} \quad = \quad \{^{\varrho}\boldsymbol{C} \; ; \; \varrho = 1, 2, \dots, N\} \quad . \quad (25.45)$$

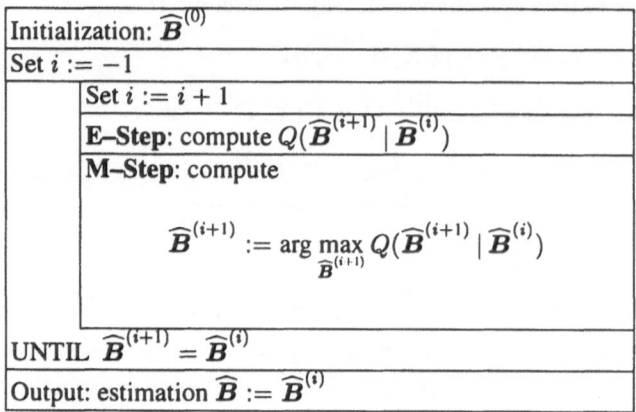

Initialization: $\widehat{\boldsymbol{B}}^{(0)}$
Set $i := -1$
Set $i := i + 1$ **E–Step**: compute $Q(\widehat{\boldsymbol{B}}^{(i+1)}\mid\widehat{\boldsymbol{B}}^{(i)})$ **M–Step**: compute $$\widehat{\boldsymbol{B}}^{(i+1)} := \arg\max_{\widehat{\boldsymbol{B}}^{(i+1)}} Q(\widehat{\boldsymbol{B}}^{(i+1)}\mid\widehat{\boldsymbol{B}}^{(i)})$$
UNTIL $\widehat{\boldsymbol{B}}^{(i+1)} = \widehat{\boldsymbol{B}}^{(i)}$
Output: estimation $\widehat{\boldsymbol{B}} := \widehat{\boldsymbol{B}}^{(i)}$

Figure 25.12 EM algorithm

The maximum likelihood approach for parameter estimation will maximize the objective function

$$L(\{{}^{1}\boldsymbol{X}, {}^{2}\boldsymbol{X}, \ldots, {}^{N}\boldsymbol{X}\}, \boldsymbol{B}) = \sum_{\varrho=1}^{N} \log p({}^{\varrho}\boldsymbol{X}\mid\boldsymbol{B}) \qquad (25.46)$$

in the presence of multiple observations. The influence of multiple observations on the EM algorithm and especially on the Q–function can be seen, if we take a closer look at its definition. Using (25.40) we obtain

$$Q(\widehat{\boldsymbol{B}}^{(i+1)}\mid\widehat{\boldsymbol{B}}^{(i)}) = \int \prod_{\rho=1}^{N} p({}^{\rho}\boldsymbol{Y}\mid{}^{\rho}\boldsymbol{X}, \widehat{\boldsymbol{B}}^{(i)}) \sum_{\varrho=1}^{N} \log p({}^{\varrho}\boldsymbol{X}, {}^{\varrho}\boldsymbol{Y}\mid\widehat{\boldsymbol{B}}^{(i+1)}) \, d^{1}\boldsymbol{Y} \, d^{2}\boldsymbol{Y} \ldots d^{N}\boldsymbol{Y}$$

$$= \sum_{\varrho=1}^{N} \int \prod_{\rho=1}^{N} p({}^{\rho}\boldsymbol{Y}\mid{}^{\rho}\boldsymbol{X}, \widehat{\boldsymbol{B}}^{(i)}) \log p({}^{\varrho}\boldsymbol{X}, {}^{\varrho}\boldsymbol{Y}\mid\widehat{\boldsymbol{B}}^{(i+1)}) \, d^{1}\boldsymbol{Y} \, d^{2}\boldsymbol{Y} \ldots d^{N}\boldsymbol{Y}$$

$$= \sum_{\varrho=1}^{N} \underbrace{\prod_{\substack{\rho=1\\\rho\neq\varrho}}^{N} \int p({}^{\rho}\boldsymbol{Y}\mid{}^{\rho}\boldsymbol{X}, \widehat{\boldsymbol{B}}^{(i)}) \, d^{\rho}\boldsymbol{Y}}_{=\,1} \underbrace{\int p({}^{\varrho}\boldsymbol{Y}\mid{}^{\varrho}\boldsymbol{X}, \widehat{\boldsymbol{B}}^{(i)}) \log p({}^{\varrho}\boldsymbol{X}, {}^{\varrho}\boldsymbol{Y}\mid\widehat{\boldsymbol{B}}^{(i+1)}) \, d^{\varrho}\boldsymbol{Y}}_{=\,{}^{\varrho}Q(\widehat{\boldsymbol{B}}^{(i+1)}\mid\widehat{\boldsymbol{B}}^{(i)})}$$

$$= \sum_{\varrho=1}^{N} {}^{\varrho}Q(\widehat{\boldsymbol{B}}^{(i+1)}\mid\widehat{\boldsymbol{B}}^{(i)}) \quad ,$$

where ${}^{\varrho}Q(\widehat{\boldsymbol{B}}^{(i+1)}\mid\widehat{\boldsymbol{B}}^{(i)})$ denotes the Kullback Leibler statistics corresponding to ${}^{\varrho}\boldsymbol{X}$. This result shows that in case of multiple observations, EM iterations have to maximize the sum of single Q–functions ${}^{\varrho}Q(\widehat{\boldsymbol{B}}^{(i+1)}\mid\widehat{\boldsymbol{B}}^{(i)})$ associated with single elements of the sample data, and provides the necessary mathematical tools for the computation of iterative estimation algorithms. We can explicitly derive formulas which allow the estimation of statistical parameters of mixtures and HMMs. It is a hard computation to get these formulas. For that reason, we will only show one detailed example. Other re–estimation — usually without derivations, but sufficient for implementation purposes — can be found in standard speech recognition literature.

We restrict the discussion to the estimation of discrete assignment probabilities $p(\zeta_\lambda)$. In fact, without any independency assumptions, exponentially many parameters have to be estimated. The application of the missing information principle requires the identification of the observable and hidden parts, which are denoted by $^\varrho X$ and $^\varrho Y$. The observable random variables are N feature sequences, i.e.,

$$^\varrho X \;=\; [^\varrho c_k]_{k=1,2,\ldots,^\varrho m} \quad , \tag{25.47}$$

and the hidden part is characterized by the assignment function ζ_λ, which is considered to be a random vector. The densities $p(^\varrho X, {}^\varrho Y | B)$ and $p(^\varrho Y | {}^\varrho X, B)$ required for the computation of the Q–function are therefore:

$$p([^\varrho c_k]_{k=1,2,\ldots,^\varrho m}, {}^\varrho \zeta_\lambda | B_\lambda) \;=\; p(^\varrho \zeta_\lambda) \prod_{k=1}^{^\varrho m} p(^\varrho c_k | a_{\lambda, {}^\varrho \zeta_\lambda(^\varrho c_k)}) \quad . \tag{25.48}$$

Using the identity

$$p(^\varrho Y | {}^\varrho X, B) \;=\; \frac{p(^\varrho X, {}^\varrho Y | B)}{p(^\varrho X | B)} \;=\; \frac{p(^\varrho X, {}^\varrho Y | B)}{\int p(^\varrho X, {}^\varrho Y | B)\, d^\varrho Y} \quad , \tag{25.49}$$

we get

$$p(^\varrho \zeta_\lambda | [^\varrho c_k]_{k=1,2,\ldots,^\varrho m}, B_\lambda) \;=\; \frac{p([^\varrho c_k]_{k=1,2,\ldots,^\varrho m}, {}^\varrho \zeta_\lambda | B_\lambda)}{\sum\limits_{^\varrho \zeta_\lambda} p([^\varrho c_k]_{k=1,2,\ldots,^\varrho m}, {}^\varrho \zeta_\lambda | B_\lambda)}$$

$$=\; \frac{p(^\varrho \zeta_\lambda) \prod\limits_{k=1}^{^\varrho m} p(^\varrho c_k | a_{\lambda, {}^\varrho \zeta_\lambda(^\varrho c_k)})}{\sum\limits_{^\varrho \zeta_\lambda} p(^\varrho \zeta_\lambda) \prod\limits_{k=1}^{^\varrho m} p(^\varrho c_k | a_{\lambda, {}^\varrho \zeta_\lambda(^\varrho c_k)})} \quad . \tag{25.50}$$

The required Q–function thus is

$$Q(\widehat{B}_\lambda^{(i+1)} | \widehat{B}_\lambda^{(i)}) \;=\; \sum_{\varrho=1}^{N} {}^\varrho Q(\widehat{B}_\lambda^{(i+1)} | \widehat{B}_\lambda^{(i)})$$

$$=\; \sum_{\varrho=1}^{N} \sum_{^\varrho \zeta_\lambda} p(^\varrho \zeta_\lambda | [^\varrho c_k]_{k=1,2,\ldots,^\varrho m}, \widehat{B}_\lambda^{(i)})\, \log p([^\varrho c_k]_{k=1,2,\ldots,^\varrho m}, {}^\varrho \zeta_\lambda | \widehat{B}_\lambda^{(i+1)}) \tag{25.51}$$

$$=\; \sum_{\varrho=1}^{N} \sum_{^\varrho \zeta_\lambda} \frac{\widehat{p}^{(i)}(^\varrho \zeta_\lambda) \prod\limits_{k=1}^{^\varrho m} p(^\varrho c_k | \widehat{a}_{\lambda, {}^\varrho \zeta_\lambda(^\varrho c_k)}^{(i)})}{\sum\limits_{^\varrho \zeta_\lambda} \widehat{p}^{(i)}(^\varrho \zeta_\lambda) \prod\limits_{k=1}^{^\varrho m} p(^\varrho c_k | \widehat{a}_{\lambda, {}^\varrho \zeta_\lambda(^\varrho c_k)}^{(i)})}\, \log\left(\widehat{p}^{(i+1)}(^\varrho \zeta_\lambda) \prod\limits_{k=1}^{^\varrho m} p(^\varrho c_k | \widehat{a}_{\lambda, {}^\varrho \zeta_\lambda(^\varrho c_k)}^{(i+1)}) \right)$$

Since the arguments of the logarithm in (25.51) are products, we obtain

$$\log\left(\widehat{p}^{(i+1)}(^\varrho\zeta_\lambda)\prod_{k=1}^{^\varrho m}p(^\varrho c_k|\widehat{a}^{(i+1)}_{\lambda,^\varrho\zeta_\lambda(^\varrho c_k)})\right) =$$

$$= \log\,\widehat{p}^{(i+1)}(^\varrho\zeta_\lambda)+\sum_{k=1}^{^\varrho m}\log\,p(^\varrho c_k|\widehat{a}^{(i+1)}_{\lambda,^\varrho\zeta_\lambda(^\varrho c_k)}) \qquad (25.52)$$

The maximization of the Q–function (25.51) with respect to $p(\zeta_\lambda)$ has to be done such that the constraint $\sum_{\zeta_\lambda}p(\zeta_\lambda)=1$ holds. Usually the optimization of continuous functions is based on the computation of partial derivatives and their zero–crossings. According to Appendix (C.5) Lagrange multipliers are appropriate for considering constraints on the required parameters. For an arbitrary but fixed assignment ζ_λ we get the following closed–form re–estimation formula using the partial derivative and the result of the example in Appendix (C.5):

$$p^{(i+1)}(\zeta_\lambda) = \frac{\displaystyle\sum_{\varrho=1}^{N}\frac{\widehat{p}^{(i)}(\zeta_\lambda)\prod_{k=1}^{^\varrho m}p(^\varrho c_k|\widehat{a}^{(i)}_{\lambda,\zeta_\lambda(^\varrho c_k)})}{\displaystyle\sum_{^\varrho\zeta_\lambda}\widehat{p}^{(i)}(^\varrho\zeta_\lambda)\prod_{k=1}^{^\varrho m}p(^\varrho c_k|\widehat{a}^{(i)}_{\lambda,^\varrho\zeta_\lambda(^\varrho c_k)})}}{\displaystyle\sum_{\varrho=1}^{N}\sum_{^\varrho\zeta_\lambda}\frac{\widehat{p}^{(i)}(^\varrho\zeta_\lambda)\prod_{k=1}^{^\varrho m}p(^\varrho c_k|\widehat{a}^{(i)}_{\lambda,^\varrho\zeta_\lambda(^\varrho c_k)})}{\displaystyle\sum_{^\varrho\zeta_\lambda}\widehat{p}^{(i)}(^\varrho\zeta_\lambda)\prod_{k=1}^{^\varrho m}p(^\varrho c_k|\widehat{a}^{(i)}_{\lambda,^\varrho\zeta_\lambda(^\varrho c_k)})}} . \qquad (25.53)$$

At first sight, this formula seems quite complicated. The numerator includes the "probability" to observe the assignment ζ_λ given the sequences of observations. The denominator denotes the probability to observe the feature sequence for *any* and *unknown* assignment. In fact this intuitive principle holds also for the estimation of probabilities related to pairwise independent assignments, and the input and transition probabilities of hidden Markov models.

Assignments induce a random vector. Let $(l_1,l_2,\ldots,l_m)^T$ be such a random vector. Statistical independent assignments allow the following factorization

$$p((l_1,l_2,\ldots,l_m)^T) = \prod_{k=1}^{m}p(l_k) . \qquad (25.54)$$

Since $l_k=1,2,\ldots,n_\lambda$, the parameters which have to be estimated are: $p(1),p(2),\ldots,p(n_\lambda)$. For this special case, formula (25.53) reduces to:

$$\widehat{p}^{(i+1)}(l) = \frac{\text{expected number of assigning a feature to }c_{\lambda,l}}{\text{number of features}} .$$

In case of HMMs, assignments show dependencies of first order. The parameters are $p(1),p(2),\ldots,p(n_\lambda)$, and $p(l'|l'')$ where $l',l''=1,2,\ldots,n_\lambda$. The EM algorithm leads to the famous Baum–Welch formulas, which are

$$\hat{p}^{(i+1)}(l) \;=\; \frac{\text{expected number of assigning the first feature to } c_{\lambda,l}}{\text{number of features}}$$

and

$$\hat{p}^{(i+1)}(l'|l'') = \frac{\text{expected number of assigning a feature to } c_{\lambda,l''} \text{ and its successor to } c_{\lambda,l'}}{\text{expected number of assigning a feature to } c_{\lambda,l''}}$$

These estimation formulas show a remarkable property which is important with respect to an object–oriented implementation: the concrete representation of features' densities $p(c|a_{\lambda,l})$ is not required. Only a function which allows the evaluation of these densities for a given feature is necessary. For the computation of the parameters $a_{\lambda,l}$, however, we need the knowledge of the parametric densities $p(c|a_{\lambda,l})$. If, for instance, normally distributed features are assumed, the estimation of $a_{\lambda,l}$ corresponds to the computation of the mean vector and the covariance matrix. These formulas are omitted here. We recommend [Hua90] for further explanations.

25.9 An Object–Oriented Implementation of Hidden Markov Models

Single density functions, mixture densities, hidden Markov models, and its generalization are probability density functions from an abstract point of view. For all statistical models, we need inference algorithms which allow the efficient computation of density values for given observations. Furthermore, parameter estimation algorithms are required, and we have to consider different types of density functions, like ergodic or left–right HMMs, mixtures of Gaussians, mixtures of discrete probabilities etc.. The algorithms should be implemented as general as possible. For instance, the estimation of transition probabilities of HMMs can be implemented without specifying the output density functions. The use of virtual functions allows such implementations.

The suggested class hierarchy for statistical models is shown in Figure 25.13. We define an abstract base class `Density` including the pure virtual function `probability` which evaluates the probability density function for a given observation. Therein an observation is an instance of the class `RandomVariable`. Histograms, Gaussian densities, hidden Markov models as well as mixtures of densities are density functions and therefore derived classes. In Chapter 24 we have already discussed the code of base class `Density` and the derived density class `Gaussian` (c.f. Program 195). An HMM, for instance, is defined by the initial probabilities, the transition probabilities, and a vector of output densities — one density for each state. These state densities can be Gaussians, histograms, mixtures or any other type of densities, even HMMs. This required recursive structure is provided by the suggested class hierarchy. Each class

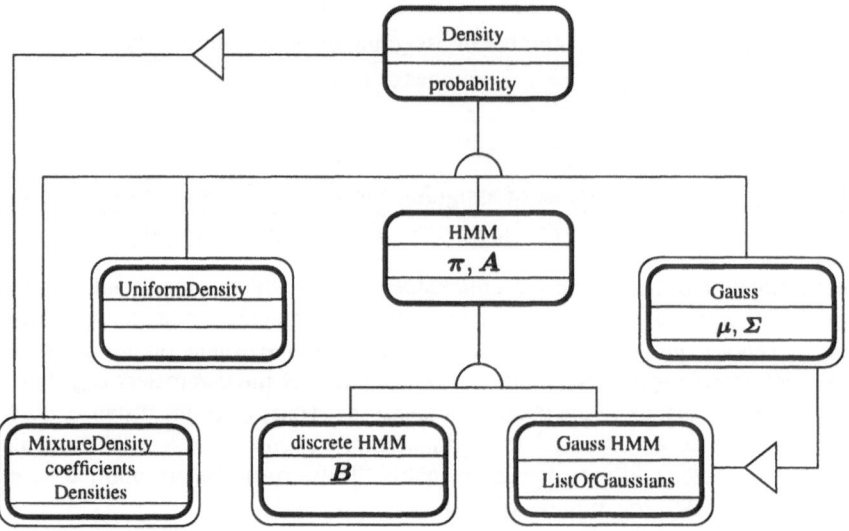

Figure 25.13 Class hierarchy for density functions

derived from the base class `Density` can be used within the density vector of the internal representation of HMMs.

In addition to classes for statistics, the implementation uses the class `SeqCltn` from NIHCL to represent sequences of output symbols in the Baum–Welch training method. As in the case of the class `Bag` in Sect. 24.2 this implies that these symbols are objects in the sense of NIHCL.

Exercises

25.a   Can you tell which speech signal in Figure 25.2 shows an Austrian accent?

25.b   Discuss basic similarities and the differences between the dynamic programming approach, the product of mixtures, and the forward algorithm.

25.c   Apply the ideas of the forward algorithm and dynamic programming to find an algorithm, which computes the most probable sequence of HMM states for a given observation. Show that this algorithm — which is the well–known *Viterbi algorithm* [Nie90a] — is bounded by $\mathcal{O}(mn_\lambda^2)$. Compare your result with the algorithm you get, if statistically independent assignments are considered.

25.d   Use the class hierarchy of Figure 24.6, and adapt your implementation of DTW such that you can use the class for nearest neighbor classifiers.

```
class HMM : public Density {
 public:
   Vector<double>  H_Pi;      // initial probability of states
   Matrix<double>  H_A;       // matrix including transition probabilities
   Vector<Density> H_P;       // ordered set of densities (class Density!)
 public:
  HMM(void);
  HMM(int NumberOfStates); // initialize Vectors and Matrices
  HMM(const HMM & g);
  HMM(const Vector<Density> & l, const Vector<double> & w, Matrix<double> & t);
  virtual ~HMM(void);
  const Vector<double> & pi(void) const;
  const Matrix<double> & A(void) const;
  const Density &        P(void) const;
  virtual double probability(const RandomVariable & feature) const;
  // forward--backward algorithm
  void state_sequence(const RandomVariable & feat, SeqCltn & seq) const;
  // Viterbi algorithm
  void BaumWelchTraining(const SeqCltn & obs);
  // for discrete probabilities
};
```

25.e Define a class for discrete hidden Markov models. Which member variables are needed? Implement methods for learning the parameters of a hidden Markov model given a set of observation sequences. Use the cited literature and define methods for computing the probability that a given HMM has generated an observed sequence of features.

25.f Implement the dynamic time warping algorithm using different types of neighborhoods and distance measures.

26 Advanced Topics

Object–oriented programming in C++ is much easier if a general class library for common programming tools is used, as, for example, NIHCL [Gor90]. The image processing classes in ἵππος [Pau92b] use the NIHCL library and provide an environment for object–oriented image processing. Recently, hidden Markov models (HMM), hierarchies of segmentation algorithms, and an object–oriented knowledge base have augmented ἵππος to an object–oriented image analysis system.

In this chapter we survey systems which we have been implemented based on the ideas introduced in the previous chapters. Each system has its own scientific goal and purpose; all share the implementation platform and the software resources. None of the systems we describe in detail; the goal of this chapter is to demonstrate that the ideas introduced in this book can be useful for the solution of real–world problems related to pattern recognition. This is to encourage the reader to apply object–oriented techniques to his own problems.

At the end of the chapter we outline further C++ features and future language trends.

26.1 Segmentation into Lines and Arcs

In [Har96], the operator hierarchy as sketched in Program178 was implemented completely. Figure 26.1 shows a subtree of the class hierarchy: edge detection, line following, gap closing, etc. — as introduced in the previous chapters, are declared as classes. The figure also shows classes for converting a segmentation object into a new one; using a so called "split and merge" algorithm [Hor74], chain coded lines are converted to sequences of straight lines and circular arcs.[1] The algorithm first detects corners on the chain (c.f. Sect. 22.9) and approximates the links between two corners.

The segmentation object is then passed to a split–and–merge procedure [Pav77; p. 179–184] to approximate the line by line segments. Only the approximation error Theta and the minimum segment length minSeg are specified in the abstract base class SplitAndMerge (Figure 26.1). The algorithm can use any approximation for the segment which defines a distance measure to the chain coded line, such as simple straight line approximations or circular arcs (Sect. 22.8) [Har96]. Examples illustrating this approach are shown in Figure 26.2.

---

[1] The algorithm can be found in various text books.

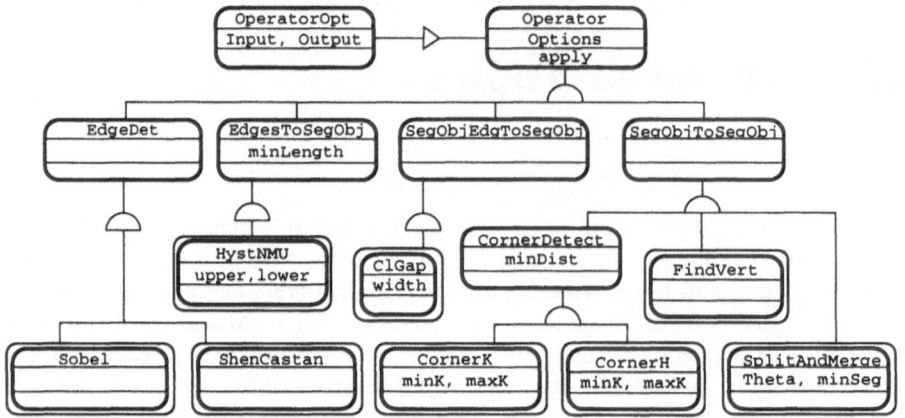

Figure 26.1 Subtree of the operator hierarchy for image segmentation from [Har96]

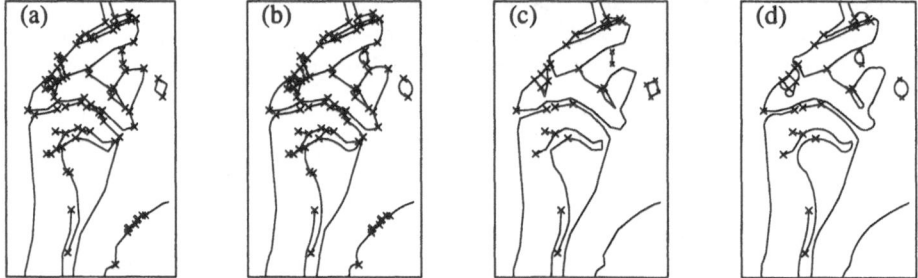

Figure 26.2 Different approximations: (a,b): k–curvature, (c,d): H–curvature, (a,c): straight lines, (b,d): straight lines and arcs. Junctions are marked as crosses.

26.2   Stereo Images

Humans as well as many animals have not only one, but two visual sensors which each provide images as described in Sect. 1.6. We saw stereo imaging already in Sect. 18.8. In addition to the model for the sensor, the geometric relation of the two image planes has to be added to the model of the visual system.

As one can easily experience when we close first the left eye and then the right, the three–dimensional world is mapped to two images which have some part in common, but each misses some part which is present in the other. The basic problem — called the correspondence problem — of stereo processing is to identify the pixels in the left and right image which belong to the same point in the three-dimensional world.

In Figure 26.3 middle we see a stereo (color) image which is a normalized version of the two images on the left, and the segmentation into chain codes (right). The approximation into sequences of straight lines is shown in Figure 26.4 as well as the approximation as straight lines and circular arcs; an automatic matching procedure [Beß96] assigns sets of lines in one image to sequences in the other in order to compute range information from the so called *disparity*, i.e. the difference in position of the matched primitives in both images. One remarkable fact is that an approximation by lines and arcs improves stereo matching, although no curved line is present in the object.

Figure 26.3   Stereo image and its segmentation into straight lines using the algorithms of Sect. 26.1.

The edge detector described in Sect. 21.1 can easily be extended to work on color images. We compute the edge strength for each color channel separately. For each pixel location we check for the maximum result in the color channels and use this result as well as the corresponding edge orientation as the values for the edge element. This idea was applied to detect the lines in Figure 26.4.

26.3   Region Segmentation

In the previous chapters we described how images can be segmented into lines and various other features related to lines. An alternative to this approach is to segment the image into regions which are similar with respect to a similarity measure. The classical approach is the the split–and–merge procedure for regions [Hor74] which creates a set of regions.

In [Pau92b] it was shown that the segmentation object (Program 171) has all the required methods for storing arbitrary segmentation results, including regions. Similarly to a

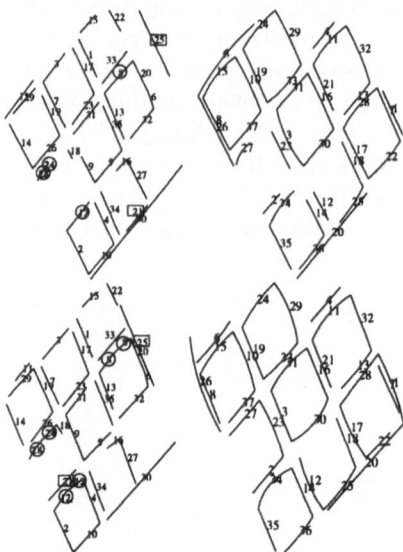

Figure 26.4 Matched lines in the segmentation of the left and right stereo image. Left: sequences of straight lines; right: sequences of straight lines and circular arcs. Boxes mark errors in the match, circles mark cases where more than one segment was present in the sets to be matched.

class for the representation of lines, a class for region representation has to be created which can be specialized to well–known representation schemes, such as quadtrees. Figure 26.5 (left) shows a color image[2] and a segmentation into regions based on color information (right). Since the algorithm in [Den95] uses a quadtree, only a rectangular subimage is segmented. The result is stored in a segmentation object containing the contours as chain codes (Figure 26.5 (middle)).

26.4   Active Vision

For active vision we often need motor controlled devices, such as pan–tilt–units or stereo cameras with motor lenses (c.f. Sect. 6.8). Programming of motor control is often a tedious work when it comes to hardware protocols. It can be facilitated when motors, joints of a device, axes, lenses, etc. are encapsulated as classes and access is provided by simple operators. Assigning an integer to a stepper motor object can then move the device to the desired position.

---

[2]printed as gray–scale image

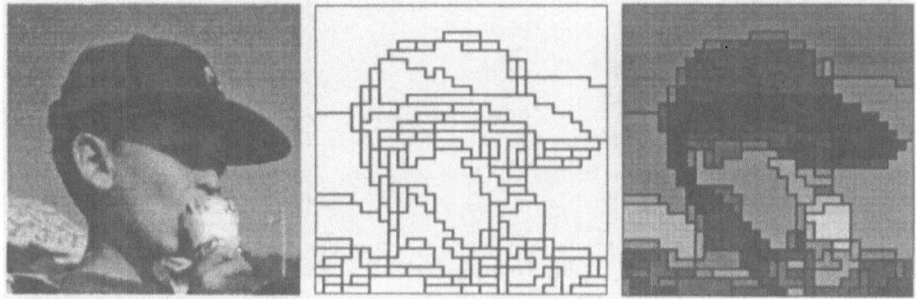

Figure 26.5 Color image segmented into regions and representation by contours

Such programming is used in [Ahl96, Den97]. [Den97] actively moves a pan–tilt unit such that it keeps a moving person in the center of the field of view or tracks any other object. The tools used there are so called "active contours" [Kas88] which in [Den97] are also modelled as a hierarchy of classes.

We recommend that stereo images are derived as a class from the class `Image` and further specialized to color–stereo images and gray–level–stereo images. The same idea can be applied to image sequences which are required in real–time vision and in active vision.

26.5 Semantic Networks

Knowledge based pattern analysis of images or speech signals as outlined in Sect. 6.7 requires that knowledge about the problem domain is represented in the computer in an explicit way, i.e., a knowledge base has to be implemented.

To give two examples: For the analysis of images captured inside an office, it can be useful to model a chair and a table in the knowledge base; each object can have parts (e.g. the legs) or can be specialized (e.g. a desk is a special table). For the analysis of an utterance from a dialog in a travel agency, the system might model the dialog act "train connection" consisting of a departure time and date, a departure and goal city, and optionally a seat preference (smoker or non–smoker).

A well established formalism for the representation of such facts are *semantic networks* [Nie86]. So called concepts (the chair, table, dialog in the examples) are connected by links which express that one concept is part of the other or is a specialization. A semantic net formalism tailored to the purpose of pattern analysis was introduced in [Nie90b]; these ideas were translated to an object–oriented implementation in [Win94]. Naturally, parts are implemented as members and specializations are mapped to inheritance.

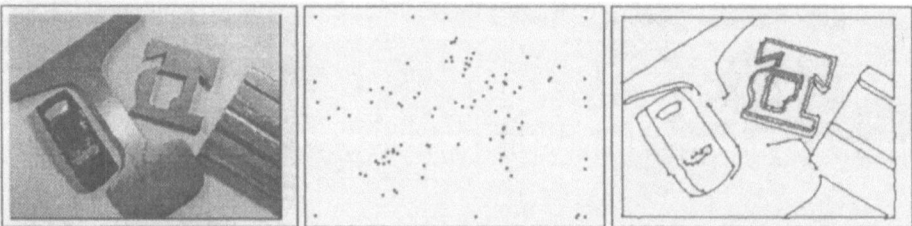

Figure 26.6 Localization of objects with heterogeneous background (left: gray–level image, middle: segmentation result, right: localized object)

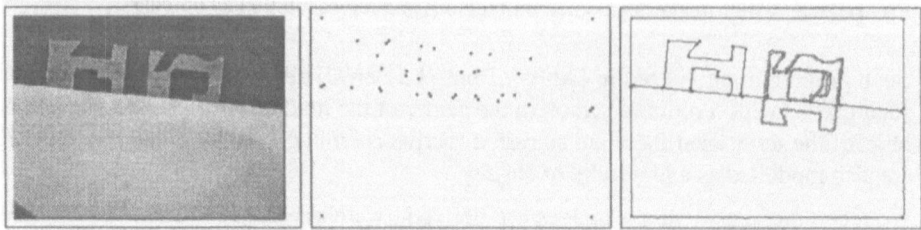

Figure 26.7 Localization of partially occluded objects and heterogeneous background (left: gray–level image, middle: segmentation result, right: localized object)

26.6 Statistical Object Recognition and Localization

An alternative to the explicit representation of knowledge using geometric or structural descriptions has recently gained more attention: as mentioned in Chapter 25, hidden Markov models were successfully applied in speech analysis.

A similar approach for image analysis was described in [Hor96a]. Features which can be detected in images were modelled taking into account the errors due to segmentation, occlusion, projection, and the object's pose (rotation and translation). In particular, mixture densities (c.f. Sect. 25.3) were used for this purpose. Figure 26.6 and Figure 26.7 show some scenes, where object localization is based on statistical methods using point features which result from image segmentation, as introduced in the previous chapters and outlined in Sect. 26.1. In contrast, Figure 26.8 includes examples of probabilistic pose estimation avoiding segmentation.

Only by an object–oriented implementation, this rather complex system was kept modular and parts of it could be reused in other projects. In addition to the statistical models (Sect. 25.3) which were implemented as classes, classes for optimization were provided. A combination of statistical methods and semantic networks is described in [Hor96b].

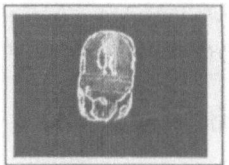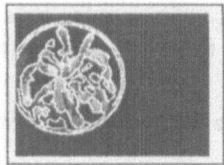

Figure 26.8 Localized objects in gray–level images without segmentation

26.7 Artificial Neural Networks

Instead of statistical classification, which was described in Chapter 24 and which was applied to object recognition in Sect. 26.6, many people prefer to use artificial neural networks (ANNs) for classification, e.g. in [Has94]. The relation between both approaches is described in [Che91].

Like statistical models such as HMMs, ANNs can be trained based on learning data and their behavior will then be verified using test data. The design of ANNs is usually done with an ANN–simulator, such as SNNS.[3] A terse description of ANNs for pattern understanding is given in [Nie90a; p. 199–205].

Of course, implementations in C++ for ANNs exist [Wel94, Mas93] and can be applied for pattern recognition purposes.

26.8 Advanced C++ Features

The C++ features described in this book are those language constructs which are used in most of the programs that we know. More sophisticated syntax is supported by the language. We only briefly mention some which might be interesting for complex systems and refer to [Str91].

One example are pointers to members or pointers to member functions, which have a weird syntax, but are occasionally useful.

Another possibility is to define a free store management by overloading the operators `new` and `delete`.

Introducing nested classes may sometimes reduce the number of global names.

Many extra rules are required when multiple inheritance is used in a programming system. Scoping rules, access regulations, etc. have to be carefully inspected before one decides to use this kind of design.

---

[3] Available from `http://www.uni-stuttgart.de`.

Overloading of many operators is possible in addition to the ones we introduced in the text. For operators which can be either prefix or postfix, a special syntax for declaration was provided.

Function templates are possible similar to the class templates introduced in Sect. 11.2.

26.9   The Future of C++

The C++ language had two major revisions already. In the first version, no multiple inheritance was possible. In the next revision, multiple inheritance was introduced and templates were added a little later.

More changes are discussed in the appendix of [Str91]. A forthcoming standard will most likely incorporate new ideas, such as dynamic type information (*rtti*, runtime type information). Casting will be more secure using an extended syntax which makes use of this new information.

When properly encapsulated, such changes can be already emulated in existing programs and upon availability in the language, can then be changed easily. One such example is the isA function of NIHCL introduced in Sect. 15.2; this function can simply be replaced by rtti.

As already mentioned at several places in the text, exception handling is a powerful tool which will be supported in the language. This is of practical use for real–time systems, such as dialogue systems or image analysis systems in autonomous ground vehicles.

Part V
Appendix

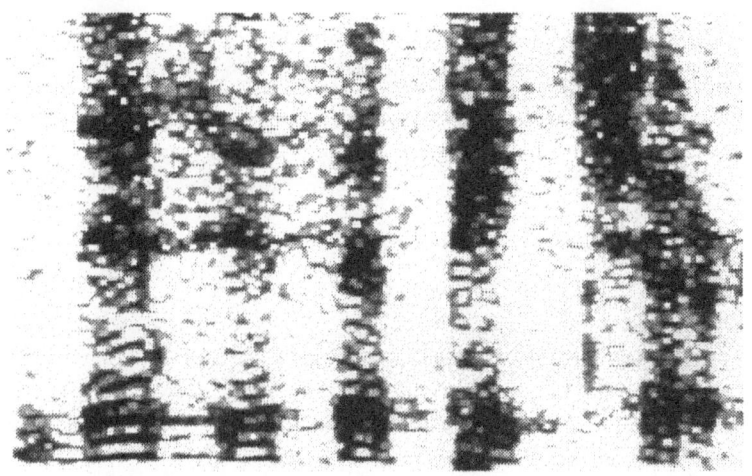

Erosion applied to spectrogram shown on page 291

In the appendix we list sources which can be used to complete the examples in the previous chapters. We describe how interested readers may access further information and request software via international computer networks. We will introduce basic software development tools.

A Software Development Tools

In this appendix we describe some tools provided by the operating system Unix. First we introduce how teamwork is supported by file version and access control. Furthermore, some tools are explained for creation and management of huge program systems and the use of libraries.

A.1 Groups and ID's with Unix

Every user of a Unix system has a user name, which is a textual equivalent of a unique user number (user ID, uid).[1] Users may be joint to groups, which also have a name and a number (group ID, gid). A user may be member of several groups; this is recorded in the file /etc/group. Upon login, the user is assigned to its uid and gid according to the file /etc/passwd.

Every file in the directory tree of the system is owned by a user. The uid is recorded with the file. The file is also assigned to a group[2]. Possibly different rights may be granted on a particular file for the owner, the group, and all other users. Read, write, and execute permissions may be set or refused independently to all of them (Figure A.1, see the manual entry for chmod). Defaults for the settings may be given (see the manual for umask). New files inherit the user and group ID of the user creating the file. The commands chown and chgrp allow change of these settings.[3]

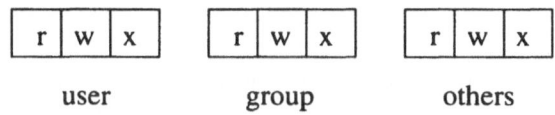

user   group   others

Figure A.1 Read (r), write (w), and execute (x) permissions with Unix

On BSD systems, gid and uid of new files are set according to the settings of the current directory. On SYS5 systems, the user may also use the command newgrp.

---

[1] As usual: there are exceptions to this rule.
[2] Try ls -l to see the user and group assignments of the file.
[3] Permission to use these commands varies between Unix–flavors.

A.2   Program Building with `make`

In the programming phase of a system, interfaces often have to be modified. Necessarily, adaption of the other – dependent – modules should be done to preserve consistency. Unix provides the powerful program `make`[4] to detect and update those modules which are out of date after such a change. This program `make` is useful for the development of small programs; it is even more required for large modular programs.

For example, you might have implemented a lot of modules which can be compiled separately into object code. In C/C++ those object files end in `.o`. In the linking stage several object files can be involved. Thus, the programmer has to make sure that a change of the object files will be followed by a new linkage of the program. The tool `make` supports the management of those dependencies. The implementor defines the file dependencies in a `Makefile` once, and describes the commands to be executed as well.

The file `Makefile` in the actual directory is read by the tool `make`. A `Makefile` can in general contain five different kinds of lines: comments, target lines, command lines, macro definitions, and include lines. If something in the dependency graph has changed, i.e. the latest modification of a file is more recent than the modification time of files which depend on this target, the call of `make` will cause execution of all commands which are required for the update.

- dependencies:
  Dependencies describe how one file target depends on another file. The target specification starts on the first column of the Makefile and is followed by a colon. After the colon, a list of dependencies can be given.
  `target : list of files`
  If a target does not have any dependents specified after the separator ":" on the target line all commands associated with the actual are executed.

- commands:
  `<TAB> command`
  The lines including shell commands follow the target line and begin with a `<TAB>` symbol. The command lines can be continued across more than one line by ending each line with a backslash.

  Target lines with their subsequent command lines are called *rules*.

- Lines starting with a # are treated as comment lines.

We now give an example and explain the actions specified in the `Makefile`. We deal with a program `prog.c`, the related object file `prog.o` and an executable `prog`. These files are related as follows:

---

[4]Also included in most computer environments.

```
# Simple make file for building prog
prog    : prog.o
        cc -o prog prog.o
prog.o : prog.c
        cc -c prog.c
```

- If the program `prog` has to be generated, it is necessary to produce the object file `prog.o`.

- If the file `prog.c` will be changed, `prog.o` has to be generated again.

- If the file object file `prog.o` is younger than `prog`, `prog` has to be linked.

A typical simple `Makefile` is shown in Program 199. The execution of the program make without further arguments causes the first rule of the make file to be evaluated. By providing the target of generation on the command line, you can select special rules of the `Makefile`. For instance, the command `make prog` generates the executable program `prog`, assumed the actual version does not exist, yet. If you simply call `make prog.o`, only the compilation of `prog.o` is done. The command lines are normally printed before they are executed. Further options and facilities can be found in the Unix manual.

A.3   The Use of Libraries

Programs and modules developed by a team can result in many files which have to be written into an archive. For example, object files which have to be linked with other programs should be collected into one archive. Unix provides a tool which allows the generation and the management of those archives. The tool `ar -r file lib` will add or replace the file `file` in the library `lib` and `ar -d file lib` for deleting the file `file` from the library. The table of contents of the archive file can be printed using the command `ar -t lib`.

A single module *contained* in a library can also be target of a `makefile` rule. The library name followed by the name of the module in parentheses has to be specified on the left side of a `make`–rule. This is of course different from specifying the library as a target; the date stamps of the modules are used, rather than those of the library file. In Program 200 this feature is shown; the `make` variables `$@` and `$%` represent the library target and the module name.[5]

---

[5]Make has many more of such short forms for targets and dependents; see the manual for details!

```
LIB=mylib.a

$(LIB)(module.o) : module.c
     cc -o module.c
     ar -ruv $@ $%
```

200

A.4   Version and Access Control with rcs

RCS is very useful for teamwork. It allows easy sharing of code which is readable for all and writable for only one of the group at a time. Let us asume you use a file called file. RCS will then create another file called file,v either in the current directory or in a subdirectory RCS if this is already present. The three basic programs for RCS are:

- ci (check in) which returns an edited version of file to the RCS file file,v and stores the changes,
- co (check out) which returns a saved version of file,v to file, Normally, this file will be read–only. If you supply the option -l, the file will be owned by you and you will have write access.
- rcs (revision control system) which does administration on file,v.

Their function is shown in Figure A.2. Common abbreviations in the diagram are ci -u file which is equivalent to the sequence

ci file; co file;

the command ci -l file stores the file and locks it. This is equivalent to

ci file; co -l file.

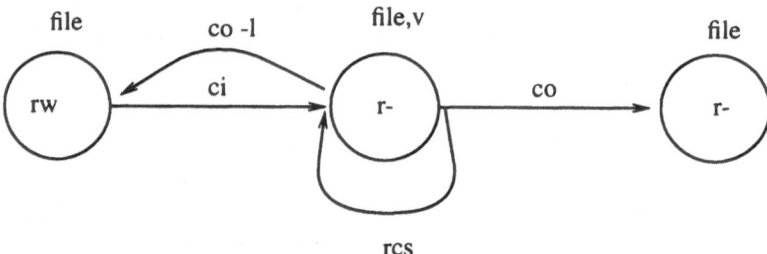

Figure A.2 RCS commands and file mode; the letters in the circles represent the file permissions.

Program 201 shows a combination of Makefiles and rcs. The strings $@ and $? are handy shortcuts for the target and the dependent of the rule. The version information

```
# Makefile for use with rcs
# RCS will fill and update in the following strings
# $Revision: 3.20 $
# $Author: paulus $
prog    : prog.o
          cc -o $@ $?
prog.o : prog.c
          cc -c $?
prog.c  : prog.c,v
          co $?
```

in this makefile is again inserted by rcs. In addition, rcs fills certain strings with values which can be used for documentation and information purposes. Further rcs tools inspect the version file; see the manuals for details on rcsdiff, rcsmerge, and rlog.

A.5 Teamwork

We now describe the strategy for teamwork using rcs under Unix. First, ask the system manager to establish a group for your team. This group will be permanent in the system.

Every time you want to do group work you have to perform the following steps:

- Join the group
  In BSD systems this will be done by changing the current directory to one which belongs to the group.
  In System V system you will have to do an explicit change by newgrp.

- Set default write permissions to the group (using umask).

- If you start with a new subject, create a subdirectory for the work with group ownership of the new group which has write permissions for the group.

- Use rcs for all files which are created or modified by the editor (i.e. source files, makefiles etc.).

B   Source Code and Tools

Various tools were mentioned in the book which can assist programming or pattern processing. Many of them are in the public domain and can be copied freely.

B.1   List of Tools

A very nice interactive facility for image processing and segmentation is the Khoros system [Ras92]. The system is very large and requires a Unix workstation with X11. Programs for almost all image processing issues addressed in this book can be found in this system. The system is written in C and some parts are included in Fortran.

The NIHCL system which was used in Part II of the book is also available in the public domain with full source code.

The GNU tools are available at many places under the so called "copyleft".

The TEX macros for structograms can be found in ftp sites for TEX, at least in Germany.

The program xfig is a drawing tool for Unix. Segmentation results in this book have been converted to xfig graphics format and then to PostScript.

B.2   How to get the sources

The programs Khoros, NIHCL cdecl, xfig, etc. were mentioned in the text. They are all available for Unix only. In order to get them, connect to your nearest ftp site. Most of these programs should be available there. If not, try to find them with archie or xarchie.

All examples printed in this book are available by ftp as well from
           ftp faui57.informatik.uni-erlangen.de .

This site can also be accessed from the world wide web using the address
           http://www5.informatik.uni-erlangen.de .

They can be compiled and run on MS-DOS as well using DJ's g++ GNU compiler.

B.3   X11

Various packages exist for the display and interactive manipulation of images on the screen. To list some of them which use the X11 windows system which is most common under Unix:

- `xv`
- `ImageMagick`
- `Khoros`

These programs can also be found on ftp sites.

B.4   Slides

If you want to use the book for teaching, you might want to get the program examples in source code (Sect. B.2). We also provide a postscript version of slides which we use for teaching. They include all examples, figures, tables, and explanatory text. They are available on request from the authors.

B.5   Addresses

Dr.–Ing. Dietrich Paulus & Dr.–Ing. Joachim Hornegger
Lehrstuhl für Mustererkennung (Informatik 5)
Martensstr. 3
D–91058 Erlangen
Germany
Phone: + 49 (9131) 85–7775
Fax: + 49 (9131) 303811
email: `paulus@informatik.uni-erlangen.de`
email: `hornegger@informatik.uni-erlangen.de`

B.6   Headers and Source Files

When you want to build your own system from the exercises and examples, you should start with the source code provided by ftp. The assignment of file names to the examples is shown in Table B.1. Those files which are never referenced are dummies,

Matrix.h	104 110
Options.h	175
complex.h	115
AtomLine.h	170
AtomObj.h	169
Chain.C	164 165
Chain.h	161 163
Edge.h	166
EdgeImage.h	138
GeoObj.h	168
GrayLevelImage.h	160
HipposObj.h	159
LineRep.h	162
Matrix.C	105
Matrix.h	104
Object.C	143
Object.h	142 145
PointXY.C	86
PointXY.h	85
SegObj.h	171
Sobel.C	187 187 182
ipop.h	178 181 186 188
testprog.C	175 176 177 179

Table B.1 List of header files and corrseponding examples

usually containing an empty class declaration. A list of programming examples and the corresponding page numbers can be found on p. 397.

C Formulas

C.1 Lookup Table Transformation

The solution of the system of equations on p. 254 is as follows:

$$
\begin{aligned}
f_0 \;=\;& a, &\text{(C.1)}\\
f_1 \;=\;& -\frac{1}{K}(-255^3 b^2 e + 255^3 b^2 a + 255^3 d^2 c - 255^3 d^2 a - b^3 d^2 f + 255^2 b^3 e \\
& -255^2 b^3 a - 255^2 d^3 c + b^3 d^2 a + b^2 d^3 f - b^2 d^3 a + 255^2 d^3 a &\text{(C.2)}\\
f_2 \;=\;& \frac{1}{K}(255 b^3 e + b^3 da - 255 b^3 a - b^3 df - 255^3 be - d^3 ab + bd^3 f + \\
& 255^3 ba + 255^3 dc + 255 d^3 a - 255^3 da - 255 d^3 c), &\text{(C.3)}\\
f_3 \;=\;& -\frac{1}{K}(255 b^2 e - 255 b^2 a + 255^2 dc - b^2 df + b^2 da \\
& -255 d^2 c - 255^2 be + 255^2 ba &\text{(C.4)}\\
& +d^2 bf - d^2 ba + 255 d^2 a - 255^2 da),
\end{aligned}
$$

where

$$
K \;=\; 255 bd\left(-d^2 b + 255^2 b + 255 d^2 + b^2 d - 255^2 d - 255 b^2\right). \tag{C.5}
$$

C.2 Marginal Density

The mixture

$$
p(c) \;=\; \sum_{\kappa=1}^{K} p(\Omega_\kappa) p(c|\Omega_\kappa) \tag{C.6}
$$

is a density function, since

$$
\int p(c)\, dc \;=\; \sum_{\kappa=1}^{K} p(\Omega_\kappa) \underbrace{\int p(c|\Omega_\kappa)\, dc}_{=\,1} \;=\; \sum_{\kappa=1}^{K} p(\Omega_\kappa) \;=\; 1 \;. \tag{C.7}
$$

C.3   Identity

$$\sum_{l_1=1}^{n}\sum_{l_2=1}^{n}\cdots\sum_{l_m=1}^{n}\prod_{k=1}^{m}x_{k,l_k} \;=\; \sum_{l_1=1}^{n}\sum_{l_2=1}^{n}\cdots\sum_{l_{m-1}=1}^{n}\prod_{k=1}^{m-1}x_{k,l_k}\left(\sum_{l_m=1}^{n}x_{m,l_m}\right)$$

$$= \left(\sum_{l_1=1}^{n}x_{1,l_1}\right)\left(\sum_{l_2=1}^{n}x_{2,l_2}\right)\cdots\cdots\left(\sum_{l_m=1}^{n}x_{m,l_m}\right)$$

$$= \prod_{k=1}^{m}\sum_{l=1}^{n}x_{k,l} \quad.$$

C.4   Property of the H–Function

For the H–function $H(\widehat{\boldsymbol{B}}^{(i+1)}|\widehat{\boldsymbol{B}}^{(i)})$ the following inequality holds:

$$H(\widehat{\boldsymbol{B}}^{(i+1)}|\widehat{\boldsymbol{B}}^{(i)}) \le H(\widehat{\boldsymbol{B}}^{(i)}|\widehat{\boldsymbol{B}}^{(i)}) \quad ; \tag{C.8}$$

this can be shown by a simple use of the definition of $H(\widehat{\boldsymbol{B}}^{(i+1)}|\widehat{\boldsymbol{B}}^{(i)})$:

$$H(\widehat{\boldsymbol{B}}^{(i+1)}|\widehat{\boldsymbol{B}}^{(i)}) - H(\widehat{\boldsymbol{B}}^{(i)}|\widehat{\boldsymbol{B}}^{(i)}) =$$

$$= \int p(\boldsymbol{Y}|\boldsymbol{X},\widehat{\boldsymbol{B}}^{(i)})\log p(\boldsymbol{Y}|\boldsymbol{X},\widehat{\boldsymbol{B}}^{(i+1)})\,d\boldsymbol{Y}$$

$$- \int p(\boldsymbol{Y}|\boldsymbol{X},\widehat{\boldsymbol{B}}^{(i)})\log p(\boldsymbol{Y}|\boldsymbol{X},\widehat{\boldsymbol{B}}^{(i)})\,d\boldsymbol{Y}$$

$$= \int\left(\log p(\boldsymbol{Y}|\boldsymbol{X},\widehat{\boldsymbol{B}}^{(i+1)}) - \log p(\boldsymbol{Y}|\boldsymbol{X},\widehat{\boldsymbol{B}}^{(i)})\right)p(\boldsymbol{Y}|\boldsymbol{X},\widehat{\boldsymbol{B}}^{(i)})\,d\boldsymbol{Y}$$

$$= \int\left(\log\frac{p(\boldsymbol{Y}|\boldsymbol{X},\widehat{\boldsymbol{B}}^{(i+1)})}{p(\boldsymbol{Y}|\boldsymbol{X},\widehat{\boldsymbol{B}}^{(i)})}\right)p(\boldsymbol{Y}|\boldsymbol{X},\widehat{\boldsymbol{B}}^{(i)})\,d\boldsymbol{Y} \quad.$$

Now we make use of the well–known inequality (c.f. Figure C.1)

$$\log x \le x - 1 \quad, \tag{C.9}$$

and get

$$\log\frac{p(\boldsymbol{Y}|\boldsymbol{X},\widehat{\boldsymbol{B}}^{(i+1)})}{p(\boldsymbol{Y}|\boldsymbol{X},\widehat{\boldsymbol{B}}^{(i)})} \le \frac{p(\boldsymbol{Y}|\boldsymbol{X},\widehat{\boldsymbol{B}}^{(i+1)})}{p(\boldsymbol{Y}|\boldsymbol{X},\widehat{\boldsymbol{B}}^{(i)})} - 1 \quad ; \tag{C.10}$$

therefore,

$$H(\widehat{\boldsymbol{B}}^{(i+1)}|\widehat{\boldsymbol{B}}^{(i)}) - H(\widehat{\boldsymbol{B}}^{(i)}|\widehat{\boldsymbol{B}}^{(i)}) \le \int\left(\frac{p(\boldsymbol{Y}|\boldsymbol{X},\widehat{\boldsymbol{B}}^{(i+1)})}{p(\boldsymbol{Y}|\boldsymbol{X},\widehat{\boldsymbol{B}}^{(i)})} - 1\right)p(\boldsymbol{Y}|\boldsymbol{X},\widehat{\boldsymbol{B}}^{(i)})\,d\boldsymbol{Y}$$

$$= \underbrace{\int p(\boldsymbol{Y}|\boldsymbol{X},\widehat{\boldsymbol{B}}^{(i+1)})\,d\boldsymbol{Y}}_{=\,1} - \underbrace{\int p(\boldsymbol{Y}|\boldsymbol{X},\widehat{\boldsymbol{B}}^{(i)})\,d\boldsymbol{Y}}_{=\,1} \;=\; 0 \quad.$$

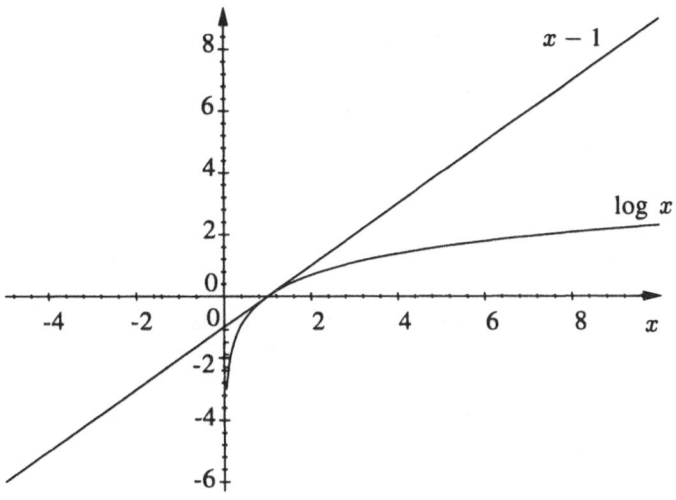

Figure C.1 Illustration of the inequality: $\log x \leq x - 1$

C.5 Lagrange Multiplier

Optimization problems in pattern recognition often have to be solved with constrained parameters. The introduction of Lagrange multipliers allows the computation of objective functions which include the predefined constraints. The following example shows the basic idea of this technique.

Discrete probabilities, for instance, have to sum up to one, i.e.,

$$\sum_{i=1}^{n} p_i = 1 \quad .$$ (C.11)

(C.12)

If we have to maximize the objective function

$$p(p_1, p_2, \ldots, p_n) = \sum_{i=1}^{n} a_i \log p_i$$ (C.13)

with respect to $p_1, p_2, \ldots, p_n$ where $a_i > 0$, $i = 1, 2, \ldots, n$, we maximize instead

$$p_{\text{Lagrange}}(p_1, p_2, \ldots, p_n) = \sum_{i=1}^{n} a_i \log p_i + \eta \left(\sum_{i=1}^{n} p_i - 1 \right)$$ (C.14)

where $\eta \in \mathbf{R}$ denotes the *Lagrange multiplier*. The maximum can be computed equating partial derivatives to zero, i.e.,

$$\frac{\partial p_{\text{Lagrange}}}{\partial p_i} = \frac{a_i}{p_i} - \eta = 0 \ . \tag{C.15}$$

By summing over all p_i, we get

$$\eta \sum_{i=1}^{n} p_i = \sum_{i=1}^{n} a_i \ , \tag{C.16}$$

and due to (C.11)

$$\eta = \sum_{i=1}^{n} a_i \ . \tag{C.17}$$

Using this result in above equation (C.15), we obtain finally

$$p_i = \frac{a_i}{\sum\limits_{i=1}^{n} a_i} \ . \tag{C.18}$$

D Notation

We use the notation as suggested by many mathematical books and as used in many books on pattern recognition, speech processing, and in image processing. The notation is summarized in Table D.1.

Text	Explanation
`virtual`	programming code as well as keywords, class names, etc. is written in `teletype` letters
a	*scalar values* are written in mathematic font (italics)
x	*column vectors* are written lower case characters in bold mathematic font (italics)
A	*matrices* are written capital letters in bold mathematic font (italics)
$A^\mathrm{T} c^\mathrm{T}$	denotes transposed vectors and matrices.
a_{ij}	denotes the *matrix elements* and the matrix A can be written as $[a_{ij}]_{1 \le i \le N, 1 \le j \le M}$
$(A)_{ij}$	this notation is occationally used to denote the element at position (i, j) in the matrix; this is useful when instead of A we have an expression (e.g. $(AA^\mathrm{T})_{ij}$).
$\mathbf{R}$	denotes *real numbers*
$\mathbf{C}$	denotes *complex numbers*
i	denotes $\sqrt{-1}$ for complex numbers
A	*sets* are like matrices written in capital letters and typed in bold face

Table D.1 Notation used in the book

Bibliography

[Ahl96]   U. Ahlrichs, J. Denzler, R. Kompe, and H. Niemann. Sprachgesteuerte Fovealisierung
          und Vergenz. In B. Mertsching, editor, *Aktives Sehen in technischen und biologis-
          chen Systemen*, Proceedings in Artificial Intelligence, pages 52–59, Sankt Augustin,
          Dezember 1996. Infix. (*Ref. on p. 358*)

[Aho74]   A. V. Aho, J. E. Hopcroft, and J. D. Ullman. *The design and analysis of computer
          algorithms*. Addison–Wesley, Reading, MA, 1974. (*Ref. on p. 141, 147*)

[Ale94]   J. C. Alexander and J. Menon, editors. *Current Topics of Pattern Recognition Re-
          search*, volume 1. Research Trends, Trivandrum, India, 1994. (*Ref. on p. 383, 386*)

[And58]   T. W. Anderson. *An Introduction to Multivariate Statistical Analysis*. Wiley Publica-
          tions in Statistics. John Wiley & Sons, Inc., New York, 1958. (*Ref. on p. 283*)

[Arp92]   R. B. Arps and W. K. Pratt, editors. *Image Processing and Interchange: Implementa-
          tion and Systems*, San Jose, CA, 1992. SPIE, Proceedings 1659. (*Ref. on p. 381, 382,
          386, 387*)

[Arv91]   J. Arvo, editor. *Graphics Gems II*. The Graphics Gems Series, A Collection of Practical
          Techniques for the Computer Graphics Programmer. Academic Press, London, 1991.
          (*Ref. on p. 380, 388, 389*)

[Ary94]   S. Arya, D. M. Mount, N. S. Netanyahu, R. Silverman, and A. Wu. An optimal
          algorithm for approximate nearest neighbor searching. In *Proceedings of the Fifth
          Annual ACM–SIAM Symposium on Discrete Algorithms*, pages 573–582, Arlington,
          Virginia, January 1994. SIAM. (*Ref. on p. 324*)

[Bal82]   D. H. Ballard and C. M. Brown. *Computer Vision*. Prentice-Hall, Englewood Cliffs,
          NJ, 1982. (*Ref. on p. 272, 274, 295, 335*)

[Bau67]   L. E. Baum and J. A. Eagon. An inequality with applications to statistical prediction
          for functions of Markov processes and to a model for ecology. *Bull. Amer. Math. Soc.*,
          73:360–363, 1967. (*Ref. on p. 340*)

[Bel67]   R. Bellman. *Dynamische Programmierung und selbstanpassende Regelprozesse*. R.
          Oldenbourg Verlag, München, Wien, 1967. (*Ref. on p. 333, 335*)

[Bel89]   Z. W. Bell. A Bayesian/Monte Carlo segmentation method for images dominated by
          Gaussian noise. *IEEE Transactions on Pattern Analysis and Machine Intelligence*,
          11(9):985–990., September 1989. (*Ref. on p. 88*)

[Ber87]   F. Bergholm. Edge focussing. *IEEE Transactions on Pattern Analysis and Machine
          Intelligence*, 9(6):726–741, 1987. (*Ref. on p. 261*)

[Beß96]   R. Beß, D. Paulus, and H. Niemann. 3D recovery using calibrated active camera. In
          Proceedings of the International Conference on Image Processing (ICIP), volume II,
          pages 855 – 858. IEEE Computer Society Press, Lausanne, Schweiz, September 1996.
          (*Ref. on p. 356*)

[Big89]   N. L. Biggs. *Discrete Mathematics*. Clarendon Press, Oxford, 1989. (*Ref. on p. 333,
          335*)

[Bir83]   G. M. Birtwistle, O. Dahl, B. Myrhang, and K. Nygaard. *Simula Begin*. Auerbach Publ. Inc., Philadelphia, PA, 1983. (*Ref. on p. 106*)

[Boo91]   G. Booch. *Object Oriented Design*. Benjamin/Cummings, Redwood City, CA, 1991. (*Ref. on p. 100, 105*)

[Bov87]   A. Bovik, T. Huang, and D. Munson. The effect of median filtering on edge detection. *IEEE Transactions on Pattern Analysis and Machine Intelligence*, 9(2):181–194, 1987. (*Ref. on p. 237*)

[Bra78]   Walter S. Brainerd. *Fortran 77 Programming*. Harper and Row, New York, 1978. (*Ref. on p. 89*)

[Bre87]   J. E. Bresenham. Ambiguities in incremental line rastering. *Computer Graphics and Applications*, 7(5):31–43, 1987. (*Ref. on p. 229*)

[Bre88]   P. Bremaud. *An Introduction to Probabilistic Modeling*. Undergraduate Texts in Mathematics. Springer, Heidelberg, 1988. (*Ref. on p. 85, 86*)

[Bro85]   I. N. Bronstein and K. A. Semendjajew. *Taschenbuch der Mathematik*. Harri Deutsch, Thun, 1985. (*Ref. on p. 137, 283*)

[Brü90]   H. Brünig. Konzeption und Realisierung einer flexiblen Bildsegmentierung. PhD thesis, IMMD 5 (Mustererkennung), Universität Erlangen–Nürnberg, Erlangen, 1990. (*Ref. on p. 2, 165, 239, 240, 268, 269*)

[Bub96]   T. Bub and J. Schwinn. Verbmobil: The Evolution of a Complex Large Speech-to-Speech Translation System. In *Proc. Int. Conf. on Spoken Language Processing*, volume 4, pages 1026–1029, Philadelphia, Oktober 1996. IEEE Computer Society Press. (*Ref. on p. 6*)

[Bun92]   H. Bunke, editor. *Advances in Structural and Syntactic Pattern Recognition*, Series in Machine Perception and Artificial Intelligence, Singapore, 1992. World Scientific Publishing. (*Ref. on p. 62, 63*)

[Bur83]   P. J. Burt and E. H. Adelson. The Laplacian pyramid as a compact image code. *IEEE Transactions on Communications*, 31(4):532–540, 1983. (*Ref. on p. 243, 244*)

[Bus92]   R. Busch. Editorial. *Informatik Spektrum*, 15(5):253–254, 1992. (*Ref. on p. 99*)

[Can86]   J. F. Canny. A computational approach to edge detection. *IEEE Transactions on Pattern Analysis and Machine Intelligence*, 8(6):679–698, 1986. (*Ref. on p. 278*)

[Cap91]   R. Capelli. Fast approximation to arcus tangent. In Arvo [Arv91], pages 389–391. (*Ref. on p. 170*)

[Car91]   I. C. Carlsen and D. Haaks. IKS^{PFH} — concept and implementation of an object–oriented framework for image processing. *Computers and Graphics*, 15(4):473–482, 1991. (*Ref. on p. 69*)

[Cha91]   V. Chandran and S. Elgar. Shape discrimination using invariants defined from higeher order spectra. In *International Conference on Acoustic, Speech & Signal Processing*, volume 5, pages 3105–3180, Toronto, May 1991. (*Ref. on p. 301*)

[Cha92]   V. Chandran and S. Elgar. Position, rotation, and scale invariant recognition of images using higher order spectra. In *International Conference on Acoustic, Speech & Signal Processing*, volume 5, pages 213–216, San Francisco, March 1992. (*Ref. on p. 301*)

[Che91] C. H. Chen. On the relationships between statistical pattern pecognition and artificial neural networks. *International Journal of Pattern Recognition and Artifical
Intelligence*, 5(3):655–661, 1991. (*Ref. on p. 360*)

[Chi83] R. Chien and C.-L. Yeh. Quantitative evaluation of some edge preserving noise
smoothing techniques. *Computer Graphics and Image Processing (CGIP)*, 23:67–91,
1983. (*Ref. on p. 237*)

[Cla92] A. F. Clark. Image processing and interchange — the imaging model. In Arps and
Pratt [Arp92], pages 106–116. (*Ref. on p. 127*)

[Coa90] P. Coad and E. Yourdon. *Object-oriented analysis*. Prentice Hall, Englewood Cliffs,
NJ, 1990. (*Ref. on p. 100, 102, 103, 104*)

[Cog87] J. M. Coggins. Integrated class structures for image pattern recognition and computer
graphics. In K. Gorlen, editor, *Proceedings of the USENIX C++ Workshop*, pages
240–245, Santa Fe, NM, 9.-10. November 1987. (*Ref. on p. 69*)

[Coo65] J. Cooley and J. Tukey. An algorithm for the machine computation of complex Fourier
series. *Mathematical Computation*, 19(6):297–381, 1965. (*Ref. on p. 135, 147*)

[Dan90] P.-E. Danielsson and O. Seger. Generalized and separable Sobel operators. In H. Free-
mann, editor, *Machine Vision for Three–Dimensional Scenes*, pages 347–380. Academic Press, San Diego, 1990. (*Ref. on p. 168*)

[Dav78] L. Davis and A. Rosenfeld. Noise cleaning by iterated local averaging. *IEEE Transactions on Systems, Man, and Cybernetics*, 8(9):705–710, 1978. (*Ref. on p. 238,
239*)

[Dec95] J. December. *Presenting Java*. Sams net publ., Indianapolis, IN, 1995. (*Ref. on p.
106*)

[Dem77] A.P. Dempster, N.M. Laird, and D.B. Rubin. Maximum Likelihood from Incomplete Data via the EM Algorithm. *Journal of the Royal Statistical Society, Series B
(Methodological)*, 39(1):1–38, 1977. (*Ref. on p. 345, 346*)

[DeM79] T. DeMarco. *Structured Analysis and System Specification*. Prentice–Hall, Englewood
Cliffs, NJ, 1979. (*Ref. on p. 99*)

[Den94] J. Denzler and H. Niemann. A two-stage real time object tracking system. In Pavešić
et al. [Pav94]. (*Ref. on p. 68*)

[Den95] J. Denzler, B. Heigl, and D. Paulus. Farbsegmentierung für aktives Sehen. In
V. Rehrmann, editor, *Erster Workshop Farbbildverarbeitung*, volume 15 of *Fach-
berichte Informatik*, pages 9–12, Universität Koblenz–Landau, 1995. (*Ref. on p. 357*)

[Den97] J. Denzler. *Active Vision for Real–Time Object Tracking*. Dissertation, IMMD 5
(Mustererkennung), Universität Erlangen–Nürnberg, Erlangen, June, 1997. (*Ref. on
p. 358*)

[Der90] R. Deriche. Fast algorithms for low-level vision. *IEEE Transactions on Pattern
Analysis and Machine Intelligence (PAMI)*, 12:78–87, 1990. (*Ref. on p. 278*)

[Der91] R. Deriche. Optimal edge detection using recursive filtering. In *Proceedings of the
1st International Conference on Computer Vision (ICCV)*, pages 501–505, London,
1991. IEEE Computer Society Press. (*Ref. on p. 278*)

[Dev96] L. Devroye, L. Györfi, and G. Lugosi. *A Probabilistic Theory in Pattern Recognition*, volume 31 of *Applications of Mathematics, Stochastic Modelling and Applied
Probability*. Springer, Heidelberg, 1996. (*Ref. on p. 88, 313*)

[Dob91] M. R. Dobie and P. H. Lewis. Data structures for image processing in C. *Pattern Recognition Letters*, 12:457–466, 1991. *(Ref. on p. 69)*

[Dud73] R. O. Duda and P. E. Hart. *Pattern Classification and Scene Analysis*. John Wiley & Sons, Inc., New York, 1973. *(Ref. on p. 85, 88, 135, 168, 293)*

[Ekl82] J.-O. Eklundh, T. Elfving, and S. Nyberg. Edge detection using the Marr/Hildreth operator with different sizes. In *Proceedings of the 6th International Conference on Pattern Recognition (ICPR)*, pages 1109–1111, München, 1982. IEEE Computer Society Press. *(Ref. on p. 261)*

[Fah94] L. Fahrmeir and L. Tutz. *Multivariate Statistical Modelling Based on Generalized Linear Models*. Springer Series in Statistics. Springer, Heidelberg, 2 edition, 1994. *(Ref. on p. 89)*

[Fal95] D. Falavigna. Comparision of different HMM based methods for speaker verification. In *Proceedings of the 4th Conference on Speech Communication and Technology*, pages 371–374, Madrid, 1995. *(Ref. on p. 293)*

[Fan73] C. G. Fant. *Speech Sounds and Features*. MIT Press, Cambridge, Massachusetts, 1973. *(Ref. on p. 304)*

[Fis88] A. S. Fisher. *CASE*. John Wiley & Sons, Inc., New York, 1988. *(Ref. on p. 31)*

[Fre80] H. Freeman. Analysis and manipulation of lineal map data. In H. Freeman and G. G. Pieroni, editors, *Map Data Processing*, pages 151–168, New York, 1980. Academic Press. *(Ref. on p. 201, 281)*

[Fuk90] K. Fukunaga. *Introduction to Statistical Pattern Recognition*. Academic Press, Boston, 1990. *(Ref. on p. 85, 256, 323)*

[Gal91] D. Le Gall. MPEG: A video compression standard for multimedia applications. *Communications of the Association for Computing Machinery*, 34(4):47–58, April 1991. *(Ref. on p. 127)*

[Gel94] E. S. Gelsema and L. N. Kanal, editors. *Pattern Recognition in Practice IV: Multiple Paradigms, Comparative Studies and Hybrid Systems*, volume 16 of *Machine Intelligence and Pattern Recognition*, Amsterdam, June 1994. Elsevier. *(Ref. on p. 319)*

[Gis94] H. Gish and Schmidt M. Text–independent speaker identification. In *IEEE Signal Processing Magazine*, pages 18–32, October 1994. *(Ref. on p. 293)*

[Gol83] A. Goldberg and D. Robson. *Smalltalk-80: The Language and its Implementation*. Addison-Wesley, Reading, MA, 1983. *(Ref. on p. 106)*

[Goo69] N. Goodman. *Languages of Art. An Approach to a theory of symbols*. Oxford Univ. Press, New York, 1969. *(Ref. on p. 3)*

[Gor90] K. E. Gorlen, S. Orlow, and P. S. Plexico. *Data Abstraction and Object–Oriented Programming in C++*. John Wiley and Sons, Chichester, 1990. *(Ref. on p. 179, 184, 185, 187, 190, 355)*

[Gut78] J. V. Guttag and J. J. Horning. The algebraic specification of abstract data types. *Acta Informatica*, 10:27–52, 1978. *(Ref. on p. 102)*

[Har88] R. Haralick and J. Lee. Context dependent edge detection. In ICPR 88 [ICP88], pages 203–207. *(Ref. on p. 261)*

[Har92] R. M. Haralick and V. Ramesh. Image understanding environment. In Arps and Pratt [Arp92], pages 159–167. (*Ref. on p. 69*)

[Har96] M. Harbeck. *Objektorientierte linienbasierte Segmentierung von Bildern*. Shaker Verlag, Aachen, 1996. (*Ref. on p. 289, 355*)

[Has94] A. Hasegawa. Image recognition by neural networks. In Alexander and Menon [Ale94], pages 237–250. (*Ref. on p. 360*)

[Hau84] R. Hauser. A stochastic approach to edge detection. In *Proceedings 7th Int. Conf. on Pattern Recognition*, pages 52–54, Montreal, 1984. IEEE Computer Society Press. (*Ref. on p. 261*)

[He91] Y. He and A. Kundu. 2–D shape classification using hidden Markov models. *IEEE Transactions on Pattern Analysis and Machine Intelligence*, 13(11):1172–1184, 1991. (*Ref. on p. 345*)

[Hec82] P. Heckbert. Color image quantization for frame buffer display. *Computer Graphics*, 16(3):297–307, July 1982. (*Ref. on p. 255*)

[Hor74] S. L. Horowitz and T. Pavlidis. Picture segmentation by a directed split-and-merge procedure. In *Proc. 2nd International Joint Conference on Pattern Recognition*, pages 424–433, Kopenhagen, 1974. (*Ref. on p. 355, 357*)

[Hor93a] J. Hornegger and D. Paulus. Detecting elliptic objects using inverse Hough–transform. In *Image Processing: Theory and Applications*, pages 155–158. Elsevier, Amsterdam, 1993. (*Ref. on p. 274*)

[Hor93b] J. Hornegger and D. Paulus. Surface segmentation and classification of 3D shapes using dynamic programming. *Pattern Recognition and Image Analysis*, 3(3):328–332, 1993. (*Ref. on p. 335*)

[Hor94] J. Hornegger and H. Niemann. The missing information principle in computer vision. *International Journal of Computing and Information Technology*, 2(3):201–209, 1994. (*Ref. on p. 320*)

[Hor96a] J. Hornegger. *Statistische Modellierung, Klassifikation und Lokalisation von Objekten*. Shaker, Aachen, 1996. (*Ref. on p. 320, 345, 360*)

[Hor96b] J. Hornegger, E. Nöth, V. Fischer, and H. Niemann. Semantic network meet Bayesian classifiers. In B. Jähne, P. Geißler, H. Haußecker, and F. Hering, editors, *Mustererkennung 1996*, pages 260–267, Berlin, September 1996. Springer. (*Ref. on p. 360*)

[Hou62] P. V. C. Hough and A. Arbor. Method and means for recognizing complex patterns. Technical report, US Patent 3069654, 1962. (*Ref. on p. 272*)

[Hu97] J. Hu and H. Yan. Polygonal approximation of digital curves based on the principles of perceptual organization. *Pattern Recognition*, 30(5):701–718, May 1997. (*Ref. on p. 281, 287*)

[Hua88] J. Huang and D. Tseng. Statistical theory of edge detection. *Computer Vision, Graphics and Image Processing (CVGIP)*, 43:337–346, 1988. (*Ref. on p. 261*)

[Hua90] X. D. Huang, Y. Ariki, and M. A. Jack. *Hidden Markov Models for Speech Recognition*. Number 7 in Information Technology Series. Edinburgh University Press, Edinburgh, 1990. (*Ref. on p. 61, 304, 351*)

[Hue73] M. H. Hueckel. A local visual operator which recognizes edges and lines. *JACM*, 18:634–647; erratum in Vol. 21, p. 350, 1974, 1973. (*Ref. on p. 260*)

[ICP88]   *Proceedings of the 9th International Conference on Pattern Recognition (ICPR)*, Rome, 1988. IEEE Computer Society Press. (*Ref. on p. 382, 386*)

[Ill87]   J. Illingworth and J. Kittler. The adaptive Hough transform. *IEEE Transactions on Pattern Analysis and Machine Intelligence*, 9(5):690–698, 1987. (*Ref. on p. 274*)

[Jäh93]   B. Jähne. *Digital Image Processing — Concepts, Algorithms, and Scientific Applications*. Springer, Heidelberg, 1993. (*Ref. on p. 6, 298*)

[Jai90]   A. K. Jain. *Fundamentals of Digital Image Processing*. Prentice Hall, 1990. (*Ref. on p. 298*)

[Jai97]   A. K. Jain and D. Zongker. Feature selection: Evaluation, application, and small sample performance. *IEEE Transactions on Pattern Analysis and Machine Intelligence*, 19(2):153–158, February 1997. (*Ref. on p. 294*)

[Jak94]   A. Jaklič, A. Leonardis, and F. Solina. Object–oriented analysis and design of image segmentation package. In *3rd Electrotechnical and Computer Science Conf. ERK*, volume B, pages 23–26, Portorož, Slovenia, 1994. (*Ref. on p. 69*)

[Jen85]   K. Jensen and N. Wirth. *Pascal User Manual and Report*. Springer-Verlag, New York, 1985. (*Ref. on p. 35*)

[Joh87]   M. E. Johnson. *Multivariate Statistical Simulation*. Probability and Mathematical Statistics. John Wiley & Sons, Inc., New York, 1987. (*Ref. on p. 226*)

[Joh93]   R. Johnsonbaugh and M. Kalin. *Applications programming in ANSI C*. Macmillan, New York, 2 edition, 1993. (*Ref. on p. 17*)

[Kan90]   K. Kanatani. *Group–Theoretical Methods in Image Understanding*. Springer, Heidelberg, 1990. (*Ref. on p. 228*)

[Kas88]   M. Kass, A. Wittkin, and D. Terzopoulos. Snakes: Active contour models. *International Journal of Computer Vision*, 2(3):321–331, 1988. (*Ref. on p. 358*)

[Kem97]   M. Kempe. Ada 95 reference manual, 1997. http://lglwww.epfl.ch/Ada/rm95. (*Ref. on p. 106*)

[Ker78]   B. W. Kernighan and D. M. Ritchie. *The C Programming Language*. Prentice-Hall Software Series, Englewood Cliffs, NJ, 1978. (*Ref. on p. 17*)

[Kir90]   H. Kirchner. Blockmatching with column and row oriented optimization. *Proc. of the 3rd Int. Workshop on Time–Varying Image Processing and Moving Object Recognition, May 29-31 1989, Florence, Italy*, pages 280–288, 1990. (*Ref. on p. 295*)

[Kle95]   R. Klette and P. Zamperoni. *Handbuch der Operatoren für die Bildbearbeitung*. Vieweg, Braunschweig, 2 edition, 1995. (*Ref. on p. 231*)

[Knu73]   D. E. Knuth. *The Art of Computer Programming*, volume 2: Seminumerical Algorithms. Addison–Wesley, Reading, MA, 1973. (*Ref. on p. 226*)

[Koe96]   D. Koelma. *A Software Environment for Image Interpretation*. PhD thesis, Faculteit der Wiskunde, Informatica, Natuurkunde en Sterrenkunde, Amsterdam, 1996. (*Ref. on p. 69*)

[Kro79]   L. I. Kronsjö. *Algorithms: Their Complexity and Efficiency*. John Wiley & Sons, Inc. John Wiley & Sons, Inc., Chichester, 1979. (*Ref. on p. 147*)

[Kun87]   A. Kundu and S. Mitra. A new algorithm for image edge extraction using a statistical classifier approach. *IEEE Transactions on Pattern Analysis and Machine Intelligence*, 9(4):569–577, 1987. (*Ref. on p. 261*)

[Luo94] A. Luo. *Helligkeitsbasiertes Rechnersehen zur direkten Ermittlung räumlicher Eigenschaften*. Verlag Shaker, Aachen, 1994. (*Ref. on p. 237*)

[Mac81] R. Machuca and A. Gilbert. Finding edges in noisy scenes. *IEEE Transactions on Pattern Analysis and Machine Intelligence*, 3(1):103–111, 1981. (*Ref. on p. 237*)

[Mao92] J. Mao and A. K. Jain. Texture classification and segmentation using multiresolution simultaneous autoregressive models. *Pattern Recognition*, 25(2):173–188, 1992. (*Ref. on p. 309*)

[Mar76] A. Martelli. An application of heuristic search methods to edge and contour detection. *Comm. ACM*, 19:335–345, 1976. (*Ref. on p. 272*)

[Mar80] D. Marr and E. Hildreth. Theory of edge detection. *Proceedings Royal Society London B*, 207:187–217, 1980. (*Ref. on p. 165, 174, 261*)

[Mar82] D. Marr. *Vision: A Computational Investigation into the Human Representation and Processing of Visual Information*. W.H. Freeman and Company, San Francisco, 1982. (*Ref. on p. 61*)

[Mas93] T. Masters. *Practical neural network recipes in C++*. Academic Press, Inc., Boston, 1993. (*Ref. on p. 361*)

[May96] St. Mayer. Farbbasierte Objektlokalisierung mit einer aktiven Kamera. Student's thesis, IMMD 5 (Mustererkennung), Universität Erlangen–Nürnberg, Erlangen, 1996. (*Ref. on p. 257*)

[Mey91] A. Meystel. *Autonomous Mobile Robots, Vehicles with Cognitive Control*, volume 1 of *World Scientific Series in Automation*. World Scientific, Singapore, 1991. (*Ref. on p. 6*)

[Moo79] R. K. Moore. A Dynamic Programming Algorithm for the Distance Between Two Finite Areas. *IEEE Transactions on Pattern Analysis and Machine Intelligence*, 1(1):86–88, 1979. (*Ref. on p. 335*)

[Mun92] J. Mundy, T. Binford, T. Boult, A. Hanson, R. Veveridge, R. Haralick, V. Ramesh, C. Kohl, D. Lawton, D. Morgan, K Price, and T. Strat. The image understanding environments program. In *Image Understanding Workshop*, pages 185–214, Hawaii, Jan. 1992. (*Ref. on p. 69*)

[Mus96] D. R. Musser and A. Saini. *STL tutorial and reference guide*. Addison-Wesley, Reading, Mass., 1996. (*Ref. on p. 179, 192*)

[Nag79] M. Nagao and T. Matsuyama. Edge preserving smoothing. *Computer Graphics and Image Processing (CGIP)*, 9:394–407, 1979. (*Ref. on p. 237*)

[Nev80] R. Nevatia and R. Babu. Linear feature extraction and description. *Computer Graphics and Image Processing (CGIP)*, 13:257–269, 1980. (*Ref. on p. 259, 262, 267, 268*)

[Ney84] H. Ney. The use of a one-stage dynamic programming algorithm for connected word recognition. *IEEE Transactions on Acoustics, Speech and Signal Processing*, 32(2):263–271, 1984. (*Ref. on p. 335*)

[Nie74] H. Niemann. *Methoden der Mustererkennung*. Akademische Verlagsgesellschaft, Frankfurt, 1974. (*Ref. on p. 284*)

[Nie83] H. Niemann. *Klassifikation von Mustern*. Springer, Heidelberg, 1983. (*Ref. on p. 13, 61, 62, 85, 88, 91, 95, 141, 147, 151, 249, 276, 294, 308, 309, 313, 315, 318, 319, 330*)

[Nie86]   H. Niemann, A. Brietzmann, U. Ehrlich, and G. Sagerer. Representation of a con-
           tinuous speech understanding and dialog system in a homogeneous semantic net
           architecture. In *Proc. ICASSP 86*, pages 1581–15584. Tokio, 1986. (*Ref. on p. 359*)

[Nie90a]   H. Niemann. *Pattern Analysis and Understanding*. Springer, Heidelberg, 1990.
           (*Ref. on p. 7, 8, 13, 63, 64, 66, 67, 135, 214, 278, 293, 294, 298, 304, 309, 313, 329,
           335, 336, 352, 361*)

[Nie90b]   H. Niemann, G. Sagerer, S. Schröder, and F. Kummert. ERNEST: A Semantic Network
           System for Pattern Analysis. *IEEE Trans. Pattern Analysis and Machine Intelligence*,
           9:883–905, 1990. (*Ref. on p. 70, 103, 192, 359*)

[Nöt90]   E. Nöth. *Prosodische Information in der automatischen Spracherkennung, Berech-
           nung und Anwendung*. Niemeyer, Tübingen, 1990. (*Ref. on p. 66*)

[Opp75]   A. V. Oppenheim and R. W. Schafer. *Digital signal processing*. Prentice-Hall,
           Englewood Cliffs NJ, 1975. (*Ref. on p. 147, 151*)

[Ost91]   W. Osten. *Digitale Verarbeitung und Auswertung von Interferenzbildern*. Akademie
           Verlag GmbH, Berlin, 1991. (*Ref. on p. 301*)

[Ous94]   J. K. Ousterhout. *Tcl and the Tk toolkit*. Addison-Wesley, Reading, Mass., 1994.
           (*Ref. on p. 219*)

[Pap91]   A. Papoulis. *Probability, Random Variables, and Stochastic Processes*. Electrical
           Engineering: Communications and Signal Processing. McGraw–Hill, New York, 3
           edition, 1991. (*Ref. on p. 85*)

[Pau92a]   D. Paulus. Object oriented image segmentation. In *Proc. of the 4ᵗʰ Int. Conf. on
           Image Processing and its Applications*, pages 482–485, Maastrich, Holland, 1992.
           (*Ref. on p. 197*)

[Pau92b]   D. Paulus. *Objektorientierte und wissensbasierte Bildverarbeitung "Object–oriented
           and knowledge based image processing"*. Vieweg, Braunschweig, 1992. (*Ref. on p.
           38, 65, 69, 130, 197, 207, 211, 355, 357*)

[Pau92c]   D. Paulus and H. Niemann. Iconic–symbolic interfaces. In Arps and Pratt [Arp92],
           pages 204–214. (*Ref. on p. 197, 211*)

[Pau94]   D. Paulus and H. Niemann. Object–oriented programming for image analysis. In
           Alexander and Menon [Ale94], pages 185–204. (*Ref. on p. 69*)

[Pav77]   T. Pavlidis. *Structural pattern recognition*. Springer-Verlag, Berlin Heidelberg New
           York, 1977. (*Ref. on p. 355*)

[Pav94]   N. Pavešić, H. Niemann, D. Paulus, and S. Kovaćić, editors. *3–D Scene Acquisi-
           tion, Modeling and Understanding, Proceedings of the Second German–Slovenian
           Workshop*, Ljubljana, Slovenia, June 1994. IEEE Slovenia Section. (*Ref. on p. 230,
           381*)

[Pen86]   A. P. Pentland, editor. *From Pixels to Predicates – Recent Advances in Computational
           and Robot Vision*, Norwood, New Jersey, 1986. Ablex Publishing Corporation. (*Ref. on
           p. 293*)

[Pip88]   J. Piper and D. Rutovitz. An investigation of object-oriented programming as the basis
           for an image processing and analysis system. In ICPR 88 [ICP88], pages 1015–1019.
           (*Ref. on p. 69*)

[Pit93]   I. Pitas. *Digital Image Processing Algorithms*. Prentice Hall, New York, 1993. (*Ref. on
           p. 298, 335*)

[PJ80]   M. Page-Jones. *Practical Guide to Structured System Design*. Prentice–Hall, Engle-
          wood Cliffs, NJ, 1980. (*Ref. on p. 99*)

[Pos90]   S. Posch. *Automatische Bestimmung von Tiefeninformation aus Grauwert-
          Stereobildern*. Deutscher Universitäts Verlag, Wiesbaden, 1990. (*Ref. on p. 295*)

[Poy92]   C. A. Poynton. An overview of TIFF 5.0. In Arps and Pratt [Arp92], pages 150–158.
          (*Ref. on p. 5, 127*)

[Poy95]   C. A. Poynton. colorspace-faq, May, 28 1995.
          http://www.inforamp.net/~poynton/Poynton-colour.html.
          (*Ref. on p. 128, 129*)

[Pra80]   M. Prager. Extracting and labeling boundary segments in natural scenes. *IEEE
          Transactions on Pattern Analysis and Machine Intelligence*, 2(1):16–27, 1980. (*Ref. on
          p. 240*)

[Pra91]   W. K. Pratt. *Digital Image Processing*. John Wiley & Sons, Inc., New York, 2 edition,
          1991. (*Ref. on p. 5, 225*)

[Pra95]   W. K. Pratt. *The PIKS Foundation C Programmers Guide*. Manning, Greenwich,
          1995. (*Ref. on p. 127*)

[Pre70]   J. M. S. Prewitt. Object enhancement and extraction. *Picture Processing and Psy-
          chopictorics*, pages 75–149, 1970. (*Ref. on p. 168, 259*)

[Pre92]   W. H. Press, B. P. Flannery, S. Teukolsky, and W. T. Vetterling. *Numerical Recipes -
          the Art of Numerical Computing, C Version*. Cambridge University Press, Cambridge,
          2 edition, 1992. (*Ref. on p. 58, 151, 283*)

[Rab88]   L. R. Rabiner. Mathematical foundations of hidden Markov models. In H. Niemann,
          M. Lang, and G. Sagerer, editors, *Recent Advances in Speech Understanding and
          Dialog Systems*, volume 46 of *NATO ASI Series F: Computer and System Sciences*,
          pages 183–205. Springer, Heidelberg, 1988. (*Ref. on p. 135, 293, 340*)

[Rab93]   L. Rabiner and B. H. Juang. *Fundamentals of Speech Recognition*. Prentice Hall,
          Englewood Cliffs, NJ, 1993. (*Ref. on p. 14, 329, 336, 340, 345*)

[Ram72]   U. Ramer. An iterative procedure for polygonal approximation of plane curves.
          Computer Graphics and Image Processing (CGIP), 1:244–256, 1972. (*Ref. on p. 287*)

[Ras92]   J. R. Rasure and M. Young. Open environment for image processing and software
          development. In Arps and Pratt [Arp92], pages 300–310. (*Ref. on p. 69, 218, 370*)

[Red84]   R. A. Redner and H. F. Walker. Mixture densities, maximum likelihood and the EM
          algorithm. *Society for Industrial and Applied Mathematics Review*, 26(2):195–239,
          1984. (*Ref. on p. 321*)

[Rim91]   R. D. Rimey and M. Brown. Controlling eye movements with hidden Markov models.
          International Journal of Computer Vision, 7(1):47–65, January 1991. (*Ref. on p. 6*)

[Rip96]   B. D. Ripley. *Pattern Recognition and Neural Networks*. Cambridge University Press,
          Cambridge, 1996. (*Ref. on p. 294*)

[Rit86]   X. Ritter, P. Gadev, and J. Davidson. Automated bridge detection in flir images. In
          Proceedings 8th Int. Conf. on Pattern Recognition, pages 862–864, Paris, 1986. IEEE
          Computer Society Press. (*Ref. on p. 259*)

[Rob77]   G.S. Robinson. Edge detection by compass gradient masks. *Computer Graphics and
          Image Processing (CGIP)*, 6:492–501, 1977. (*Ref. on p. 259*)

388

[Ros71] A. Rosenfeld and M. Thurston. Edge and curve detection for visual scene analysis. *IEEE Transactions on Computers*, 20:562–569, 1971. (*Ref. on p. 289*)

[Ros82] A. Rosenfeld and A. Kak. *Digital Picture Processing*. Academic Press, New York, 1982. (*Ref. on p. 260*)

[Rum91] J. Rumbaugh. *Object-oriented modeling and design*. Prentice-Hall, Englewood Cliffs, NJ, 1991. (*Ref. on p. 100*)

[Rum96] J. Rumbaugh. To form a more perfect union: Unifying the OMT and Booch methods. *Journal of Object Oriented Programming*, 8(8):14–18, January 1996. (*Ref. on p. 100*)

[Sar94] K. B. Sarachik. An analysis of the effect of Gaussian error in object recognition. PhD thesis, Department of Electrical Engineering and Computer Science, Massachusetts Institute of Technology, AI Lab., Cambridge, Massachusetts, 1994. (*Ref. on p. 88*)

[Sch77] J. Schürmann. *Polynomklassifikatoren für die Zeichenerkennung*. R. Oldenbourg-Verlag, München, 1977. (*Ref. on p. 317, 318, 319*)

[Sch78] J. Schürmann. A Multifont Word Recognition System for Postal Address Reading. *IEEE Transactions on Computers*, 27:721–732, 1978. (*Ref. on p. 6*)

[Sch90] N. Schneider. *Kantenhervorhebung und Kantenverfolgung in der industriellen Bild-verarbeitung*. Fortschritte in der Robotik, 6. Vieweg, Braunschweig, 1990. (*Ref. on p. 37*)

[Sch92] R. J. Schalkoff. *Pattern Recognition – Statistical, Structural and Neural Approaches*. Wiley Publications in Statistics. John Wiley & Sons, Inc., New York, 1992. (*Ref. on p. 294, 313, 319*)

[Sch95] E. G. Schukat–Talamazzini, J. Hornegger, and H. Niemann. Optimal linear feature transformations for semi–continuous hidden Markov models. In *Proceedings of the International Conference on Acoustics, Speech, and Signal Processing (ICASSP)*, volume 1, pages 369–372, Detroit, Mai 1995. IEEE Computer Society Press. (*Ref. on p. 345*)

[Ser88] J. Serra. *Image Analysis and Mathematical Morphology*. Academic Press, London, 1988. (*Ref. on p. 237*)

[Set91] I. K. Sethi and A. K. Jain, editors. *Artificial Neural Networks and Statisitcal Pattern Recognition*, volume 11 of *Machine Intelligence and Pattern Recognition*, Amsterdam, 1991. Elsevier. (*Ref. on p. 319*)

[She86] J. Shen and S. Castan. An optimal linear operator for edge detection. *Computer Vision, Graphics and Image Processing (CVGIP)*, 5:109–114, 1986. (*Ref. on p. 278*)

[She88] J. Shen and S. Castan. Further results on drf method of edge detection. *Proc. Computer Vision, Graphics and Image Processing, Miami*, 6:223–225, 1988. (*Ref. on p. 278*)

[Shi87] Y. Shirai. *Three–Dimensional Computer Vision*. Springer, Heidelberg, 1987. (*Ref. on p. 176*)

[Shl88] S. Shlaer and S. J. Mellor. *Object-oriented systems analysis*. Yourdon, Englewood Cliffs, NJ, 1988. (*Ref. on p. 100*)

[Sho91] K. Shoemake. Faster fourier transform. In Arvo [Arv91], pages 368–370. (*Ref. on p. 151*)

[Spr79] M. D. Springer. *The Algebra of Random Variables*. Wiley Publications in Statistics. John Wiley & Sons, Inc., New York, 1979. (*Ref. on p. 227*)

[ST95]   E. G. Schukat-Talamazzini. *Automatische Spracherkennung – Grundlagen, statistische Modelle und effiziente Algorithmen.* Künstliche Intelligenz. Vieweg, Braunschweig, 1995. (*Ref. on p. 14, 70, 88, 293, 294, 296, 297, 304, 305, 309, 329, 336, 345*)

[Str91]   B. Stroustrup. *The C++ Programming Language,* 2nd edition. Addison-Wesley, Reading, MA, 1991. (*Ref. on p. 18, 23, 45, 74, 78, 82, 106, 114, 154, 162, 163, 180, 361, 362*)

[Swa91]   M. J. Swain and D. H. Ballard. Color indexing. *International Journal of Computer Vision,* 7(1):11–32, November 1991. (*Ref. on p. 256*)

[Tal93]   R. Talluri and J. K. Aggarwal. Position estimation techniques for an autonomous mobile robot – a review. In C. H. Chen, L. F. Pau, and P. S. P. Wang, editors, *Handbook of Pattern Recognition & Computer Vision,* pages 769–801, Singapore, 1993. World Scientific Publishing. (*Ref. on p. 6*)

[Tan93]   M. A. Tanner. *Tools for Statistical Inference: Methods for the Exploration of Posterior Distributions and Likelihood Functions.* Springer Series in Statistics. Springer, Heidelberg, 1993. (*Ref. on p. 89, 320*)

[The89]   L.W. Therrien. *Decision, Estimation, and Classification.* John Whiley & Sons, Inc., New York, 1989. (*Ref. on p. 294, 313*)

[Udu91]   J. K. Udupa and G. T. Herman. *3D Imaging in Medicine.* CRC Press, Boca Raton, 1991. (*Ref. on p. 6*)

[Vap96]   V. N. Vapnik. *The Nature of Statistical Learning Theory.* Springer-Verlag, Heidelberg, 1996. (*Ref. on p. 85, 314*)

[Wal90]   G. Wallace. Overview of the JPEG (ISO/CCITT) still image compression standard. In *Electronic Image Science and Technology,* pages 97–108. SPIE Proceedings 1244, Santa Clara, CA, Feb. 1990. (*Ref. on p. 127*)

[War97]   V. Warnke, S. Harbeck, E. Nöth, and H. Niemann. Topic spotting using subword units. In *Proceedings des 9–ten Aachener Kolloquiums "Signaltheorie" Bild- und Sprachsignale,* pages 287–290, Aachen, 1997. (*Ref. on p. 293, 294*)

[Weg87]   P. Wegner. Dimensions of object–based language design. *OOPSLA '87 Conference Proceedings, SIGPLAN,* 22(12):168–182, 1987. (*Ref. on p. 100*)

[Wel94]   S. T. Welstead. *Neural network and fuzzy logic applications in C/C++.* John Wiley & Sons, Inc., New York, 1994. (*Ref. on p. 361*)

[Wel95]   W. M. Wells III, W. E. L. Grimson, R. Kikinis, and F. A. Jolesz. Adaptive segmentation of MRI data. In N. Ayache, editor, *Computer Vision, Virtual Reality and Robotics in Medicine,* volume 905 of *Lecture Notes in Computer Science,* pages 59–69, Heidelberg, 1995. Springer. (*Ref. on p. 6*)

[Win94]   A. Winzen, D. Paulus, H. Niemann, and V. Fischer. Semantische Netze für die Bildanalyse: Objektorientierte Realisierung mit paralleler Kontrolle. In H. Wedekind, editor, *Verteilte Systeme,* pages 371–386. BI Wissenschaftsverlag, Mannheim, 1994. (*Ref. on p. 359*)

[Wir83]   N. Wirth. *Programming in Modula 2.* Springer-Verlag, Heidelberg, 1983. (*Ref. on p. 102*)

[Wu83]   C. F. J. Wu. On the convergence properties of the EM algorithm. *The Annals of Statistics,* 11(1):95–103, 1983. (*Ref. on p. 347*)

[Wu91] X. Wu. Efficient statistical computations for optimal color quantization. In Arvo [Arv91], pages 126–133. (*Ref. on p. 256*)

[Wys82] G. Wyszecki and W. S. Stiles. *Color Science: Concepts and Methods, Quantitaive Data and Formulae*. John Wiley & Sons, Inc., New York, 2 edition, 1982. (*Ref. on p. 128*)

[XDR88] Sun Microsystems Inc., Stanford. *RFC External Data Representation Standard: Protocol Specifications*, sun os 4 manuals, network programming, part 2 edition, 1988. (*Ref. on p. 208*)

[Xu96] G. Xu and Z. Zhang. *Epipolar Geometry in Stereo, Motion and Object Recognition — A Unified Approach*, volume 6 of *Computational Imaging and Vision*. Kluwer Academic Press, Dordrecht, 1996. (*Ref. on p. 295*)

[Yam81] G. Yamg and T. Kuang. The effort of median filtering on edge location estimation. *Computer Graphics and Image Processing (CGIP)*, 15:224–245, 1981. (*Ref. on p. 237*)

[Yam91] H. Yamada and K. Yamamoto. Recognition of Echocardiograms by a Dynamic Programming Matching Method. *Pattern Recognition*, 24(2):147–157, 1991. (*Ref. on p. 335*)

[You96] S. Young, J. Jansen, J. Odell, D. Ollason, and P. Woodland. *The HTK Book*. Entropic Cambridge Research Laboratory Ltd., Cambridge, 1996. (*Ref. on p. 329*)

[Zam91] P. Zamperoni. *Methoden der digitalen Bildverarbeitung*. Vieweg, Braunschweig, 1991. (*Ref. on p. 281*)

[Zim96] W. Zimmer and E. Bonz. *Objektorientierte Bildverarbeitung*. Carl Hanser Verlag, München, 1996. (*Ref. on p. 69*)

List of Figures

List of Tables

List of Programs

Index